Praise for The Innovator's Prescription

Every American who's looking for the smartest ways to transform our health system should read The Innovator's Prescription.
—**Newt Gingrich**, Former Speaker of the House and Founder, Center for Health Transformation

A compelling framework for legislators, regulators, payers, providers, and society at-large to debate meaningful reform for our ailing health-care system.
—**David Snow**, Chairman and CEO, Medco

The Innovator's Prescription *is a timely and insightful manifesto for a much-needed revolution in health care.*
—**Steve Case**, Co-Founder, former Chairman and CEO, America Online and Founder, Revolution LLC

The Innovator's Prescription *offers a road map to the dramatic changes in health-care delivery, costs, and policy we can expect in the next couple of years. Well worth the effort to read and study it.*
—**John W. Brown**, Chairman, Stryker Corporation

The Innovator's Prescription *sets out a reform map that calls for government, employers, providers, and patients to change their traditional ways, shaking the status quo to its very roots. For anyone seeking real change, this book should be on your list.*
—**John Iglehart**, Founding Editor, *Health Affairs* and National Correspondent, *New England Journal of Medicine*

The authors provide a very original analysis and a road map through the labyrinth of health care to better care at lower cost. Everyone seriously looking for that road must read this book.
—**Dr. Alain Enthoven**, Professor of Public and Private Management, Emeritus, Stanford University

Christensen's new book draws lessons from a variety of industries to offer up a refreshing take on the importance—and feasibility—of reengineering delivery to reduce the cost of care.
—**Dr. Mark D. Smith**, President and CEO, California HealthCare Foundation

This book does the best job of describing the current situation in health care I've ever read; it's accessible, understandable, and thoughtful. I don't agree with all of Professor Christensen's observations and recommendations, but his book will make anyone who cares about these issues think.
—**Charles D. Baker**, President and CEO, Harvard Pilgrim Health Care

The
Innovator's
Prescription

A Disruptive Solution for Health Care

Clayton M. Christensen
Jerome H. Grossman, M.D. & Jason Hwang, M.D.

New York   Chicago   San Francisco   Lisbon   London
Madrid   Mexico City   Milan   New Delhi
San Juan   Seoul   Singapore
Sydney   Toronto

The **McGraw·Hill** Companies

Copyright © 2009 by Clayton M. Christensen, Jerome Grossman and Jason Hwang. All rights reserved. Printed in the United States of America. Except as permitted under the United States Copyright Act of 1976, no part of this publication may be reproduced or distributed in any form or by any means, or stored in a data base or retrieval system, without the prior written permission of the publisher.

1 2 3 4 5 6 7 8 9 0 DOC/DOC 0 10 9 8

ISBN 978-0-07-159208-6
MHID   0-07-159208-3

McGraw-Hill books are available at special quantity discounts to use as premiums and sales promotions, or for use in corporate training programs. For more information, please write to the Director of Special Sales, Professional Publishing, McGraw-Hill, Two Penn Plaza, New York, NY 10121-2298. Or contact your local bookstore.

This book is printed on recycled, acid-free paper.

Library of Congress Cataloging-in-Publication Data

Christensen, Clayton M.
 The innovator's prescription : a disruptive solution for health care / by Clayton M. Christensen, Jerome H. Grossman, Jason Hwang.
  p. cm.
 ISBN 0-07-159208-3 (alk. paper)
 1. Health services administration. 2. Public health administration. 3. Disruptive technologies. I. Grossman, Jerome H. II. Hwang, Jason. III. Title.
 RA971.C56 2009
 362.1--dc22

2008043957

Acknowledgments

I was an innocent bystander in 1998, happily ensconced in the study of innovation at the Harvard Business School when Professor Elizabeth Armstrong of the Harvard Medical School changed my career with an irresistible invitation: "Everyone else is trying to solve the problems of expensive, inaccessible health care by studying health care. I'd bet that if you stood aside the industry and examined it through the lenses of your research on innovation, you'd be able to see things that others can't see." A short while later Dr. Jerry Grossman, then a Fellow at Harvard's Kennedy School of Government, made the same invitation. Jerry was a physician, had been CEO of one of Boston's major hospitals, founder of a leading health benefits plan, chairman of the Federal Reserve Bank of Boston, and a director of several of America's leading health-care companies. I decided if men and women of this stature saw potential in this approach to one of the world's most vexing problems, I ought to accept their invitation.

My concern a decade ago was whether my research on innovation and management was insightful and robust enough that it would help us understand the root causes of this industry's problems. That challenge proved to be simple, however, when compared with the unfathomable, interdependent technological and economic complexity of the health-care enterprise. Wrapping my brain around the whole of it took $3.1416\times$ more time, and $10\times$ more intellectual energy than I had imagined it could. Making health care affordable and accessible is a challenge of monstrous proportions—far beyond the most intractable of the problems I had previously tried to study.

Too often scholars succumb to complexity of this sort by offering simplistic solutions to incorrectly defined problems. We have been determined not to do this—but instead to wrestle with and boil down the complexity in order to distill from it the essence of the problems—so that we could recommend solutions that would address them at their root. My colleagues and I wrote my previous books ourselves, and generally vetted them only with a small group of advisors and critics before publishing them to the world. But that approach wouldn't work here. Over a hundred friends have helped us do this. These include leaders of medical schools, some of the world's most respected scientists, administrators of great hospitals and health-care companies, practicing physicians and nurses, irreverent, free-thinking and risk-taking entrepreneurs and investors, large and small employers and insurers, and insightful analysts. They have patiently taught us, allowed us to stress-test our ideas against their experience, and helped us conceptually take apart and then reconstruct the industry so that we could understand how the pieces have worked together in the past, and how they must do so in the future. We have listed below the names of many of those who have helped us in these ways. We hope they can see their imprint on this work and that each can feel our gratitude for their selfless service to us and to this Cause.

Jerry Grossman passed away nine years into this decade-long project. It's impossible to describe the marvelous workings of Jerry's mind. He helped us see connections across each element of the system from perspectives that only his divergent mind could take. That a man of his scope and stature would join with me in this enterprise has been an extraordinary honor. Though he is no longer with us, I know that he still lives, and I hope this book brings honor to him and his wonderful family. His daughter Kate has worked with us to be sure her father's mind and voice have been reflected and preserved herein as faithfully as possible. Jason Hwang, MD-MBA, is one of the best students I've ever had at the Harvard Business School. I am deeply grateful that he would step away from his intended career to stay with me after graduation to wrestle these problems to the ground. He beat them up again and again until they confessed the truth. Jason is a true genius, a patient and perceptive colleague. I love working with him.

My son Matt Christensen, my wife Christine, and my Innosight colleagues Matt Eyring and Steve Wunker—each of whom understands my research on innovation better than I do—pored over and poked holes in every paragraph of this book. My friends Lewis Hassell, Gilbert Tang, Jason Sanders, and Jeremy Friese—all of them busy medical doctors—did the same, as did Tom Armstrong, one of Boston's leading venture capitalists. The published version of this book is vastly improved over the drafts that they worked on, because of their help. I am grateful to Lisa Stone and JaNeece Thacker for keeping us organized; to Danny Stern and Whitney Johnson for creating so many opportunities for us to present our ideas to audiences that could help us sharpen them better; and to Mary Glenn, our editor at McGraw-Hill, for so patiently and so competently whipping our work into shape. Our children Ann, Michael, and Katie prepared the index of this book, and patiently let me talk through with them each piece of the logic. Our son Spencer, currently a missionary in Taiwan, has helped me immeasurably with his prayers. I am grateful to my family for the light and richness they bring to my life.

My teaching colleagues at the Harvard Business School—Steve Kaufman, Willy Shih, and Ray Gilmartin—have sharpened our body of understanding about innovation far beyond the limits of my own perspective and experience. I love working with and supporting them.

Dr. Ronald Arky has helped me live free of the complications of Type I diabetes for nearly 30 years. Dr. Michael Kjelsberg saved my life when a clot completely blocked the left anterior descending artery in my heart. Dr. James Karlson sewed my shattered elbow together with Kevlar, rendering my arm fully functional instead of useless. Dr. Sherleen Chen brought brightness and clarity to my right eye, which otherwise would now be blind. Drs. Callie Taffe and Charles Blatt keep me tuned up. The nurses, technicians, and support staff behind these experts are miracle workers, too. These all have preserved, extended, and enriched my life. I thank them. I dedicate this work to Dr. Jerry Grossman and to these wonderful doctors and caregivers who have preserved my life and my abilities far beyond what nature otherwise would have allowed. I hope that through this book, in some small measure I might repay them, by freeing their abilities from the limits that the health-care system within which they work has often imposed. May God bless each of them, and all of those who are engaged in this vast effort to preserve and enrich the lives of mankind.

Clayton M. Christensen
Boston, Massachusetts

■ ■

I've been leading up to this book for 42 years. In 1966, fresh from my medical training, I took a job at Massachusetts General Hospital (MGH) where I divided my time between the Laboratory of Computer Science and the practice of internal medicine. At the lab, I developed an automated medical record for the brand new Harvard Community Health Plan, an early HMO. Along with other young physicians, with the wise mentoring of John Stoeckle, we started a group practice, and I began managing more and more outpatient functions at the MGH. With others from the lab, I founded a software company called Medical Information Technology (commonly known as MEDITECH), which serves health-care organizations worldwide. By 1970, I was set on my career path of combining the art of hospital management with the new information technologies rapidly coming into use.

After 13 years at the MGH, I moved across town to the New England Medical Center (now known as Tufts Medical Center), where I became president and CEO. Here, with the support of an innovative board and leadership team, I found the perfect place to meld my interest in technology and health-care delivery. The Medical Center gave me unlimited opportunities to test and apply many of my theories about how high-quality health care could be delivered more efficiently using information technology and systems engineering.

During my years as hospital president, I became involved with three other organizations that vastly deepened my understanding of management, technology, and health-care delivery systems. In 1980, thanks to Howard Cox, I was asked to join the board of the Stryker Corporation, a Fortune 500 medical device company. During my 28 years at Stryker, I learned an immense amount working alongside its wise and innovative leader, John Brown. In 1984, I was elected to the Institute of Medicine of the National Academy of Sciences, and over the next 24 years, I had the privilege of serving on numerous committees both at the Institute of Medicine and the National Academy of Engineering. I owe a huge debt to the leaders and staff of the National Academies, and especially to Proctor Reid. Finally, in 1990, I was asked to join the board of the Federal Reserve Bank of Boston, and then to serve as its chair. Both Cathy Minehan and Lynn Browne taught me a great deal of what I know about economics and the constructive role of good regulation.

After retiring from hospital management, I joined the Harvard Kennedy School as the Director of the Health Care Delivery Policy Program (HCDP). I am grateful to the people at the Harvard Kennedy School who gave me the intellectual space to develop my ideas of how health care can be transformed in the United States: Joseph Nye, David Ellwood, John Ruggie, Jack Donahue, and Scott Leland. I offer a deep thanks to each HCDP member and guest speaker, for the spirited and rigorous discussions we had over the years. I especially thank Karen Tracy, Karen Eggleston, and Cara Helfner, without whom the work of HCDP would not have gone so well or so smoothly. Many of the ideas developed through the HCDP Program have found their expression in this book.

During my tenure at the Harvard Kennedy School, I continued to enjoy other opportunities to explore how health care could or should be conducted throughout the United States. In particular, I highly valued my time on the board of the Mayo Clinic, where many innovations in health-care delivery are already in place, and extend my appreciation to Mayo's President & CEO, Denis Cortese, and his colleagues, who allowed me to wade through their data and systems for the last five years. I also am grateful for my collaboration with Alain Enthoven, which most recently included work on a report for the Committee for Economic Development.

While the thoughts that go into this project started forming over four decades ago, the seed for this book specifically began to grow when, after I arrived at the Harvard Kennedy School, I met Clay Christensen. One of my greatest joys comes from the opportunity to collaborate with great thinkers from other fields to further inform and develop my research and thoughts on the medical-care industry, and I was excited to have the chance to examine health-care delivery systems through Clay's lens of disruptive innovation. Through Clay, I met Jason Hwang. He has been invaluable to this book: developing and melding first drafts; culling research, reports, and real-world examples to support our theories; and managing the daunting editorial process.

In addition to the partnership and collaboration of my co-authors, it would not have been possible to produce this book without the generous and able help of many people. I'm grateful to a wonderful cohort of friends and colleagues who provided us with carefully considered, thoughtful feedback which helped clarify our writing and ideas. Denis Cortese, Proctor Reid, and Gordon Vineyard all read multiple chapters, provided extensive notes, and were invaluable sounding boards. In addition, I am indebted to John Brown, for his review of our medical devices chapter; Jon Kingsdale, for his passionate thoughts on reimbursement; and Karen Eggleston, for her astute comments on our chronic disease chapter. I owe all the readers a debt of gratitude for their willingness to help make this project as articulate, well-reasoned, and coherent as possible. I also offer sincere thanks to Cara Helfner, whose many hours of research and work on the endnotes helped ensure clarity and credibility; and to Whitney Johnson and Lisa Stone for all their help coordinating the endorsements.

I offer very special thanks to Karen Tracy, who has worked alongside me for 29 years with good humor and patience, keeping me organized and on track throughout my adventures in health care. I have been fortunate to work with someone as wise and sensible as Karen, who has been the calm in the eye of the storm throughout our many years together.

Over a 42-year career, I was lucky to be given many opportunities to serve—in hospitals, government, the corporate world, think tanks, banking, and academia. In all of these settings, I have been blessed with colleagues, those named here and many others, who constantly challenged my thinking and helped me develop, amend, and revise my ideas. To every one of them, I am extremely grateful.

My deepest thanks go to my family: my youngest daughter, Amelia, for being a fellow risk taker and for sharing my sense of adventure; my middle daughter, Kate, who shepherded this book through to publication in its final months, acting as my voice and representative; and my oldest daughter, Elizabeth, for her willingness to take intellectual journeys with me as I explored disparate disciplines and sectors in search of new approaches to transforming the health-care system.

Finally, I would like to thank my wife, Barbara, for her role in this book. From our very first date, in the summer of 1966, we debated about various models of health-care delivery systems from our disparate political perspectives. For the next 42 years, we refined one another's ideas, became better thinkers from challenging one another, and had lots of fun in the process. Together we raised our three wonderful daughters, and we are unabashedly proud that the interest and passion for public policy that has animated our lives and careers is living on in each of them.

Jerome H. Grossman, M.D.
Cambridge, Massachusetts

■ ■ ■

After reluctantly leaving clinical practice behind to attend Harvard Business School in 2004, I could never have anticipated the path that my career subsequently took. In the summer of 2006, I was generously given a most-unexpected opportunity to work with two of the brightest, most talented individuals I have ever had the great fortune to know. It was as though two Oscar-winning actors had just handed me an all-access pass to the studio lot, together with an assignment to help them compose a movie script whose first act was already being reviewed by critics everywhere. The process of researching and writing *The Innovator's Prescription* was an experience that was alternately terrifying and exhilarating— a constant, *ex post* critique of everything about a health-care system that I had grown to love, combined with a forward-looking compulsion to make it everything that it could be.

I shared my two-and-a-half-year journey of reflection and exposition with two wonderful, illustrious co-authors, Clayton Christensen and Jerome Grossman. When I enrolled in Clay's class as a second-year business school student, little did I know that we would soon form a collaboration to try to change the health-care system. What I realized very quickly, however, was that Clay's ideas would forever have a profound effect on the way I approach problems and their solutions—in work and in life. My respect and admiration for Clay have only grown since then, and I am distinctly privileged to have had the chance to work with such an honorable, giving gentleman.

Unfortunately, Jerry was called away from this earth far too soon. His passing was a tragic and immense loss for all of us, yet the impact he left behind was immeasurable. He influenced not just health care, but public education, finance, and everything he touched. Jerry was instrumental in opening doors that I never even knew existed, and, in the writing of this book, he often served as the yang to Clay's yin. Clay and I did everything in our power to ensure that this book would be remembered as Jerry's Ninth Symphony, leaving his tremendous legacy intact and allowing him, much as in life, the final word.

I owe tremendous gratitude to the same individuals already thanked by my colleagues, and there are several others who warrant special acknowledgment. Kate Sutliff, Jerry's daughter, ably stepped in to help us complete her father's work during a time of great sorrow. Mary Glenn, Danny Stern, and their respective teams at McGraw-Hill and Stern + Associates expertly guided us along this immense undertaking. Whitney Johnson was the ball of energy that frequently re-energized and re-focused the team. Bern Shen served as the calm voice of impartiality, providing reasoned counsel whenever needed. Lisa Stone, JaNeece Thacker, and Karen Tracy managed to inject stability when there seemed to be nothing but chaos and always made certain things got done. My colleagues at Innosight LLC, including Mark Johnson, Scott Anthony, Matt Eyring, and Steve Wunker, served both as sources and sounding boards for our ideas. And I offer a special thanks to Michael Horn, who co-founded Innosight Institute with me and, in the process of toiling as a fellow starving writer on his own book *Disrupting Class*, became a trustworthy and valued friend.

Finally, I must thank the people who helped guide me at the head of this winding but worthwhile path: my teachers, colleagues, and patients at the University of Michigan Medical School and University of California, Irvine Medical Center; my physician friends who continue to struggle to deliver perfect results in an imperfect system; and, of course, my family, whose love and support always ensured that I had a working compass and a running start.

Jason Hwang, M.D.
Cambridge, Massachusetts

The authors would like to thank the following individuals for their contribution and support.

Arshad Ahmed	Valerie Fleishman	Steve Neeleman
Mara Aspinall	Steven Fransblow	Chris O'Connell
Charlie Baker	Erez Gavish	Reed Quinn
JoAnn Baker	Ray Gilmartin	Saquib Rahim
Nancy Barrand	Ginger Graham	Noah Roberts
Keith Batchelder	Andy Grove	Mary Kate Scott
David Bjorkman	Richard Hamermesh	Michael Segal
Richard Bohmer	Aviad Haramati	Jay Silverstein
Kevin Bolen	Lucie Heinzerling	Kanwarjit Singh
Chris Boyce	Michael Howe	Mark Smith
Bruce Bradley	Dennis Hunter	David Snow
Joe Camaratta	Brent James	Steven Spear
Chris Coburn	John Kaegi	Michael Stapley
Delos Cosgrove	John Kenagy	Peter Stebbins
Deborah Danoff	Wolfgang Kleitmann	David Sundahl
Ricky Da Silva	Raju Kucherlapati	Paul Tarini
Keith Dionne	Margaret Laws	Ferris Taylor
Ken Dobler	Jeff Levin-Scherz	Joe Turk
Bruce Donoff	Armando Luna	Janice Uhlig
Nathan Estruth	Marie Mackey	Nick Valeriani
Colin Evans	Mike Mahoney	Thomas Viggiano
Robert Falcone	Nita Maihle	Bill Weldon
Lynn Feldman	Joseph Martin	Linda Hall Whitman
Stephen Field	Michael McGranaghan	Woody Woodburn
Elliott Fisher	Ed Miller	Leslie Yee

Partial support for the production of this book was provided by the California HealthCare Foundation. Information about the Foundation is available at www.chcf.org.

Contents

Introduction

In 1970 the cost of health care in the United States accounted for approximately 7 percent of gross domestic product. In 2007 it accounted for 16 percent of America's GDP. Normally, we view it as good news when an industry gains "share of wallet" in such a manner because it indicates that enterprises are making products or services that customers value and seek to purchase. At one level, therefore, we ought to be treating the fact that Americans are spending more of their income on health care as good news. They value good health. They're certainly better off spending it on health than many other diversions. But at another level this news is terrifying. We note just four frightening factors.

1. The growth in health-care spending in the United States regularly outpaces the growth of the overall economy. Over the last 35 years, while the nation's spending on all goods and services has risen at an average annual rate of 7.2 percent, the amount spent on health care has grown at a rate of 9.8 percent.[1] As a consequence, an increasing proportion of Americans simply cannot afford adequate care. Many efforts

to contain overall costs have the effect of making care inaccessible on a convenient and timely basis for *all* of us—even for those who can pay for it.

2. Second, if federal government spending remains a relatively constant percentage of GDP, the rising cost of Medicare within that budget will crowd out all other spending except defense within 20 years.[2]

3. The third factor that engenders fear is that the burden of covering the costs of health care for employees, retirees, and their families is forcing some of America's most economically important companies to become uncompetitive in world markets. Health-care costs add over $1,500 to the cost of every car our automakers sell, for example.

4. The fourth frightening factor, about which few people are aware, is that if governments were forced to report on their financial statements the liabilities they face resulting from contractual commitments to provide health care for retired employees, nearly every city and town in the United States would be bankrupt. There is no way for them to pay for what they are obligated to pay, except by denying funding for schools, roads, and public safety, or by raising taxes to extreme levels.[3]

Health care is a terminal illness for America's governments and businesses. We are in *big* trouble.

The rest of the world isn't far behind. Nationalized health systems such as those in Canada and the United Kingdom generally seem good at making everyday care conveniently accessible to most people. Some appear to maintain a better balance between general and specialty care than the United States. However, budget limitations continue to result in long lines for specialty services and technologically advanced care.[4] The straits in which Canada's public, paid-for system finds itself, for example, prompted Chief Justice Beverly McLachlin of the Supreme Court of Canada to opine in 2005 that "access to a waiting list is not access to health care."[5] Even in the U.K., where the National

Health Service has made impressive strides in cutting wait times and upgrading facilities, the dramatically increased cost has not been offset by improved productivity.[6]

We look to each other for answers that nobody seems to have. Even while many Americans have begun to look to a single-payer, government-controlled health system as an answer to the crisis in the United States, some governments with nationalized systems have recently introduced competing private insurance plans that offer their citizens a wider array of choices. And in developing countries, the notion of somehow replicating the systems of the developed world is simply unthinkable. Their only option seems to be adequate care for the rich and little for everyone else.

The U.S. system's cost is fueled by a runaway reactor called fee-for-service reimbursement. It has taught us that the economist Jean Baptiste Say was right, at least for this industry: when care-givers make more money by providing more care, supply creates its own demand. By some estimates, a staggering 50 percent of health care consumed seems to be driven by physician and hospital supply, not patient need or demand.[7]

Those fighting for reform have few weapons for systemic change. Most can only work on improving the cost and efficacy of their piece of the system. There are very few system architects among these forces that have the scope and power of a commanding general to reconfigure the elements of the system.

Perhaps most discouraging of all, however, is that there is no credible map of the terrain ahead that reformers agree upon and trust. They are armed with data about the past, and they have become accustomed to reaching consensus for action when the data are conclusive. But because there are no data about the future, there is no map available to convincingly show these reformers which of the pathways ahead of them lead to a dead end and which constitute a promising road to reform. And few have a sense for the interconnectedness of these pathways. As the prophet of Proverbs said, "Where there is no vision, the people perish."[8]

So why this book? There is little dispute that we need a system that is competitive, responsive, and consumer-driven, with clear metrics of value per dollar being spent.[9] Our hope is that *The Innovator's Prescription* can provide a road map for those seeking innovation and reform—an accurate description of the terrain ahead, about which data are not yet available. Much of today's political dialogue on health-care reform centers on how to pay for the cost of health care in the future. This book offers the other half of the equation: how to innovate to reduce costs and improve the quality and accessibility of care. We don't simply ask how we can *afford* health care. We show how to make it *affordable*—less costly and of better quality.

Almost every day somewhere in the United States, a group of health-care reformers convenes a conference. We've attended many of these. Nearly without exception the participants talk past each other. This one focuses on the uninsured poor, that one on prescription coverage for the elderly, another on overuse of expensive diagnostics technology, and still someone else on the cost of end-of-life care. Someone decries the perversions of fee-for-service reimbursement, while someone else bewails the failings of capitation.

They talk past one another because they don't share a common language and a common understanding of the root causes of these problems. Unable to agree on the problem, and without a language for understanding one another, they find it impossible to articulate and agree upon promising solutions. We hope this book helps these reformers understand the root causes of America's health-care malaise so they can frame solutions that stanch the problems at their source. And we hope to give them a common language so that we understand one another and can work cooperatively.

The approach we take in *The Innovator's Prescription* is unique. We have not studied health care to derive solutions for health care. Rather, our aim is to examine this industry through the lenses of general models of managing innovation that have emerged from 20 years of studying these problems at Harvard Business School and the Kennedy School of Government at Harvard. These models have been insightfully applied to industries as diverse as national defense, automobiles, financial services, telecommunications, computer hardware and software, public education, and steel. They have been used to help entire national economies remain competitive and prosperous. They have helped companies innovate in industries that are heavily regulated, as well as in those that are not. We use these models in this book first to explain the root causes for why health care has become progressively expensive and inaccessible. With the causes of these problems defined, we then draw upon these models to show how to solve them.[10]

What follows is a summary of our primary assertions, in order to give our readers a road map of sorts for this book. The subsequent chapters then offer deeper analyses of the problems and solutions, from as many perspectives as possible.

AFFORDABILITY AND CONVENIENT ACCESSIBILITY

The problems facing the health-care industry actually aren't unique. The products and services offered in nearly every industry, at their outset, are so complicated and expensive that only people with a lot of money can afford them, and only people with a lot of expertise can provide or use them. Only the wealthy had access to telephones, photography, air travel, and automobiles in the first decades of those industries. Only the rich could own diversified portfolios of stocks and bonds, and paid handsome fees to professionals who had the expertise to buy and sell those securities. Quality higher education was limited to the wealthy who could pay for it and the elite professors who could provide it. And more recently, mainframe computers were so expensive and complicated that only the largest corporations and universities could own them, and only highly trained experts could operate them. (We will come back to this last example, below.)

It's the same with health care. Today, it's very expensive to receive care from highly trained professionals. Without the largesse of well-heeled employers and governments that are willing to pay for much of it, most health care would be inaccessible to most of us.

At some point, however, these industries were transformed, making their products and services so much more affordable and accessible that a much larger population of people could purchase them, and people with less training could competently provide them and use them. We have termed this agent of transformation *disruptive innovation*. It consists of three elements (shown in Figure I.1).

1. **Technological enabler.** Typically, sophisticated technology whose purpose is to simplify, it routinizes the solution to problems that previously required unstructured processes of intuitive experimentation to resolve.
2. **Business model innovation.** Can profitably deliver these simplified solutions to customers in ways that make them affordable and conveniently accessible.
3. **Value network.** A commercial infrastructure whose constituent companies have consistently disruptive, mutually reinforcing economic models.[11]

In the middle of these three enablers are a host of regulatory reforms and new industry standards that facilitate or lubricate

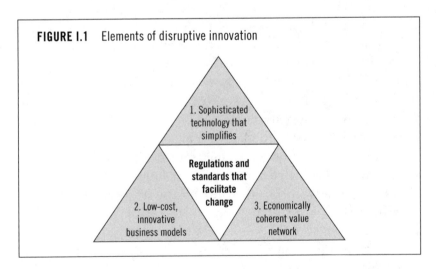

FIGURE I.1   Elements of disruptive innovation

interactions among the participants in the new disruptive industry.

To illustrate how these enablers of disruptive innovation can combine to transform a high-cost, expertise-intensive product into one that is much more affordable and simple, let's briefly review how it transformed digital computing.

The Computer Revolution

Until the 1970s there were only a few thousand engineers in the world who possessed the expertise required to design mainframe computers, and it took deep expertise to operate them. The business model required to make and market these machines required gross profit margins of 60 percent just to cover the inherent overhead. The personal computer disrupted this industry by making computing so affordable and accessible that hundreds of millions of people could own and use computers.

The technological enabler of this disruption was the microprocessor, which so simplified the problems of computer design and assembly that Steve Wozniak and Steve Jobs could slap together an Apple computer in a garage. And Michael Dell could build them in his dorm room.

However, by itself, the microprocessor was not sufficient. IBM and Digital Equipment Corporation (DEC) both had this technological enabler inside their companies, for example. DEC eschewed business model innovation and tried instead to commercialize the personal computer from within its minicomputer business model, a model that simply could not make money if computers were priced below $50,000. IBM, in contrast, set up an innovative business model in Florida, far from its mainframe and minicomputer business units in New York and Minnesota. In its PC business model, IBM could make money with low margins, low overhead costs, and high unit volumes. By coupling the technological and business model enablers, IBM transformed the computing industry and much of the world with it, while DEC was swept away.[12]

And it wasn't just the makers of expensive computers that were swept away. The systems of component and software suppliers, and the sales and service channels that had sustained the mainframe and minicomputer industries, were all disrupted by a new supporting cast of companies whose economics, technologies, and competitive rhythms matched those of the personal computer makers. An entire new value network displaced the old network.

1. DISRUPTIVE TECHNOLOGICAL ENABLERS IN HEALTH CARE

Our bodies have a limited vocabulary to draw upon when they need to express that something is wrong. The vocabulary is comprised of physical symptoms, and there aren't nearly enough symptoms to go around for all of the diseases that exist—so diseases essentially have to share symptoms. When a disease is only diagnosed by physical symptoms, therefore, a rules-based therapy for that diagnosis is typically impossible—because the symptom is typically just an umbrella manifestation of any one of a number of distinctly different disorders.

The technological enablers of disruption in health care are those that provide the ability to precisely diagnose by the *cause* of a patient's condition, rather than by physical symptom. These technologies include molecular diagnostics, diagnostic imaging technology, and ubiquitous telecommunication. When precise diagnosis isn't possible, then treatment must be provided through what we call *intuitive medicine*, where highly trained and expensive professionals solve medical problems through intuitive experimentation and pattern recognition. As these patterns become clearer, care evolves into the realm of evidence-based medicine, or *empirical medicine*—where data are amassed to show that certain ways of treating patients are, on average, better than others. Only when diseases are diagnosed precisely, however, can therapy that is predictably effective for each patient be developed and standardized. We term this domain *precision medicine*.[13]

As we'll see in Chapter 2, disruption-enabling diagnostic technologies long ago shifted the care of most infectious diseases from intuitive medicine (when diseases were given labels such as "consumption") to the realm of precision medicine (where they can be defined as precisely as different types of infection, different categories of lung disease, and so on). To the extent that we know what type of bacterium, virus, or parasite causes one of these diseases—and when we know the mechanism by which the infection propagates—predictably effective therapies can be developed—therapies that address the cause, not just the symptom. As a result, nurses can now provide care for many infectious diseases, and patients with these diseases rarely require hospitalization. Diagnostics technologies are enabling similar transformations, disease by disease, for families of much more complicated conditions that historically have been lumped into categories we have called cancer, hypertension, Type II diabetes, asthma, and so on.

2. DISRUPTIVE BUSINESS MODEL INNOVATIONS

In health care, however, many technological enablers have not yet been translated into lower-cost, higher-quality, more accessible services. The reason? Because of the factors we will explore in this book, the delivery of care has been frozen in two business models—the general hospital, and the physician's practice—both of which were designed a century ago, when almost all care was in the realm of intuitive medicine.

The lack of business model innovation in the health-care industry—in many cases because regulators have not permitted it—is the reason health care is unaffordable. Chapters 1, 3, 4, and 5 describe what these business model innovations might look like and suggest pathways by which entrepreneurs and regulators can accelerate the processes of disruption that have already begun in every branch of the health-care industry.

Generically, there are three types of business models: *solution shops, value-adding process* (VAP) *businesses,* and *facilitated networks.*[14] The two dominant provider institutions in health care—general hospitals and physicians' practices—emerged originally as solution shops. But over time they have mixed in value-adding process and facilitated network activities as well. This has resulted in complex, confused institutions in which much of the cost is spent in overhead activities, rather than in direct patient care. For each to function properly, these business models must be separated in as "pure" a way as possible.

Solution Shops

These "shops" are businesses that are structured to diagnose and solve unstructured problems. Consulting firms, advertising agencies, research and development organizations, and certain law firms fall into this category. Solution shops deliver value primarily through the people they employ—experts who draw upon their intuition and analytical and problem-solving skills to diagnose the cause of complicated problems. After diagnosis, these experts recommend solutions. Because diagnosing the cause of complex problems and devising workable solutions has such high subsequent leverage, customers typically are willing to pay very high prices for the services of the professionals in solution shops.

The diagnostic work performed in general hospitals and in some specialist physicians' practices are solution shops of sorts. Highly trained experts amass information from imaging and other monitoring equipment, analysis of blood and tissue samples, and personal physical examinations. They'll then intuitively develop hypotheses of the causes of patients' symptoms. When the diagnosis is only an uncertain hypothesis, these experts typically test the hypothesis by applying the best available therapy. If the patient responds, it verifies the hypothesis. If not, the experts iterate through cycles of hypothesis testing in an attempt to diagnose and resolve the problem.

Payment almost always is made to solution shop businesses in the form of fee for service. We've observed that consulting firms such as Bain and Company occasionally agree to be paid in part based upon the results of the diagnosis and recommendations their teams have made. But that rarely sticks, because the outcome depends on many factors beyond the correctness of the diagnosis and recommendations, so guarantees about total costs and ultimate outcomes can rarely be made.

Value-Adding Process Businesses

Organizations with value-adding process business models take in incomplete or broken things and then transform them into more complete outputs of higher value. Retailing, restaurants, automobile manufacturing, petroleum refining, and the work of many educational institutions are examples of VAP businesses. Some VAP organizations are highly efficient and consistent, while others are less so.[15]

Many medical procedures that occur after a definitive diagnosis has been made are value-adding process activities. These range from a nurse prescribing medication to cure strep throat after it was diagnosed by a rules-based diagnostic test, to hernia repair, angioplasty, and laser eye surgery. VAP procedures are possible only after a definitive diagnosis has been made first—quite often in a solution shop. When VAP procedures such as these are organizationally separated from those of solution shops, overhead costs drop dramatically: focused VAP clinics typically can deliver comparable care at prices that are half of those incurred in hospitals and physicians' practices in which VAP and solution shop business models are conflated. Institutions such as the Minute-Clinic, Shouldice Hospital, eye surgery centers, and certain focused heart health and orthopedic hospitals are examples of value-adding process businesses.[16]

VAP businesses typically charge their customers for the *output* of their processes, whereas solution shops must bill for the cost of their inputs. Most of them even guarantee the result.[17] They can do this because the ability to deliver the outcome is embedded in repeatable and controllable processes and the equipment used in those processes. Hence, restaurants can print prices on their menus, and universities can sell credit hours at guaranteed prices. Manufacturers of most products publish their prices and guarantee the result for the period of warranty.

Since they operate in the realms of empirical and precision medicine, VAP businesses in the health-care industry can do the same thing. MinuteClinic posts the prices of every procedure it offers. Eye surgery centers advertise their prices; and Geisinger's heart hospitals can specify in advance not just the price of an angioplasty procedure, but can guarantee the result. In a new and remarkable agreement with several European governments, Johnson & Johnson has guaranteed that its new drug Velcade will effectively treat a specific form of multiple myeloma that can be diagnosed with a particular biomarker—or it will refund to the health ministry the cost of the full course of therapy. J&J can do this because the treatment is undertaken after a definitive diagnosis has been made.[18]

Many who have written about the problems of health care decry the fact that the value of health-care services being offered by hospitals and doctors is not being measured. To them, we would explain that the reason isn't that these providers don't *want* to provide measurable value; they simply *can't*, because under the same roof they have conflated fundamentally different business models whose metrics of output, value, and payment are incompatible with one another.

Facilitated Networks

These are enterprises in which people exchange things with one another. Mutual insurance companies are facilitators of networks: customers deposit their premiums into the pool, and they take claims out of it. Participants in telecommunications networks send and receive calls and data among themselves; eBay and craigslist are network businesses. In this type of business, the companies that make money tend to be those that facilitate the effective operation of the network. They typically make money through membership or user fees.

Networks can also be an effective business model for the care of many chronic illnesses that rely heavily on modifications in patient behavior for successful treatment. Until recently, however, there have been few facilitated network businesses to address this growing portion of the world's health-care burden.

Organizations like dLife, which facilitates the networking of people with diabetes and their families, are evolving toward models that can deal with the particular challenges in treating these chronic illnesses.[19] Waterfront Media and WebMD are building facilitated networks for patients with chronic diseases. Harnessing a vast array of patient data, they're building the capability for patients to find "someone like me." This will allow patients to compare progress in treating their disease with directly comparable patients, and ultimately enable those patients to communicate with and learn from each other. The physicians' practice business model is a horrible mismatch with the nature of care for many chronic diseases. Facilitated network business models in health care can be structured to make money by keeping people well; whereas solution shop and VAP business models make money when people are sick.[20]

So what's the answer? The health-care system has trapped many disruption-enabling technologies in high-cost institutions that have conflated two and often three business models under the same roof. The situation screams for business model innovation. The first wave of innovation must separate different business models into separate institutions whose resources, processes, and profit models are matched to the nature and degree of precision by which the disease is understood. Solution shops need to become focused so they can deliver and price the services of intuitive medicine accurately. Focused value-adding process hospitals need to absorb those procedures that general hospitals have historically performed after definitive diagnosis. And facilitated networks need to be cultivated to manage the care of many behavior-dependent chronic diseases. Solution shops and VAP hospitals can be created as hospitals-within-hospitals if done correctly.

The reason why this basic segregation of business models must occur from the outset of disruption is that it will enable accurate measurements of value, costs, pricing, and profit for each type of business. A second wave of disruptive business models can then emerge within each of these three types. Powerful online tools can walk physicians through the process of interpreting symptoms and test results to formulate hypotheses, then help them define the additional data they need to converge upon definitive diagnoses. This will enable lower-cost primary care

physicians to access the expertise of—and thereby disrupt—
specialist practitioners of intuitive medicine. Likewise, ambulatory clinics will disrupt inpatient VAP hospitals. Retail providers
like MinuteClinic, which employ nurse practitioners rather than
physicians, need to disrupt physicians' practices.[21]

Hospitals and physicians' practices have long defended themselves under the banner, "For the good of the patient." Yet, for
the good of the patient, do we really need to leave *all* care in the
realm of intuitive medicine? Much technology has moved past
this point, and health-care business models need to catch up.
Two landmark reports from the Institute of Medicine—*Crossing
the Quality Chasm* and *To Err Is Human*—shattered the myth that
ever-escalating cost was the price Americans must pay to have the
high-quality care that only full-service hospitals staffed by the
best doctors can provide.[22]

3. A DISRUPTIVE VALUE NETWORK: SYSTEMIC REFORM VS. PIECEMEAL INSERTION

The third enabler of disruption is the coalescence of an independent value network around the new disruptive business
models through which care is delivered. Disruptions are rarely
plug-compatible with the prior value network, or commercial
ecosystem. When disruptive innovators assume that relying on
the existing value network is a cheaper, faster way to succeed,
they invariably find that ensconcing their "piece" of the system
into the old value network kills their innovation—or it co-opts
and reshapes their disruptive business model so that it conforms
to that system. Vice versa never happens.

Figure I.2 depicts the systemic change inherent in the new
disruptive value network for health care. This diagram is a sim-
plification of a complicated system whose details are explained
in the chapters that follow. Nonetheless, it highlights how many
elements of the new system will need to change in concert in
order for any of the individual elements to have the desired effect.
Disruption means that many distinctly different business models
will provide care. But this reflects an important step in all of the

disruptive transformations we have studied: the benefits of these focused models will be a dramatic reduction in overhead costs and improvements in quality grounded in better integration. Personally controlled electronic health records and significant reform of the reimbursement and insurance systems are essential in this new value network because they will connect the constituent providers and lubricate the functioning of the system.

Many of the elements of the new disruptive value network depicted on the right side of Figure I.2 have been attempted. The problem is, innovators typically have followed a strategy of individually exchanging, or "hot swapping," themselves for the established institutions in the current value network—the system on the left. And they just don't fit. One by one these reformers have faced a losing battle in their attempts to disrupt the incumbent system from within it. The history of disruption speaks powerfully and unambiguously on this topic: in order to succeed,

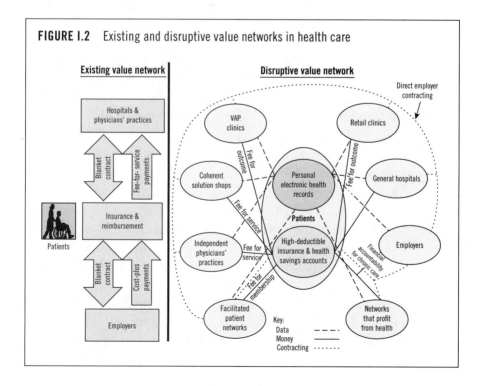

FIGURE I.2 Existing and disruptive value networks in health care

disruptive solutions need to be knit together in a new value network. When this is accomplished, as with all disruptions, patients and providers will be drawn one by one from the old system into the new.

AMASSING THE POWER TO EXECUTE DISRUPTION

In Chapter 6 we will explore how to "make it happen." Disruption can take decades if independent disruptive companies rely on other independent companies to put in place, piece by piece, the other components of the value network depicted on the right side of Figure I.2. Companies that aspire to a faster solution to these problems will need to *integrate*—combining, through a coordinated effort, the business models that must comprise the disruptive value network.[23] This requirement for corporate integration will not be a mandate forever, but it is crucial now. If the generals lack the scope and power to reconfigure today's disparate troops, the forces of reform will remain mired with incompatible agendas, fighting with one another and working on their individual pieces of the problem.

The current health-care system generally is modular. Specialized companies operate hospitals, process paperwork, negotiate blanket service contracts, and manage outpatient and retail clinics. Most doctors' offices are set up as independent businesses. Each can improve its piece of the system, but that's all. When there are interdependencies among the elements of the disruptive value network—meaning that one cannot occur unless others do—the speed of disruption is significantly accelerated if an integrated entity wraps its arms around all the elements in order to orchestrate the changes. As an illustration, when color television was invented, nobody would buy color TVs because no network was broadcasting in color. And networks would not broadcast in color because nobody owned color televisions. It took David Sarnoff—whose company, RCA, acquired NBC—to implement color television in that chicken-and-egg situation. Similarly, health-care systems will need to integrate so they can wrap their arms around all the pieces of the system that must be interdependently reconfigured.

The key dimension of integration will be the creation of integrated fixed-fee providers—companies that own hospitals and employ doctors and, most importantly, do not operate on a fee-for-service basis. Rather, they charge their members a fixed annual fee to provide all the care they will need. These organizations—of which there are a few, such as Kaiser Permanente—are structured to profit from members' wellness, rather than their sickness. Their structure gives them the incentive to create and direct patients to lower-cost business models.

Where providers do not create an integrated fixed-fee system to oversee this systemic overhaul, we can expect more and more major employers to integrate backward and begin providing the primary level of health care for their employees. This trend has already begun, and will accelerate. Employers make money when their employees are healthy and productive. Even though many of them *say* they want to be freed from the burden of paying for employees' health care, if you watch what major employers *do*, they invest heavily to attract, train, and retain the best employees possible. As a result, employers increasingly are integrating backward to contract directly with hospitals and clinics themselves, cutting insurance companies out of the decision-making loop. This integration enables them to direct employees to those providers—be they solution shops, value-adding process clinics, or networks—whose capabilities and costs are best-suited to the problem.

Some dismiss the potential of this backward integration as an activity that is far from the "core competence" of these corporations. But such integration is in fact quite common. Chapter 6 shows that business history is replete with examples of companies that integrated backward in order to ensure a reliable, cost- and performance-effective supply of critical inputs. The notion of sticking with your "core competence" is actually a recent and alarmingly backward-looking one. Many of history's most successful companies followed a much more forward-looking mantra: if it's a critical problem to solve, we'd better develop the competence to solve it. It is in this tradition that more and more employers are backward-integrating into providing health care.

This need for integration exists only when reliable, cost-efficient providers of critical inputs are not available, and when there is a need to change the system's architecture. Once the business models of the new system become ensconced and their interactions become predictable, the system will dis-integrate, and companies will specialize once again.

CHANGES IN THE INFRASTRUCTURE AROUND HEALTH CARE

Clearly, there is no silver bullet that can cure what ails health care. As depicted in Figure I.1, the cure involves three enablers: technology, a business model, and a commercial ecosystem that we call a value network. Putting them together can best be done by integrated companies. But with enablers come constraints. Even the most integrated and powerful entities in the industry will find their progress impeded unless additional innovations that attack these infrastructural constraints are put into place. These were depicted as the middle triangle in Figure I.1, and we will explore them in Chapters 7 through 11. Together with the enablers, these comprise the best map we can draw of the terrain of reform ahead.

Reforming the Reimbursement System

Most discussions about reforming our health-care system hit a dead end when the participants realize that the reimbursement system will simply not allow it. The prices at which reimbursement occurs determine which products and services are profitable, and which are not. Because people will predictably do more of what is profitable and less of what isn't, the system of reimbursement in the United States constitutes one of the most powerful and pervasive schemes of macro- and microlevel regulation that humanity has ever devised.

Health insurance emerged in the 1920s—alongside fire, life, disability, and auto insurance—as a self-purchased product to protect against the unlikely possibility of a disastrously expensive health problem. After legislation in 1943 made health benefits a tax-free form of compensation, employers increasingly used health insurance as a tool for attracting and retaining the best possible employees.[24] Through the 1960s and 1970s, employer-provided insurance against catastrophic events evolved into comprehensive coverage that paid for all health-care costs, large and small. We show in Chapter 7 that the "job" for which employers use health insurance is to attract and retain the best employees possible. Although employers complain about the costs of health care and make noises about wishing to unshackle themselves from that burden, few would probably ever choose to do so—because health coverage is a key weapon required to win the war for talent. That's the good news.

The bad news is that the insertion of massive insurance/reimbursement firms between patients and caregivers over the last three decades has obfuscated all sense of whether the value of services offered is a good deal or a bad one. The dominant payment mechanism today remains fee for service, which defines a simple formula by which providers can prosper: the more services you provide, and the higher the price of these services, the more money you make. It encourages providers not to offer as much care as is needed, but to offer as much care as possible. It is akin to spraying jet fuel on the explosion in health care costs.

The lubricants of efficiency in free-market capitalism are prices that provide accurate, autonomous signals about where, when, and how to create and deploy value-creating innovations. But not only are these prices invisible to most patients and purchasers, most of the prices that claims processors pay are not set by market forces at all. Rather, they are administered prices calculated by Medicare and the insurance industry using pricing algorithms similar to those used in communist systems. The most deleterious effect of these pricing mechanisms is that it's difficult to implement disruptive innovations, which are the key to ushering in affordable health care.

In Chapter 7 we'll discuss a combination of two major interdependent streams of innovation—high-deductible insurance coupled with health savings accounts on the payments side, and disruptive business model innovations on the provider side—that would be a far more effective system for governments and employers to make quality health care affordable. Unless both sides of this reform are done in concert, however, both will fail, because consumers will find themselves paying out of pocket for inconvenient, expensive options that far exceed what they can afford or are willing to pay.

Reformers who focus solely on how to pay for rising health-care costs fail to address the root problems of why care is so costly to begin with. Overcoming this interdependent nature of reimbursement requires integration and the development of a congruent value network. If we don't address the inseparability of this challenge, we run the risk of setting up a system that in fact constitutes "coverage without care."[25]

Perhaps more important, a payment system that incorporates health savings accounts aligns consumer incentives, both financially and behaviorally, giving consumers the freedom to participate in their care or to outsource the decision making to a medical home or health advisor. Regional or national markets set up to encourage and inform consumer choices will help foster these critical decisions.[26]

Role of Information Technology in the Disruption of Health Care

Information technology will play two crucial roles in facilitating the emergence of disruptive business models. First, IT will be the enabling mechanism that shifts the locus of care, when this is desirable and feasible, from solution shops to facilitated networks. It will enable doctors, nurses, and patients to help each other; and it will provide the enabling fuel for primary care doctors to disrupt specialists, and for nurse practitioners to disrupt doctors. Second, the transition from medical records based on pen and paper to ones that are portable, easily accessible, and interoperable will not just substantially reduce the costly paperwork that burdens today's caregivers. It will be the primary mechanism of coordination among the providers in the disruptive value network, as depicted in Figure I.2. These will make it easier to avoid costly mistakes, and will enhance the involvement of patients in their own care.

IT and Facilitated Networks

There are two levels in many disruptive transformations of industries. In most disruptions, companies with lower-cost business models emerge at the bottom of a market in simple applications and gradually move up-market to disrupt the established competitors. Toyota did this to General Motors. Canon did it to Xerox. Sun Microsystems did it to Digital Equipment. Disruptions such as these transform markets with expensive, complicated products that could be used only by a few people with a lot of money and a lot of skill, into markets where far more people with less money and skill can own and use the products. In this stage of disruption, however, the *type* of business model remains the same. In these examples, the disruptees and the disruptors both made their cars, photocopiers, and computers in value-adding process business models.

A second level of disruptive transformation comes when not just *buying* and *using* the product become affordable and simple, but *developing* the product becomes inexpensive and simple as well. When this happens, the type of business model shifts from a solution shop or value-adding process business to a facilitated network business. For example, it used to be very complicated to produce and sell albums in the music recording industry. Production and distribution were value-adding process businesses in which only a limited number of companies participated. MP3 technology, however, made it so simple to record and distribute music that any band with a basement or garage can do it. YouTube led to a similar change in the development and distribution of video: anyone armed with a webcam can do it.[27] In both these industries, networks have emerged so that the participants can exchange content and items of value with each other.

The Internet is enabling the emergence of facilitated networks in health care as well. As mentioned previously, Web sites like dLife.com and Crohns.org enable patients to teach each other how to live with their diseases. Professional networks enable physicians to share insights from patient case studies with each other, without enduring the cumbersome rules and delays entailed in conventional academic publishing. And through expert systems, content and judgment previously available only to specialist physicians become easily accessible to generalist physicians, their assistants, and their patients. As these networks grow, the center of gravity for the care of many chronic diseases will increasingly shift from solution shop business models to facilitated networks.

Evolution of Patient Health Records

The second role for IT in transforming the cost and quality of health care is through the enhancement of medical records. In its most basic form, an electronic medical record (EMR) is simply the electronically stored version of what has always been recorded with pen and paper. However, as the EMR movement gains ground, a medical record known as the personal electronic health record (EHR) has come to the fore. The ability to customize and focus the EHR on consumer involvement may allow it to overcome many of the hurdles that have slowed the adoption of EMRs.[28]

In some countries, such as Denmark, EMRs are pervasively kept in a standard format so any physician in any facility can instantly access the medical records of any patient. We suggest in Chapter 4 that, for good reason, we can expect the major integrated health-care organizations in the United States only to create and employ proprietary EMR systems. The reason is that when software is implemented in complex, established health systems, the power of the existing organizational structures and processes will force the records system to conform itself to them, rather than vice versa. Standard-format EMRs will flourish, however, in a new system of disruptive business models, because the processes and structures of those businesses are in flux and can therefore conform to the architecture of the EMRs.

A more flexible format may have already arrived in the form of the above-mentioned EHRs, whose growth mirrors the exponential growth rate of adoption that characterizes all disruptive innovations. Rather than using data provided and controlled by independent hospitals and physician practices as its foundation, the EHR collects data from all providers and shifts control of the medical record to patients. In bypassing the integrated structure of the existing value network and storing the data in open-source formats, the EHR facilitates connections among the new business models that will comprise the new disruptive value network in health care.

New EHR tools have recently been launched by Microsoft and Google, and innovators like Docvia have enabled patients anywhere in the world to manage their health using the Internet or their mobile phones for less than 10 cents per encounter. The potential changes that consumer involvement can bring are striking. For example, this technology has contributed to a substantial reduction in mother-to-child HIV transmission in large areas of sub-Saharan Africa. Most significantly, this technology appeals to all levels of society, both the very rich and very poor, paving the way for the much anticipated and long overdue transformation of medical records.

The Future of the Pharmaceutical and Medical Devices Industries

Five significant changes loom in the future of the pharmaceutical industry.

The first is that the advent of precision medicine heralds product-line fragmentation in pharmaceuticals. Volumes per therapeutic compound will drop significantly, as the number of therapeutic compounds expands. Blockbuster drugs will become rare. This will necessitate a reshaping of the business model of today's major pharmaceutical companies because—to borrow words from oil exploration—in the future there will be fewer big gushers to cover the costs of drilling a lot of dry holes.[29]

The second of the significant changes we foresee is that the trend already apparent on television, in which drug companies market their products directly to patients rather than through doctors and hospital formularies, is likely to become more widespread. Provided also with sophisticated information and decision-making tools, empowered patients will make self-diagnosis an increasingly common point of entry into the health-care system.

The third and fourth changes are related. In contrast to the past, when diagnostic products were regarded as unattractive stepchildren, in the future diagnostics will become quite profitable relative to therapeutics. In other solution shop businesses, customers are willing to pay high prices to firms like McKinsey & Company for precise diagnoses of their problems—because the value of defining and solving the right problem is immense. The modest profitability of diagnostic products and services has been an artifact of today's reimbursement system. This will change as the disruptions described above are implemented.

The fourth change is that because it appears to be a profit-maximizing move based upon data from the past, most of today's leading pharmaceutical companies are dis-integrating—choosing to outsource, step by step, drug discovery and development, the management of clinical trials, and the manufacture of their products. What drives this "shedding" of activity after activity is that revenues are unaffected by this outsourcing, while profits seem to improve. We show in Chapter 8 however, that where, in the past, sales and marketing muscle was the unassailable strength of major pharmaceutical companies, this is rapidly becoming commoditized by massive distribution and pharmacy benefit management companies like Medco. And what was a complex cost center to pharmaceutical executives in the past—the management of clinical trials and the concomitant development of precision diagnostics—is likely to become the core of profit generation in the future. The major companies, in summary, are exiting the wrong part of the business.

Fifth, and finally, generics competitors are disrupting companies that develop, manufacture, and market patented drugs. It's well known that generics manufacturers move in the day after the patent protection of drugs expires. Often, the price of these drugs will drop by as much as 80 percent, literally overnight. What is not widely appreciated, however, is that several major generics manufacturers, primarily in Israel and India, are moving up-market, developing their own proprietary products as they pursue greater profitability.

The reason they can do this is that the U.S. government allows our pharmaceutical companies to price their proprietary products high enough not just to recoup the cost of developing those specific drugs, but the cost of developing and testing all of the drugs that failed to make it to market as well. Most other governments—including that of Canada—have few pharmaceutical companies they must assist in this way. As a result, their national health systems negotiate much lower prices for patented drugs than those that are allowed in America. This constitutes a very real tax that American consumers pay to subsidize pharmaceutical research for the world. There is some evidence that this practice of subsidizing pharmaceutical companies' R&D costs in fact has allowed their work to become relatively inefficient. Disruptive, formerly generic competitors whose governments do not offer these subsidies of research costs seem able to develop new proprietary drugs at a cost 40 percent lower, on average, than that of U.S. companies.

Medical Devices and Diagnostic Equipment

We show in Chapter 9 that the use of devices and diagnostic equipment will *decentralize*—playing out a typical pattern of innovation. At the beginning stages of most modern industries, the initial products are so complicated and expensive that things become *centralized*: we take the problems to the solution.

By way of illustration, in the formative years of the telecommunications and photocopying industries, we took our messages to the Western Union telegraph office and our originals to the corporate photocopy center. Activity in the industry subsequently became centralized to economize on the high fixed costs of the equipment and the operators. While the vendors of those expensive, centralized products work to make them even better, disruptive innovators, by making the products simpler and more affordable, drive a decentralization of the industry—bringing the solution ever closer to the problem or the need.

For example, in telecommunications, the telephone made it possible for people to communicate over long distances from their homes rather than the telegraph office. With mobile phones, we don't have to be home; we can communicate from our pockets and purses. Canon brought photocopying to the closet around the corner; and the Hewlett-Packard ink-jet printer put it on our desktops. A new company, Zink, is now bringing photocopying to our briefcases. This pattern of centralization-decentralization characterizes the history of innovation in most industries.

The same pattern has begun to play itself out in medical devices and diagnostic equipment. Blood and tissue testing, and most imaging services, are at present centralized industries. Great opportunities for disruptive growth are arising as companies focus on point-of-care diagnostics and on in-office imaging technologies. This is a key technological enabler that will fuel professionals to do ever more sophisticated procedures in lower-cost venues of care, and it will enable lower-cost caregivers to disrupt their higher-cost colleagues.

Developments in medical devices will change the essence of expertise in certain branches of medical practice. Interventional radiology, for example, is driven by such new diagnostic imaging technologies. Historically, the domain of radiologists was the operation of X-ray machines and interpretation of the images they generated. However, imaging technologies such as ultrasound and CT scanners have become so good that radiologists can get shockingly clear images not just of bones, but of deep tissues and organs. These imaging modalities had primarily been used diagnostically. Increasingly, however, radiologists and other nonsurgeons are using these techniques to guide minimally-invasive surgical tools. Because the doctor can clearly see the tools and target tissues on a television screen, executing a perfect procedure becomes much easier.

Already this is beginning to blur the boundaries between certain surgical specialties whose boundaries have generally been drawn around parts of the body, and it will undoubtedly change the nature of training required to perform surgery—obscuring the line between surgeons and nonsurgeons. As an example, in the past, most hysterectomies were done by gynecologists. Now, interventional radiologists, using ablation techniques to treat uterine fibroids, are more and more obviating the need to perform total hysterectomies.

Changes in Medical Education

Today's medical training reflects three realities of the early 1900s, when the basic architecture of our medical schools' curricula was put in place. The first of these realities was that medical practice in the first decades of the twentieth century was an intuitive art, not a science—meaning that the ability to deliver care was embedded in the caregivers, not in rules, processes, and equipment. Hence, medical training was organized to train doctors to work individually and intuitively. The second former reality was that students finished their work on the farm in the fall, and therefore needed to start their schooling in batches. The third was that when the architectures of today's medical school curricula were established, most diseases were acute, so the full course of many diseases could be observed within the hospitals where the doctors-in-training worked.

The future world in which today's medical students will practice will be substantially different from the world for which medical schools are preparing them. One dimension of difference is that many diseases that are in the realms of intuitive and empirical medicine today will have migrated toward the domain of precision medicine 20 years from now. As a result, many diseases will eventually be diagnosed and treated by nurse practitioners and physician assistants. Organizing and supervising the work of paraprofessionals will be a major dimension of most physicians' jobs.

Another difference is personal versus process expertise. There will always be a need for deeply experienced, intuitively expert physicians to do the work of solution shops. Many diseases will continue to defy precision medicine, and new diseases will emerge. Today's methods of preparing medical students to work as individuals are generally appropriate for those who will work in solution shops—though we will likely need fewer such physicians 30 years from now than are needed today. But most physicians in the future will work in settings where much of the ability to deliver care will be better embedded in processes and in equipment, rather than exclusively resident in individuals' capacities. No medical school that we know of has yet established a course in which students can learn how to design self-improving processes that prevent mistakes from occurring.

We note in Chapter 10 that because today's reimbursement schedules make specialist careers much more lucrative than the careers of primary care physicians, the graduates of U.S. medical schools are moving decisively "up-market," choosing training to become specialists. As a result, about half of all new primary care doctors that begin practicing in the United States today were trained in foreign medical schools—primarily in the Caribbean, Latin America, and India. Those schools are getting very good, and they are disrupting the U.S. schools, starting in the tier of the market that is economically least attractive to the incumbents.

The reason why this is a serious development for our medical training establishment is that a host of technological enablers will fuel the disruption of specialists by primary care physicians in the future. In addition, these same technological advances will enable nurse practitioners and physician assistants to disrupt primary care physicians. And yet we have a chronic shortage of nurses in the United States too—which again is filled primarily by immigrant nurses trained in places like the Philippines. A key driver of this shortage is the limited faculty capacity of U.S. nursing schools. In sum, this means that the United States is shifting its medical education resources to train more of the professionals we'll need fewer of, and training fewer of those we will need more of in the future.

The Impact of Regulation on Disruption Innovation in Health Care

In the final chapter we consider the regulatory barriers to disruptive change, identify eight categories of regulations that now impede disruption and must be changed, and propose a model for how these changes can be made. As with many of the findings in this book, we show that health care honestly isn't that different from other industries: the pattern of regulation in health care matches that of many other industries in which the public interest may not be addressed through normal market mechanisms. Regulation in these industries typically goes through three stages:

1. **Foster.** Subsidize the creation of the industry.
2. **Stabilize and assure.** Strengthen the participants; ensure that all who should have access in fact do; and make sure that the products are safe and effective.
3. **Afford.** Encourage competition that will reduce prices.

A major class of government subsidies of America's health-care system occurs directly through the National Institutes of Health, and indirectly through the high prices that our government allows on patented drugs in order to fund ongoing research and development within our pharmaceutical companies. Together, these subsidies fund a large share of the research that has begun transforming medical practice from intuition to precision. This subsidy of basic and applied research, and of product development and testing, truly constitutes an extraordinary gift to the people of the world.[30] We recommend one change in how this subsidy is administered. In fields in which breakthroughs are needed, research at the *intersection* of scientific disciplines, and not just research that deepens knowledge within disciplines, needs its separate channel of review so such projects can more readily receive funding.

As mentioned previously, by setting the rates of reimbursement for providers of products and services, the Centers for Medicare and Medicaid Services (CMS) exerts powerful regulatory control over what providers will and will not do. Furthermore, government-sponsored health plans like state Medicaid programs and the Veterans Health Administration have policies that guarantee best-in-market prices from their suppliers through a system of price ceilings and rebates. For example, most Medicaid programs stipulate that, at the end of each quarter, the prices they pay to suppliers must be written down to the lowest prices charged to any other customer. While this ostensibly ensures that Medicaid automatically pays the lowest price for everything it buys, its inadvertent effect is to make discounting extremely expensive for providers of health-care products and services. It instills extraordinary pricing "discipline" among competitors in the hospital, pharmaceutical, and medical device industries that executives in other industries—airlines, for example—can only dream about.

Much of the government's regulatory energy currently focuses on ensuring that providers and products are safe and effective. When medicine is in the intuitive realm, the best mechanism for accomplishing this is to regulate *who* can provide care. Regulatory focus is on the inputs or resources used in the process—primarily the training and qualifications of the doctors who provide the care. When care of a disorder has moved into the realm of empirical medicine, the emphasis of regulation needs to focus less on the qualifications of the providers and more on *how* they do their work—on the processes being followed. This is because following best-practice processes is the key to getting the best outcomes most consistently, when medical practice is empirical. Finally, when a disorder has advanced into the realm of precision medicine, regulation most productively focuses on *what*—on the outcomes—rather than on inputs or processes.

In many areas the progress of medical science now calls for the body of medical regulation to shift focus toward reducing costs. We show in Chapter 11 that economists-turned-deregulators are often guided by too simple a model when they attempt this, in that they believe that simply intensifying competition will bring about lower prices. In reality, when regulators try to intensify *sustaining* competition in an industry, the result typically is *higher* prices. Regulations that provide an incentive for general hospitals to compete more intensely against other general hospitals, for example, will send them rushing up-market toward ever more profitable services. It has been a *disruptive* competition that has reduced costs dramatically in literally *every* historical instance in which regulators have sought to reduce prices.

A key reason why regulatory change persistently lags behind the progress of medical science is that those who would be disrupted by the shift in regulatory focus have a lot to lose, and for the good of the provider they adroitly preserve regulations that initially had been adopted for the good of the patient. Our research has shown that the power of those ensconced behind the protection of these regulations almost *never* yields to a direct assault on the regulation. Rather, the regulations are toppled only when disruptive innovators find applications or markets beyond the reach of the regulators. They succeed in that context—and the regulation ultimately succumbs to the evidence. We give case histories in this final chapter of instances in which regulations that barred lower-cost health-care providers from entering a market were toppled through this strategy.

SUMMARY

The challenge that we face—making health care affordable and conveniently accessible to most people—is not unique to health care. Almost every industry began with services and products that were so complicated and expensive to provide and consume that only people with a lot of skill and a lot of money could participate. The transformational force that has brought affordability and accessibility to other industries is disruptive innovation. Today's health-care industry screams for disruption. Politicians are consumed with how we can afford health care. But disruption solves the more fundamental question: How do we make health care affordable?

Most disruptions have three enablers: a simplifying technology, a business model innovation, and a disruptive value network. The technological enabler transforms a technological problem from something that requires deep training, intuition, and iteration to resolve, into a problem that can be addressed in a predictable, rules-based way. Diagnostic abilities are the technological enablers of disruption in health care. Precise definition of the problem, in this and in every industry, is a prerequisite to the development of a predictably effective solution.

In the past, business model innovation was common in health care. When the technological enablers for the diagnosis and treatment of infectious diseases emerged, most patient care was transferred away from hospitals to doctors' offices, and away from the doctors to the nurses. However, business model innovation has stalled in the last three decades. Regulations and reimbursement systems currently trap in high-cost venues much care that could be provided in lower-cost, more convenient business models. Other disruptions fail because they lack new value networks that combine business models into coherent ecosystems that allow them to disrupt their predecessors.

Three key lessons from the history of disruptive innovation are particularly important in the disruption of health care. The first is that while the technological enablers almost always emerge from the laboratories of leading institutions in the industry, the business model innovations do not. Almost always these are forged by new entrants to the industry. Regulators must beware, therefore, of attempts by the leading institutions to outlaw business model innovation. Regulation should facilitate it. What is in the interest of society most often does not coincide with the self-perceived interests of the leading institutions.

The second key lesson is that disruption rarely happens piecemeal, where stand-alone disruptions are plugged into the existing value network of an industry. Rather, entirely new value networks arise, disrupting the old. Hence, disruptive business models such as value-adding process clinics, retail clinics, and facilitated networks must be married with disruptive innovations in insurance and reimbursement in order to reap the full impact in cost and accessibility. At the outset, knitting all these pieces together will require a much higher degree of integration than has been the norm in the health-care industry. Difficult though it will be, these providers need to disrupt themselves. Employers will need to play a more proactive role in orchestrating the emergence of this new value network, compared to the reactive posture they have taken in the past.

Finally, we have seen a pervasive pattern in *every* industry that has been transformed through disruption. This same pattern characterizes what has happened to date with disruptive initiatives in health care. The energies, talent, and resources of the leading organizations in an established system *always* are absorbed in improving their best products, which are sold to address the most demanding applications in the industry. Why? Because the high end of most markets is where the most attractive profits are made, serving the most profitable customers. When a disruptive technological enabler emerges, the leaders in the industry disparage and discourage it because, with its orientation toward simplicity and accessibility, the disruption just isn't capable of solving the complicated problems that define the world in which the leading experts work.

Always, the technological enablers of disruption are successfully deployed against the industry's simplest problems first. They then build commercial and technological momentum upon that foothold and improve, progressively displacing the old, high-cost approach application by application, customer by customer, disease by disease. Apple sold its Apple IIe personal computer as a toy to children, not to the accounting departments of major banks. Nucor cut its teeth on concrete reinforcing bars, not the sheet steel that fed Ford. Cisco deployed its switches to route data, not voice—because data didn't care about the router's four-second latency delay, whereas voice telecommunications did. Target started by selling things like paint, hardware, and simple kitchen supplies, not designer clothing. JCB transformed the digging of big holes not by aspiring to use hydraulics technology to excavate massive underground parking garages upon which skyscrapers would be built. JCB started by digging one-foot trenches to run water lines from homes to the pipes under the street. Toyota's launch vehicle was a Corona, not a Lexus.

Health care is no different. An illustration: angioplasty has transformed the interventional care of coronary artery disease— making it *much* more affordable and *much* more convenient for *many* more people to receive effective treatment.[31] It was initially deployed against partially occluded, easy-to-access coronary arteries. Luckily, angioplasty wasn't blocked from the market just because it couldn't beat the gold standard of open-heart bypass surgery, which was unquestionably the best way to resolve intractable blockages in complicated locations. But step by step, stent by stent, the minimally invasive approach has improved to the point where fewer and fewer people need bypass surgery. Now, pharmaceuticals, including lipid-lowering agents such as Lipitor, are disrupting angioplasty in the same manner. They were not withheld from the market because they couldn't dissolve defiant arterial blockages. But deployed as prevention, patient by patient, these "statins" demonstrate reabsorption of athero-sclerotic plaques that can obviate the need for angioplasty.

Doctors and hospitals, regulators, and policy makers need to convert to this religion because it isn't myth: it is true. The fact that cost-lowering, accessibility-enhancing disruptive enablers can address only the simplest of problems at the outset is indeed a gospel of good news. It frees physicians and hospitals to focus their energies on what they do best—tackling complex medical problems and moving more and more problems along the spectrum from intuitive toward precision medicine. However, in the history of health care, industry leaders have repeatedly lobbied for legislation and regulation that block disruptive approaches from being used anywhere until they are certifiably good enough to be used everywhere. This traps the industry where it began, in the expertise-intensive world of high costs.

Generally, the leading practitioners of the old order become the victims of disruption, not the initiators of it. But properly educated, the leaders of the existing systems can take the lead in disrupting themselves—because while leaders instinctively view disruption as a threat, it always proves to be an extraordinary growth opportunity. Hence, IBM played a huge role in creating the personal computer industry; the department store Dayton-Hudson launched Target; and Hewlett-Packard created and grew to dominate the disruptive ink-jet printer business. When they follow the rules we've described in our research, the leaders in the old indeed can become the leaders of the new.

The forces of health-care reform have had no credible map of the terrain ahead. Our hope is that this book can serve as the map. We hope this map inspires some of you to step to the front and become leaders in a coordinated revolution, because the reforms that make health care affordable and accessible are indeed possible.

NOTES

1. According to the Kaiser Family Foundation and the Centers for Medicare and Medicaid Services, the average annual growth rate in national health expenditures was 9.8 percent in nominal terms between 1970 and 2005. The nominal growth rate of GDP was 7.4 percent over the same period. See *Health Care Costs: A Primer*, Kaiser Family Foundation, August 2007.

2. David Walker, comptroller general of the United States, estimates that the federal government would have to set aside $23 to $28 trillion today to meet the underfunded promises of Medicare. Walker was interviewed on *60 Minutes* on July 8, 2007, about the future effects of Medicare on the nation's economy: http://www.cbsnews.com/stories/2007/03/01/60minutes/main2528226.shtml.

3. Unfunded and unrecognized pension obligations. See D'Angelo, G., "State and Local Governments Must Address Unfunded Health Care Liabilities," Heritage Foundation WebMemo #1808, February 11, 2008. Accessed at http://www.heritage.org/research/healthcare/wm1808.cfm.

4. Schoen, Cathy, et. al., "Toward Higher-Performance Health Systems: Adults' Health Care Experiences in Seven Countries, 2007," *Health Affairs*, vol. 26, no. 6 (2007), 717–34.

5. "Unsocialized Medicine," *Wall Street Journal*, June 13 2005, A12.

6. "NHS Audit: Big Spender, Unwise Spender," *The Economist*, September 13, 2007.

7. Brownlee, S., *Overtreated: Why Too Much Medicine Is Making Us Sicker and Poorer*, Bloomsbury USA, September 2007.

8. *Holy Bible*, Book of Proverbs, 29:18.

9. The leading and most articulate spokesperson for consumer-driven health care is Professor Regina Herzlinger of Harvard Business School. Her books on this topic include *Consumer-Driven Health Care: Implications for Providers, Payers, and Policy-Makers* (San Francisco: Jossey-Bass, 2004); and *Who Killed Health Care?: America's $2 Trillion Medical Problem—and the Consumer-Driven Cure* (New York: McGraw-Hill, 2007). See also Porter, M., and Teisberg, E., *Redefining Health Care: Creating Value-Based Competition on Results* (Boston: Harvard Business School Press, 2006).

10. In this book we do not describe the data and the analytics through which these models were derived, because they have been thoroughly documented in a range of books and academic publications. In this book we *illustrate* the workings of these models and theories by drawing on examples that are familiar to many readers. These illustrations aren't offered as proof of the validity of these models, however. Readers who want further documentation and analysis should first study Christensen, Clayton M. (1997), *The Inno-*

vator's Dilemma, and Christensen, Clayton M., and Michael Raynor (2003), *The Innovator's Solution* (both published by Harvard Business School Press, Boston). Footnotes in those books can lead curious readers even more deeply into the academic papers through which these models were originally published.

11. Stabell and Fjeldstad describe the value network or commercial system a "system of interlinked chains" (Stabell, Charles. B., and Fjeldstad, Ø. D., "Configuring Value for Competitive Advantage: On Chains, Shops and Networks." *Strategic Management Journal*, May 1998), which Porter labels the value system (Porter, Michael, *Competitive Advantage*. New York: The Free Press (1985):34).

12. We refer interested readers to Christensen, Clayton M., *The Innovator's Dilemma*, op.cit.

13. It is important to keep in mind that the progression from one end of this spectrum to the other is an incremental process. There remains a significant number of patients—16 to 20 percent, according to Groopman, J., *How Doctors Think*, Houghton Mifflin Company (March 2007)—who still require intuitive care to reach a definitive diagnosis. However, by applying rules of thumb and other heuristics, the work that many physicians do today has actually progressed through the intuitive and empirical phases and is very nearly precision, or rules-based, medicine.

14. We are deeply indebted to our friend Øystein Fjeldstad of the Norwegian School of Management, who developed and taught us this framework. We'll explain these concepts more deeply in later chapters. Those interested in Fjeldstein's framework should also read Stabell, C. B., and Fjeldstad, Ø. D., "Configuring Value for Competitive Advantage: On Chains, Shops and Networks." *Strategic Management Journal*, May 1998.

15. Most concepts of strategy were derived from the study of VAP businesses. See, for example, Porter, Michael, *Competitive Advantage*. New York: The Free Press (1985). More recently, Professor Tom Eisenmann at Harvard Business School has done similarly insightful work on strategy in Network businesses. There has been much less Porter- and Eisenmannesque work done on strategy in solution shop businesses.

16. Our colleague Regina Herzlinger, building upon earlier work by Harvard Business School professor Wickham Skinner, has written extensively on the value of focus. See Herzlinger, R., *Market-Driven Health Care: Who Wins, Who Loses in the Transformation of America's Largest Service Industry*. Reading, Massachusetts: Addison-Wesley (1997).

17. Abelson, Jenn, "Shift in Health-Cost Focus Is Said to Show Promise." *New York Times*, July 12, 2007.

18. The treatment of this specific form of multiple myeloma isn't yet in the realm of *precision* medicine—but it is solidly in the empirical world. Johnson & Johnson therefore cannot guarantee that *every* patient will be healed. But the biomarker diagnosis is unambiguous, and Velcade is efficacious a high enough percentage of the time so that J&J can build into its product pricing the probability of Velcade not working with a small percentage of patients.

19. dLife at http://www.dlife.com, provides newsletters, recipes, forums, a national weekly television show and radio station, and online educator-customized interactive tools for providers and patients.

20. Another example is Revolution Health, which recently merged with Waterfront Media. Together they offer online communities of blogs, forums, groups, and people with similar goals. Members are encouraged to start a new group.

21. Bohmer, Richard, "The Rise of In-Store Clinics—Threat or Opportunity?" *New England Journal of Medicine*, vol. 356, no. 8 (2007): 765-68.

22. Committee on Quality of Health Care in America, *Crossing the Quality Chasm: A New Health System for the 21st Century*, Washington, DC: Institute of Medicine, National Academy Press, 2001; and Kohn, Linda T., Janet M. Corrigan, and Molla S. Donaldson, eds., *To Err Is Human: Building a Safer Health System*, Washington, DC: Committee on Quality of Health Care in America, Institute of Medicine, National Academy Press, 1999.

23. The term "integrated" likely has different meanings to our readers who are physicians and those who are businesspeople. To physicians, an integrated approach in health care entails mustering a team of caregivers from many potentially relevant specialties in order to give the patient every dimension of care he or she might need. To a businessperson, integration involves operationally knitting together insurance, hospitals, physician-employees, outpatient surgery centers, and retail clinics under one corporate umbrella. Our usage of the term is in the business sense.

24. Special Ruling, October 26, 1943, CCH Federal Tax Service, vol. 443, paragraph 6587.

25. A phrase originated by Dr. Marcia Angell, former executive editor of the *New England Journal of Medicine*.

26. Committee for Economic Development Report, October 2007.

27. The first level of disruption in the movie industry occurred when Pixar and similar studios, using digital animation, disrupted traditional animation studios like Disney. Both were value-adding process businesses, however. YouTube shifts the business model to a facilitated network.

28. Raymond, Brian, "Realizing the Transformative Potential of Personal Health Records," Kaiser Permanente Institute for Health Policy, Oakland, CA, 2007. See also Mandl, K. D. and I. S. Keohane, "Tectonic Shifts in the Health Information Economy," *New England Journal of Medicine*, vol. 358, no. 16, April 17, 2008, 1732–37.

29. This will not always be exactly the case, as we describe in Chapter 8. New types of blockbuster drugs will arise. For example, the Elan Pharmaceutical drug Tysabri, marketed by Biogen-Idec, has been shown to effectively treat patients with multiple sclerosis, Crohn's Disease, rheumatoid arthritis, and certain other diseases. The reason seems to be that these are different symptomatic manifestations of the same fundamental causal disorder, which is a particular type of inflammation in the nervous system.

30. This subsidy is akin to what was done in telecommunications. For nearly half of the twentieth century the government intentionally kept the prices of long-distance telephony high—in part to subsidize local phone service, but also to cover the cost of AT&T's Bell Laboratories. A great number of the technological and scientific discoveries in the history of microelectronics were developed at Bell Laboratories and then licensed to the world at extraordinarily low prices.

31. Some recent studies purport to show that angioplasty is just as costly on a per-patient basis as open-heart surgery. We contend that even if these studies are accurate, it is simply the result of pricing and profit distortions of the present reimbursement system.

Chapter 1

The Role of Disruptive Technology and Business Model Innovation in Making Products and Services Affordable and Accessible

In the 15 years since we first introduced the term "disruptive technology" into the lexicon of business management, there has probably been as much confusion about it as there has been clarity because the terms "disruption" and "technology" carry many prior connotations in the English language. Disruption connotes something "upsetting" and "radically different," among other things. And to many, "technology" connotes revolutionary ways of doing things that are comprehensible only to Ph.D. scientists and computer nerds. As a result of these other connotations of the words we chose, many who have only casually read our research have assumed that the concept of disruptive innovation refers to a radically new technology that tips an industry upside down.

But we have tried to give the term a very specific meaning: "disruption" is an innovation that makes things simpler and more affordable, and "technology" is a way of combining inputs of materials, components, information, labor, and energy into outputs of greater value. Hence, every company—from Intel to Wal-Mart—employs technology as it seeks to deliver value to its customers. Some executives believe that technology can solve the challenges of growth and cost that confront their firms or industries. Yet this is rarely the case. Indeed, widely heralded technologies often fall short of the expectation that they will transform an industry. Anyone who has been inside a modern hospital, for example, has noted the myriad sophisticated technologies at work today, yet health care only seems to get more expensive and inaccessible. The reason is that the purpose of most technologies—even radical breakthroughs—is to *sustain* the functioning of the current system. Only *disruptive* innovations have the potential to make health care affordable and accessible.

In this chapter we first review the concept of disruptive innovation and its constituent elements. We then zero in on the concept of a business model, showing that it is composed of four elements—a value proposition, and the resources, processes and profit formula required to deliver that value proposition to targeted customers. Because business model innovation is the crucial ingredient in harnessing a disruptive technology in order to transform an industry, we then describe three different classes of business models around which the health-care industry will be organized in the future. Along the way, we offer illustrations from other industries showing that when innovators stop short of business model innovation, hoping that a new technology will achieve transformative results without a corresponding disruptive business model and without embedding it in a new disruptive value network or ecosystem, fundamental change rarely occurs. In other words, disruptive technologies and business model innovations are both necessary conditions for disruption of an industry to occur. We close the chapter by explaining the process by which existing companies and their leaders can create new business models that match the degree of disruption needed.

In the subsequent five chapters we will build upon the foundation we lay out in this one. Chapter 2 explores the technological enablers of disruption in health care. Chapters 3 and 4 show how the business models of hospitals and physicians' practices must change in order to harness the power of disruption to make health care affordable and conveniently accessible, while Chapter 5 addresses the type of business model innovation necessary to transform the management of chronic disease. Finally, Chapter 6 explores which companies and industry executives are and are not in a position to lead these disruptive innovations—and what they need to do to get the job done.

THE DISRUPTIVE INNOVATION THEORY

The disruptive innovation theory explains the process by which complicated, expensive products and services are transformed into simple, affordable ones. It also shows why it is so difficult for the leading companies or institutions in an industry to succeed at disruption. Historically, it is almost always new companies or totally independent business units of existing firms that succeed in disrupting an industry.

The theory's basic constructs are depicted in Figure 1.1, which charts the performance of a service or product over time. First, focusing on the graph in the back plane of this three-dimensional diagram, there are two types of improvement trajectories in every market. The solid line denotes the pace of improvement in products and services that companies provide to their customers as they introduce newer and better products over time. Meanwhile, the dotted lines depict the rate of performance improvement that customers are able to utilize. There are multiple dotted lines to represent the different tiers of customers within any given market, with the dotted line at the top representing the most demanding customers and the dotted line at the bottom representing customers who are satisfied with very little.

As these intersecting trajectories of the solid and dotted lines suggest, customers' needs in a given market application tend to be relatively stable over time. But companies typically improve their products at a much faster pace so that products that at one point weren't good enough ultimately pack together more features and functions than customers need. A useful way of visualizing this is to note how car companies give customers new and improved engines every year, but customers simply cannot use all of this improvement because of speed limits, traffic jams, and police officers.

Innovations that drive companies up the trajectory of performance improvement, with success measured along dimensions historically valued by their customers, are said to be sustaining innovations. Some of these improvements are dramatic breakthroughs, while others are routine and incremental. However, the competitive purpose of all sustaining innovations is to maintain the existing trajectory of performance improvement in the established market. Airplanes that fly farther, computers that process faster, cellular phone batteries that last longer, and televisions with larger screens and clearer images are all sustaining innovations. We have found in our research that in almost every case the companies that win the battles of sustaining innovation are the incumbent leaders in the industry. And it seems not to matter how technologically challenging the innovation is. As long as these innovations help the leaders make better products which they can sell for higher profits to their best customers, they figure out a way to get it done.

The initial products and services in the original "plane of competition" at the back of Figure 1.1 are typically complicated and expensive so that the only customers who can buy and use the products, or the only providers of these services, are those with a lot of money and a lot of skill. In the computer industry, for example, mainframe computers made by companies like IBM comprised that original plane of competition from the 1950s through the 1970s. These machines cost millions of dollars to purchase and millions more to operate, and the operators were highly trained professionals. In those days, when someone needed to compute, she had to take a big stack of punched cards to the corporate mainframe center and give it to the computer expert, who then ran the job for her. The mainframe manufacturers focused their innovative energies on making bigger and better mainframes. These companies were very good, and very successful, at what they did. The same was true for much of the

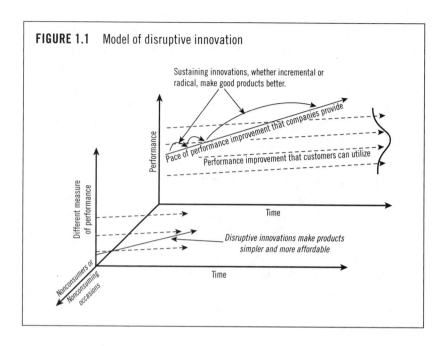

FIGURE 1.1 Model of disruptive innovation

history of automobiles, telecommunications, printing, commercial and investment banking, beef processing, photography, steel making, and many, many other industries. The initial products and services were complicated and expensive.

Occasionally, however, a different type of innovation emerges in an industry—a disruptive innovation. A disruptive innovation is *not* a breakthrough improvement. Instead of sustaining the traditional trajectory of improvement in the original plane of competition, the disruptor brings to market a product or service that is actually *not as good* as those that the leading companies have been selling in their market. Because it is not as good as what customers in the original market or plane of competition of Figure 1.1 are already using, a disruptive product does not appeal to them. However, though they don't perform as well as the original products or services, disruptive innovations are simpler and more affordable. This allows them to take root in a simple, undemanding application, targeting customers who were previously nonconsumers because they had lacked the money or skill to buy and use the products sold in the original plane of competition. By competing on the basis of simplicity, affordability, and accessibility, these disruptions are able to establish a base of customers in an entirely different plane of competition, as depicted in the front of Figure 1.1. In contrast to traditional customers, these new users tend to be quite happy to have a product with limited capability or performance because it is infinitely better than their only alternative, which is nothing at all.

The personal computer is a classic example of a disruptive innovation. The first personal computers (PCs), like the Apple IIe, were toys for children and hobbyists, and the first adult applications were simple things like typing documents and building spreadsheets. Any complex computational problem still had to be served by the back plane of competition, where experts with mainframe computers ran the jobs for us. However, the performance of these simple PCs just kept getting better and better. As they became good enough, customers whose needs historically had required the more expensive mainframe and minicomputers were drawn one by one, application by application, from the back into the front plane of competition.

None of the customers of mainframe or minicomputer companies like Control Data Corporation (CDC) and Digital Equipment Corporation (DEC) could even use a personal computer during the first 10 years that PCs were made; PCs just weren't good enough for the problems they needed to solve. When CDC and DEC listened to what their best customers needed, there was no signal that a personal computer was important—because it *wasn't* to *them*. And when they looked at the financials, the personal computer market looked bleak. The $800 in gross margin that could be earned from selling a personal computer paled in comparison to the $125,000 in margin per unit that DEC could earn when it sold a minicomputer, or to the $800,000 in margin that Control Data could earn when it sold a mainframe.

Eventually, every one of the makers of mainframe and minicomputers was killed by the personal computer. But they weren't killed simply because the margins and volumes were different. The PC simply got better at doing more things. And it wasn't because the technology was difficult; in fact, given their industry expertise, companies like DEC could build some of the best PCs in the world. But it never made business sense for them to pursue the personal computer market. Even when PCs were becoming good enough to do much of what mainframes and minicomputers could do, the business model at companies like DEC could only prioritize even bigger and faster mainframes or minicomputers.

The only one of these companies that didn't fail was IBM, which for a time became a leader in personal computers by setting up a completely independent business unit in Florida and giving it the freedom to create a unique business model and compete against the other IBM business units.

The Kodak camera, Bell telephone, Sony transistor radio, Ford Model T (and more recently Toyota automobiles), Xerox photocopiers, Southwest Airlines' affordable flights, Cisco routers, Fidelity mutual funds, Google advertising, and hundreds of other innovations, all did or are doing the same thing. They used disruption to transform markets that had been dominated by complicated, expensive services and products into simple and affordable ones.

In each of these cases, the companies that had successfully sold their products or services, often dominating industries for decades, almost always died after being disrupted. Despite their stellar record of success in developing sustaining innovations, the incumbent leaders in an industry just could not find a way to maintain their industry leadership when confronted with disruptive innovations. The reason, again, is not that they lack resources such as money or technological expertise. Rather, they lack the motivation to focus sufficient resources on the disruption.

During the years in which a commitment to succeed with a new innovation needs to be made, disruptions are unattractive to industry leaders because their best customers can't use them and they are financially less attractive to incumbents than sustaining innovations. In a company's resource allocation process, proposals to invest in disruptive innovations almost always get trumped by next-generation sustaining innovations simply because innovations that can be sold to a firm's best customers for higher prices invariably appear more attractive than disruptive innovations that promise lower margins and can't be used by those customers. In the end, it takes disruptive innovations to change the landscape of an industry dramatically.

An industry whose products or services are still so complicated and expensive that only people with a lot of money and expertise can own and use them is an industry that has not yet been disrupted. This is the situation in legal services, higher education, and, yes, health care. The overarching theme of this book, however, is that these processes of disruption are beginning to appear in health care. One by one, disorders that could be treated only through the judgment and skill of experienced physicians in expensive hospitals are becoming diagnosable and treatable by less expensive caregivers working in more accessible and affordable venues of care. True to form, most of these innovations are being brought into the industry by new entrants, and they are being ignored or opposed by the leading caregiving institutions for perfectly rational reasons.

WHAT IS A BUSINESS MODEL AND HOW IS IT BUILT?

We mention above that of all the companies that made mainframe computers, IBM was the only one to become a leading maker of minicomputers; and of all the companies that made minicomputers, IBM was the only one that became a leading maker of personal computers. The reason is that IBM was the only company that invested to create new business models whose capabilities were tailored to the nature of competition in these disruptive markets. The others, if they attempted at all to participate in these emerging market segments, did so by trying to commercialize the disruptive products from within their existing business model.

So what is a business model? It is an interdependent system composed of four components, as illustrated in Figure 1.2.[1] The starting point in the creation of any successful business model is its *value proposition*—a product or service that can help targeted customers do more effectively, conveniently, and affordably a job that they've been trying to do. Managers then typically need to put in place a set of *resources*—including people, products, intellectual property, supplies, equipment, facilities, cash, and so on— required to deliver that value proposition to the targeted customers. In repeatedly working toward that goal, *processes* coalesce. Processes are habitual ways of working together that emerge as employees address recurrent tasks repeatedly and successfully. These processes define how resources are combined to deliver the value proposition. A *profit formula* then materializes. This defines the required price, markups, gross and net profit margins, asset turns, and volumes necessary to cover profitably the costs of the resources and processes that are required to deliver the value proposition.

Over time, however, the business model that has emerged begins to determine the sorts of value propositions the organization can and cannot deliver. While the starting point in the creation of a business model is the value proposition, once a business model has coalesced to deliver that value proposition, the causality of events begins to work in reverse, and the only value propositions that the organization can successfully take to market are those that fit the existing resources, processes, and profit formula. In other words, the available business model is often the constraint to the realization of a disruptive technology's full potential.

A business model innovation is the creation of a new set of boxes, coherently established to deliver a new value proposition.[2] Because the value proposition is the starting point for every business model, in the next few pages we take you on a deep dive into the concept of "helping customers do more effectively, conveniently, and affordably *a job they've been trying to do.*" Understanding the job that customers are trying to do is critical to

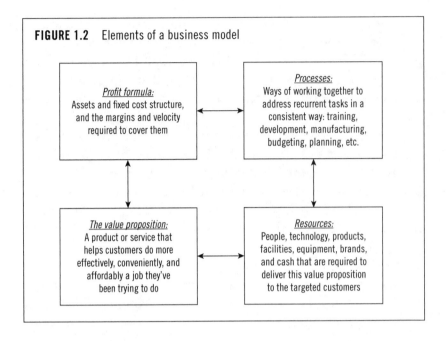

FIGURE 1.2   Elements of a business model

Profit formula:
Assets and fixed cost structure, and the margins and velocity required to cover them

Processes:
Ways of working together to address recurrent tasks in a consistent way: training, development, manufacturing, budgeting, planning, etc.

The value proposition:
A product or service that helps customers do more effectively, conveniently, and affordably a job they've been trying to do

Resources:
People, technology, products, facilities, equipment, brands, and cash that are required to deliver this value proposition to the targeted customers

successful innovation, and we draw upon this concept in several of the subsequent chapters.

Understanding the Job-to-Be-Done

The way in which companies choose to define market segments is a crucial strategic decision, because it influences which products they develop, drives the features of those products, and shapes how they are taken to market.

Most marketers divide their markets into categories based on the characteristics of their products or customers. Automakers, for example, segment their markets by product characteristics. There are subcompacts, compacts, midsize and full-size cars; minivans, SUVs, luxury vehicles, and sports cars. They can tell you exactly how large each segment is and which competitor has what share. With this framing of the market's structure, they try to beat the competitors in their segments by adding more features faster and at the lowest cost. Meanwhile, other companies segment their markets based on the characteristics of their customers. There are low-, middle-, and high-income segments; the segment of 18- to 34-year-old women; and so on. Or, in the business-to-business world, they'll segment by small, medium, and large enterprises, industry verticals, and so on. Almost all managers frame their market's structure by product category and/or customer category because if you're *in* the company looking out on the market, this is indeed how things appear to be structured.

The problem with segmentation schemes such as these is that this is not at all what the world looks like to customers. Stuff just happens to customers. *Jobs* arise in their lives that they need to do, and they *hire* products or services to do these jobs. Marketers who seek to connect with their customers need to see the world through their eyes—to understand the jobs that arise in customers' lives for which their products might be hired. The job, and *not* the customer or the product, should be the fundamental unit of marketing analysis.

To illustrate what a job is and how much clearer the path to successful innovation can be when marketers segment by job, we offer illustrations below from the fast food and textbook industries, where companies historically have segmented markets by product and customer categories but would greatly benefit from segmenting by job.

Hiring Milkshakes

A chain of fast-food restaurants some time ago resolved to improve sales of its milkshake.[3] Its marketers first defined the market segment by product—milkshakes—and then segmented it further by profiling the customer most likely to buy milkshakes. They would then invite people who fit this profile to suggest how the company could improve the milkshakes so they'd buy more of them. The panelists would give clear feedback, and the company would improve its product—but this had no impact on sales whatsoever.

One of our colleagues then spent a long day in a restaurant to understand the jobs that customers were trying to get done when they "hired" a milkshake. He chronicled when each milkshake was bought, what other products the customers purchased, whether they were alone or with a group, whether they consumed it on the premises or drove off with it. He was surprised to find that over 40 percent of all milkshakes were purchased in the early morning. These early-morning customers almost always were alone; they did not buy anything else; and they left the restaurant to consume the milkshake in their cars.

The researcher returned the next day to interview the morning customers, milkshakes in hand, as they emerged from the restaurant. He essentially asked (in language that they would understand), "Excuse me, but could you please tell me what job you were needing to get done for yourself when you came here to hire that milkshake?" As the customers struggled to answer, he'd help them by saying, "Think about a recent time when you were in the same situation, needing to get the same job done, but you didn't come here to hire a milkshake. What did you hire?" Most of them, it turned out, bought it to do a similar job: they faced a long, boring drive to work. One hand had to be on the steering wheel, but they had an extra hand and there was nothing in it. They needed something to do with that hand to keep them occupied during the drive. They weren't hungry yet, but knew that they'd be hungry by 10:00 A.M., so they needed something now that would stay in their stomach for the morning. And they faced constraints: they were in a hurry, they were wearing work clothes, and they had (at most) one free hand.

In response to the researcher's query about what other products they hired to do this job, the customers realized that sometimes they hired bagels to do the job. But bagels were dry and tasteless. Bagels with cream cheese or jam resulted in sticky fingers and gooey steering wheels. Sometimes these commuters bought a banana, but it didn't last long enough to solve the boring-commute problem. Doughnuts didn't carry people past the 10:00 A.M. hunger attack. A few had hired a candy bar to do the job, but it made them feel so guilty that they didn't do it again. The milkshake, it turned out, did the job better than any of these competitors. It took people 20 minutes to suck the viscous milkshake through the thin straw, thus addressing the boring-commute problem. It could be eaten cleanly with one hand. And though they had no idea what the milkshake's ingredients were, they did know that at 10:00 A.M. on days when they had hired a milkshake, they didn't feel hungry. It didn't matter that it wasn't a healthy food, because becoming healthy wasn't the job they were hiring the milkshake to do.

Our colleague observed that, at other times of the day, parents often bought milkshakes, with a meal, for their children. What job were the parents trying to do? They felt like mean parents because they had been saying no to their children all week long, and they hired milkshakes as an innocuous way to placate their children and to feel like loving parents. The researchers observed that the milkshakes didn't do this job very well, though. They saw parents waiting impatiently after they had finished their own meal while their children struggled to suck the thick milkshake up through the thin straw.

Customers were hiring milkshakes for two very different jobs. But when marketers had asked a busy father who needs a time-consuming milkshake in the morning (and something very different later in the day) what attributes of the milkshake they should improve upon, and when his response was averaged with those of others in the same demographic segment, it led to a one-size-fits-none product that didn't do well either of the jobs for which it was being hired.

Once the company understood the *jobs* that the customers were trying to do, however, it became very clear which attributes of the milkshake would do the job even better, and which improvements were irrelevant. How could it better tackle the boring-commute job? Make the shake even thicker, so it would last longer. And swirl in tiny chunks of fruit, nuts, or candy so that the drivers would occasionally suck chunks into their mouths, adding a dimension of unpredictability and anticipation to their monotonous morning routine. Just as important, it could move the dispensing machine in front of the counter and sell customers a prepaid swipe card so that they could dash in, gas up, and go without getting stuck in the drive-through lane. Addressing the other job to be done with the children would entail a very different product, of course.

As Peter Drucker said, "The customer rarely buys what the company thinks it is selling him."[4]

Understanding the job and improving the product so that it would do the job better would enable the company's milkshakes to gain share against the *real* competition—not just competing chains' milkshakes, but doughnuts, bagels, bananas, and boredom. This would grow the category, which brings us to an important point: job-defined markets are generally much larger than product category-defined markets. Marketers who are stuck in the mental trap that equates market size with product categories don't understand who they are competing against or how to enhance the value of their product, from the customer's point of view.

Before it understood the job for which its milkshake was being hired in the morning, the company had *thought* it was integrated. It sold a dizzying array of sandwiches, side dishes, salads, drinks, and desserts. But this integration simply helped it to do anything for anyone, and not very well. This mode of integration simply pitted its plethora of products into a product-for-product competition—against bananas, doughnuts, bagels, breakfast drinks, coffee, diet cola, and other fast-food products. But once it understood the morning commute job, the restaurant chain could integrate *differently*—linking together an optimized product, a delivery mechanism, and a payments system that together did the job perfectly—in a way most makers of the competing products couldn't replicate because they didn't see the rationale. Proprietary integration of the company's resources, processes, and profit formula in order to do a job that the customer is trying to do is the essence of competitive advantage.

Connecting with Customers Who Don't Have a Job

Very often, customers will tell market researchers, "Sure, I'd buy that product," and then they don't. Why? A second case history provides some clues.

In the past decade the college textbook companies together have spent several billion dollars creating Web sites where students can explore more deeply topics that can be covered at only a cursory level in the textbook. In a geography textbook, for example, only about 10 pages can be allocated to the Amazon rain forest because there is so much other geography to cover. But thank goodness for the Internet. At the end of the text on the Amazon rain forest is a Web site address, which students can visit to get almost limitless additional information about the rain forest. Overwhelmingly, students and their professors indicated during market research interviews that they would love to have that capability.

It has turned out, however, that very few students ever click on those links. Why? What most students really are trying to get done in their lives (as evidenced by what they do, rather than what they say) is simply to pass the course without having to read the boring textbook at all. They *should* have a limitless appetite for learning—but they don't.

So what's the solution? Face the facts. When you help customers do more affordably, conveniently, and effectively a job that they have been *trying* to get done, they will pay a premium price, digest all kinds of instructions, and change lots of habits in order to get the job done better and faster. But when your product helps them do a job that they've *not* been trying to do, selling your product is akin to an uphill death march through knee-deep mud.

This doesn't mean that the idea of online or electronic books is dead. It simply means that if textbook companies wanted students to start using their Internet-based learning materials, they need to package them in a way that helps college students do the job that they're trying to do. In this case, you'd create a facility called Cram. com with the objective of helping college students cram for their exams more effectively, with less effort, later in the semester. These customers would be willing to pay steep prices for this assistance. The stereotypical student would feverishly log on to Cram.com two days before his final. The screen would ask, "What course are you trying to cram for?" The student would click on "College Algebra." The next page would ask, "Which of these textbooks did your old professor think you'd have read by now?" After he clicked on the title, the next page would ask, "Now, which of these problems is giving you a hard time?" The student would click on one that is vexing him, and the next pages would nurse him through the problem, giving him tricks and methods for solving it.

Next year, like any disruptive company, Cram.com would need to improve its products—to make it even easier to cram even later in the semester, with even better results. Within a few years, you might see a couple of students in their college bookstore anguishing over whether they should really pay $129 for a textbook. Another student, walking by, would notice their pain and offer, "I wouldn't buy the book. I took that course last semester, and I just used Cram.com from the beginning—and it worked great." Bingo. The disruption of a horrifically expensive industry would be underway.

The graveyard of failed products and services is populated by things that people *should* have wanted—if only they could have been convinced those things were good for them. The home-run products in the marketing hall of fame, in contrast, are concepts that helped people more affordably, effortlessly, swiftly, and effectively do what they already had been trying to get done.

In ensuing chapters, readers will find that understanding the job that customers are trying to do is a major issue in *every* healthcare innovation. Many wellness programs that seek to ameliorate or stave off the onset of certain chronic diseases stumble, for example, because for a great many people who are obese, are addicted to tobacco, or who suffer from coronary artery disease, becoming healthier isn't a job that they're prioritizing—until they become sick. Indeed, as we show in our discussion of chronic disease in Chapter 5, for certain patients, financial health is a much more pressing job-to-be-done than physical health. Our analysis in Chapter 7 explains the reason why health savings accounts have been adopted more slowly than expected: because they're being marketed into a product category, and not positioned to fulfill a job-to-be-done.

There are three levels in the architecture of every job. The highest level is the job itself—the basic, root problem the customer needs to resolve, or the result he or she needs to achieve. Once innovators understand the job, they can then burrow into the second level of the architecture: What functional, social, and emotional experiences in purchasing and using the product do we need to provide the customer in order to get the job done perfectly? Knowing what these experiences need to be gives product designers and marketers a sense of "true north" as they delve into the detail at the third level of the architecture: the specific characteristics, features, and technologies that comprise the product and how it is sold and used. If a feature helps provide one of the experiences that is required to get the job done perfectly, it will enhance the product's success. If not, then it will add cost and complexity to the product that customers don't value. Understanding the job to be done provides a sense of "true north" to innovators.

What this means is that convenience and cost are not jobs. Convenience is an experience that must be provided to get some, but not all, jobs done well. And cost, likewise, is a feature of products that customers will assess when deciding what product to hire to do a job.

Jobs exist independently of a market for products that can be hired to do them. By illustration, since the days of Julius Caesar there's been an I-need-to-get-this-from-here-to-there-with-perfect-certainty-as-fast-as-possible job. Caesar's only option was to put someone he trusted in a chariot pulled by a fast horse and order him to go like crazy. When FedEx came along, a huge new *market* was created—but the *job* had always been there. And the job exists independently of customers as well. Not every person has this job to do, and those who find themselves needing to do this job don't need to do it every day.

THE IMPORTANCE OF THE BUSINESS MODEL IN DISRUPTIVE INNOVATION

In our research on disruptive innovation, as noted earlier, the only instances in which the original market leader in the back plane of Figure 1.1 also became the subsequent leader in the new disruptive plane of competition occurred when the leader set up a completely autonomous business unit whose value proposition focused on a job to be done. This independent business unit was given the freedom to create a different profit formula, permitting it to make money on lower margins than the parent ever could. This required, in turn, processes and resources that were markedly different and that could deliver the disruptive value proposition under the new profit formula.

The history of innovation is littered with companies that had a disruptive technology within their grasp but failed to commercialize it successfully because they did not couple it with a disruptive business model. An example of a disruptive technology that withered in the absence of a disruptive business model occurred at Nypro, a successful manufacturer of high-precision plastic products in Clinton, Massachusetts. The Nypro business model, which it replicates in each of its 60-plus plants around the world, centers on a single *value proposition*: making ultra-high-precision parts in high volumes for the world's largest product companies, including Nokia (mobile phones), Hewlett-Packard (printer components), and Eli Lilly (insulin injection pens). To make high volumes of precise parts at low costs for customers such as these, Nypro utilized *resources* such as multicavity molds that could yield as many as 32 parts with a single stroke of its molding machines. In order to squeeze plastic into that many cavities, Nypro's molding machines had to inject the plastic at very high pressures—meaning the machines had to be huge and powerful. And because the technology was so complex, the *processes* that developed at Nypro involved long setup times to ensure that perfect parts were made in each of the molds' cavities. For Nypro's plant managers, this meant that very long runs of standard parts were extremely attractive, because the company's *profit formula* necessitated high yields and equipment utilization to support the cost of its resources.

In the mid-1990s Nypro's founder and CEO, Gordon Lankton, foresaw a change in the company's future: the product markets

of Nypro's customers were beginning to fragment. This por-
tended that the market for parts produced in high volumes would
diminish, giving way to a much wider variety of parts produced
in shorter production runs. To help Nypro catch this new wave
of growth and deliver this new value proposition, Lankton's
engineers developed a new injection molding machine dubbed
Novaplast. It used only four-cavity molds that could be snapped
into place quickly and filled precisely with low pressures. Its
features were cleverly designed to produce a wide variety of low-
volume parts without the cost penalties that would have been
incurred by using the larger and more powerful machines.

Lankton considered building a special plant with its own sales
force to pursue this high-variety, low-volume-per-part business,
but he ultimately decided instead to leverage the company's
existing resources, such as its sales and manufacturing infrastructure, offering to lease the Novaplast machine on attractive
terms to his plant managers. Only nine plant managers took
Lankton up on his offer, and seven of them returned the machines
after just three months, complaining that there was no business
to keep the machines utilized. When Lankton inquired why the
other two plants kept their Novaplast machines, he learned those
plants had previously struggled to use traditional 32-cavity molds
to produce the extremely thin plastic liners that were inserted
inside AA battery canisters. It turned out, serendipitously, that
the Novaplast machine could make those standard, high-volume
parts with much higher yields.

Why did so few plant managers take the Novaplast machine in
the first place? Despite the burgeoning market for high-variety,
low-volume-per-part products, orders to produce a wide variety
of parts in low volumes simply weren't attractive to Nypro plant
managers. They weren't consistent with Nypro's business model,
because they didn't support the existing profit formula and help
the company's plants make money in the way they were structured
to make money. Why did seven of the nine plants conclude there
was no demand for low-volume parts, even though the company's
CEO had already seen that there was booming demand? Because

selling low-volume parts didn't fit the compensation structure of the Nypro sales force. The salespeople had little reason to push a large number of low-volume products when all the incentives of the sales process were aligned with turning out high-volume runs for their existing customers. Finally, the two plants that actually kept their Novaplast machines only did so because they were able to use the machine by plugging the resource right into their existing business model—thereby making extremely high volumes of precision thin-walled battery liners.

In other words, those within a business model cannot disrupt themselves. Managers can only implement new technologies in ways that sustain the model within which they work. Although the Novaplast machine was capable of attacking the growing wide-variety, low-volume-per-part market, the business model in which it was ensconced was not. Lankton's vision actually proved correct: the market for high-variety, low-volume parts grew significantly, while the market for standard, high-volume parts declined. Yet the only way Nypro could have attacked that market would have been to embed the Novaplast machine within an autonomous business model whose profit formula, processes, and resources were optimized for the disruptive value proposition.[5]

A TYPOLOGY OF BUSINESS MODELS

Professor Øystein Fjeldstad of the Norwegian School of Management and his colleague Charles Stabell have developed a framework that defines three general types of job-focused business models: shops, chains, and networks. For purposes of added clarity in this book, we refer to these three types as solution shops, value-adding process (VAP) businesses, and facilitated networks.[6] As we will demonstrate, these are fundamentally different institutions, in terms of their purpose, where their capabilities reside, and the formulas by which they make money.

Solution Shops
Solution shops are institutions structured to diagnose and recommend solutions to unstructured problems. Certain consulting

firms, advertising agencies, research and development organizations, and many law practices are examples of solution shops. The ability to deliver value to customers resides primarily in the firms' resources, the most significant of which is the people these firms employ—experts who draw upon their intuition, training, and analytical and problem-solving skills to diagnose the cause of complicated problems and then recommend solutions. The work they do for each customer tends to be unique and can vary from project to project, firm to firm.

Almost always, solution shops charge their clients on a fee-for-service basis. Consulting firms will occasionally make a portion of their fees contingent upon the successful results of their recommendations, but such arrangements rarely are satisfactory for either party—there are simply too many variables in addition to the consultants' diagnoses and recommendations that affect the outcome. Because diagnosing the cause of complex problems and devising workable solutions have such high subsequent leverage, customers typically are quite willing to pay very high prices for the services of solution shops—often topping $1,000 per hour for the services of a partner at a leading consulting or law firm.

The diagnostic activities in general hospitals and much of the work done in specialist physicians' practices are solution shop activities. In Chapter 2, we give the work done in medical solution shops a new label: intuitive medicine. In these institutions, highly trained experts use their intuition to synthesize data from a wide range of analytical and imaging equipment, and from personal examinations of the patient. They will then distill hypotheses of the causes of patients' symptoms from these data. When the diagnosis has only the precision of a hypothesis, these experts typically test the hypothesis by applying the most appropriate therapy. If the patient responds, the hypothesis is essentially verified. If not, the experts must then iterate through cycles of hypothesis testing until the diagnosis can be made with as much certainty as possible.

We show in Chapter 5 that there are today only a few entities in health care that qualify as true, coherent solution shops. Most intuitive medicine, unfortunately, is practiced in a disconnected way by individual specialists.

Value-Adding Process Businesses

The second type of business model is the value-adding process (VAP) business. *VAP businesses* transform inputs of resources—people, materials, energy, equipment, information, and capital—into outputs of higher value. Retailing, restaurants, automobile manufacturing, petroleum refining, and the work of many educational institutions are examples of value-adding process businesses. Because value-adding process organizations tend to do their work in repetitive ways, the capability to deliver value tends to be embedded in processes and equipment. They are not nearly as dependent upon the instincts of people as is the case with solution shop businesses. Because of this, VAP businesses that focus on process excellence can consistently deliver high-quality services and products at lower cost, using methods that are far less susceptible to the variability that often vexes businesses whose results primarily depend on their employees' intuition. Of course, outcomes can still vary, because some value-adding process organizations are more efficient and consistent than others.[7]

Many medical events and procedures are in fact value-adding process activities in that what needs to be done can be verified ahead of time and that a relatively standardized process can be followed to rectify the problem. Certainly, the diagnosis of many problems and the decisions about how to solve them must often still be made in the solution shops of hospitals or physicians' practices. But whenever a definitive diagnosis can be made, the treatment that follows can typically be performed in a value-adding process organization. Just like the more familiar examples of value-adding process models employed by restaurants, business schools, or automobile manufacturers, a patient is brought in, a relatively standard sequence of events is performed, and then the patient is "shipped" out the door.

When value-adding process procedures like the ones described above are delivered by business models that are organizationally independent from solution shops, the overhead cost of the value-adding process work drops dramatically. As a case study in Chapter 3 demonstrates, focused value-adding process hospitals and clinics often can deliver care at prices that are 40 to 60 percent below those incurred in hospitals and physicians' practices, where the value-adding process and solution shop business models are typically intermingled.[8] Retail clinics such as RediClinic and MinuteClinic (which was acquired in 2007 by CVS-Caremark); surgical specialty hospitals like Shouldice Hospital and some orthopedic hospitals; ambulatory surgical centers including many eye surgery clinics; and medical specialty hospitals like cardiology hospitals and cancer centers are all part of a growing number of value-adding process businesses in the health-care industry.[9] And the patients and diseases that can be managed by VAP businesses are not necessarily limited to the simple end of the spectrum. Transplant services are now often managed as a bundle of services and priced per outcome in a VAP model.[10]

Because their ability to deliver value to customers tends to be embedded in equipment and processes rather than the individual intuition of people, value-adding process businesses typically bill their customers for results, not inputs. Often, the product or outcome is priced in advance, and because costs and outcomes are relatively predictable, most value-adding process organizations can guarantee their products. If they don't work or should they break, they'll be replaced or repaired free of charge. While most general hospitals charge on a fee-for-service basis for everything they do, many value-adding process hospitals have begun to charge their patients on a fixed-price basis for each procedure offered. And they guarantee the result. In February 2006, Geisinger Health System's ProvenCare program began charging insurers a flat rate for elective heart bypass surgeries, effectively providing a 90-day warranty for its work.[11]

The employees of Toyota, which is probably the best value-adding process company in the world, follow a standard process religiously in everything that they do—from training employees to maintaining and repairing equipment to designing and making cars. The reason they adhere to standard processes isn't to make the work mindless, however. Rather, they have concluded that doing it the same way every time actually constitutes a controlled experiment by which they test over and over whether doing it that way yields a perfect result. In less mature or experimental processes, where unanticipated problems can arise, Toyota designs methods to respond to these problems in a consistent way—to test whether their method of solving unanticipated problems is a reliable method for doing so. By the same token, we should not expect value-adding process clinics to be manned with robotic personnel who cannot respond to unanticipated problems that might arise during the course of a procedure. Instead, they should be much more able to anticipate and address the unexpected problems that will undoubtedly arise, but in a predictably effective way. These core principles of the Toyota Production System have already been applied to processes within hospitals like Virginia Mason Medical Center in Seattle and the University of Pittsburgh Medical Center to improve quality of outcomes and patient safety.[12]

Facilitated Network Businesses

The third type of business model, *facilitated networks*, comprise institutions that operate systems in which customers buy and sell, and deliver and receive things from other participants.[13] Much of consumer banking is a network business in which customers will make deposits and withdrawals from a collective pool. Casinos, Second Life, and multiplayer Internet games could also be termed facilitated networks. Approximately 40 percent of the GNP in many economies is generated by facilitated network businesses.[14]

The companies that make money in network industries are the ones that organize, facilitate, and maintain the effective operation of the networks. Whereas solution shops price on a fee-for-service basis, and value-adding process businesses can price on a fee-for-outcome standard, facilitated networks typically make money through membership or transaction-based fees.

In many network business models, the dependency among customers is the main product delivered. Said another way, the networked users themselves are the key part of the product, and the "size and composition of the customer base are therefore the critical driver[s] of value." Whereas most of the economics literature on the subject of network externalities addresses the size of the network, the compatibility of members is more important.[15]

As we discuss further in Chapter 5, facilitated networks are now beginning to emerge in health care to address problems in very new ways. Some network businesses tie professionals together to help support each other as they do their work. Sermo, an online community of physicians,[16] and some disease management organizations have taken preliminary steps to facilitate provider networks. Other networks are organized around patients and specific conditions. In many cases, they offer an effective business model for the care of chronic diseases, particularly those which demand from patients and their families significant behavioral changes.[17] Examples include social networking Web sites such as PatientsLikeMe.com, which focuses on communities of patients with multiple sclerosis, amyotrophic lateral sclerosis (Lou Gehrig's disease), Parkinson's disease, and HIV; and CarePlace, which connects users with rare diseases.[18] Meanwhile, Waterfront Media and WebMD are harnessing vast amounts of patient and insurer data to generate an extensive facilitated network that will offer patients the ability to find "someone like me." Patients will be able to compare their own progress against directly comparable patients and teach and learn from each other.[19]

Until now, the care of patients with chronic diseases has been centered in physicians' practices, but these solution shops are simply ill-equipped to meet many of the demands of chronic disease care. Just as value-adding process hospitals can outperform solution shops by delivering higher-quality outcomes at far lower costs, facilitated networks can improve quality and reduce costs for certain chronic diseases by a similar magnitude.[20]

THE DISRUPTION OF BUSINESS MODELS

Most historical examples of disruptive innovation have occurred within a single type of business model. The Boston Consulting

Group disrupted McKinsey within the solution shop class of business models. Toyota has disrupted Ford, and Medco is disrupting retail pharmacies within the class of value-adding process business models. Traditional wire-line telephone companies, which are network facilitators, were disrupted by the wireless carriers, which in turn are being disrupted by Skype, which is facilitating a mobile network using voice over Internet protocol (VOIP).

However, a more fundamental disruption occurs when one type of business model displaces another. eBay is a network facilitator, for example, but it is disrupting certain retail and distribution channels that historically were configured as value-adding process businesses.[21] The top section of Figure 1.3 gives some examples of disruptions in a variety of industries that occurred *within* a business model type. The examples in the bottom section are companies that transformed, or are transforming, the type of business model. When disruption occurs *across* different classes of business models, the gains in affordability and accessibility are even more profound than when disruption occurs within the same type of business model.

The appendix to this chapter briefly summarizes why we classified the disruptive companies in Figure 1.3 in the way that we did.

Business Model Innovation in Health Care

We foresee three phases of disruptive business model innovation in health care, which together hold the potential to reduce costs by between 20 and 60 percent, depending on the situation—while at the same time improving the quality and efficacy of care received.[22] The first phase will entail carving hospitals apart, creating coherent rather than disjointed solution shops, value-adding process businesses, and facilitated networks as focused business models. These will employ similarly qualified doctors, but their significantly lower overhead burden qualifies them as disruptive relative to our hospitals as they currently work. Second, we foresee lower-cost disruptive business models emerging within each of these

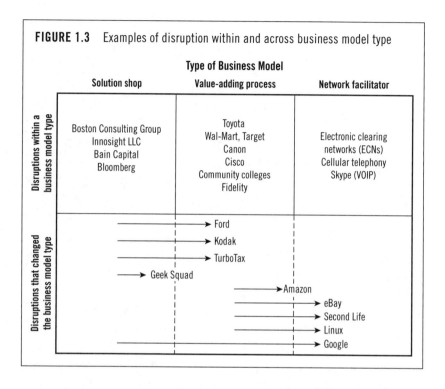

FIGURE 1.3   Examples of disruption within and across business model type

categories—disruptors akin to those companies in the top row of Figure 1.3. Among solution shops, for example, a telemedicine-based institution would be a disruptive business model to the diagnostic activities of certain hospitals and physicians' practices. Ambulatory and mobile clinics will represent value-adding process business models that can disrupt specialty hospitals, and so on. The third phase of disruption will occur across business model types. Retail clinics, for example, transfer the ability to care for rules-based disorders from solution shops to value-adding process businesses. Firms like SimulConsult, through which the published research of thousands of specialist physicians is integrated on the computers of primary care physicians, disrupts the solution shop of specialists with a professional network business model. We explore each of these possibilities in greater depth in subsequent chapters of this book—after we examine the role of technological enablers in disruption in Chapter 2.

The Disruption of Angioplasty

A narrowing of the arteries, whether caused by cholesterol deposition, high blood pressure, or myriad other causes, is a common problem that can affect blood vessels throughout the body. When intervention is warranted, the typical treatment involves inserting a catheter, inflating a balloon to expand the narrowed portion of the vessel, and inserting a stent to keep the area propped open. Yet today, though the same technologies and techniques are used, a patient who needs angioplasty of the heart will see an interventional cardiologist; a patient who needs angioplasty of the kidney might see an interventional radiologist; a patient who needs angioplasty of a carotid artery in the neck may visit a vascular surgeon; and a patient with peripheral disease, such as in the leg, could be treated by any one of the three.

Much of this care is delivered today through solution shops that are organized around disease type or medical specialty. For example, cardiologists practicing angioplasty have been disrupting cardiac surgeons practicing coronary artery bypass grafting (CABG) for 25 years. But this has largely occurred *within* the solution shop business model of the general hospital. However, we propose that these vascular interventions may be better suited for new disruptive business models that compete across very different categories.

The first phase of disruption will involve the separation of the different business model types currently housed within general hospitals. Specialty heart hospitals were among the first focused value-adding process business models to break off from general hospitals, but disruption within this category can continue to affect how care is delivered.

For example, as the field of angioplasty has developed, we've learned that the traditional categories of competition no longer make sense. Rather than cardiology, radiology, and vascular surgery patients, the competitive category is really the same for all of these patients—blood vessels. Patients undergoing this procedure, beginning with those with stable disease and low risk of complications, would be much better served by seeing a "vascular interventionalist" who does nothing but angioplasties day in and day out in a value-adding process business, surrounded by support staff who are experts in managing all the processes of angioplasty care, no matter which organ system happens to be involved. By reframing the categories of competition, the value-adding process business model allows you to bring scale and lower overhead costs to areas where you didn't have it before.

Because these patients no longer need to be located with all the other processes meant to handle complex patients, they can be treated in a lower-cost, ambulatory facility. This new business model would be even more focused on a select few processes than the specialty cardiology hospitals that already exist today, and they would essentially disrupt other value-adding process businesses.

Eventually, the vascular interventionalist we describe here may not even need to be a physician. A skilled interventionalist primarily requires video-gaming-like skills that a nonphysician could acquire through practice, and this would result in even further disruption of other, more costly value-adding process businesses. Peripheral vascular occlusive disease (PVOD) tends to be the simplest of the vascular diseases that undergo angioplasty and would be the most likely category of patients to be managed under a nonphysician technician first. However, we can foresee even multivessel cardiac cases eventually being handed off to a technician, while an interventional cardiologist will be involved, perhaps just as a supervisor, in those cases where there is a higher risk for complications.[23]

Of course, cardiologists, radiologists, and surgeons should continue managing the most complex vascular diseases, particularly when there are unpredictable interdependencies such as unstable disease or high risk for undesirable outcomes. But the number of patients who require their costly expertise will diminish over time as more care is handed off to value-adding process businesses that can focus on very specific procedures and techniques that cut across traditional disciplines and specialties—and that can deliver better outcomes at lower cost.[24]

Whether the changes described here would naturally lead to yet another phase of disruption across business model types remains to be seen. It's difficult to imagine today what that would look like, but we'll know it when we see it, and we hope our readers too will spot the opportunity when it does arrive.

APPENDIX

Disruptive Companies Arrayed in Figure 1.3

Amazon.com. Book and music retailing historically were value-adding process businesses. With its ratings system, discussion groups, and a network of resellers called Amazon Marketplace, Amazon is pushing these VAP activities toward a network facilitator business model. MP3 and electronic publishing technologies are enabling artists and authors to create and sell their own content to each other through the network that Amazon is facilitating.

Bain Capital. Bain Capital today is one of the world's largest private equity and leveraged buyout firms. In the investment business, the vertical axis on the diagram of disruption is the size of the company receiving the investment. Partners with limited time and lots of money to put to work will always opt to make a larger investment over a smaller one. Bain started by making rather small investments in start-ups like Staples, instead of attempting a head-on attack against Kohlberg Kravis Roberts & Co. Then little by little it raised more and more money, going after larger and larger deals.

Bloomberg. Bloomberg LLC started selling simple, low-value-added data to financial analysts, who used the data to analyze the problems and opportunities facing the companies in which they were considering investing. Gradually, Bloomberg integrated into its systems the ability to perform analyses so that anyone today who has a Bloomberg terminal simply needs to push a button to get even the most sophisticated of those analyses that previously had required a Wharton MBA.

Boston Consulting Group (BCG). In the consulting business, the vertical axis on the diagram of disruption is the size of the project. Given the choice, the partners (who are the salespeople) would much prefer to sell large projects to clients than small ones. When BCG entered the market in 1963 with a product offering in a new field it called "strategy," McKinsey was caught flat-footed for about 15 years. It's not that the McKinsey staff lacked the intellectual horsepower to compete against BCG in the strategy market. It's because strategy projects are inherently smaller than are operations improvement, postmerger integration, and reorganization projects. After establishing a foothold, BCG was able to move up-market, and now it does *lots* of operations and postmerger integration work—and less strategy work.

Canon. Photocopying formerly had been in the province of complex, electromechanical high-speed photocopiers made by Xerox, housed in corporate photocopy centers, and operated by technicians. Whereas IBM and Kodak attacked Xerox in a head-on battle of sustaining innovation (and got bloodied), Canon disrupted Xerox by starting with simple table-top boxes that were so slow and limited in their capabilities that none of Xerox's customers could use them. But the Canon machines were so simple and affordable that they could be located just around the corner from one's office. As they got better and faster, Canon's convenient, local machines began to pull jobs, one by one, away from the high-speed copy center.

Cellular telephony. Wireless telephones disrupted wire-line telephony—starting out as big, clunky car phones that often dropped calls when switching from one cell to the next. However, this was an application where wire-line phones were impossible. Then, little by little, the cell phones improved, to the point that many people no longer have wire-line phones.

Cisco. Because Cisco's router "packetized" information in virtual envelopes, addressed them, and then fanned them out over the Internet, it took about three seconds for the packets to arrive at their destination, be ordered correctly, and then opened and read. This was too slow for voice, but for data it was much faster than prior options (airmail). Makers of circuit-switching equipment for voice, such as Lucent, Nortel, and Alcatel, were disrupted as the router and its packet-switching technology ultimately became good enough for voice as well as data.

Community colleges. These schools don't operate under the cost burdens of full-time, research-oriented faculty. They simply teach—and do it quite well, often online. And they are booming. Many graduates of four-year universities took some or all of their first two years of general education at a community college, where credits for similar basic courses cost much less than they do at four-year schools. Many community colleges have subsequently become four-year universities.

eBay and PayPal. Retailing historically has been a value-adding process business. eBay started by facilitating a network through which people could exchange collectibles with each other. The range of products exchanged through the eBay network has gradually increased to encompass cars, boats, and even homes. Many companies now use eBay as their primary sales channel. Meanwhile, eBay's subsidiary PayPal is also a network facilitator business, disrupting the networks of Visa, MasterCard, and American Express, which are network facilitator businesses themselves.

Electronic clearing networks. ECNs are electronic, automated securities exchanges that are disrupting the NASDAQ exchange, which itself has been disrupting the New York Stock Exchange. Leading ECNs include Direct Edge, BATS trading, and Bloomberg Tradebook.

Fidelity Investments. The ability to own a diversified equity portfolio originally was limited to those with a very large net worth. Through its no-load mutual funds, Fidelity enabled a much larger population of people to become diversified equity investors. Fidelity is now being disrupted by Vanguard, which itself is being disrupted by exchange-traded funds (ETFs).

Ford. Henry Ford's Model T decisively transferred the design and manufacture of automobiles out of mechanics' garages, where artisans produced them one at a time. Their solution shops were disrupted by a value-adding process business model.

Geek Squad. This unit of the electronics retailing giant Best Buy is trying to routinize the installation and repair of home entertainment and computer systems—activities that historically had been addressed through small solution shops.

Google. Historically, most advertising and brand-building were done in the province of advertising agency solution shops. Google is transforming these activities into facilitated networks.

Innosight. For the same reasons that enabled the Boston Consulting Group to disrupt McKinsey, Innosight is on a trajectory by which it is disrupting the innovation and strategy consulting business. The company bases its work on theories of strategy and innovation, including those of Clayton Christensen, rather than approaching problems through data analysis. As a consequence, Innosight's work is priced substantially lower, and major consulting firms simply walk away.[25]

Kodak. Prior to 1890, most photographs were taken and developed in a solution shop environment by artists such as Matthew Brady. George Eastman disruptively transformed photography into a value-adding process business by selling film and an inexpensive Brownie-brand camera to the masses. Customers simply had to mail their shot rolls of film back to Kodak, where the photos were processed and returned to them.

Linux. Computer operating systems historically have been a value-adding process product. Linux is disrupting Microsoft's Windows by shifting the business model type to a facilitated network in which network participants build, improve, and use the product.

Second Life. Pixar, using digital technology, disrupted Disney Studios, which had developed animated content by hand. Both were value-adding process businesses. Second Life is a 3-D virtual world created by its residents, who use tools provided by the network facilitator to create their own animated content and to exchange and interact with others.

Skype. Owned by eBay, Skype is an in-type disruption of one facilitated network business by another. Voice-over-Internet-protocol (VOIP) telephony accounts for a growing share of global telephony traffic, and Skype has already begun its march into the markets of wireless carriers with Skype-branded phones that use VOIP technology.

Toyota. Toyota did not become the world's most profitable automobile manufacturer by attacking Mercedes, Cadillac, and BMW with its Lexus. Rather, it started at the low end of the market with a little subcompact branded Corona. Then it moved up-market with models whose American brands were Tercel, Corolla, Camry, Avalon, 4Runner, RAV4, and *then* the Lexus. Every once in a while General Motors and Ford would look at Toyota coming up from below and send down a Chevette or Pinto to compete against Toyota. But when the Americans compared the profitability of those subcompacts with the profitability of larger, more powerful SUV and luxury vehicles, it made no sense to defend the low end of the marketplace. Today, Toyota is being disrupted by Hyundai and Kia, which are being disrupted by Chery from China and the Tata Nano in India.

TurboTax. Intuit, which owns TurboTax, is shifting the tax preparation business from the solution-shop realm of tax advisors and preparers to a relatively automated, do-it-yourself value-adding process.

Wal-Mart and Target. Discount retailers are disrupting full-service department stores like Macy's. Until the 1960s, department stores sold the full "merchandise mix." This ranged from branded hard goods on the low-margin end—items like paint, hardware, kitchen utensils, toys, and sporting goods—to harder-to-merchandise soft goods like clothing and cosmetics, which were more difficult, and therefore more profitable, to sell. Discount retailers originally came in at the low end, focusing on branded hard goods that were already so familiar to users that they sold themselves. The department stores quickly fled up-market and became retailers of clothing and cosmetics exclusively. Now the discounters, especially Target, are moving resolutely into fashion soft goods.

NOTES

1. We owe enormous gratitude to Mark Johnson, our colleague and chairman of Innosight, for his development of the business model innovation framework. See Johnson, M. *Seizing the White Space: Business Model Innovation for Transformative Growth and Renewal* (Boston, Massachusetts: Harvard Business School Press, 2009).

2. Typically, new-to-the-world business models are formed in the counterclockwise sequence as described. Some disruptive business model innovations, however, are built in a clockwise sequence. Disruption starts with a value proposition for a product or service that is much more affordable and simpler than those available previously. The disruptive innovators then specify the profit formula required to profitably hit the price envisioned in the value proposition. This then defines the sorts of processes the firm will need and the levels of resources required in order to profitably deliver the value proposition.

3. The descriptions of the product and company in this example have been disguised. We thank Rick Pedi and Bob Moesta of Pedi, Moesta & Associates for sharing this case with us and permitting us to publish it in disguised form. Though each has used different words for the phenomenon, the concepts presented in this section have been taught by a number of different scholars, including Ted Levitt and Peter Drucker. Though they are not as well known, we acknowledge the roles that Rick and Bob played in articulating this way of thinking, and we thank them again for their tutelage.

4. Drucker, Peter F., *Managing for Results*, London: Heinemann, 1964.

5. See Christensen, Clayton M., and Rebecca Voorheis, "Managing Innovation at Nypro, Inc. (A)," Harvard Business School case #9-696-061, and Christensen, Clayton M., "Managing Innovation at Nypro, Inc. (B)," Harvard Business School case #9-697-057.

6. We are deeply indebted to our friend Øystein Fjeldstad of the Norwegian School of Management, who developed and then taught us of this framework. Those interested in this framework should also read Stabell, Charles B., and Øystein D. Fjeldstad, "Configuring Value for Competitive Advantage: On Chains, Shops and Networks," *Strategic Management Journal*, May 1998. Professor Fjeldstad chose the terms *value shops, value chains*, and *value networks* for these three types of business models. He has graciously given us permission to use different names for each type. The reason we felt it necessary was that Michael Porter has applied the term "value chain" differently in some of

his writings to the activities that occur across an entire supply chain. Similarly, Clayton Christensen used the term "value network" to apply to the set of businesses in a value chain that have mutually supportive and compatible business models. In many ways the names chosen by Professors Fjeldstad and Stabell are more elegant and simpler than the ones we've used here.

7. See, for example, Porter, Michael E., *Competitive Advantage* (New York: The Free Press, 1985).

8. For example, early data from a two-year study of claims at MinuteClinic, conducted by HealthPartners, revealed that visits cost $18 less than visits to other primary care clinics. Kershaw, Sarah, "Tired of Waiting for a Doctor? Try the Drugstore," *New York Times*, August 23, 2007, A1. The reimbursement for a 10-minute physician outpatient/office visit is roughly $60 according to the 2008 Medicare Physician Fee Schedule (this is the amount of reimbursement for CPT 99213 at the nonfacility price, which reflects most small physician practices). Private insurers will reimburse largely in accordance with the Medicare schedule. The $18 difference between MinuteClinic and a primary care clinic would equate to approximately 30 percent savings. The Fee Schedule is available at http://www.cms.hhs.gov/PFSlookup/. In 1985, CardioVascular Care Providers, a bundled pricing plan for coronary artery bypass grafting at the Texas Heart Institute, had a combined facility and physician fee of $13,800 versus the average Medicare payment of $24,588—about 44 percent lower. See Edmonds, Charles, and Grady L. Hallman, "CardioVascular Care Providers: A Pioneer in Bundled Services, Shared Risk, and Single Payment," *Texas Heart Institute Journal*, vol. 22, no. 1, 1995. 72–76. In Chapter 3, we examine cost reductions at Shouldice Hospital.

9. Our colleague Regina Herzlinger, building upon earlier work by Harvard Business School professor Wickham Skinner, has written extensively on the value of focus. See Herzlinger, Regina, *Market-Driven Health Care: Who Wins, Who Loses in the Transformation of America's Largest Service Industry* (Reading, Massachusetts: Addison-Wesley, 1997).

10. We refer readers to the work of our colleague Michael Porter, who has emphasized the importance of creating competition based on value and results, using in particular the field of organ transplantation as a case study.

11. Abelson, R., "In Bid for Better Care, Surgery with a Warranty," accessed from http://www.nytimes.com/2007/05/17/business/17quality.html on August 14, 2008.

12. Our colleagues Richard Bohmer and Steve Spear have both researched and written extensively about the applications of the Toyota Production System in health care. More about these two particular examples can be found in Harvard Business School Publishing case #606044, "Virginia Mason Medical Center," by Richard Bohmer and Erika M. Ferlins; and Thompson, D. N., G. A. Wolf, and S. J. Spear, "Driving Improvement in Patient Care: Lessons from Toyota," *Journal of Nursing Administration*, vol. 33, 2003, 585–95.

13. "Customers" can include individual consumers and/or businesses. Thus, while networks of consumers are perhaps the most familiar examples, companies can also facilitate B-to-B and B-to-C networks. Øystein Fjeldstad has described to us the eventual migration of any value network into facilitated networks that connect individual consumers, solution shops, and value-added process businesses. Readers who wish to learn more about network businesses can also study the work of Harvard Business School professor Tom Eisenmann, which is available primarily in the form of cases and notes from Harvard Business School Publishing Company.

14. Estimate based on data from the U.S. Department of Commerce, Bureau of Economic Analysis. See *Income and Employment by Industry*, Washington, DC: Bureau of Economic Affairs, accessed from http://www.bea.gov/scb/pdf/2007/08%20August/0807_account_6. pdf on August 28, 2008. The calculation was made by combining the contributions to national income from the information, finance, insurance, real estate, rental, and leasing sectors; and fractions of wholesale trade, retail trade, transportation and warehousing, professional and business services, as well as education services, health care, and social assistance. The sum was then compared to the total national income without capital consumption adjustment.

15. Stabell, Charles B., and Øystein D. Fjeldstad, "Configuring Value for Competitive Advantage: On Chains, Shops and Networks," *Strategic Management Journal*, May 1998, 431.

16. Sermo at http://www.sermo.com, is a community of over 70,000 physicians, all authenticated and credentialed at the time of their registration, who exchange thoughts and opinions via online bulletin boards.

17. Some chronic diseases, particularly those less dependent on behavior modification, may be well suited for value-adding process businesses.

18. We thank Graham Pallett of Carol.com for bringing our attention to PatientsLikeMe. com. See also Goetz, Thomas, "Practicing Patients," *New York Times Magazine*, March 23, 2008. Careplace (http://www.careplace.com/home) was launched in 2006 and encourages users to share similar experiences and concerns by joining online communities organized by health topics and conditions.

19. This was one of the value propositions of Revolution Health, which merged its online activities with Waterfront Media in 2008. It offers online communities of blogs, forums, groups, and people with similar goals.

20. As we discuss in Chapter 5, facilitated networks have the potential to commoditize expertise and decentralize resources. Based on observations of other industries, we can expect the per-transaction cost to decrease tremendously once facilitated networks are established.

21. While Christensen's studies of disruption have focused primarily on disruptions within a type of business model, Professor Fjeldstad has taught us that disruption of shops by chains (which we call value-adding process businesses), and of chains by networks, causes a more fundamental transformation of a firm or industry's value configuration. Professor Fjeldstad's current research agenda includes understanding value configuration transformation at both the firm and the industry level. Readers interested in studying this concept more deeply should read Fjeldstad, Øystein D., and Christian Ketels, "Competitive Advantage and the Value Network Configuration," *Long Range Planning*, vol. 39, 2006, 126.

22. We explore the source of these cost reductions further in Chapter 3, when we discuss the disruption of general hospitals by focused, value-adding process hospitals.

23. The number of vessels should not even be the primary determinant of complexity in angioplasty. There is, of course, correlation between multivessel disease and risk for complications, but from a technical standpoint, a case involving one vessel should be no different from one involving four vessels.

24. Similar handoffs already exist, but only within and across solution shops like hospitals and specialty practices. For example, there are criteria and algorithms for PVOD (based on guidelines from the Inter-Society Consensus for the Management of Peripheral Artery

Disease, also known as TASC) that help determine when patients should be managed by surgical bypass grafting rather than angioplasty. Of course, proper incentives need to be in place for these waves of disruption to occur. In Chapters 6 and 7 we discuss corresponding changes in the employer purchasing and insurance systems that will be necessary for such disruptions to succeed. Our thanks to Dr. Mohan Nandalur for sharing his clinical knowledge and experiences.

25. One of the coauthors of this book, Jason Hwang, works at Innosight LLC and at an affiliate called the Innosight Institute, a nonprofit organization whose purpose is to continue to develop the ideas presented in this book and to help a broad community of health-care reformers understand and implement our recommendations.

Chapter 2

The Technological Enablers of Disruption

Each disruption is composed of three enabling building blocks: a technology, a business model, and a disruptive value network. While Chapter 1 deals with business models, this chapter focuses on the technological enablers that form the backbone of disruptive business models. These technological or methodological enablers allow the basic problems in an industry to be addressed on smaller scale, with lower costs, and with less human skill than historically was needed. These technologies sometimes come from years of work in corporate research and development (R&D) labs. Others are licensed or bought, and, on occasion, technology can be repurposed from an entirely different industry.

The health-care industry is awash with new technologies—but the inherent nature of most is to sustain the current way of practicing medicine. However, the technologies that enable precise diagnosis and, subsequently, predictably effective therapy are those that have the potential to transform health care through disruption. We begin this chapter with a general review of what makes a technology disruptive and how that technology converts complex intuition into rules-based tasks. We then introduce a three-stage framework for characterizing the state of technology in the treatment of various diseases. This framework asserts that the treatment of most diseases initially is in the realm of experimentation based on *intuition*. Care then transitions into the realm of probabilistic or *empirical* medicine; and ultimately it becomes rules-based *precision* medicine. After explaining this framework, we then review the history of infectious diseases to show how technological enablers based on precise diagnosis caused care to pass through these stages. Moving to the present, we show how similar transitions are now afoot in the care of diabetes, breast cancer, and AIDS. Next, we redefine the concept of *personalized* medicine and show how information technology is enabling facilitated networks to deliver true personalization. Finally, we sketch out a preliminary map of the state of knowledge of a range of diseases, allowing us to project what technological breakthroughs will enable the further disruption of today's health-care business models.[1]

WHAT MAKES A TECHNOLOGY DISRUPTIVE?

There is a clear pattern in the long and arduous process by which an industry eventually transforms the body of knowledge upon which it is built from an art into a science. In the earliest stages of most industries, the extent of understanding is little more than an assortment of observations collected over many generations. With so many unknowns, the work to be done is complex and intuitive, and the outcomes are relatively unpredictable. Only skilled experts are able to cobble together adequate solutions, and their work proceeds through intuitive trial-and-error experimentation. This type of problem-solving process can be costly and time-consuming, but there is little alternative when the state of knowledge is still in its infancy.

Over time, however, patterns emerge from these intuitive experiments. Defining these patterns that correlate actions with the outcomes of interest makes it much easier to teach people how to solve the problems. There is as yet no cookbook that can guarantee success every time, but the scientists can often state the probability of an outcome, given the actions that have been taken. Ultimately these patterns of correlation are supplanted with an understanding of causality, which makes the result of given actions highly predictable. Work that was once intuitive and complex becomes routine, and specific rules are eventually developed to handle the steps in the process. Abilities that previously resided in the intuition of a select group of experts ultimately become so explicitly teachable that rules-based work can be performed by people with much less experience and training. Problem solving becomes focused on root cause mechanisms, replacing activities that were grounded in conjecture and correlation.

The term "technology" that we use here might refer to a new piece of machinery, a new production process, a mathematical equation, or a body of understanding about a molecular pathway. However, at the heart of this evolution of work is the conversion of complex, intuitive processes into simple, rules-based work, *and* the handoff of this work from expensive, highly trained experts to less costly technicians. The cases that follow illustrate how disruptive technologies enable this transformation and eventually lead to the emergence of successful business models that are able to capture the advantages of rules-based work.[2]

DuPont's Miracle of Science

Founded in 1802 as a manufacturer of gunpowder, DuPont operated several industrial laboratories to expand its understanding and capabilities in materials science. Building on the discovery of synthetic rubber, DuPont's scientists conducted research on polymers at the company's Experimental Station through the 1930s. DuPont evaluated over 100 different polyamides before finding new fibers that were adequately stable for commercial development and production. This resulted in the invention of the world's first synthetic textile fiber, nylon, in 1935. The success of that discovery led to further polymer research that ultimately yielded DuPont's acrylic fiber in 1944 and Dacron polyester fiber in 1946. The work that led to these inventions was a classically intuitive, trial-and-error process of problem solving. During those decades, there were only a limited number of scientists in the world with sufficient expertise to push the work forward, and DuPont employed most of them. As a result, DuPont dominated the synthetic fibers industry.

As DuPont's scientists continued to practice their craft, however, and as the fields of quantum mechanics and molecular physics became better understood and applied, the cause-and-effect relationship between a polymer's molecular structure and the fiber's physical properties became more clearly understood. Scientists codified which arrangements of molecules and specific chemical bonds defined a polymer's strength, melting point, and stiffness. This understanding of polymer chemistry ultimately enabled scientists to reliably predict the physical properties of a fiber before it was created—enabling the design and production of application-specific fibers with less trial-and-error experimentation than ever before. The development of DuPont's Nomex, a heat-resistant fiber that could serve as a fire retardant, and Kevlar, a fiber five times stronger than steel, both resulted from this progress in polymer science.[3]

Today, engineers at DuPont and in many other companies rely on computer modeling to assist in the creation of novel compounds with the exact properties that are desired. To a growing extent, success requires at least as much, and perhaps more, familiarity with the software than the intuition or knowledge of physics and chemistry that those first scientists had drawn upon at DuPont's Experimental Station. In other words, the intuition and expertise of DuPont's engineers ultimately were captured in software that has diffused around the world, enabling many more engineers to discover new synthetic materials more rapidly and efficiently than could have been imagined 50 years before.

The impact of this progress on our well-being is simply extraordinary. In the 1950s, wood, metal, paper, rubber, stone, and ceramics (including glass and cement) were the primary materials available for building and covering things. Today, our lives are made incredibly efficient and comfortable by materials whose durability, flexibility, strength, appearance, and cost were inconceivable a generation ago. This enrichment did not come from replicating the costly expertise of DuPont's scientists, however. It came from scientific progress that commoditized their expertise, thereby enabling many more scientists and technicians to continue building on their initial work.

Automobile Design

A second example of how scientific and technological progress can transform the fundamental nature of an industry's core technological problem is the process of designing automobiles. BMW triumphantly announced several years ago that its automobile models could now be designed so realistically on computers that its engineers could crash-test the cars virtually, on an engineering workstation.[4] This enables BMW's engineers to optimize their designs for safety before a physical model is even made. That's the good news for BMW. It is *much* less expensive to design safe, attractive, high-performance cars on a computer than to build and crash physical prototypes. The bad news is that once the algorithms of design have been codified so completely that a computer can guide much of this work, such technology enables a *lot* of people—not just BMW engineers—to design comparable cars.

Made possible by advances in technology and science, the migration of problem solving from a small group of experts to a larger population of less-expensive providers who simply have to follow the rules is a widespread foundational phenomenon that underlies the transformation of industries ranging from animation to architecture to aviation; and from telecommunications to taxes.

HOW THE ART OF MEDICINE BECOMES A SCIENCE

In spite of all of the money and effort devoted to biomedical research in today's academic medical institutions, pharmaceutical companies, and biotechnology firms, the outcomes of many commonly prescribed therapies are not very satisfying. For example, over 60 percent of all patients being treated for Type II diabetes have blood sugars that exceed the recommended level, putting them at significantly elevated risk of developing heart disease, kidney failure, blindness, and other long-term complications of uncontrolled diabetes.[5] Despite the use of medications, the blood pressure in as many as 58 percent of patients being treated for hypertension (depending upon which study is consulted) does not conform to the recommended target of below 140/90.[6] Even though billions of dollars are spent to purchase lipid-lowering drugs, only 17 percent of patients with heart disease—those most in need of good control—ever reach the goals for cholesterol management established by national guidelines.[7] Among patients diagnosed with depression, only half report a 50 percent improvement in symptoms after using anti-depressant medications, and of those, 10 percent relapse within six months. What is more baffling is that 32 percent of patients who received a placebo *also* experienced a 50 percent improvement in symptoms.[8] Table 2.1 chronicles the story more completely.

The statistics in Table 2.1 are not the results of poor patient compliance or variations in clinical care; all these patients were enrolled in clinical trials where medication use was closely monitored and where the physicians conducting the studies treated patients according to fixed protocols established by the clinical trial investigators.

Why, despite the billions being spent, does medical science still seem at best to be an art? A significant reason lies in our inability to precisely diagnose disorders such as those listed above based on their actual root causes, which may be genetic, infectious, or quite possibly to the result of something still unknown to medical science. But it is only when precise diagnosis is possible that consistently effective therapy is possible. Until this happens, many of those afflicted with disorders such as these can be treated only

Table 2.1
Patient response rates to a major drug in selected categories of therapy

Category of disease	% who respond to therapy
Pain treated with analgesics (COX-2 inhibitors)	80%
Asthma	60%
Cardiac arrythmias	60%
Schizophrenia	60%
Migraine (acute)	52%
Migraine (prophylaxis)	50%
Rheumatoid arthritis	50%
Osteoporosis	48%
Hepatitis C	47%
Alzheimer's disease	30%
Oncology	25%

Source: Spear, Brian B., et. al., " Clinical Application of Pharmacogenetics," Trends in Molecular Medicine, vol. 7, issue 5, 2001, pp. 201–04. (The source of data in this article was the Physicians' Desk Reference, Thomson Health Care.)

with the trial-and-error guesswork that pervades clinical decision making today.

THE SPECTRUM FROM INTUITIVE TO PRECISION MEDICINE

It turns out that the human body has a very limited vocabulary from which it can draw when it needs to declare the presence of disease. And to a confusing degree, the body often inarticulately "slurs" its expressions that disease is afoot. Fever, for example, is one of the "words" through which the body declares that something inside isn't quite right. The fever isn't the disease, of course. It is a symptomatic manifestation of a variety of possible underlying diseases, which could range from ear infections to Hodgkin's lymphoma. Medications that ameliorate the fever don't cure the disease. And a therapy that addresses one of the diseases whose symptom is a fever (as ampicillin can cure an ear infection) may not adequately cure many of the other diseases that also happen to declare their presence with a fever.

As scientists work to decipher the body's limited vocabulary, they are teaching us that many of the things we thought were diseases actually are not. They're symptoms. For example, we have learned that hypertension is like a fever—it is a symptomatic expression of a number of distinctly different diseases. There are many more diseases than the number of physical symptoms that are available, so the diseases end up having to share symptoms. One reason why a therapy that effectively reduces the blood pressure of one patient is ineffective in another may be that they have different diseases that share the same symptom. Another reason, which we discuss toward the end of the chapter, may be that they are genetically different in their physiologic metabolism of the drug itself.[9] When we cannot properly diagnose the underlying disease or fully understand the context in which the patient may or may not be able to respond to treatment, the sorts of rules-based processes that emerged for synthetic fibers and computers to this point have proved impossible in medicine. As a result, effective care generally could only be provided through the intuition and experience of highly trained (and expensive) caregivers—medicine's equivalent of the pioneering scientists and engineers at DuPont, BMW, and in IBM's mainframe computer business.

In this book, we define *intuitive medicine* as care for conditions that can be diagnosed only by their symptoms and only treated with therapies whose efficacy is uncertain. By its very nature, intuitive medicine depends upon the skill and judgment of capable but costly physicians. Not surprisingly, that skill and judgment is heavily influenced by where and when practitioners were trained, where they practice, the relative supply of human and physical capital, how caregivers are paid, and how updated they are with the latest medical advancements.[10,11]

At the other end of the spectrum, we define *precision medicine* as the provision of care for diseases that can be precisely diagnosed, whose causes are understood, and which consequently can be treated with rules-based therapies that are predictably effective. The science of precisely diagnosing diseases by the pathophysiology through which they arise and propagate does not ensure that a predictably effective therapy can be developed, of course, but it sure helps. In other words, precise diagnosis is necessary but not sufficient for treatment of a disease to be at the precision end of the spectrum.

As we show below, progress along the spectrum between intuitive and precision medicine is the primary mechanism through which technological enablers can lead the disruption of existing health-care business models.[12]

Intuitive and precision medicine are not binary states, of course. There is a broad domain in the middle that we term *empirical medicine*. The practice of empirical medicine occurs when a field has progressed into an era of "pattern recognition"—when correlations between actions and outcomes are consistent enough that results can be predicted in probabilistic terms. When we read statements like, "Reduction to normal levels occurred in 73 percent of patients who took this medication," or, "98 percent of patients whose hernias were repaired with this procedure experienced no recurrence within five years, compared to 90 percent for the other method," we're in the realm of empirical medicine. Empirical medicine enables caregivers to follow the odds, but not to guarantee the outcome.[13]

Scientific progress takes us along the continuum from intuitive to empirical and ultimately to precision medicine.[14] In most cases, precise diagnosis must precede predictably effective therapy.[15] And in order to achieve that degree of precision, technology must progress interactively on three fronts. As the following case histories illustrate, the first front is an understanding of what causes the disease; the second is the ability to detect those causal factors; and the third is the ability to treat those root causes effectively.

How Precision Medicine Has Transformed the Field of Infectious Diseases

Infectious diseases were the first to yield to precise diagnoses. The earliest diagnostic categorization schemes for infectious diseases were based on factors such as immorality and weakness of faith, unsanitary conditions in the city, exposure to affected individuals, or contact with certain insects and animals (anthrax pneumonia was once called "wool sorters' disease"). These diagnoses were reasonable given the state of knowledge—and therapy was sometimes successful.

However, progress was finally unleashed when, by using microscopes and various staining techniques, scientists realized that people were surrounded by a sea of microorganisms, both harmless and deadly. Some of these microbes caused diseases with overlapping symptoms, but identification of the particular organism involved offered clues to the aggressiveness and spread of the disease and the patient's general prognosis. Over time, this would translate to tailored antibiotic therapy based on the species of organism and, more recently, on the molecular subtype and resistance profile of the involved strain.

Precise diagnosis enabled consistently effective therapy. This took time, as Figure 2.1 shows—Leeuwenhoek saw his first microbes in his primitive microscope 250 years before Fleming discovered penicillin.

The potential for precision medicine as a technological enabler to dramatically reduce overall health-care costs is illustrated by what has happened to the cost of treating infectious diseases. In

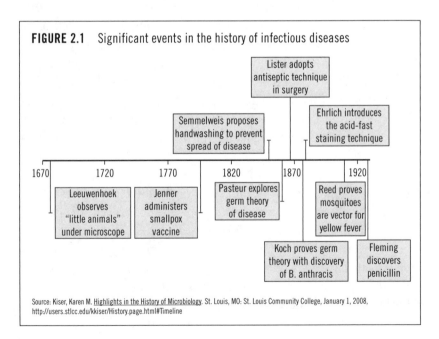

FIGURE 2.1 Significant events in the history of infectious diseases

Lister adopts antiseptic technique in surgery

Semmelweis proposes handwashing to prevent spread of disease

Ehrlich introduces the acid-fast staining technique

1670   1720   1770   1820   1870   1920

Leeuwenhoek observes "little animals" under microscope

Jenner administers smallpox vaccine

Pasteur explores germ theory of disease

Reed proves mosquitoes are vector for yellow fever

Koch proves germ theory with discovery of B. anthracis

Fleming discovers penicillin

Source: Kiser, Karen M. Highlights in the History of Microbiology. St. Louis, MO: St. Louis Community College, January 1, 2008, http://users.stlcc.edu/kkiser/History.page.html#Timeline

constant dollars, the cost of diagnosing and treating these diseases has declined by about 5 percent per year since 1940—step by step, disease by disease, as scientific progress has shifted these disorders from intuitive toward precision medicine.[16] Diseases like tuberculosis, diphtheria, cholera, malaria, measles, scarlet fever, typhoid, syphilis, poliomyelitis, yellow fever, smallpox, and pertussis (whooping cough) once accounted for the lion's share of health-care costs. Now they amount to a blip in the U.S. health-care budget.

Tuberculosis: From Consumption to Cure

Until the early twentieth century, tuberculosis was known as "consumption," so named because the disease caused its victims to waste away. Given the limited understanding of the disease, however, what was called consumption also likely referred to cases of lung cancer, pneumonia, and bronchitis, all of which could present with overlapping symptoms. Still other diseases that were once categorized as kidney failure, bone disease, or a skin disease thought to be curable by the touch of royalty ended up being tuberculous nephritis, Pott's disease, and scrofula, respectively—all manifestations of unrecognized, untreated tuberculosis.

Long feared as one of the great microbial killers of mankind, tuberculosis itself would soon begin to fall victim to our curiosity. By the second half of the nineteenth century, there was strong suspicion that tuberculosis was an infectious disease, often spreading through crowded cities. Measures were taken to prevent public spitting, and sanitariums were established to offer fresh air, exercise, and good nutrition to the afflicted. Though the level of understanding and treatment had progressed slightly, the inability to precisely diagnose and specifically treat meant that tuberculosis continued to kill without mercy.

By the end of the nineteenth century, two discoveries dramatically altered the landscape. In 1882, Robert Koch identified the bacteriological cause of disease, Mycobacterium tuberculosis, moving the level of understanding to the organism.[17] This was soon followed by Wilhelm Roentgen's discovery of the X-ray in 1895, which enabled clinicians to examine and diagnose lung disease in far more sophisticated ways.

In 1906, the Bacillus Calmette-Guerin (BCG) vaccine offered the first form of targeted prevention, although it was imperfectly targeted since it was prepared from a related bacteria strain that infected cows. However, after years of experimentation, an arsenal of antibiotics was discovered that could successfully treat tuberculosis: streptomycin in 1944, isoniazid in 1952, and rifampin in 1963.

However, although these antibiotics were extremely successful in treating tuberculosis initially, they too were imperfect. A disease thought to be headed toward eradication soon began to put up a fight. Multidrug-resistant strains of tuberculosis were first noted in 1970, and increasing rates of infection in the 1980s were soon found to coincide with the rising number of immunosuppressed HIV patients. Clearly, though the number of victims is no longer overwhelming, the battle against tuberculosis is not yet over, and we should be prepared to move toward even more specific and targeted weapons as time goes on.

The result of this prolonged attack on infectious disease through diagnostic and therapeutic innovation is the dramatic decline in mortality from infectious diseases shown in Figure 2.2 (although readers should note the tremendous increase in 1918, which is discussed in endnote 16). Diseases such as cervical cancer and stomach ulcers, whose causes used to be uncertain and whose treatments were unpredictable, have also been shown to be infectious diseases. The former is now preventable through vaccination, and the latter treatable through antibiotics. More recently, scientific progress was able to rapidly shift AIDS and SARS toward the precision end of the spectrum too.[18, 19]

Cancer's Movement Toward Precision Medicine

Cancer has begun to yield to a similar revolution in the precision of diagnosis and efficacy of treatment. Just as the invention of

FIGURE 2.2 Mortality rates from infectious disease in the United States, 1900–2000

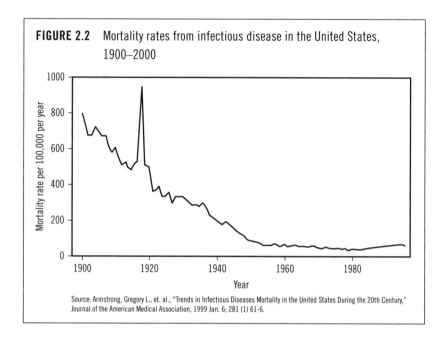

Source: Armstrong, Gregory L., et. al., "Trends in Infectious Diseases Mortality in the United States During the 20th Century," Journal of the American Medical Association, 1999 Jan. 6; 281 (1) 61-6.

the microscope and subsequent discovery of antibiotics drove infectious diseases toward the precision end of the spectrum, a deeper understanding of molecular biology and the human genome is enabling scientists and clinicians to begin diagnosing and treating cancers based upon their molecular characteristics rather than gross anatomical observations. For example, we used to think that leukemia was a disease diagnosed by visually observing an excessive number of white blood cells. Now we know this preponderance of abnormal white blood cells, like a fever, is a vague "word" that the human body utters when one of 38 different cancers of the blood occurs (and there are likely many more yet undiscovered). Each of these specific diseases can be characterized by the molecular pathways by which the cancer propagates, and each can be detected by a pattern in which certain genes express themselves.

As a result, now we know why in the past a course of therapy that would cure one leukemia patient could not save the life of another: they had different diseases, and we just didn't know it.

These diseases were in the realm of intuitive medicine—standardized therapy was not only inadvisable, it was impossible. However, members of this set of diseases are yielding one by one to precision medicine, as molecular diagnostics paves the way for predictably effective therapy. Gleevec (imatinib) from Novartis is such a therapy—predictably effective for one type of leukemia called chronic myeloid leukemia (CML) that depends on a particular molecular pathway that can be inhibited by imatinib.[20] Figure 2.3 chronicles the important milestones in the ongoing process of transforming this collection of diseases from intuitive to precision medicine.

In a similar way, we now know that breast cancer, like leukemia, is not a single disease. Rather, it denotes a geographic location in which a range of microscopically unique tumors can arise. Medical historians have discovered recorded cases of breast cancer dating back to 490 B.C. Based on its destructive and unpredictable effects, breast cancer (or almost any cancer for that matter) was viewed as a death sentence. It remains one of the most feared diseases among women today.

In 1985, scientists discovered that a specific receptor on the surface of cells, called human epidermal growth factor receptor 2 (HER2), was produced in excess in about 20 to 25 percent of breast tumors—suggesting to them that these tumors might be a different disease, defined by a unique molecular pathway through which those tumors propagated. In 1998, Genentech received Food and Drug Administration (FDA) approval to market trastuzumab under the brand name Herceptin. The drug is an antibody designed to specifically halt the growth of breast cancer cells by attaching to the HER2 receptors on the surfaces of those cancer cells. The result has been a dramatic improvement in the survival rate of the patients who have that specific form of breast cancer. Herceptin is better tolerated and safer than chemotherapy or surgery since it is better able to address the disease at the molecular level. For patients who are

HER2-positive, determined by specific molecular testing for the receptor or its precursor gene, Herceptin has essentially become a rules-based treatment, and the result is a vastly improved probability of survival with fewer side effects.[21] Eventually, given the right tools, the treatment for HER2-positive breast cancer will increasingly move out of the hands of oncologists and into the realm of generalists.[22]

Links to cigarette smoking, hormone replacement therapy, and specific genes like BRCA-1 and BRCA-2 indicate many possible causes of other forms of breast cancer. These explanations to date have been incomplete, overlapping, and often confusing. As a result, the primary defense against breast cancer has been to discover it early through mass screening efforts using mammography. The need to cast such a wide net is an indication that, though science has made significant progress, there is much diagnostic uncertainty yet to resolve.

Bernadine Healy, former head of America's National Institutes of Health, summarized this progress against cancer in a reflection upon her own battle with a brain tumor: "Sifting through the

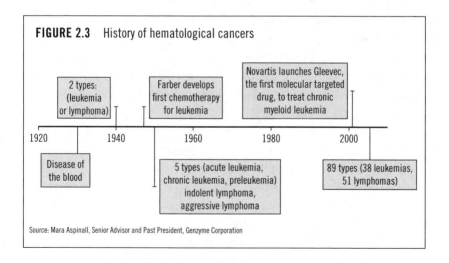

FIGURE 2.3   History of hematological cancers

Source: Mara Aspinall, Senior Advisor and Past President, Genzyme Corporation

genetic and molecular profiles of individual cancers has exposed a big secret that misled many treatments of the past: What seem to be identical tumors under the microscope can be markedly different where it really matters, in the genes and proteins. This is a crucial discovery, explaining for the first time why a tumor melts away under a particular therapy while another of the same type is barely touched; and why one tumor returns in a few years and yet another disappears for a lifetime."

It enables, Healy continued, "a re-thinking of the traditional treatment approach, in which any and all cells with rapidly replicating DNA—malignant or not—are attacked as if they were known enemies of the body. The new era instead relies upon an army of laser-like drugs, some old, some new, and some yet to be devised, that specifically target deranged genetic pathways and swoop in for the kill, leaving the innocent bystanders intact."[23]

Indeed, what we have learned in recent decades is that while the body had seemed quite inarticulate when we were only able to discern what it was saying by magnifying and measuring what we could see, feel and hear, the body is delightfully articulate at the level of genetic expression.[24] Over time, as scientists use molecular biology and imaging diagnostics to push one disease after another from the intuitive toward the precision end of the spectrum, the mortality rate for other diseases will decline just as it did for infectious diseases a century earlier. In fact, this has already begun for cancer. From 1995 to 2004, the overall number of deaths from the 15 deadliest cancers decreased by an average annual rate of 1.2 percent.[25]

The reason why investments to gain this knowledge are so important, from the point of view of efficacy and economy, is that as diagnosis and treatment become simpler and more proven, care of these diseases can be shifted from the most expensive specialists to less expensive generalists, and ultimately to nurses and the patients themselves.[26] Hence, as has already happened with many infectious diseases, precision medicine, when embedded within the sorts of business model innovations described in Chapter 1, will ultimately cause more costs in our health-care system to decline as well.

We emphasize that this progress, in American football terms, is being ground out in a cloud of dust, yard by yard, play by play, and that negative yardage is common. As we are learning in our efforts to help patients with AIDS, precision diagnostics enable, but do not guarantee, the development of predictably effective therapies. Sometimes in our efforts to eradicate a disease, touchdown plays are called back as the bacteria, protozoan parasites, or viruses that cause a disease evolve to become resistant to previously effective treatments. Such is the case with malaria, which stubbornly resists precise interventions.

How soon will precision medicine affect the cost, quality, and accessibility of health care? The reality is that it is already here—the patterns of rules-based work and innovation described earlier have already profoundly shaped the diagnosis and treatment of diseases like diabetes mellitus—where the contrast between Type I and Type II diabetes care illustrates the impact rules-based work can have on the care for two seemingly similar diseases.[27,28]

The Sweet Science of Diabetes

The early days of diabetic care involved significant uncertainty. The exact etiology of diabetes was unknown, and until the late 1800s, it was thought to be a kidney disease rather than a pancreatic hormone (insulin) deficiency. For centuries, diabetics could be diagnosed only by tasting a urine sample to assess its sweetness. Treatment was intuitive. Some physicians would experiment with dietary restrictions; others focused on personal hygiene. Others offered opium as a treatment. This trial-and-error problem solving led to extremely variable degrees of success in treatment and an inability to improve the overall standard of care. Worse yet, it fostered a high number of "quack" remedies which preyed on the hopes of desperate patients who had fallen victim to poorly understood diseases such as diabetes.[29]

Fortunately, as physicians came to understand more about diabetes and its treatment, their decision-making process began to change. One of the most important medical breakthroughs in history took place in 1922, when Canadian physician Sir Frederick Grant Banting and medical student Charles Best successfully treated a 14-year-old boy with insulin-containing pancreatic material extracted from dogs.[30] Their work defined the pathophysiology of diabetes and linked it to a universal treatment. While physicians could once reasonably argue in favor of one therapy over another, even a layperson would soon be able to identify insulin as the only acceptable treatment for diabetes.

However, researchers soon began to understand that diabetes was a more complex disease than they had initially believed. The insulin seemed to restore vitality to once-cachectic children,[31] yet there were other diabetics who seemed far less responsive to insulin. While they also had the same elevated blood glucose and physical symptoms, these patients were typically diagnosed with diabetes in adulthood and were often overweight. Physicians ultimately decided that there were two types of diabetes—childhood-onset and adult-onset, insulin dependent and non-insulin dependent; Type I and Type II.[32]

Despite ongoing research, there remains today a stark contrast in the level of understanding, and hence treatment, of these two diabetic populations. It is now known that a Type I diabetic has high glucose levels because the pancreas has lost the ability to produce insulin due to an autoimmune reaction. Although not strictly curative, insulin provides a method of treatment that can be entirely rules-based because it directly addresses the root cause of the disease.[33]

A critical reason why this diagnostic and therapeutic progress is important is that it makes it possible to deliver care through a different business model. Patients with diabetes can measure their own glucose levels at home with an electronic meter. Based on this reading, they can self-administer specific quantities of insulin which can be determined and prescribed by algorithm. Before long, the patients become expert in managing their own glucose levels (more so than the physician) and can recite a list of rules that govern their regimen. It is the Type I diabetic, not the physician, who knows exactly how much insulin she needs after consuming a bowl of cereal. In other words, responsibility for the care of the Type I diabetic has shifted from the physician to the patient.

In contrast, many challenges in the diagnosis and treatment of Type II diabetics remain in the realm of intuitive medicine, in the hands of professionals who use their medical expertise to solve complex problems. Some Type II diabetics are obese, while others are not. Some are diagnosed in adulthood, but an increasing number are now identified in childhood. Some require insulin, while others can be treated with oral medications or diet alone. In other words, the term "Type II" likely refers to a mélange of as many as 20 different disorders that may prove one day to have different molecular root causes and therefore require different treatments.[34] Because the scientific understanding necessary to distinguish among these variants does not yet exist, precision treatment is impossible. For now, scientists will continue to refer to the disease as "multifactorial," and people who have this form of diabetes will need to rely on the intervention of experts to guide treatment.

The Mystery of Ward 86

When a mysterious illness began to appear in Ward 86[35] of San Francisco's General Hospital in the early 1980s, the hospital's best experts were put to the test. In 1981, the disease was called GRID (gay-related immune deficiency) because scientists could base their diagnoses only on observable symptoms and demographic data. Without a clear root cause for the disease, physicians had to categorize at-risk individuals by these attributes. The common rule of thumb was to screen patients for the "four Hs": heroin user, hemophiliac, homosexual, and Haitian. These early victims of AIDS were extremely sick, and, despite the best efforts of dedicated physicians, most of them died.[36]

It is critical not to advocate rules-based treatment when the science relating to a disease is still intuitive. Yet in the past 25 years, just a blip in the overall history of infectious diseases, the diagnosis, treatment, and prevention of AIDS have evolved dramatically. Human immunodeficiency virus (HIV) was discovered as the root cause; molecular targets for pharmaceutical intervention were identified, and successful treatment protocols were developed. Though a cure or vaccine had yet to be discovered, the care surrounding HIV quickly became codified such that more and more generalists could manage the disease. Patients with HIV were living longer, and much of their treatment was shifted from intensive care and inpatient wards to outpatient clinics.

While HIV care has not yet reached the point where medicine can claim victory, the relatively quick progression toward greater precision care is also a likely indicator that past experience from dealing with other infectious diseases has shortened the period of intuitive medicine and experimentation necessary before rules-based care can develop. The world's quick mobilization in response to SARS (sudden acute respiratory syndrome) is another example of this increasingly rapid cycle time.

PERSONALIZING MEDICINE

Another term, "personalized medicine," is often used for this phenomenon that we're calling "precision medicine." The reason we decided to coin a new term is that most precisely diagnosed diseases are in fact not uniquely personal. The same causal mechanism that predictably yields to the same therapy can be at work in many different people. As we soon discuss, the precise biological definition of a disease also does not incorporate "personalization" that takes into account how an individual patient might *respond* to a particular treatment.[37] However, unlike precision medicine, personalization refers to both biological and nonbiological issues that can affect an individual's response to a treatment.[38]

For example, in the case of Type I diabetes that we just reviewed, the *diagnosis* of the disease is in precision medicine. There is no ambiguity: if the islet cells of your pancreas are unable to produce sufficient insulin, you have Type I diabetes.[39] But the therapy still must be *personalized* for each patient. Patients in excellent physical condition typically need less insulin per calorie of carbohydrate ingested because their tissues are more sensitive to the presence of insulin, compared to patients who don't regularly exercise.

Personalization to some degree has always been a part of care delivery, of course, even though it may not feel like we always get the personal attention we desire. Physicians will avoid prescribing medications that could trigger a drug allergy, for example, or modify dosing based on the patient's age, weight, or kidney or liver function. However, just as diagnosis has progressed beyond observable symptoms, the assessment of an individual's specific response to treatment has begun to move to more sophisticated levels. This personalization of therapy can involve tailoring treatment either on the molecular level, or, as we will explain, based on socioeconomic and other nonbiologic factors that extend far beyond a clinician's normal realm of expertise—and therefore require new business models to deliver that care.

One of the most well-studied examples of tailoring therapy to the molecular mechanisms that affect response to therapy involves a drug called warfarin, a blood-thinner used by approximately 2 million new patients every year in the United States to prevent blood clotting, stroke, and heart attacks.[40] However, the optimal dose of warfarin differs from patient to patient, and improper levels can cause serious problems—doses that are too high can cause deadly bleeding, while doses that are too low can lead to blood clotting diseases that the warfarin was meant to prevent. Studies have found that testing for variations in two genes (CYP2C9 and VKORC1) can help determine whether an individual will metabolize warfarin differently from others, and testing patients for these genetic variants prior to starting warfarin therapy would allow physicians to adjust their doses appropriately.[41] A report from the American Enterprise Institute-Brookings Joint Center for Regulatory Studies estimated that integrating genetic testing into warfarin therapy would save $1.1 billion annually in the United States and prevent 85,000 cases of serious bleeding and 17,000 strokes each year.[42] However, these specific improvements in care will come not from improving diagnosis, since the set of diseases being treated with warfarin remains the same, but rather from a greater understanding of how patients respond to some of our most commonly applied treatments.[43]

For most services in other industries, people think of personalization as an attempt by the company or its employees to acknowledge and respond to a customer's specific situation and circumstances. If a grocery store clerk offers to carry an elderly woman's shopping bags to her car, we would say that he has offered personalized service that was tailored to her needs. In the same sense, sometimes there is an entirely different, "nonmedical" set of characteristics that can affect the course of a patient's treatment. Complex human behaviors such as compliance, motivation, and learning also influence outcomes. These in turn can be traced back to factors including family imprinting, the presence or absence of a social support system, financial resources, or previous experiences with the health-care system. In other words, there are a lot of things that can affect the outcome of a treatment, and many of them cannot be resolved through precision medicine. These are also the issues that very often frustrate health-care workers because they are so difficult to understand and control. Patients rightfully become frustrated as well when they discover that their sophisticated and expensive health-care system can't seem to understand the problem.

In health care the degree of personalization typically has stopped at the biologic level, despite the fact that so many nonphysiological factors can affect outcomes and patient satisfaction. Social workers and other allied health professionals help to bridge this gap, but those systems are overwhelmed and can only help the outliers. Personalization is certainly not yet a matter of routine in health-care delivery. New business models are needed—particularly facilitated networks of professionals and patients enabled by information technology, as we discuss in Chapter 5.

"Someone Like Me"

Under the traditional health-care delivery model, there are only a few ways that a doctor and patient can fine-tune the treatment plan. Most often the plan is slowly adjusted over a series of appointments through a process of trial and error. This is expected of treatments for conditions that are only within or just beginning to move away from intuitive medicine, such as congestive heart failure and diabetes. However, even for more rules-based conditions like middle-ear and upper-respiratory-tract infections, high cholesterol, and high blood pressure, treatment plans often need to be adjusted for circumstances that go beyond the capabilities of precision medicine. The patient might only be able to afford generic drugs, or her busy schedule might prevent her from appearing at all of her physical therapy appointments, or she may have an intense distrust of hospitals because of a family member's past experience.

Doctors are accustomed to focusing on easily measurable markers such as vital signs and laboratory values, and the increasing significance of precision medicine means that ever more emphasis is being placed on such objective, straightforward criteria. And even though some doctors do try to account for some of the psychosocial factors that can influence outcomes, recognition often comes too late in the treatment process. Success is too heavily dependent on whether the physician is even aware of the impact of these "secondary" issues and how to counteract them. This is perhaps one of the main reasons why so many patients have taken such a great interest in participating in their own health care—not to challenge the physician's decision-making authority, but to complement it.

Professional and patient-centric network business models must play a greater role in the care of chronic diseases. Support groups in which patients can discuss the different circumstances that affect their treatment have long been a fertile ground for identifying effective solutions outside of the physician's office, often without expert guidance. Interestingly, this model has proven especially successful for addiction and psychiatric therapy—conditions which are perhaps more entrenched in intuitive medicine than any others. A key to the success of these networks is their ability to help patients find "someone like me," with whom they can identify and whose successful approach to the disease can serve as a role model for them to follow. Historically this option has only been viable when there has been a critical mass of patients locally with shared characteristics. However, the Internet is now bringing this level of personalized medicine to the rest of health care by extending the reach for "someone like me" across the globe.

Traditional media such as written publications, radio, and television are much like a typical visit to a doctor's office—the information tends to flow only in one direction. Early health-care Web sites were similar, acting primarily as information depositories meant for passive absorption by their users. However, social networking Web sites and newer "Web 2.0" services have taken the Internet far beyond its initial incarnation for most users as a one-way reference tool. In health services, this networking capability and collective intelligence are beginning to create the personalized health-care experience so many patients seek.

As mentioned earlier, online network facilitators are using their vast data processing capabilities to help users find "someone like me." Using self-reported personal health records and anonymous data from insurance billing claims, they can even provide metrics through which a patient can compare herself to her peers. Combining these data with predictive modeling tools, they can calculate the probability of disease and suggest the most beneficial ways of mitigating that risk with a more comprehensive view than any doctor could offer. It's not a far stretch to begin incorporating into these models less traditional health factors. As their databases become more sophisticated, the accuracy of matches and predictions will continue to improve.

Before the advent of such tools, a patient had to rely on a physician's expert opinion, which was built out of a largely random collection of book knowledge, clinical experience, heuristics, rules of thumb, and dumb luck.[44] Whether a physician could prescribe the right treatment the first time often depended on whether he happened to have experienced a similar case in the past. But the odds of finding that similar case are now dramatically improved with tools that help patients identify each other through their common circumstances. Instead of waiting for the circumstances to declare themselves and become potentially life-threatening, patients and doctors can hopefully use these new resources to carry out the promise of truly personalized, precision medicine.

THE PRESENT AND FUTURE OF PRECISION MEDICINE

There are three prominent implications of the fact that scientific progress in imaging, molecular medicine, and biochemistry has long been shifting diseases along the spectrum from intuitive toward precision medicine. First, research that enables precision diagnosis should take highest priority for funding by entities such as the National Institutes of Health. This includes basic science research which naturally leads to future technologies that enable precision care, such as the investment made in the Human Genome Project, which led to the spinoff of many critically important developments in medicine. We also show, in Chapter 8, that whereas diagnostics historically has been a far less profitable business for the pharmaceutical industry than the therapeutics business, in the future that tendency will reverse. The reason is that in the past the industry's profit structure has been largely determined by autocratic reimbursement policies that do not reflect the value created by products and services. On average, reimbursement formulas accord greater profit to therapeutics than to diagnostics. Indeed, when health care was largely in the realm of intuitive medicine, diagnosis and treatment were interwoven. It was impossible to parse reimbursement between the two. But when solution shops are separated from value-adding process activities, as we describe in Chapter 3, it will be possible. And our theories of innovation suggest that diagnosis will become one of the most profitable parts of the value chain for pharmaceutical companies.[45] This implies that pharmaceutical companies and academic researchers who focus their research and development energies will find that creating the precise diagnostics that fuel the growth of precision medicine will be most profitable in the future.

The second implication is that regulatory bodies such as the FDA in the United States need to change their posture about the role of clinical trials in research toward precision medicine. In the past, clinical trials were lined up in a serial mode, *after* research and development had been completed. If too small a percentage of patients responded to the drug, it was not approved—the result of trials has typically been a go-for-all/no-go-for-all decision. Instead, as we show in Chapter 8, trials need to be included as an integral part of the R&D process. If a trial shows that only 16 percent of patients responded to the therapy, in all probability the other 84 percent had a different disease from those who were helped. Such results from a trial ought to be celebrated as an opportunity to search for the biomarkers that would enable precise diagnosis.[46]

The third implication is that health-care executives need to aggressively couple the development of business model innovations with the progress that diseases are making along the spectrum from intuitive to empirical to precision medicine. We outline this mandate more completely in Chapters 3, 4, and 5.

Progress Toward Precision Medicine and the Potential for Business Model Innovation

To illustrate the latent potential that already exists for business model innovation, we've arrayed along two dimensions in Figure 2.4 a sampling of diseases. The current state of "diagnosability" of these diseases is mapped along the horizontal axis. At the left-most extreme are disorders that can be diagnosed only through the iterative testing of intuitive hypotheses. Diseases toward the right are those whose molecular etiology is relatively well understood and verifiable. The vertical axis of this chart plots the current efficacy of therapy. Diseases positioned at the bottom of the chart can be treated only experimentally: what works on one patient might not work on another; and sometimes there are no known effective therapies. Treatment for diseases in the middle is currently palliative (meaning that symptoms can reliably be alleviated); and treatment is curative for diseases we've plotted toward the top. The location of various diseases in the matrix is intended simply to be illustrative, rather than exact. It is the consensus of a set of professionals whose opinions we have sought. Figure 2.4 offers only a snapshot in time of this sampling of diseases. The chart is in fact quite dynamic, with diseases constantly migrating to new positions over time, as noted earlier.

Those diseases for which care is essentially rules-based— ranging from strep throat to Gaucher's disease—are clustered in the upper-right region. Much of the diagnosis and treatment of these diseases is rules-based and no longer requires significant expertise. Diseases still requiring complex problem solving remain in the lower-left corner where the intuition of skilled specialists is essential. These include amyotrophic lateral sclerosis

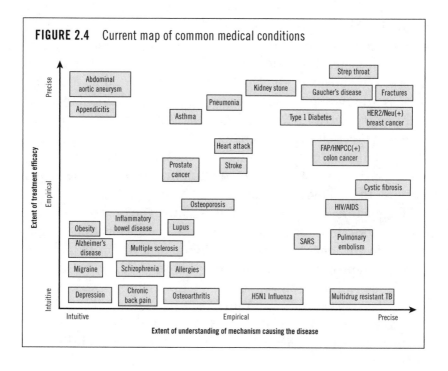

FIGURE 2.4 Current map of common medical conditions

(ALS, or more commonly known as Lou Gehrig's disease) and psychiatric conditions such as bipolar disorder. The etiology of some diseases—like infection by the Ebola virus—is understood and diagnosable, but currently cannot be treated with predictable efficacy. These are in the lower-right portion of the chart. And there are some diseases, in the upper left, where a dependable therapy works, and yet we're not quite sure why. By categorizing diseases in this manner, we hope to illustrate which diseases can be transferred to new business models of health-care delivery and which ones deserve more research dollars to push them toward precision care.

Note that the diseases tend to lie along the diagonal from the lower left to the upper right—suggesting that the ability to diagnose precisely generally, though not always, enables the development of a predictably effective therapy.

As a general rule, imaging technologies give us a much more accurate characterization of how anatomy and symptoms are linked; but molecular medicine often will be the technology through which causality can be understood. Tumors and things like aortic aneurysms, for example, are symptoms of a deeper, causal mechanism. These disorders can be identified and characterized by imaging. But their *cause* is not yet well understood. This is why we state at the beginning of this chapter that the technological enabler for disruption in health care is the ability to diagnose precisely, which then opens the door for development of a predictably effective therapy. The three specific streams of technology that can enable this revolution are molecular medicine, imaging technologies, and ubiquitous connectivity.

If regulators, policy makers, and executives do not seek business model innovation for diseases that move toward the upper-right region in this chart, the potential returns, in terms of reduced cost and improved accessibility, for society's massive investments in science and technology, will be small. As each disease moves along the spectrum from intuitive to precision medicine, fewer people with highly specialized expertise are needed to solve the challenges that the particular disease presents. Individuals with less specific training become capable of delivering care which was once restricted to the experts. Nurse practitioners and physician assistants can do the work once performed by physicians. As was the case in organic fibers and computers, reduced cost and improved accessibility of quality health care will not come from replicating the expertise and costs of today's best physicians. These can only come, very frankly, from scientific progress that "commoditizes" their expertise, making it accessible at low cost to many more patients. Specialists working in the finest medical centers will always be needed to treat those diseases remaining in the realm of intuitive medicine, of course—and surely, new, poorly understood diseases will continue to emerge. But it makes no sense for regulation, reimbursement, habit, or culture to imprison care in the realm of intuition when it has moved a significant distance along the spectrum.

There are countless examples of such shifts in the locus of care. Angioplasty has enabled cardiologists to treat many patients who would otherwise have been under the care of a cardiothoracic surgeon or who were ineligible for surgery altogether. Effective HIV medications, genotyping, and routine viral load surveillance have enabled primary care physicians to manage as outpatients those who were once complex inpatient cases treated by infectious disease specialists.[47] Physician assistants, rather than primary care physicians, can adjust blood pressure medications or perform a diabetic patient's routine examinations with less waiting time in the clinic. Nurses can perform tests for strep throat and prescribe pharmaceutical treatment at low-cost, conveniently located retail kiosks. Consumers can buy a pregnancy test kit from the drugstore and perform at home tests that previously had to be professionally administered in a hospital lab.

A map from the previous century would look quite different from the one we present in Figure 2.4. Diseases like the plague, smallpox, and polio are just three of many ailments, so feared long ago, which have become historical footnotes because of the success of the microbe hunters of modern medicine. These diseases represent only a microscopic share of the health-care system's expenditures today, and they are hard to find on charts categorizing diseases of modern time. There is every reason to believe that imaging and molecular diagnostics, as technological enablers of future disruptive innovations in health care, can have similar impact.

NOTES

1. This touches on principles first outlined in *The Innovator's Solution* about the conservation of attractive profits and skating to where the money will be. As technologies commoditize expertise, those technologies themselves occupy the new value-delivering positions in the value network. As a result, profits would be expected to flow to those areas.
2. We thank our colleague Dr. Richard Bohmer for first articulating this three-staged pattern for us. It was originally published in Christensen, Clayton M., et al., "Will Disruptive Innovations Cure Health Care?" *Harvard Business Review*, vol. 78, no. 5, Sept.–Oct. 2000, 102–17.
3. With Kevlar, for example, DuPont was able to deliberately work toward the goal of developing a fiber with specific properties—in this case, one that was stiff yet heat resistant. The work was not entirely straightforward, however, still requiring tremendous intuition in determining which steps to take. The story of Kevlar's development can be found at Tanner, David, "The Kevlar Innovation," *R&D Innovator*, vol. 4, no. 11, Nov. 1995.
4. Thomke, Stefan, "The Crash in the Machine," *Scientific American*, March 1999.
5. Kahn, Steven E., et al., "Glycemic Durability of Rosiglitazone, Metformin, or Glyburide Monotherapy," *New England Journal of Medicine*, vol. 355, no. 23, Dec. 7, 2006, 2427–43. This study evaluated the long-term efficacy of oral monotherapy in patients with type II diabetes mellitus. After four years of treatment with escalating doses as deemed clinically appropriate, 40 percent of the 1,456 patients receiving rosiglitazone, 36 percent of the 1,454 patients receiving metformin, and 26 percent of the 1,441 patients receiving glyburide had a glycated hemoglobin level of less than 7 percent.
6. Kearney, Patricia M., et al., "Worldwide Prevalence of Hypertension: A Systematic Review," *Journal of Hypertension*, vol. 22, no. 1, Jan. 2004, p.11–19. This study examined the worldwide awareness, prevalence, and treatment of hypertension. Control of hypertension (defined as <140/90 while on medication) was found to vary from 5.4 percent in Korea to 58 percent in Barbados.
7. Fletcher, Barbara, et al., "Managing Abnormal Blood Lipids: A Collaborative Approach," *Circulation*, vol. 112, no. 20, 2005, 3184–3209. The authors proposed a new approach to managing cholesterol after previous studies (National Health and Nutrition Examination Survey [NHANES III] and Lipid Treatment Assessment Project [L-TAP]) demonstrated only 16.6 to 18 percent of patients with heart disease were able to reach treatment targets established by the NCEP ATP III (National Cholesterol Education Program Adult Treatment Panel III). In turn, the same studies found that 30.2 to 37 percent of high-risk patients and 68 to 72.8 percent of low-risk patients were able to reach their targets.
8. See Thase, Michael E. and John A. Rush, "Treatment-Resistant Depression," in Bloom, Floyd E. and David J. Kupfer, eds., *Psychopharmacology: The Fourth Generation of Progress*

(New York: Raven Press, 1995); and Williams, John W. Jr., et al., "A Systematic Review of Newer Pharmacotherapies for Depression in Adults: Evidence Report Summary: Clinical Guideline, Part 2," *Annals of Internal Medicine*, vol. 132, no. 9, 2000, 743–56. This study evaluated SSRIs and newer antidepressants: 51 to 54 percent of patients experienced a 50 percent improvement in symptoms; 10 percent of patients in active treatment relapsed within 24 weeks; 32 percent who received placebo experienced at least a 50 percent improvement in symptoms.

9. The differences in diseases and outcomes are also affected by nonbiological characteristics. We discuss these additional factors later in this chapter, and discuss how to manage them in Chapter 5 within the context of caring for chronic diseases.

10. A range of studies has shown that there often are profound regional differences in clinical practice in these intuitive fields of medicine that defy standardization. For example, the number of spinal surgeries performed within a community can range from 0.6 to nearly 5.0 per 1,000 Medicare patients. The fact that one is over 10 times more likely to have spinal fusion surgery in Idaho Falls, Idaho, than in Bangor, Maine, suggests that in the practice of intuitive medicine the focus of a doctor's training and the mechanisms for making money are part of the intuition used to decide which therapy will be most efficacious for the patient. For more information see Weinstein, James N., et al., "United States' Trends and Regional Variations in Lumbar Spine Surgery: 1992–2003," *Spine*, vol. 31, no. 23, 2006, 2707–14.

11. Appleby, Julie, "Back Pain Is Behind a Debate," *USA Today*, October 17, 2006.

12. Another term, "personalized medicine," is often used for this phenomenon that we're calling "precision medicine." The reason we decided to coin a new term is that most precisely diagnosed diseases are in fact not uniquely personal. The same causal mechanism that predictably yields to the same therapy can be at work in many different people. As we shall soon discuss, the precise biological definition of a disease also does not incorporate "personalization," that is, how an individual patient might *respond* to a particular treatment. Thus we concluded that the term "precision medicine" more accurately connotes the nature and enabling potential of scientific and technological progress in health care, while "personalized medicine" should refer to the additional aspect of incorporating biological and nonphysiological issues that deal with an individual's *response* to precise care.

13. Another reason we use "empirical medicine" rather than "evidence-based medicine" is that the degree to which the evidence is convincing varies by disease and over time. The situations in which the probabilities of the desired outcome are so high that every caregiver should play those odds by following those "best practice" procedures are a subset within a broader territory between intuitive and precision medicine, where correlations are clear enough so outcomes can be expressed probabilistically. Of course, intuition still must be exercised in the realm of empirical medicine.

The practice of empirical medicine was spawned by researchers at Canada's McMaster University, led by David Sackett and Gordon Guyatt in the early 1990s. They proposed that there was sufficient medical knowledge and experience that we could begin to apply statistical analysis to both diagnosis and treatment of specific conditions. They reasoned that using double-blind prospective studies—the gold standard of methods— was neither feasible nor moral. Instead, they looked retrospectively and brought together large numbers of articles from the clinical literature, performed meta-analyses on them, and began to publish the best demonstrated algorithms from these analyses. Their earliest syntheses of these studies were primitive, but they improved over time. Soon, other researchers began to develop methods, such as registries and cohort observational studies, that were well-suited for prospective short-term projects. From there they have evolved into a more formal discipline, evidence-based medicine. Guyatt coined the term, "evidence-based medicine" in Guyatt, Gordon H., et al. "Evidence-Based Medicine. A New Approach to Teaching the Practice of Medicine," *JAMA*, 268 (1992):2420-25.

14. Although the dominant current flows from intuitive to empirical and finally to precision medicine, occasionally a disease can flow the other way. For example, the evolution of new bacteria that are resistant to certain antibiotics can cause a regression back to empirical and even intuitive medicine, as physicians cannot accurately predict that a given treatment will cure any particular patient.

15. While it is possible to achieve rules-driven care without precision diagnosis, such care is at best empirically driven and reliant upon mechanisms and explanations for disease that could be gravely misunderstood.

16. Of course, the estimates used here can vary, depending on incubation period, virulence, vector organism, mode of transmission, and so on. Nevertheless, the typical cost trend for infectious diseases crosses three phases. Initially, the cost of care tends to be low, while the etiology and pathophysiology are still unknown. Next, these patients can be stabilized, often at high cost through hospitalization, but the primary cause is still unknown or untreatable. Finally, once the cause becomes known and treatable, costs typically decline significantly; if a preventive measure like vaccination becomes available, costs plummet even faster. For example, polio vaccines have saved the U.S. health-care system $810 billion in the past 50 years and will have saved an estimated $1 trillion by 2015. See Shankar, Vivek, "U.S. Saved 135,000 Lives, $810 Billion Using Polio Vaccines." Polio Survivors and Associates, January 23, 2007, accessed from http://www. rotarypoliosurvivors.com/PDF/US%20Saved%20135%20000%20Lives%20%20 $810%20Billion%20-%20Polio%20Vaccines.pdf on August 30, 2008. The cost savings have been even more dramatic for HIV/AIDS patients. From early 1991 to late 1992 the cost of treating AIDS patients from the time of diagnosis until death fell by 32 percent, from $102,000 to $69,000. The average number of hospital days fell from 52 days to 35 days. See Hellinger, Fred J., "The Lifetime Cost of Treating a Person with HIV," *Journal of the American Medical Association*, vol. 270, July 1993, 474–78. Finally, between 1954 and 1997 antimicrobials reduced new cases of active tuberculosis by 32 percent, mortalities by 81 percent, lost life-years by 87 percent, and cost of medical treatment by 76 percent. Total financial burden of illness, including the value of lost life-years, decreased (in 1997 dollars) from $894 billion to $128 billion. This equates to an average yearly decline of 4.4 percent in the cost of treatment and overall burden of disease. See Javitz, Harold S. and Marcia M. Ward, "Value of Antimicrobials in the Prevention and Treatment of Tuberculosis in the United States," *International Journal of Tuberculosis and Lung Disease*, vol. 6, no. 4. April 2002, 275-88.

17. Koch, Robert, "Die Aetiologie der Tuberculose," *Berlin klin. Wochschr*, vol. 19, 1882, 221.

18. On the other hand, we must also not be so hubristic to believe that our current categorization scheme is absolutely correct. After all, each method of the past was at some point supported with some type of evidence and believed to be correct by seemingly reasonable people. The best we can hope to do is constantly push both our diagnostic and therapeutic

understanding forward. If we fail to do so, the consequences can be grave. There remains a continuing threat of new infections that extend beyond the boundaries of our scientific understanding and ability to treat. For example, Influenza A subtype H5N1, also known as Avian flu, is currently beyond our treatment capability, even though we are able to precisely diagnose the pathogenesis. Without effective prevention or treatment, the prevailing fear is that it may one day create a terrifying spike in mortality, mirroring the one caused by the Spanish influenza pandemic of 1918 (as shown in Figure 2.2). Even diseases like tuberculosis, once thought to be close to defeat, are capable of mounting a resurgence if our treatments fail to precisely match the resistance profiles we have identified.

19. Central to the transformation of infectious disease medicine was the predictable and routine identification of the agent or organism responsible for a disease, usually through culture in a laboratory, followed by an assessment of which medications were most likely to be effective against that organism. Evidence thus accumulated over time in a given location became the source of data that determined the initial, empiric treatment of a patient with pneumonia, for example. An "antibiogram" from a hospital lab, based on such data, gave physicians a snapshot of which organisms were likely to be present and which drugs were most likely to be effective. While empirical treatment was typically the first step, treatment would then progress to a more precise pathway as the individual patient's culture results and specific drug sensitivity information became available from the laboratory. It is this adoption of molecular methods into microbiology laboratories today that will continue to narrow the window between an empiric treatment and a precision one. Identifying the molecular signature of a microbe within each patient sample will allow physicians to determine sooner what treatment will be best for the patient, whether that treatment happens to be a customized immunologic molecule or a long-known chemical agent like penicillin.

20. More specifically, Gleevec targets a subtype of CML patients who possess a certain genetic mutation known as the "Philadelphia Chromosome." However, 95 percent of CML patients share this mutation, making the drug quite effective for the overall CML population. For more information, see "How Gleevec Works," at http://www.gleevec.com/info/ag/index.jsp and "The Philadelphia Chromosome and CML" at http://www.medscape.com/viewarticle/408451_5.

21. Even when the unique pattern of genetic expression for each of these tumors that occur in the breast has been characterized, and when predictably effective Herceptinlike therapies have been developed, we may not be home free. This is because the tumor itself can be a symptom of a deeper causal mechanism. Many scientists theorize that a large number of cancers and other diseases will eventually be attributable to infectious diseases. Nevertheless, until the cause(s) of the tumor is understood, prevention is difficult and recurrence can still occur in affected patients.

22. Even Herceptin will eventually be viewed as insufficient treatment, since it only attacks a nonspecific receptor and not a genetic target unique to a breast cancer cell. See Jeffrey, Stephen, "Cancer Therapy: Take Aim," *Economist* (2007).

23. Healy, Bernadine, "Cancer and Me," *U.S. News and World Report,*" April 9, 2007, 60-68. This source was excerpted from her book, *Living Time: Faith and Facts to Transform Your Cancer Journey* (New York: Bantam, 2007).

24. Historically, we have diagnosed and categorized diseases based only on phenomena observable to the five senses. For example, the sweet taste of a patient's urine and the smell

of ketones in his or her breath were reliable indicators of diabetes. Even the roentenogram (now more commonly known as the X-ray), which was so lauded as a new way for doctors to diagnose disease, was merely an extension of how our eyes could detect abnormalities.

25. A significant portion of this progress has been achieved through prevention—discouraging cancer-causing behaviors such as smoking and prolonged exposure to the sun, and removing known carcinogens from the environment—based on a deeper understanding of risk factors for disease. In addition, a measurable reduction in the mortality rate of select cancers can now be attributed to improved, targeted drugs.

26. Furthermore, vaccinations given by nurses are an even greater disruption in terms of creating value, since prevention of disease obviates any need for intuitive diagnosis and treatment downstream.

27. Schaffer, Amanda, "In Diabetes, a Complex of Causes," *New York Times*, October 16, 2007.

28. Manning, Anita, "Islets Could Be a Key to Diabetes Cure," *USA Today*, November 13, 2007.

29. "American Medical Association Publishes 'Nostrums and Quackery' Warning the Public Against Humbugs," *New York Times*, January 14, 1912, SM7.

30. Banting, Frederick G., et al., "The Internal Secretion of the Pancreas," *American Journal of Physiology*, vol. 59, no. 479, 1922. For his revolutionary discovery, Sir Frederick G. Banting (as well as his laboratory sponsor John Macleod) was awarded the Nobel Prize in Medicine in 1923.

31. *Cachectic* means inability to be nourished.

32. Again, the attempt the categorize disease based solely on observable symptoms leads to labels that are overlapping and confusing, as we shall soon see.

33. It can also be argued that the true "root cause" has yet to be identified, since the etiology of the autoimmune reaction is unclear. For example, if a virus is eventually found to be the inciting cause, then a vaccine or antiviral medication would be a more appropriate treatment.

34. This estimate was given in personal conversations between 2000 and 2002 with Dr. Keith Dionne, who at the time worked as a senior scientist at Millennium Pharmaceuticals in Cambridge, Massachusetts.

35. Some background information comes from the historical records of San Francisco General Hospital (http://www.library.ucsf.edu/collres/archives/ahp/sfgh.html). Ward 86 was the area of the hospital where some of the nation's first AIDS patients congregated.

36. In 1981, 91 percent (247 of 270 of AIDS patients) died within six months of diagnosis. In 1982, 87 percent (886 of 1,014); in 1983, 87 percent (2,459 of 2,822); in 1984, 81 percent (4,611 of 5,695). Centers for Disease Control and Prevention, HIV/AIDS Surveillance Report, 1987 edition, 5. Accessed from http://www.cdc.gov/hiv/topics/surveillance/resources/reports/pdf/surveillance87.pdf. It should be noted that death counts from HIV/AIDS varied slightly across the earliest annual reports, as diagnosis was still difficult to make, and many cases could be added only retrospectively.

37. In other words, a population of patients can be divided into categories based on precise disease pathways, but they can also be independently divided into categories based on how they will respond to precision therapies. It is actually an overlapping subset of patients (with as few as one member) between these two categorization schemes who will benefit the most from a particular personalized treatment plan.

38. We acknowledge the fact that many researchers appear to combine the concepts of precise definition of disease pathways and the precise response of patients to therapy. Both elements of diagnosis and treatment have been drilled down increasingly to their molecular and genetic levels over the last decade, so it is understandable why they are often thought of as combined notions under the general heading of personalized medicine. However, we believe it is important to keep these concepts separate, as technological enablers can independently come from either side to further the progression to new, disruptive models of care.

39. Even this categorization of Type I diabetes has multiple etiologies, including autoimmune disease, infection, trauma, or toxins. Thus far, increasing the precision of diagnosis beyond "insulin deficiency" does not appear to affect insulin treatment, but there is obviously still some capacity for ever-precise categorization.

40. "FDA Approves Updated Warfarin (Coumadin) Prescribing Information," FDA press release, August 16, 2007. Accessed from http://www.fda.gov/bbs/topics/NEWS/2007/NEW01684.html.

41. Schwarz, Ute I., et al., "Genetic Determinants of Response to Warfarin during Initial Anticoagulation," *New England Journal of Medicine*, vol. 358, no. 10, 999-1088.

42. McWilliam, Andrew, et al., "Health Care Savings from Personalizing Medicine Using Genetic Testing: The Case of Warfarin," American Enterprise Institute-Brookings Joint Center for Regulatory Studies, Working Paper 06-23, Nov. 2006. Accessed from: http://www.aei-brookings.org/publications/abstract.php?pid=1127.

43. Taking a lesson from our previous discussion about precision medicine, there would be potentially even greater gains to be made if we could identify exactly which patients are truly at risk for stroke, heart attack, or recurrent blood clotting.

44. We refer readers interested in the nuances of physician decision making to Groopman, Jerome, *How Doctors Think* (New York: Houghton Mifflin, 2007).

45. The theory in question is called the "Law of Conservation of Attractive Profits" and is summarized in Chapter 6 of Christensen, Clayton, and Michael Raynor, *The Innovator's Solution* (Boston: Harvard Business School Press, 2003). Michael Porter articulated his "five forces" framework in the early 1980s, showing how those forces tend to concentrate the ability to earn attractive profits at particular points in an industry's value chain, stripping them away from companies at other points in the chain. This is a valuable model, but it is static, in that it describes how things are at present. The Law of Conservation of Attractive Profits comprises the dynamic dimension of Porter's model, showing how and why those forces shift to different places in the value chain over time. In particular, it describes the mechanism by which activities become commoditized. When that happens, the places in the value chain where the products and services are not yet good enough for what the next customer in the chain needs shifts to the adjacent layer in the chain. Hence, commoditization in one layer initiates a reciprocal process of *decommoditization* in the adjacent layers. We strongly recommend that executives in the pharmaceutical and hospital industries use this theory to understand how to focus their future investments in those activities in the chain that will become decommoditized—because the future will be different from the past.

46. In a speech at Harvard Business School (HBS Health Industry Alumni Association Fourth Annual Health Care Conference, Boston, Massachusetts: Harvard Business School, November 7–8, 2003), Mark B. McClellan, former director of the Food and

Drug Administration and former director of the Center for Medicare and Medicaid Services, asserted that the FDA already has begun making progress in this direction.

47. It is interesting to note, however, how many HIV patients continue to be managed primarily by HIV specialists. This is an indication that the system has not encouraged the development of new models of care for HIV, instead relying on traditional models even when the care is no longer as complex. As we discuss in Chapter 7, the reimbursement system has much to do with encouraging this. Contrast the situation with the developing world, where in many instances a nurse prescribes the drugs and manages the care. There, a disruptive model of care arose because the alternative was no care at all.

Chapter 3

Disrupting the Hospital Business Model

Though hospitals have existed since late antiquity, the concept of the hospital as we know it today did not begin to take shape until the eighteenth century in Europe.[1] These early hospitals served a variety of purposes, including caring for the indigent and isolating contagious diseases like leprosy and tuberculosis. Unfortunately, with medicine still more an art than science, there just wasn't a lot that could be done for most of these patients. People generally thought of hospitals as places where one went to die.

However, after the late nineteenth century, with support from governments and wealthy donors, hospitals gradually began to assume their role as respected centers of scientific research, medical technology, clinical training, and specialty care. Nursing schools supplied a round-the-clock hospital staff.[2] New therapies such as insulin and penicillin emerged from research done in hospitals. There was a concerted effort to train better physicians through the use of teaching hospitals, and the increasing body of medical knowledge led to more specialization among healthcare practitioners. Hospitals became the workshops within which physicians could practice their intuitive craft. They were clinical laboratories where complex medical cases could be solved and unanticipated emergencies and complications could be resolved with as much certainty as possible.[3] This value proposition has been a great fit for solving poorly understood problems of the past, such as tuberculosis in the early 1900s, poliomyelitis in the 1950s, and AIDS in the 1980s. When these diseases were first encountered, they had to be addressed in hospitals.

If we mapped the complexity of diagnosing and treating disease on the vertical axis of the diagram of disruptive innovation, we'd see that for a century hospitals have been on a relentless up-market march on the trajectory of sustaining innovation. An administrator in one of the major Boston-area teaching hospitals estimated for us that 70 percent of the patients in his hospital today would have been in the intensive care unit 30 years ago, and that 70 percent of the patients in his ICU today would likely have been dead 30 years ago. His hospital has become extraordinarily capable of dealing with very complicated problems. But in the process of adding all of that capability and its attendant costs, the hospital has overshot what patients with straightforward disorders can utilize when they are admitted. We suspect that if his predecessor had made the same estimate 30 years ago looking back on the prior 30 years, he would have said exactly the same thing. Yesterday's frontiers are now more than adequately addressed by the capabilities of most hospitals, whose engines of progress are all focused toward the frontiers of today and tomorrow.

For reasons that are rooted primarily in regulation, contracting, pricing, and reimbursement systems, however, many of the activities that occurred at yesterday's frontiers of medicine in general hospitals are still being done in these high-cost hospitals, rather than being handed off to lower-cost, more convenient venues of care, as was done in the past. An important lesson from our studies of disruptive innovation is that the hospitals providing much of today's health care *cannot* and therefore *ought not* to be relied upon to transform the cost and accessibility of health care. Instead, hospitals need to be disrupted. We need them to cede market share to disruptive business models, patient by patient, disease by disease starting at the simplest end of the spectrum of disorders that they now serve. We will always need hospitals. We will just need fewer of them, as scientific progress continues to move more diseases along the spectrum from intuitive medicine toward precision medicine.

Indeed, disruptive innovation in health care has already started, and is accelerating as you read this book, especially in the overshot markets that hospitals no longer find profitable to serve—including wellness, urgent care, primary care, and chronic disease—areas where volume is big but profits (under the existing reimbursement model) are low relative to the business models of hospitals.

THE BUSINESS MODEL OF HOSPITALS

Why are hospitals so costly? The organizational paradigm of the general hospital coalesced in an age of intuitive medicine. The entire hospital was essentially a solution shop. But today's hospitals are substantially different. As technological and scientific progress enabled standardized processes and treatments for precisely diagnosed disorders, hospitals commingled value-adding process and solution shop activities within the same institution— resulting in some of the most managerially intractable institutions in the annals of capitalism.

Recall from Chapter 1 that every viable business model starts with a value proposition—a product or service that helps customers do more effectively, affordably and conveniently *a job that they've been trying to do.* "We will do everything for everybody" has never been a viable value proposition for any successful business model that we know of—and yet that's the value proposition managers and directors of general hospitals feel they are obligated to put forth. A *company* might want to be all things to all people, but this isn't what *customers* need. There are few patients who are searching to "hire" a health-care provider that can do everything for everyone else. Rather, customers of health-care delivery generally find themselves needing one of two jobs done. The first might be summarized as, "I need to know what the problem is, what is causing it, and what I can do to correct it." The second job would be, "Now that I know what needs to be done to fix my problem, I need it to be done effectively, affordably, and conveniently."[4]

Delivering a value proposition to do the first job requires a solution shop business model; the second job requires a value-adding process business model. We know of no business that has successfully housed two fundamentally different business models within the same operating unit. Were it not for today's tangled web of subsidies, administered prices, and regulations that constrain competition, today's general hospitals would not be economically or competitively viable.[5]

The Nature of Hospital Solution Shops

The solution shop activities within a hospital are generally those involved in diagnosing patients' problems. This requires centralized laboratories filled with the most advanced instruments to analyze blood and tissue samples, and radiology departments with the most sophisticated imaging technologies, such as computerized tomography (CT) scanners, magnetic resonance imaging (MRI) machines, and positron emission tomographic (PET) imagers.

Those who assemble and interpret the results are schooled in the arts of intuitive medicine. In some instances even the finest can't definitively diagnose the problem: the best they can do is develop hypotheses. In these instances caregivers need to test their hypotheses of what the disorder might be by experimentally treating the patients. If they respond, it verifies the hypothesis. If they don't, it signals that something else is going on, and the physicians initiate treatment for their next best hypothesis, and then the next best after that, and so on. Hence, experimental treatment, whether involving surgery, drugs, or other intervention, is an integral part of a hospital's solution shop work. It bears repeating, however: only in hypothesis testing does treatment need to be given in a solution shop model.

The typical general hospital's solution shop is set up to tackle any disorder in any part or system within the body. To deliver on this promise, a good general hospital must have one of every type of diagnostic equipment, and at least one physician from every subspecialty on staff. The capability to address such problems cannot reside in standardized *processes*. Rather, it is largely resident in the hospital's *resources*—the intuition, training, and experience of the people who practice there and the equipment at their disposal. Indeed, these individual pieces of equipment and the individual specialist physicians must be kept separate, not tightly linked by processes, in order to have the flexibility to do anything for anybody.

Value-Adding Process Activities in a Hospital

Value-adding process activities comprise the other business model in a general hospital. Their value proposition addresses the second of the jobs to be done that was noted earlier—to fix problems after definitive diagnoses have been made. Hip and knee replacement surgeries, the setting of many fractured bones, coronary artery bypass and angioplasty procedures in the heart, and surgical repairs of cataracts and hernias are examples of value-adding process activities. These activities are not unlike those that occur in a university, a manufacturing plant, or the kitchen of a restaurant. Partially complete (or partially broken) things are brought in one door. The workers pick up a set of tools, follow a series of relatively proven value-adding steps, and then ship a more complete product out the other door.

Problems Created by Commingling Business Models

When the same hospital seeks to fulfill these two very different value propositions, the consequent mandate for two types of business models creates extraordinary internal incoherence. The resources and the essential nature of the processes inherent in the two business models are different. So are their profit formulas. Solution shops need to get paid on a fee-for-service basis. Their fees cannot be based on outcomes, because many factors beyond the accuracy of diagnosis affect the results. In contrast, value-adding process businesses can routinely sell their outputs for a fixed price, and they can guarantee their results.

Many market-oriented students of our health-care systems bewail the fact that hospitals and physicians don't readily disclose the prices of what they do, or the outcomes they achieve. The value of the services being offered therefore isn't measured—and as a result, the normal market mechanisms that drive performance, efficiency, and customer-centeredness don't exist in our health-care systems.[6] What these critics have not yet understood, however, is that the value actually *cannot* be measured, because the metrics of value in the two different business models are so different.

Here's a way to visualize the impossibility: what's a better value to the consumer—a strategy study by McKinsey & Company, or a Hyundai Sonata automobile? The services of a solution shop such as McKinsey are priced on an hourly, fee-for-service basis. Whether those fees represent good or bad value is gauged by the reputation of the firm, based upon its prior work and the qualifications of its professional staff—all stacked up against the stakes involved in the project. In contrast, the price of a Hyundai car is published; whether that price reflects good or bad value can be measured by the number of full, half-full, and empty bubbles in *Consumer Reports*—all relative to the prices and bubble count of comparable vehicles.

The value of products and services can only be calculated by comparing their prices and expected outcomes, relative to the job to be done, but the jobs for which the solution shops and value-adding process services of hospitals are "hired" to do are very different. Meanwhile, reimbursement formulas typically price both types of hospital services on a fee-for-service basis, with overhead costs spread across them in highly distorted ways. The result is that the value of what general hospitals do simply cannot be measured—let alone compared.[7]

THE RIGHT KIND OF FOCUS FOR HOSPITALS

The first recommendation of this chapter is that hospitals need to deconstruct their activities operationally into the two different business models: solution shops and value-adding process activities.[8] This can be done by creating hospitals-within-a-hospital, or by building distinct facilities.[9] In either case, the work done within each business model must be organized differently, and their cost accounting and pricing systems must be separated and structured in ways appropriate to each. Our biggest and best medical centers will be able to bifurcate themselves. Smaller hospitals, however, will need to focus on becoming solution shops or value-adding process hospitals, or simply expect to be liquidated through disruption.[10] The reason why this division is such a crucial first step is that there are two different jobs-to-be-done. Only when an organization's resources, processes, and profit model are focused around a job-to-be-done can they be integrated in a correct and optimized way that does the job as perfectly as possible.

To visualize why, let's return to the efforts of the fast-food restaurant that was trying to improve the sales of its milkshakes, as recounted in Chapter 1. Analysts and executives alike *thought* that this company was an *integrated* concern. It contracted directly with potato farmers to grow potatoes that the chain had specially developed to make its french fries. It managed its own warehousing and distribution system. It operated its own management training university; offered a broad product line of many different meals, salads, drinks, and desserts; and so on. Much of this integration was in place to optimize the cost and quality of its *products*. But once the company figured out the *job* customers were hiring the milkshake to do, it realized that doing the job as perfectly as possible required a very different sort of integration. Beyond the product changes described in Chapter 1, the delivery mechanism, the payments system, and types of locations from which the milkshake could be "hired" all had to be knit together in a new and optimized way. The company, it turned out, was integrated *incorrectly*! It was only by understanding the jobs to be done that they could see how to *correctly* integrate, in order to orchestrate all of the experiences in purchase and usage that they needed to offer in order to do the job as perfectly as possible.

Separate solution shop organizations can be integrated to optimize the delivery of accurate diagnosis and recommend the most effective therapy. Impossible, you say, to create and profitably operate stand-alone solution shops? Look again. They're popping up in many places.

Solution Shop Hospitals

A friend of ours[11] has suffered from asthma for much of his life. Each specialist he saw seemed to have another possible remedy. It got to the point that he was taking multiple medications with multiple side effects, whose combined cost at one point exceeded $1,000 per month—yet he was still not well. Then he visited the National Jewish Medical and Research Center in Denver, Colorado.[12] National Jewish is a solution shop focused on pulmonary disease, particularly asthma. Like the integrated job-to-be-done optimization of the milkshake system, National Jewish is integrated in an optimal way to diagnose the root cause, and prescribe the best possible course of therapy, for disorders of the respiratory system. When our friend arrived, they administered a unique battery of tests, then assembled an allergist, a pulmonologist, and an otolaryngologist—also known as an ear, nose, and throat, or ENT, specialist—to meet together with him. They integrated their perspectives on his long medical history together with the test results, told him what was causing his symptoms, and prescribed a straightforward course of therapy that finally solved his problem.

In the general hospital systems in which our friend previously sought solutions, each of these specialists existed. But they weren't integrated in the right way. He had seen each of them individually and was passed from one individual specialist to the next. Indeed, the individuals he saw were typically trying to participate in both the solution shop and value-adding process business models in their hospitals. What these disjointed general hospital solution shops had been unable to do, a coherently integrated solution shop could readily do. Why? A key reason diseases remain in the realm of intuitive medicine is that they arise at the interdependent intersection of two or more systems of the body. Studying the disease from the perspective of only one of those systems, therefore, can't develop an integrated solution consonant with the integrated nature of the disease.

The Texas Heart Institute is a focused solution shop for cardiovascular disease. The Cleveland Clinic has created "institutes" within the clinic that are focused solution shops. One is a heart and vascular institute. Another is a neurological institute populated by neurosurgeons, neurologists, psychiatrists, and others whose work processes are integrated together in a way that optimizes diagnosis and therapeutic recommendations. The Mayo Clinic is similarly organized. Patients there are processed through solution shops whose specialists, equipment, and procedures are knitted together across each of the potentially relevant organ system specialties, in order to provide the best possible diagnosis as fast and at as low a cost as possible. Once the diagnosis and recommendations have been made, they tell their patients, in essence (and using our language), "Now this is what needs to be done. You can go over there to our value-adding process organization to have it done, where we'll charge you on a fee-for-outcome basis. Or you can return to your hometown and have it done there. Your choice."

Isn't it too expensive for Joe Average Patient to travel to these distant solution shops? No. It's cheap. Two thousand dollars for our friend to travel to Denver was a pittance to the system, compared to thousands of dollars spent on the wrong prescription drugs and devices that were the result of inaccurate, incomplete diagnoses by a stream of individually operating specialists. An accurate diagnosis ensures that you don't waste money and lives solving the wrong problem. We believe that, ultimately, focused solution shops will be able to bill fee-for-service rates that cover not just the full cost of their services, but also begin to reflect the value of their work.[13] Current reimbursement formulas constrain and distort this at present—but there is a path to circumventing those constraints, as we will outline in Chapters 6 and 7.

At the time our system of general hospitals in every community was established, medical practice was *very* intuitive. Traveling significant distances was expensive and risky for patients, and it was simply not worth the marginal benefit of seeking care in a far-off hospital. In that environment it made sense to construct general hospitals, in every community, that could do everything for everybody. But the economic and technological constraints that propelled us in that direction are no longer binding. Travel is cheap, and doctors and equipment are expensive. Yet the industry is structured around the technology and health-care economics of the 1930s, not the realities around which we should optimize today.

Value-Adding Process Clinics

Much has been made of "specialty hospitals." Some have alleged that specialty hospitals skim the most profitable patients and procedures away from general hospitals—leaving general hospitals with the obligation to provide unprofitable procedures to the sickest patients and those less able to pay for their care.[14] In addition, concerns have been raised that physicians who hold financial interests in the specialty hospitals to which they refer patients might have motives for directing care that are not necessarily in the best interests of the patients. Because of these concerns, the U.S. Congress imposed a ban on the opening of new specialty hospitals in 2003,[15] which was finally lifted in 2006, despite the lobbying efforts of the American Hospital Association (AHA) and the Federation of American Hospitals (FAH).[16]

Are specialty hospitals good or bad for health care? The "specialty versus general" categorization scheme is a faulty distinction that leads to serious misunderstanding and mismeasurement. Some specialty hospitals such as National Jewish, noted earlier, are coherent solution shops. Their focus allows them to put processes into place that integrate the work of multiple specialists in a way that optimizes delivery of the value proposition. Because the care is still the realm of intuitive medicine, and because feedback from treatment decisions is essential to the learning that takes place, diagnosis and therapy in these institutions must be one and the same. The organizational structure of coherent solution shops like National Jewish makes it possible for the patient to be in the care of a true team. On the other hand, the organizational structure of the typical general hospital, with its separate departments of specialty care, typically leaves patients in the care of individuals—often several individuals who pass the patient from one to another—since the current structure makes working together and coordinating care cumbersome.

Other specialty hospitals are value-adding process hospitals. These include surgery centers, both inpatient and ambulatory. Some of these do many types of surgery, while others specialize in a specific type. For example, the Shouldice Hospital, north of Toronto, repairs only external abdominal wall hernias. The Aravind Hospitals in India do eye surgery, and the Coxa Hospital in Finland focuses on hip and knee replacement surgery. Meanwhile, the Cancer Treatment Centers of America offers treatment for dozens of cancer types, even integrating complementary and alternative treatments not typically offered at traditional hospitals, but all in a value-adding process model aimed at following the diagnosis of cancer made elsewhere. Just as solution shops focused on a job can integrate in ways that optimize their effectiveness, VAP hospitals, because they focus on a job, can integrate in optimal ways as well.[17]

A generation ago *diagnosis* was a key reason why many surgeries were performed. Ultrasound was limited and primitive, and X-ray technology could not give doctors images of soft internal tissues—so surgeons often had to cut patients open just to see what was going on inside. Exploratory surgery was part and parcel to the solution shop activities of general hospitals. But thanks to the capabilities of ultrasound and MRI machines, and CT and PET scanners, doctors can now summon to their desktops extraordinarily clear images of internal tissues. Today, the vast majority of surgeries are performed *after* definitive diagnosis—meaning that most of these can be performed in the VAP hospitals we call surgical centers.[18]

The job-to-be-done that these hospitals address is: "I've had a definitive diagnosis. I know what needs to be done. I need to have it fixed as effectively, conveniently, and economically as possible." Because they can optimally integrate the entire process—from preadmission preparation to the surgery process to rehabilitation to discharge—value-adding process hospitals can do their work at substantially reduced cost, with *much* higher levels of quality. A hernia repair at the privately owned, for-profit Shouldice Hospital, for example, entails a four-day visit for preparation, surgery, and rehabilitation in a truly country-club-like setting.[19]

In the typical U.S. general hospital, this procedure is done on an outpatient basis. Yet the entire cost at Shouldice is *still* 30 percent lower than CPT #49560,[20] the standard reimbursement given for comparable hernia repair in the United States.[21] In the typical U.S. hospital, unanticipated complications that necessitate additional surgical intervention arise in 5 to 10 percent of cases.[22] At Shouldice, complications arise only 0.5 percent of the time.[23] The Coxa Hospital for Joint Replacement in Tampere, Finland, achieves similarly better costs than general hospitals. The 64 general hospitals in Finland that perform similar surgeries average unanticipated complication rates of 10 to 12 percent; the rate at Coxa is 0.1 percent.[24]

These differences are not simply attributable to intrinsically better and worse doctors; it's in the nature of the integration enabled by a value proposition that focuses on a specific job to be done. Doctors at Shouldice, Coxa, and other focused value-adding process hospitals may get better at doing certain procedures by doing them over and over, but *everything* within these institutions is optimized for a focused job.

One of the things Toyota taught the world is that if we do a task differently every time, it's very hard to improve the result. It's when we standardize that we're able to continuously improve and respond to unanticipated problems in predictably effective ways. This is why focused VAP clinics get so good.

Two "Yeah, but" objections are frequently leveled against arguments for focus. The first is that the kinds of focused solution shop and value-adding process hospitals described here can't handle emergencies and complications of their work—and that to be truly effective, they should be backed up with an emergency department and the full arsenal of a general hospital. It's interesting that the medical establishment long ago became comfortable with the idea that it's okay for many community hospitals not to offer the full extent of services and expertise as some of their larger brethren. But this is rarely used as an argument against the existence of community hospitals. We accept that these hospitals may not offer the full arsenal because patients who need more sophisticated care can be rushed to a tertiary care hospital.[25] There's little reason why similar transfers and referrals couldn't be made from focused hospitals as well.[26]

The second objection is that specialty hospitals and other value-adding process businesses are accused of "cherry picking" or "cream skimming" the youngest, healthiest, and most profitable patients, while the sickest patients typically go to the general hospitals. To this we say, "Of course." Patients whose multiple, interdependent illnesses ensconce them solidly in the realm of intuitive medicine need the broad and unstructured arsenal of capability that only the best tertiary care hospitals can offer. We will always need such hospitals. But because much of what is done within them today can be done elsewhere much more effectively and at much lower cost, we just don't need as many of them.

The finger pointing we have seen from general hospital executives is rooted in a faulty cost accounting and reimbursement system that maintains the commingling of business models through cross-subsidization. General hospitals ought to get paid much more than they're paid today for the complex, intuitive work that only they can do. If the business model of general hospitals today can be separated into its component value propositions with distinct business models of care delivery, and the payment system properly rewards each for their work, what seems to be cherry picking today will in reality be recognized as the efficient distribution of resources.

The business model innovations we propose here are truly disruptive, relative to the business models of general hospitals. Just as General Motors successfully lobbied in the 1970s and 1980s to install import quotas to protect themselves against disruption by Toyota, Honda, and Nissan, protests against these disruptive hospitals are perfectly predictable. But these cries are self-serving, not substantive.

In the remainder of this chapter we will first review a case history of a network of manufacturing plants operated by Michigan Manufacturing Corporation (MMC).[27] The purpose of this case study is to introduce the *cost of complexity* as a driver of overhead costs and product quality problems—which for business models like those of general hospitals are the major components of total cost. This will illustrate why we must encourage coherent solution shops and value-adding process clinics to disrupt general hospitals. Single-digit percentage improvements in costs are possible *within* the general hospital business model. But much more significant cost savings can be achieved through creating new business models. The solution to the cost problem in hospitals, in other words, is not efficiency *within* that business model. Rather, significant improvement will come only through the creation of fundamentally focused business models that in the end are highly disruptive to the present profit formulas of general hospitals. We'll see that quality comes from proper integration and that lower cost comes from overhead reduction enabled by focus.

After this case history, we'll close the chapter by describing how the first wave of disruptive hospitals—focused solution shops and value-adding process hospitals—will themselves be disrupted.

THE ORGANIZATION OF MICHIGAN MANUFACTURING CORPORATION'S PLANTS

Michigan Manufacturing Corporation manufactured automobile components such as axles, suspension systems, and gear boxes in a network of nine plants in the Midwest. MMC's plant in Pontiac,

Michigan,[28] was organized into departments (see Figure 3.1). The cut-off machines were grouped in one section, stamping machines in another, and so on—each type of machine had its own department. This departmental layout gave the Pontiac plant three advantages. First, operating the machines required extensive training and skill, and putting machines that did the same function in the same area deepened and leveraged the operators' expertise. The second advantage was equipment utilization—the machines were expensive to purchase and maintain, and grouping them by department gave a single point of responsibility for maximizing the machines' productivity. Third, the departmental layout was consummately flexible—it was capable of producing any part.

The manufacturing process always started in the office of the process engineer, who studied the part drawings and then determined the sequence of activities and procedures in order to make the part. Often, this sequence subsequently had to be revised. The figure depicts that the design of Product A, for example, required a path through the factory shown by the dashed line. Beginning at the cut-off saw, Product A, an axle, proceeds to the turning machines (or lathes), which shape its outside diameter. The product then visits the hobbing department (cutting gears), and then is heat-soaked in the annealing furnace to relax stresses in the metal. Holes are then tapped (drilled), screw threads bored, more holes tapped, and then sharp metal fragments are removed through deburring. Following a second visit to the annealing furnace and a pass through a polishing machine, the axle is ready to be shipped. Product B, a simpler bracket, needed fewer operations before it got shipped. More complicated products could be routed through the same department multiple times.

Because the Pontiac plant had at least one of every type of metal-working machine required to build axles and suspension systems, and because the departments stood independently of each other—they were not tightly coupled by processes—the company's engineers and workers could make almost anything. If the design of a particular part needed a specific operation performed, the part simply was taken to the department whose machines could do it. If another part's design didn't call for that operation, then the part never visited that department. Each time a part arrived at a department for an operation, it had to wait until a machine was available. The operator then set up the machine to perform the specified operation.

The type and sequence of operations performed on a part as it wended its way through the plant comprised a pathway. If all products made in the plant had followed the same pathway, it would be much easier to manage. True, the machine operators would have to change the settings on their machines to the particular dimensions of each different part, but they would always know who they'd receive parts from and who they needed to be given to, in order to perform the next required operation. Given the set of product designs manufactured in MMC, however, there were 20 different pathways products took through the Pontiac plant—and there could have been many more. Coordinating 20 different serpentine paths through the plant required a lot of administrative oversight and planning. Things easily got lost. Mistakes and rework were common because workers couldn't get in a standard "rhythm" of work. And bottlenecks would unpredictably arise when the same pieces of equipment were suddenly needed at the same time by products whose pathways intersected at that point.

The Value Proposition and Layout of General Hospitals

Interestingly, when we remove the labels from the machine departments in Figure 3.1 and show it, with its snakelike pathways, to a panel of friends, they are as likely to say that it is a schematic layout of a general hospital as that it represents a batch-oriented manufacturing plant.

Indeed, patients follow unique pathways through the general hospital's various departments, depending on their symptoms. One patient might visit the emergency department, then go to radiology for a CT scan, then get cycled into an operating room, then to the intensive care unit. While in the ICU, the patient may

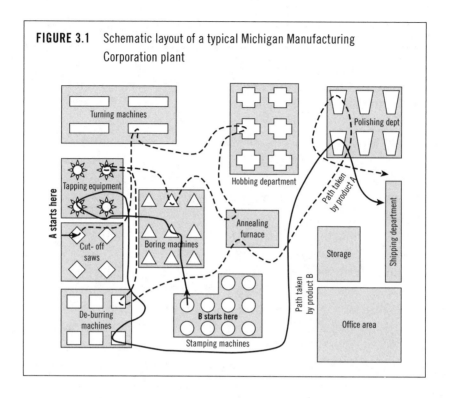

FIGURE 3.1   Schematic layout of a typical Michigan Manufacturing
Corporation plant

make several more trips to the radiology department, before being
assigned to a regular room. From there she might go to and from
a neurologist's wing of the hospital for further testing before ultimately being discharged. Another patient might get checked in,
go to a birthing room, deliver her baby, get assigned to a regular
room for 18 hours, and then be discharged. Another mother might
give premature birth—necessitating weeks of intensive neonatal
care for her baby. An otherwise healthy businessman, having failed
a cardiac stress test as part of an overnight observation for chest
pain, might need angioplasty. A heart attack victim, whose blockage
was found to defy stenting, might need to be rushed into bypass
surgery. Someone else might come for an outpatient colonoscopy.
Like the Pontiac plant, the fact that a good general hospital has
one of everything means that its professionals can build as many
solutions as technology-assisted intuitive medicine can provide.

We estimate that our best tertiary care academic medical centers manage over 100 different "service families," or different pathways of care, through their complex facilities.[29] Community hospitals are simpler, because the diseases they attempt to treat can be managed by about 40 different pathways of care.[30]

Overhead Costs at the MMC Pontiac Plant

Noelle Allen, the manager of MMC's Pontiac plant, was frustrated on a recent afternoon. Another troupe of corporate accountants had just left her office, after pointing out that in the Pontiac plant there were 6.2 dollars in overhead expenses for every dollar spent on direct labor—a ratio termed the "overhead burden rate." Pontiac's burden rate of 6.2 was the highest among the nine plants in the company's network. These overhead costs included not just utilities and depreciation, but the costs of scheduling, expediting, quality control, repair and rework, scrap, maintenance, materials handling, accounting, computer systems, and so on. Overhead comprised all costs that were not directly spent in making products. The corporate efficiency experts had warned Allen that if she couldn't get her overhead costs in line, the products made in Pontiac would be transferred to lower-cost plants in the network and Pontiac would be closed.

The quality of products made in Pontiac was also the worst in the MMC system. About 15 percent of all overhead costs were created by the need to repair and rework products that failed in the field, or had been discovered by inspectors as faulty before shipment. In other words, Allen was presiding over a mess.

In order to set prices appropriately, MMC's costing system tracked the specific cost of materials and the required amount of direct labor time spent making each of the company's hundreds of products. These were termed "direct" costs. MMC's system then multiplied the cost of the direct labor spent by the overhead burden rate, as a means of assigning to each product its "share" of overhead costs. It was difficult to attribute these overheads to any specific product, yet their magnitude needed to be allocated to products so products could be priced at levels that would cover these overheads.

Though her plant's overheads were high, it didn't appear to Noelle Allen that *any* money was being wasted. Pontiac was the original MMC plant. As demand for MMC's axles had increased, the eight newer MMC plants were built. The Pontiac plant hadn't been painted inside or out in 20 years. The landscaping was by now overrun with weeds. The receptionist in the bare-bones lobby had been replaced long ago with a paper directory and a phone. Allen herself had no secretarial assistance, and her gray World War II vintage steel desk was dented from a kick by some frustrated predecessor.

Paradoxically, the lowest-overhead plant in the MMC network, in Maysville, Ohio, had everything Pontiac didn't have: It was beautifully landscaped, the offices and reception areas were cleanly decorated, and office furniture was state-of-the-art. They had a receptionist, and the plant manager even had a secretary! And yet that plant's overhead burden rate was *one-third* the burden rate in the Pontiac plant, and the quality of its products was best in the industry.

Allen visited the Maysville plant to learn its manager's secret. After she had walked the plant floor, interviewed its foremen, and studied the production figures, the secret distilled in her mind. The Maysville plant was larger—and enjoyed certain economies of scale. More profoundly, however, she learned that the genesis of the Maysville plant had occurred in Pontiac when 15 years earlier corporate management had essentially "lifted" the two highest-volume pathways out of the Pontiac plant. When they placed those pathways into the new building they had built in Maysville, however, rather than re-creating the serpentine Pontiac map, the pathways in Maysville were stretched out in the form of two straight production lines. There were equipment types that were quite important in Pontiac's operations that didn't exist in Maysville—because those machining capabilities weren't needed, given the sequence of operations involved in Maysville's sole two pathways.

"I realized," Allen reflected, "that these two plants were organized around two very different value propositions. Pontiac's was, 'We'll make any product that anyone designs.' Maysville's was, 'If you need a product that can be made through one of these two sequences of operations and activities, we'll do it at the lowest possible cost and the highest possible quality.' You couldn't say that one value proposition was better or worse. They were just *different*."

To understand her plant's economics, Allen asked her counterparts in each of the other MMC plants for three pieces of data: their plant's overhead burden rate, its annual sales volume, and the number of different pathways that products produced in the plant might take in a typical month. To visualize the extent to which economies of scale were driving differences in overhead rates, Allen charted the overhead burden rate on the vertical axis, and plant scale—measured by annual sales—on the horizontal axis; and she located each MMC plant on this grid. (She did this on logarithmic graph paper because it made it easier to see percentage differences.)

The data, mapped in Figure 3.2, initially seemed inconclusive. While there was a general downward slope to the data that reflected scale economies, some of the larger plants, such as those in Fremont, Ohio, and Saginaw, Michigan, had relatively high overhead burden rates, while certain of the smaller plants, like the one in Lima, Ohio, seemed to be controlling overheads well.

Then, on a hunch, Allen penciled next to each plant's position the number of product families each was producing—and it all became clear. While indeed there were economies of scale, there were *countervailing costs of complexity*: the more product families produced in a plant, the higher the overhead burden rates seemed to be.

Dusting off her skills in regression analysis, she developed an equation that allowed her to predict what a plant's overhead burden rate would be, at any given level of scale and degree of product line complexity (the number of distinctly different pathways that products followed through the plant). She drew the results of this equation as the downward-sloping dotted lines on the chart, based upon the equation ln (burden rate) = 1.729 − 0.233 [ln (plant scale)] + 0.34 [ln (# product families)]. Her analysis showed that each time the scale of a plant doubled, holding the degree of pathway complexity constant, the overhead rate could be expected to fall by 15 percent. So, for example, a plant that made two families and generated $40 million in sales would be expected to have an overhead burden ratio of about 2.85, while the burden rate for a plant making two families with $80 million in sales would be 15 percent lower (2.85 × .85 = 2.42). But every time the number of families produced in a plant of a given scale doubled, the overhead burden rate soared 27 percent.[31] So if a two-pathway, $40 million plant accepted products that required two additional pathways, but that did not increase its sales volume, its overhead burden rate would increase by 2.85 × 1.27, to 3.62.

Allen's analysis helped her make sense of the Pontiac plant's situation. It was relatively small, and therefore couldn't reap some of the benefits of scale that larger plants enjoyed. And because of her charter to make so many different product families—10 times the number of the Maysville plant—her complexity costs were horrific. Indeed, there were overhead functions

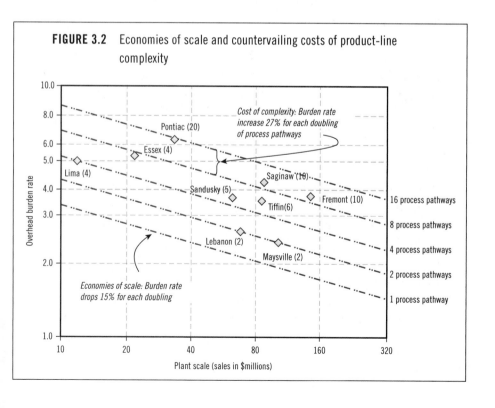

FIGURE 3.2 Economies of scale and countervailing costs of product-line complexity

in the Pontiac plant—such as schedulers, expediters, materials handlers, cost accountants, and the like—that didn't even exist in Maysville. Allen's overhead burden rate was actually significantly *less* than the equation predicted it should have been—an achievement wrought by laying off the receptionist, deferring painting and landscaping costs, and making do with her beat-up steel desk for one more year, year after year.

The Maysville and Pontiac plants comprised fundamentally different business models. The differences were rooted in their contrasting value propositions. Maysville's value proposition was making a limited range of high-volume products at low cost. In other words, it had a value-adding process business model. On the other hand, Pontiac's value proposition was to make any product it was asked to make, even in small volumes—and its business model looked a lot like a solution shop.

To deliver their value propositions, the two plants had different sets of resources—different types of employees and machines. Their processes were different. In Pontiac, the products in each family snaked their way along unique paths through the plant, and it took a lot of overhead to manage that complexity. In Maysville, the products moved rhythmically along two dedicated production lines. As a consequence, the markup required to cover the overheads in the two plants—their profit formulas— were different. It was not a story of efficiency and inefficiency. Both were quite efficient, using different business models, in delivering upon very different value propositions.[32]

Complexity-Driven Overhead Cost Structure of General Hospitals

Most hospitals do not calculate the "direct labor content" of the services they provide, and therefore don't have a Pontiac-plant equivalent "burden rate" at their fingertips to contrast the cost of directly caring for the patient, versus the complexity-driven overheads required to manage the number of pathways that patients might traverse between admission and discharge. This calculation is particularly difficult because the "direct labor" in a hospital—primarily nurses and doctors—spend a significant portion of their time in Pontiacesque overhead activities like scheduling, expediting, repair and rework, record-keeping; and moving, storing and retrieving things and people. Our best estimate, however, is that the overhead burden rate in a tertiary care hospital is about 8.0. For community hospitals it is approximately 6.0, because their breadth of service offerings is less. We estimate that the overhead burden rate for a value-adding process hospital like Shouldice is about 2.6.

Just as MMC's corporate accountants were silly to attack Noelle Allen for not controlling her overheads, it is silly to hammer general hospitals for their high costs. The overhead structure and rate of unanticipated complications are inherent to the business model that is required to deliver the value proposition general hospitals have chosen to offer—to be able to address any disorder any patient might present. Spending tens or hundreds of millions of dollars on six-sigma process consultants and IT systems will not make a significant difference in cost or quality until the solution shop and value-adding process activities of hospitals are housed in different models of care delivery.

The impact that the disruptive value-adding process clinic business model can have on the cost and quality of care is extraordinary.[33] Consider the example detailed in Table 3.1 below, which contrasts the cost of hernia repair in a typical general hospital in North America, versus the cost at Shouldice Hospital, mentioned earlier, which focuses only on surgical repair of hernias. Though there are a handful of types of external abdominal wall hernias— the only kind treated at Shouldice—all patients there follow the same pathway of care. It takes four days. The first is spent in dietary preparation. The surgery is done on the second day, and the third and fourth days are spent recovering on the hospital's country-club-like grounds. The cost: $2,300. Patient satisfaction ratings are near perfect, and the cost of malpractice litigation is virtually zero. In contrast, the same procedures done in a tertiary care general hospital cost $3,350, and are done on an *outpatient*

Table 3.1

Sources of cost differences between general and focused hospitals: an example

	Shouldice Hospital	General Hospital
Cost of materials and supplies	$200	$200
Cost of direct labor	$650	$770
Overhead costs	$1,450	$6,030
Total cost for equivalent length of stay	$2,300	$7,000
Service families offered	1	100
Overhead burden rate	2.2	7.8

As a starting point, we used figures from Herzlinger, Regina E., *Market Driven Health Care*, (Cambridge, Massachussets: Perseus, 1997). Herzlinger states that hernia repair at Shouldice Hospital costs $2,000, while at American hospitals the procedure costs between $2,400 and $15,000.

basis. If patients stayed in the general hospital for four days, the cost would be approximately $7,000. Table 3.1 shows the sources of these cost differences.[34] Low cost comes from focus. Quality comes from correct integration to get a job done.

Cost Accounting Practices at MMC and the Subsidy of Specialty Products

At MMC, most new product lines were initially produced in Pontiac.[35] When a new product's volume became large enough, MMC management essentially lifted its pathway, or sequence of operations, out of the complex Pontiac facility and moved it to a more focused plant to continue production. Whenever a high-volume product family was lifted out of the Pontiac plant, it had a wrenching effect on its economics. The reason? MMC used what one of its executives called the "peanut butter method" of overhead cost allocation. Overheads at each MMC plant were spread evenly across all products by multiplying the cost of direct labor required to make each product by the plant's overall burden rate. Hence, the fraction of the plant's overheads that each product "absorbed" was equal to the fraction of the plant's direct costs that went into each product.

A couple of years earlier, MMC executives had decided to move a product family of light-duty axles that accounted for 25 percent of Pontiac's revenue into the Lebanon plant. Allen fought that transfer tooth and nail, because that product line "absorbed" 25 percent of her overhead costs. Intuitively she sensed that if the product line were taken out, it would still leave the 25 percent of Pontiac's overhead costs behind, because that overhead was still needed to manage all the remaining product lines. And she was right. The revenues disappeared, but Pontiac's schedulers, expediters, materials handlers, and accountants seemed as frantically busy as they'd been before.

Looking back, Allen realized that most of Pontiac's overheads weren't caused by the standard, higher-volume product families. They were driven by the special, low-volume products the plant was tasked to make. When the overhead burden that the light-duty axle family had been shouldering was shifted onto Pontiac's remaining specialty products, suddenly most of them "became" unprofitable, because they were allocated more overhead costs. Customers had become so accustomed to paying a subsidized price for the specialty products, however, that it took Allen nearly two years to get those prices raised to the point where they covered the higher burden rate.

While the adjustment was painful to Noelle Allen, MMC was much better off. By addressing customers' jobs-to-be-done with business models designed to do each different job, MMC was able to price its standard, high-volume products to earn a reasonable profit over what it actually cost to make those products; and it could price the specialty products at levels reflecting what they actually cost. MMC could deliver two pure and appropriately priced value propositions to its customers.

One of MMC's major competitors at the time, Indiana Standard Inc. (ISI), operated only one plant, in Kokomo, Indiana—a huge, complex facility similar to the Fremont plant in Figure 3.2. ISI was the market leader in the type of light-duty axles that MMC had transferred from Pontiac to Lebanon. The Kokomo plant manager fought creating a focused facility for the standard, high-volume, light-duty axle family for the same reasons that had motivated Noelle Allen to oppose the transfer to Lebanon. The Kokomo plant manager *won* his argument, however, keeping *all* of ISI's volume in the single plant. When MMC transferred its light-duty axles to Lebanon and began pricing them at levels reflecting the lower overhead burden, MMC quickly stole the market for those products from ISI. When the Kokomo plant lost that volume, the profits from light-duty axles that its accountants had unwittingly used to subsidize its manufacture of specialty products also disappeared, and the company plunged into a financial crisis from which it never recovered.[36]

The measurements Allen calculated for the plants in the MMC system were subsequently found to be typical in manufacturing. As general rules, overhead costs per unit drop by 15 percent for each doubling of plant volume, and increase 25 to 30 percent each time the number of product families made in the plant is doubled.[37]

Cost Accounting Systems and the Subsidy of Specialty Services at Hospitals

With such dramatic differences between the cost of care in a general hospital versus the cost of focused providers, why aren't we aggressively shifting the care of patients into coherent solution shops and VAP clinics—especially with spiraling hospital costs strangling employers and the Medicare system? The reason is that focused hospitals—particularly VAP clinics—are disruptive relative to the business model of the general hospital. Hospital companies' motivation is to keep those high-volume procedures within the overhead-intensive general hospital because they absorb so much overhead. *Keeping high-volume procedures within general hospitals allows hospitals to subsidize the unique, low-volume specialized capabilities that are so central to the value proposition of their solution shops—being able to diagnose and embark on a therapy for anything that might be wrong.*[38]

This is a crucial insight. When regulators, policy makers, and legislators solicit testimony from the barons of the hospital industry about the desirability of these disruptive, focused business models, of course the hospital leaders are opposed to them. They give exactly the testimony that the executives of General Motors gave in the 1970s and 1980s when asked whether Toyota would be good for America. Toyota made life difficult for General Motors, of course, but history has proven that *disruptive business models have been good for America.*

What is good for our general hospitals as presently configured is *not* what is good for health care. The existence of multiple value propositions demands multiple business models.

Medical Tourism and the Globalization of the Hospital Industry

Whether it likes it or not, the hospital industry is nationalizing, and even globalizing. Attracted by the capabilities of coherent solution shops, individuals from around the world bring their complicated problems to places like National Jewish or the Mayo Clinic to have the world's best practitioners of intuitive medicine figure out what's wrong.

And a phenomenon called "medical tourism" is siphoning value-adding process procedures away from American and European general hospitals into hospitals in Singapore, Thailand, and India.[39] These hospitals represent a dramatic disruptive threat—or opportunity, depending upon your frame of reference—in part because they pay lower wages to their physicians and nurses, but primarily due to overhead cost advantages stemming from focusing on a value-adding process business model. A patient can fly first-class on Singapore Airlines, have a procedure done by world-class surgeons in world-class hospitals, recover in a nearby resort, and then return to America or Europe for one-half the cost of the procedure done locally.

As we'll discuss in Chapter 4, once the common parameters of performance can be met reliably in an industry, the definition of "quality" shifts dramatically, creating opportunities for new business models that can deliver the same performance with added convenience or, in this case, affordability and comfort. In Chapter 6 we will address the trend, which has already begun, for employers to take more extensive control over employee health care and how that will accelerate the nationalization and globalization of the hospital industry.

SECOND WAVE OF BUSINESS MODEL DISRUPTION

In most industries, when radically new technology emerges that enables people to do things that previously were impossible, the technology is so expensive and complicated, that provision of the service must be centralized. The people and the problems flow to the technology, rather than vice versa. Before the phonograph, for example, New Yorkers went to Carnegie Hall to hear high-quality music. They took their messages to the telegraph office so a skilled operator could send them. In the 1960s and 1970s we brought our computing problems in the form of punched cards to the corporate or university mainframe computing center, where an expert ran the job for us. In the 1970s and 1980s we took our originals to photocopying centers, where a technician who operated complex high-speed Xerox machines ran the job for us. People traveled to the downtown department store or a big shopping mall to buy what they needed, and then went home.

Modern health care is no different than how these other industries used to be. Our hospitals draw people with their illnesses to an expensive, central location. We collect blood and other fluid and tissue samples from dispersed doctors' offices and transport them to a central laboratory where complex, high-speed equipment performs the required analysis. Imaging equipment like MRI and CT scanners are similarly centralized. The structure of today's health-care industry is essentially structured around taking our problems to the solution.

In the other industries we've studied, disruption inverts this system, so the solution is delivered to the problem. Downloadable music on MP3 players brings high-quality music to where we live, work, and play. The telephone brought to our homes the ability to communicate instantly over long distances, and the mobile phone then brought this ability to our pockets and purses. The PC brought computing to our homes and offices, and notebooks and handheld devices have since decentralized computing to wherever we are. Canon's tabletop copiers put photocopying right around the corner from our offices, and all-in-one ink-jet printers have now brought copying home. And Internet retailing is bringing shopping to the people, rather than making people go shopping in a mall. In every case, the quality, convenience, and cost per unit consumed improved dramatically with disruption.

The first wave of disruption in the hospital industry will be the separation of business models, as described earlier, into distinct institutions, each designed to serve different value propositions. The second wave, which we'll explore more deeply in Chapter 9, will then entail taking the solution to the patients, instead of taking the patients to the solution. In the office, while the patient is there, doctors and nurses will be able to do tests and procedures that today are centralized. And decision-making algorithms will disrupt solution shops, putting the perspective of the world's most expert specialists into the hands of primary care physicians. Where the lack of technological progress limits the decentralization of these capabilities, connectivity in many instances will enable virtual decentralization—a movement commonly called *telemedicine*.

Figure 3.3 depicts the ongoing cascade of disruptions that will be required in order for health care to continue to become more affordable and accessible, without compromising on quality. Let's start at the rearmost plane of competition. First, general hospitals need to create hospitals-within-hospitals, or others must build new institutions that are focused solely on solution shop or value-adding process business models. The solution shops can integrate optimally for the practice of intuitive medicine, while the value-adding process hospitals can optimally integrate the steps in their procedures. Then technology must be brought to large group ambulatory clinics, so we can begin doing in that setting the simplest of the procedures that can only be done in hospitals now. Those clinics then need to become increasingly capable of doing ever more sophisticated procedures, drawing into that setting more and more of the activities that have historically been done in hospitals.

While the ambulatory clinics are moving up-market, we must bring technology to small groups and individual doctors' offices, so they can begin doing the simplest of things that today require a large ambulatory clinic. Then they too, enabled by technological advances, must be able to do progressively more sophisticated things, drawing procedures one by one from clinics into offices. And while doctors' offices are moving up-market, we need technologies that enable us to do in the home the simplest of the things that historically had to be done in a doctor's office; and so on.

To facilitate disruption, drug and medical device companies should focus their technology and product development efforts on bringing the location and the ability to provide care toward the front of this diagram. These technological advances are critical to this transformation of health care. Business model innovation, in the form of focus and disruption, is the mechanism by which substantial improvements in the quality and cost of health care can be achieved. Already, several companies—notably the Ethicon Endo-Surgery Division of Johnson & Johnson—have begun focusing their new product development on technologies,

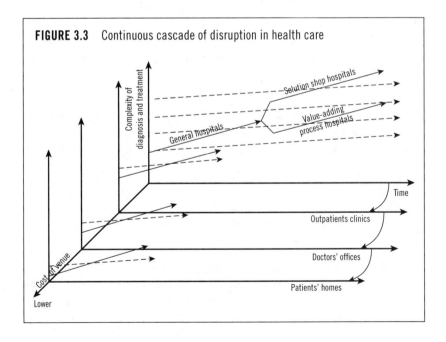

FIGURE 3.3 Continuous cascade of disruption in health care

devices, and drugs that can become the "Intel Inside" of these disruptions—the engine that propels lower-cost and more convenient venues of care to be able to do ever more sophisticated things.[40] In Chapters 8 and 9 we will revisit the roles that drug and medical device industries must play in fueling this disruption.

What Will Become of Our Hospitals?

In nearly every instance of disruption we have studied, the survival instincts of the disruptees—the prior industry leaders who are being disrupted—set in motion defensive actions intended to slow the pace of disruption. In the end, however, the advantages that disruptive competitors bring to customers in terms of quality, cost, convenience, and accessibility become so apparent that the regulations are removed and the disruption proceeds apace. This results in significant excess capacity among the companies whose business models are being disrupted, because there just isn't enough volume at the high end of their markets to support everyone. They respond by going bankrupt, merging, taking out cost and capacity, merging again to take out more cost and capacity, and so on.

Some examples: nonbank lenders such as Capital One and GE Capital used credit scoring technology to disrupt the lending market. They started with credit cards and moved up-market to auto, mortgage, and now small business loans. As the nonbanks captured the high-volume tiers of the market, the major banks have fled up-market to huge, one-of-a-kind corporate financings where margins are still sufficient to cover their high overheads. Because the volume at the high end is insufficient, the major banks have merged repeatedly to take capacity out of the system. In New York, by illustration, Manufacturers Hanover merged with Chemical Bank, which then merged with Chase, which then merged with JP Morgan, which then merged with Bank One. When you see these consolidations, they are not signs of triumph. These are companies in the throes of disruption.

Similar consolidations have occurred among the integrated steel companies as minimills disrupted them. Department stores have been merging again and again as Wal-Mart and Target have grown underneath them. The major legacy airlines have been going bankrupt and merging, as disruptive regional carriers like Southwest, RyanAir, and SkyWest secured their initial foothold on the short routes that were unattractive to the majors, and subsequently moved relentlessly up-market into longer and longer routes. This is why the world's major stock exchanges are consolidating so rapidly. They've been disrupted by electronic communications networks (ECNs).

As a general rule, the first ones to sell out at the beginning of these consolidations make good money. The last ones left standing after this consolidation typically make a lot of money too. But the ones in the middle typically bleed badly, as they try to grow and remain independent while caught between lower-cost disruptors moving up and overcrowded markets at the high end.

What does this mean for general hospitals? We will need fewer of them as the disruptive solution shops and VAP clinics grow. As they do so, the surviving general hospitals will no longer be able to offer their low-volume, nonstandard solution shop services at prices that are subsidized by high-volume work. Prices of the esoteric procedures will increase *a lot* when they must eventually carry the freight of their own overhead. This won't be bad news, however. If overconsumption of these services is a major driver of cost in today's health-care system, we will not solve the problem by continuing to subsidize their use. Judicious decisions about the value of these services will best be made when those prescribing and using them know their actual costs.

Achieving these disruptive changes to our hospital system will be extraordinarily complicated, because interdependent changes in pricing and payment methods, regulation, and certification, will all be required. Pricing, performance, and quality data need to be coupled with incentives for patients and physicians alike to make optimal decisions and trade-offs. The tremendous political clout of academic medical centers and general hospitals, often among the largest employers in any community, will prove formidable. Managing the disruptive changes posed in this chapter will be a challenge, but a feasible one if approached in the proper way, as we'll show in the subsequent chapters.

Meanwhile, expecting expensive institutions to become more cost efficient, and asking expensive professionals to take pay cuts while squeezing in more and more patients, are not viable avenues for making health care affordable and available. Affordability and accessibility come instead from disruptive innovations that enable less expensive caregivers, and less expensive venues of care, to become capable of doing progressively more sophisticated things, with equal or better quality than their high-cost counterparts.

The instinct of every leader is to frame disruption as a threat—even though it constitutes an extraordinary opportunity for growth by reaching more people more affordably.[41] If today's hospitals set up focused hospitals to disrupt themselves—just as Michigan Manufacturing Corporation set up its Maysville and Lebanon Plants—the evolution can be profitable rather than painful, because the holding company can realize the systemic benefits.

NOTES

1. Predecessors to the modern hospital were primarily associated with religious practices and provided care to the poor, as well as the sick. The hospital's secular role of only caring for the sick and using professionals trained in medicine and science did not begin to take root until the early eighteenth century.

2. Rosemary Stevens in "Past Is Prologue" credits the transformation of hospital care into its modern form to the advances in nursing first introduced by Florence Nightingale. The development of nursing schools in cities across the country enabled the corresponding growth of hospitals, in Wiener, Carolyn L. and Anselm L. Strauss, *Where Medicine Fails*, 5th ed. (Piscataway, NJ: Transaction Publishers, 1996).

3. Risse, Guenter B., *Mending Bodies, Saving Souls: A History of Hospitals*. (New York: Oxford University Press, 1999).

4. For the sake of simplicity we've broken out health-care delivery into two jobs. Some feel that emergencies comprise a third job. We have concluded, however, that emergencies can be deconstructed into one or both of these jobs. In our studies, whenever the need to get two different jobs done arises at the same time, a business model that is good at delivering a value proposition that simultaneously fulfills both jobs will emerge. This is why, for example, convenience stores and gasoline stations are becoming one and the same: people need gasoline and junk food at the same time. In this sense, there are many instances in

which patients want both jobs—diagnosis and treatment—done at the same time. We have found that when two jobs are distinct but arise at the same time, then and only then does it make sense to combine them. We will address this topic in greater detail in Chapter 7, when we discuss the likely convergence of 401(k) products and health savings accounts.

5. Hospitals themselves are responsible to a large degree for maintaining this current system of reimbursement. As we will discuss in Chapter 11, regulatory schema like the administered pricing system of health care are often used by incumbent players in anti-competitive ways to thwart disruption.

6. Porter, Michael, and Elizabeth Olmsted Teisberg, *Redefining Health Care: Creating Value-Based Competition on Results* (Boston, Massachusetts: Harvard Business School Press, 2006). In "Principles of Value-Based Competition," the authors argue that "focus should be on value for patients, not just lowering costs" and that competition ought to be based on results.

7. We say this fully cognizant of the fact that numerous academic careers, and even entire consulting practices, are devoted to measuring and comparing value across these institutions. In this chapter we argue that separating the value-adding process activities from the solution shop work, which are currently mixed together in general hospitals, will make it possible to accurately value some of the services provided by general hospitals. Until then, value can only be approximated using general estimates of cost and proxy measurements of performance and quality.

8. We are not the first to note the cost and performance advantages of focused hospitals, of course. See, for example, Harvard Business School professor Regina Herzlinger's books, *Consumer-Driven Health Care: Implications for Providers, Payers, and Policy-Makers* (San Francisco: Jossey-Bass, 2004), and *Who Killed Health Care?: America's $2 Trillion Medical Problem—and the Consumer-Driven Cure* (New York: McGraw-Hill, 2007). Professor Herzlinger built upon Bill Abernathy's groundbreaking work on the value of focus and Wickham Skinner's seminal article, "The Focused Factory," *Harvard Business Review* 52 no.3 (1974): 113–21.

9. Professor Wickham Skinner proposed this method of achieving focus without building new and separate facilities, calling it a "factory-within-a-factory." See "The Focused Factory," ibid.

10. As we have often remarked, it is unlikely that existing general hospitals will ever find sufficient reason to disrupt themselves completely. We present these concepts here as an appeal to hospitals to save themselves, while aware of the fact that more than likely disruptive change will occur through the introduction of entirely new business models.

11. This was recounted in a personal conversation with David Snow, CEO of Medco, Inc., a major mail-order pharmacy and pharmacy benefits manager.

12. Recently changed its name to National Jewish Health.

13. Although the estimated value of a solution shop will still be reliant upon the skill of employees and the reputation of the company, over time we suspect that solution shops will be able to increasingly differentiate among themselves and charge prices that better reflect the actual value they deliver.

14. "Physicians More Likely to Treat Less Acute, More Profitable Patients in Specialty Hospitals that They Own," *Health Affairs*, Web Exclusive (2005): W5-481.

15. The moratorium was active from December 8, 2003, through June 7, 2005, first enacted by the Medicare Modernization Act of 2003 and later with some restrictions extended by the Deficit Reduction Act of 2005, Public Law no: 109-171, Sec. 5006.

16. Iglehart, John K., "The Emergence of Physician-Owned Specialty Hospitals," *New England Journal of Medicine*, vol. 352, no. 1:78–84.

17. There are other types of specialty hospitals, such as those organized around pediatrics, women's health, and cardiac health. Many of these are themselves conflations of solution shop and value-adding process hospitals. We believe that the same recommendations made in the text about creating "hospitals within hospitals" apply to these institutions as well.

18. Surgery performed before a definite diagnosis is made is typically categorized as exploratory surgery. Several studies have shown that the need for exploratory surgery is declining for a variety of conditions and purposes, including cancer staging. As many as 40 to 50 percent of patients underwent exploratory surgeries for cancer staging in the early 1990s, but it's estimated that 80 percent of patients could be accurately staged using double spiral CT scanning, precluding the need for surgical exploration. See "Inroads Against a Formidable Foe," USC/Norris Comprehensive Cancer Center Report, Fall 1999, accessed from http://www.usc.edu/hsc/info/pr/ccr/99fall/inroad.html on August 28, 2008.

19. For details about Shouldice Hospital, we recommend James L. Heskett, "Shouldice Hospital Ltd.," Harvard Business School Case Study 9-683-068, April 25, 1983.

20. A Current Procedural Terminology code is assigned to all medical services and procedures for billing and administrative purposes. CPT #49560 technically refers to "Repair initial incisional or ventral hernia; reducible." CPT codes are defined and managed by the American Medical Association. The cost at Shouldice used here does not include travel expenses.

21. Studies that compare specialty versus general hospitals typically show that net profit margins in general hospitals range around 2 to 4 percent, while those at specialty hospitals usually vary between 6 to 9 percent. They therefore find only minor differences in their costs of providing comparable care. There are two serious problems with studies of this type, however. The first is that many "specialty" hospitals are themselves conflations of solution shop and value-adding process businesses. The second is that the CPT prices paid are the same, whether the procedure is done in a general or a value-adding process hospital. Hence, profit margins don't necessarily reflect inherent cost differences.

22. Recurrence rates vary widely depending on the type of repair, experience of the surgeon, general health of the patient population, and many other factors. One recent study reported that the two-year recurrence rate of open repair was 4.9 percent and of laparoscopic repair was 10.1 percent. Neumayer, Leigh, et al., "Open Mesh versus Laparoscopic Mesh Repair of Inguinal Hernia," *New England Journal of Medicine*, vol. 350, no. 18.:1819–27.

23. Shouldice reports a complication and infection rate of less than 0.5 percent and an overall recurrence rate of 1 percent on the over 300,000 hernia operations performed since 1945. See http://www.shouldice.com/admin.htm.

24. Shactman, David, "Conference Report: Specialty Hospitals, Ambulatory Surgery Centers, and General Hospitals: Charting a Wise Public Policy Course," *Health Affairs*, 24, no. 3 (2005):868-72.

25. It is interesting to note how this sorting and triaging function for many diagnoses already occurs without significant debate or call to action. For example, studies have shown that angioplasty is the optimal treatment for acute myocardial infarction when delivered within 90 minutes (Asseburg, Christian et al., "Assessing the Effectiveness of Primary Angioplasty Compared with Thrombolysis and its Relationship to Time Delay: A Bayesian

Evidence Synthesis," *Heart* 2007; 93:1244–50). Yet the response has not been to demand that a catheter lab be built within 90 minutes of every person. Instead, employing a drug that can be given without all the expertise of an interventional cardiologist, thrombolysis is used when angioplasty is not feasible.

26. Clearly, there remain advantages to having focused solution shops and value-adding process specialty hospitals located in close proximity. Integrating and linking these various business models into a coherent care delivery system will be discussed further in Chapters 6 and 7. We advocate the independent operation of these different business model types, but they may still be co-located and under the same organizational umbrella; in a hospital-within-a-hospital model, for example.

27. The name of this company is disguised. See Christensen, Clayton M., "Michigan Manufacturing Corp.: The Pontiac Plant—1988," Harvard Business School Case Study #9-694-051 (1993).

28. It's called the Pontiac plant because it is located in Pontiac, Michigan. It is not owned or operated by the Pontiac division of General Motors Corporation.

29. Furthermore, teaching hospitals must also manage the processes of training medical residents, students, nurses, and other health-care professionals, adding complexity beyond just the delivery of patient care. We will discuss in Chapter 10 how teaching hospitals can assert more control over this special value proposition.

30. Our estimate of the number of product families is based upon the number of possible sequence permutations of the departments found in a typical hospital and narrowing the list to only those sequences that would reasonably occur in the normal course of care. Definitively determining what a service family is, let alone calculating how many a given hospital provides, would comprise at least one blockbuster Ph.D. dissertation, and probably more; we invite subsequent scholars to study this question to bring more precision to these estimates. As a general rule, from our study of these phenomena in other manufacturing and service settings, these rules apply: First, a product family is defined by a unique pathway through a plant, because it is managing the tangled web of pathways that drives overhead costs. There is little correlation between the number of products or SKUs (stock-keeping units) that a group of plants make and their overhead burden rates. Multiple product models can be made by following the same sequence of operations in the plant, without affecting overhead costs significantly. When an automaker like Toyota achieves what it calls "mixed model production," different models might be sequenced one after another on the same assembly line, or within the same manufacturing cell (for a component). But the mixed models all follow the same sequence of operations, along a single line. Those factories do not have multiple intersecting assembly lines.

In comparison, a good general hospital's staff includes physicians from more than 100 subspecialties who can competently treat several thousand different diseases. This count would be the hospital's equivalent of SKU count in a factory. But there are fewer pathways, or sequences of "process steps," in a hospital than the number of diseases it can treat.

31. The equation Allen estimated through regression analysis was: ln (burden rate) = 1.729 – .233 [ln (plant scale)] + .34 [ln (# product families)]. R^2 = .94. t-statistics: scale = –5.82; product families = 7.22.

32. Toyota has become famous for its "mixed model" production capability—it can produce multiple product models on the same production line. While it in fact does have this flexibility, those lines cannot handle significant variation in the *sequence* of the production

steps. In the language of the Michigan Manufacturing case, its production lines look like those in Maysville. If Toyota wanted to introduce variability in the sequence of manufacturing steps in order to produce a different product, it would need to pull those models off the main line when the sequence needed to vary; perform those operations on different equipment (or loop them back onto earlier pieces of equipment); then reinsert them into the main flow. The more Toyota attempted to introduce variety in the sequence of production steps, the more its plant architecture would come to resemble that of the Pontiac plant.

33. While we have done our best to present accurate data here, a broad data set facilitating an apples-to-apples comparison of costs in these two business models is hard to come by. Calculated costs can be quite arbitrary because of overhead allocations. And prices for most hospital procedures are *administered*—set by regulators whose methods fail to accurately mirror market conditions that typically drive costs and pricing.

34. These estimates are the synthesis of several different methods of estimation. They include the use of Noelle Allen's algorithm, which measures overhead burden rates as a function of scale and complexity, and analysis of hospitals' financial reports.

35. There is therefore an element of research and development activity that should be prized and compensated separately from the cost accounting methods used for MMC's traditional production process. Academic medical centers and teaching hospitals find themselves in a similar situation, since their clinicians must split their time among teaching, research, and patient care duties. If teaching and research activities are simply measured as "overhead," the overhead burden rate for patient care duties will appear outrageously high, just as they did at the Pontiac plant.

36. The problems created by the "peanut butter method" of cost allocation are summarized in Johnson, H. Thomas, and Robert S. Kaplan, *Relevance Lost: The Rise and Fall of Management Accounting* (Boston, Massachusetts: Harvard Business School Press, 1987). These insights subsequently led to Professor Kaplan's system of Activity-Based Costing. See Kaplan, Robert S., and Steven R. Anderson, *Time-Driven Activity-Based Costing: A Simpler and More Powerful Path to Higher Profits* (Boston, Massachusetts: Harvard Business School Press, 2007). Using systems like activity-based costing, many businesses have been able to measure their costs and price their products much more accurately to reflect the true cost of production. However, despite the advantages of this method, hospitals have found it difficult to implement.

37. Many of these measurements were taken by Clayton Christensen and members of his project teams at the Boston Consulting Group in the 1980s—in industries as diverse as coated fabrics, construction equipment distribution, electric motors, circuit breakers, power transformers, and automobile steering gear. In fact, a key mechanism that Toyota and Honda used as they disrupted the American automobile industry was focus-enabled business model innovation. In the 1980s the value proposition that American automakers offered their customers was that they could order a wide variety of features; in 1980, 250,000 permutations and combinations of Ford Thunderbirds were offered. The Japanese typically offered seven permutations—and they organized their plants in a "manufacturing cell" layout, so that each family was manufactured in separated pathways, keeping coordinative overheads even lower.

38. There have been many examples of hospital systems that opposed new business models of care in order to protect their profitable services, even though change would have benefited the system as a whole. We thank our friend Dr. Lewis Hassell for relating one story

about Maine Medical Center's opposition to the construction of a new surgical center by the Ambulatory Surgical Centers of America that would have lowered costs to patients and the state's Department of Health and Human Services.

39. "Medical Tourism: Sun, Sand and Scalpels," *The Economist*, March 8, 2007, 62.

40. As a general principle that should guide executives of drug and device companies, disruptive innovations typically create much stronger waves of growth than sustaining innovations achieve. For example, Johnson & Johnson in the 1980s and 1990s acquired four small companies that had disruptive potential, kept them as independent organizations, and invested capital and technology into their growth. The four businesses—Lifescan blood glucose meters, Vistakon disposable contact lenses, Ethicon Endo-Surgery, and Cordis (coronary angioplasty)—have together grown at a compounded annual rate of 41 percent, and become multi-billion-dollar businesses. In comparison, all of the other businesses in J&J's Medical Devices and Diagnostics Group, according to analysts' reports, together have generated about 3.5 percent compounded annual growth over the same period through their investments in sustaining innovations.

41. Harvard Business School professor Clark Gilbert, building upon the pioneering work of Daniel Kahneman and Amos Tversky, wrote insightfully about the differences between framing disruption as a threat versus an opportunity. We strongly recommend his work. See, for example, Gilbert, Clark G., *Can Competing Frames Co-exist? The Paradox of Threatened Response* (Boston, Massachusetts: Harvard Business School Working Paper #02-056, 2002).

Chapter 4

Disrupting the Business Model of the Physician's Practice

Our call for disrupting doctors is not rooted in animosity or envy for these healers and lifesavers. Indeed, two of us are physicians and the third would have died twice, lost the use of one arm, and gone blind in at least one eye were it not for the courageous intuition of remarkable physicians. Rather, we call for disruption only because the disruption of professions is a natural and necessary step in making an industry's products and services more affordable and accessible.

It happens again and again in the world economy. Architects have been disrupted by sophisticated software that enables technicians today to design all but the largest and most unusual buildings. Disney's illustrators have been disrupted by Pixar's technicians, using digital animation. Attorneys are being disrupted by paralegals, and bank loan officers by credit-scoring algorithms. Each of these industries, and others, were defined in eras when the practices of architecture, illustration, law, lending, and so on were in the realm of intuition. In labor-intensive industries such as these the technology-enabled disruption of costly service providers and their business models has been a crucial tool for reducing costs and improving quality.

Figure 4.1 maps how the business models of physician practices will evolve disruptively. It suggests that the typical primary care physician's business consists of four different categories of health-care delivery, enumerated in the figure as follows:[1]

1. The straightforward diagnosis and treatment of disorders (generally acute ones) that are in the realm of precision medicine. Examples: ear ache, pink eye, sore throat.
2. Ongoing oversight of patients with chronic diseases. Examples: diabetes, high cholesterol, lupus, tobacco addiction, obesity.
3. Ongoing wellness examinations and disease prevention, which lead to:
4. Preliminary identification of disorders that are in the realm of intuitive medicine—some that might be handled by the primary care physician, but many of which are referred to specialists. Examples: osteoporosis, asthma, appendicitis, cancer, restless leg syndrome.

As suggested in the first component of Figure 4.1, nurse practitioners (and other physician extenders) practicing in retail clinics, should disrupt the precision medicine portion of the physician's practice. The job to be done in these instances typically is: "As quickly and conveniently as possible, please confirm my hypothesis of the disorder and prescribe a remedy." Where the functions in a doctor's office are disjointed because of their conflated business models, retail clinics, as VAP business models, can integrate the steps in this process in a way that optimizes the fulfillment of this particular job, consistently within 15 minutes or less and with no waiting.

The second major change in the primary care physician's practice will be transfer of the ongoing oversight of patients with behavior-intensive diseases to entities with a network facilitator business model (second component of Figure 4.1). This includes

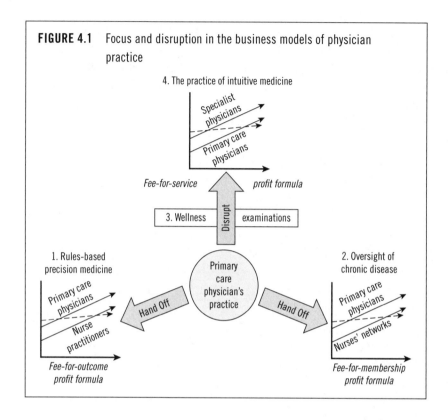

FIGURE 4.1   Focus and disruption in the business models of physician practice

4. The practice of intuitive medicine

Specialist physicians

Primary care physicians

Fee-for-service   *profit formula*

3. Wellness | Disrupt | examinations

1. Rules-based precision medicine

Primary care physicians

Nurse practitioners

Fee-for-outcome profit formula

Primary care physician's practice

Hand Off   Hand Off

2. Oversight of chronic disease

Primary care physicians

Nurses' networks

Fee-for-membership profit formula

networks of professionals who assist in disease management, such as Nashville, Tennessee–based Healthways Inc.,[2] which are structured to profit from keeping chronically ill people well. Other parts of this work will be handed off to networks of patients and their families such as PatientsLikeMe.com[3] and dLife.com,[4] through which patients help each other live with their chronic diseases. We'll discuss this handoff in care for chronic diseases more deeply in Chapter 5.

Ongoing wellness examinations (the third component), which include prevention and early detection, are often the portal through which referrals to specialists occur. These exams will remain in the province of primary care physicians, even as the treatment of rules-based disorders and the oversight of many chronic diseases get peeled away from the practices of primary care physicians. We expect, however, that primary care physicians will then disrupt the specialists' solution shops, propelled by technology that enables economical on-site testing and imaging,[5] and online diagnostic road maps that integrate large bodies of research to bring more and more diagnostic capabilities to primary care physicians (fourth component).[6]

Note that today's primary care practice has the hospitals' multibusiness model disease in spades. As we've depicted in the italicized notes in Figure 4.1, nurse practitioners in retail clinics will be disrupting a VAP business that should be billed on a fee-for-outcome basis. The handoff of care of chronically ill patients gives to disease management networks a business that is inherently compensated on a fee-for-membership basis. And the solution-shop business through which primary care doctors will disrupt specialists must use a fee-for-service profit formula.

In the remainder of this chapter we'll dive more deeply into these three projections about the future practice of primary care physicians: handoffs to nurses on the one hand and disease management networks on the other, and their disruptive invasion onto the turf of specialists. To explain why we think these are the likely pathways of disruption in the business of being a doctor, we'll draw on two models from our research on innovation. The first describes how the prevailing notion of "quality"—which we call *the basis of competition*—changes as disruption progresses in a market. The second is the concept introduced in Chapter 1 that understanding the job to be done, and not just focusing on understanding the customer, is the critical insight for innovating successfully. The bottom line of this chapter: Just as hospitals have commingled two fundamentally incompatible business models, most physicians' practices have done the same thing—combining assorted functions meant to serve distinct areas of intuitive medicine, precision medicine, chronic disease management, and wellness and prevention. For the sake of quality and cost, these have to be separated in order to integrate optimally, and then they need to be disrupted.

RETAIL CLINICS AS HARBINGER OF THE SHIFTING BASIS OF COMPETITION

One of the most consistent observations we've made in our studies of innovation is that the definition of *quality* for products and services evolves in a predictable way as disruption occurs over time. In the diagram of disruption in Figure 4.2 below, there is a *basis of competition* in every tier of every market, at any given point in time. The basis of competition is defined as the type of improvement for which customers will pay a premium price, because that improvement narrows the gap between what the customers desire in their buying and product experience, versus what they actually experience.

When companies are selling up-market on the left side of the disruption diagram—attempting to appeal to customers at a time when the best products on the market still aren't good enough— the basis of competition is performance and reliability. *Performance and reliability comprise the metrics of quality* for customers who are in the upper-left realm of the disruption diagram, and products and services that come closer to meeting what customers need on these dimensions will merit premium prices.

In contrast, on the right side of the diagram, when the performance and reliability of available products has improved beyond what customers require or can utilize, the company finds itself "marketing downward" to customers who are losing their willingness to pay higher prices for better performance.[7] As performance continues to improve, overserved customers in tier after tier will thank suppliers for giving them better products, but they will no longer pay premium prices for them. When this happens, the market does not become price-driven and commoditized. Rather, the basis of competition, or the type of improvements that do merit premium prices, changes. Customers come to value the innovations that make it easier and faster to get exactly what they need. In other words, convenience, speed, and responsiveness become the salient definitions of quality on the right-hand side of the disruption diagram, after efficacy and reliability have become more than adequate.

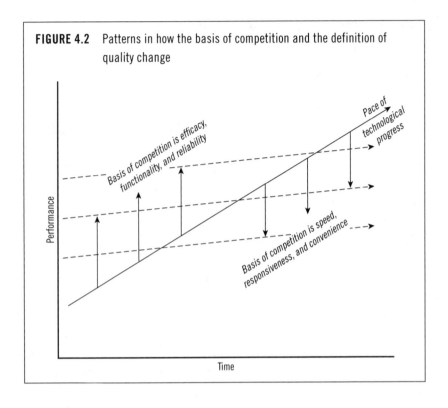

FIGURE 4.2   Patterns in how the basis of competition and the definition of quality change

For example, in the early years of personal computing, Apple Computer's products dominated the market. Apple's proprietary architecture made its products elegantly simple to use, and Apple products crashed much less frequently than competing products built around the open architecture led by IBM. Customers readily paid price premiums of 30 percent and more for Apple products because those products came closer to fulfilling the quality they demanded, which was defined in terms of performance and reliability. However, by the early 1990s Apple's computers had improved to levels beyond what customers in less-demanding tiers of the market needed—and the basis of competition changed. No longer would they pay higher prices for higher "quality" Apple products. Instead, they took their business to Dell, because its business model offered improvement on the newly salient dimensions of quality: customization and convenience.[8]

This pattern in how the basis of competition and the definition of quality evolve is common to almost every industry—from stock brokerages to consumer lending, from automobiles to the consumption of music, and from telecommunications to management education. Once things perform well and reliably enough, the spelling of the word "quality" changes to c-o-n-v-e-n-i-e-n-c-e.

The Basis of Competition in Health Care

Throughout this book we assert that conditions are ripe for disruptive business model innovation in health care. Those who oppose or declare the impossibility or inadvisability of this often rely on quality-centered arguments, claiming, for example, that the quality of care provided in a nurse-staffed retail clinic is lower than the quality of care provided in a physician's office.[9]

The essence of any good theory is that it informs those who use it how the right answer can vary, given the circumstance in which they find themselves—and that is the case here.[10] In the realm of intuitive medicine, the definition of quality and the basis of competition in health care will always be performance and reliability, because the best available care just isn't good enough yet. In this circumstance, access to the best physicians—typically judged by their education, experience, and reputation—and access to the finest academic medical centers is the essence of quality health care.

When efficacy and reliability are assured in the realm of precision medicine on the right side of the disruption diagram, however, quality health care is defined by convenience, responsiveness, and affordability. In essence, there is a hierarchy of needs that underlies changes in the basis of competition. Performance and reliability are the needs that must be met first, but once care is more than adequate in those regards, consumers *do* and *should* make their health-care decisions on the basis of speed, convenience, and affordability.[11]

We'll illustrate how the definition of quality health care can change by recounting the experience of a friend, whom we'll call

Helen, whose youngest daughter woke up on a recent winter morning with an earache. Having seen the symptoms dozens of times before, Helen called their pediatrician. "Katie has an ear ache," she said. "I bought an otoscope a few years ago because this happens so often with our children—and Katie's eardrum is bright pink. Is there any way you could just call in a prescription for ampicillin to our pharmacy?"

"No, I can't do that," the pediatrician replied. "I really need to see her."

"Can I bring her in this morning?" Helen asked. "She's in a lot of pain, and I have a busy day at work."

"Unfortunately I'm booked all day—but if you bring her in at about two o'clock, I'll see if I can work her in," was the reply.

Helen arrived with Katie at the pediatrician's office at 2:00 P.M., and waited for two hours before the doctor had time to see her. Then in 30 seconds, with one look in her ear, the doctor diagnosed, "She has an ear infection."

"That's what I told you this morning!" Helen grumbled in frustration. "We need to get home because the older kids are home from school. Can you please give us the prescription?"

The pediatrician then wrote out the prescription. After a 10-minute drive to the pharmacy and another 20-minute wait, Helen and Katie drove home with the medicine they needed. The process, which is played out tens of thousands of times every day in America, cost Helen four valuable hours. And it cost her employer, which was self-insured, $150, in addition to Helen's lost productivity.

Disruptive Retail Clinics and Quality Health Care

A short time later a retail clinic called MinuteClinic opened inside a major discount retailer near Helen's home. Staffed exclusively by nurse practitioners, the clinic had established processes to ensure that patients could be in and out in 15 minutes, without needing to make an appointment.[12] A sign on the entrance announced: WE DIAGNOSE AND TREAT THIS SPECIFIC SET OF CONDITIONS. Those listed as of April 24, 2007, are shown in Table 4.1.[13] The prices for each service were posted, varying from $39 to $79, which were approximately 40 percent lower than what physicians' practices in Helen's area were charging. In the language of this book, these are all disorders that are toward the precision medicine end of the spectrum, on the right side of the disruption diagram.

Despite the limited menu of options, these conditions represent 17 percent of all visits to primary care physicians, or about 80 million visits in all, according to Mary Kate Scott, an expert on the retail clinic industry. She estimates that, with the right enabling technologies, up to 60 to 100 conditions could eventually be managed by retail clinics like MinuteClinic.[14] The costs of managing these conditions in retail clinics are 32 to 47 percent lower than when patients visit their primary care physicians—

Table 4.1 Conditions managed by MinuteClinic

Common Illnesses	Skin Conditions	Vaccines
Allergies	Athlete's foot	DTP (diphtheria, tetanus, pertussis)
Bladder infections (females)	Cold sores	Flu (seasonal)
Bronchitis	Deer tick bites	Hepatitis A (adult)
Ear infections	Impetigo	Hepatitis A (child)
Pink eye and styes	Minor burns	Hepatitis B (adult)
Sinus infections	Minor skin infections	Hepatitis B (child)
Strep throat	and rashes	Meningitis
Swimmer's ear	Minor sunburn	MMR (measles, mumps, rubella)
Flu diagnosis	Poison ivy	Pneumonia (Oct.-Dec.)
Mononucleosis	Ringworm	Polio (IPV)
Pregnancy testing	Wart removal	TD (tetanus, diphtheria)

resulting in $3 to $4 billion in savings.[15] Further, these numbers do not reflect the savings in hidden costs, such as reducing time spent away from work, which is especially important for hourly wage workers who comprise a large portion of the uninsured. Finally, and most important, being able to access a place like MinuteClinic has a dramatic impact on a patient's sense of *well-being* that is simply not measured by dollar savings alone.

MinuteClinic publishes its patient satisfaction scores, something most traditional providers are loath to do: on a scale of 1 through 5, with 5 being "highly satisfied," its average score is above 4.9. Interestingly, even though MinuteClinic employs no doctors in its clinics, it has never been sued for malpractice. The reason is that malpractice lawsuits arise primarily in cases of misdiagnosis and flawed therapeutic judgment.[16] Because Minute-Clinic practices in the realm of precision medicine, its diagnoses are precise and its therapies predictably effective.[17]

Which of these—the doctor's practice or the retail clinic—is high quality or low quality health care, relative to the job-to-be-done?

Recent studies show that retail clinics are closer to a "new market," rather than "low-end" disruption, in that they compete predominantly against nonconsumption. For example, over 60 percent of patients who receive care at retail clinics do not have a personal care physician at all.[18] Ten problems—upper respiratory infection, sinusitis, bronchitis, pharyngitis, immunizations, middle-ear infection, outer-ear infection, conjunctivitis, urinary tract infection, and blood pressure or screening lab tests—account for 90 percent of patient visits to these clinics. In contrast, these problems are the reason for only 18 percent of patient visits to physicians' offices.

Multiple Dimensions of Quality

The jobs-to-be-done model of market segmentation that we summarized in Chapter 1 provides another useful dimension with which we can measure the quality of health care appropriately.

Every job has functional, emotional, and social dimensions. If a company hopes to sell a product or service that does the job perfectly for a customer, it needs to provide a set of experiences in purchasing and using the product that addresses each of these three dimensions, as the *customer* defines them. For some jobs, satisfying the emotional and social dimensions is a very large component of what needs to be done.

By illustration, there is a job out there in the world that we might summarize as, "I want to feel like I'm an important person, and belong to an admired and exclusive group." A person who finds herself with this job to do might hire a Gucci watch, a Versace handbag, Chanel perfume, or an Hermès silk scarf. For this job, the social and emotional dimensions are far more important than the functionality of the products. At the other end of the spectrum are jobs where functionality is paramount: "I need a place to put this trash that minimizes the mess, odor, and effort." The same customer who wears a Gucci watch, has just applied her Chanel perfume, and tied her Hermès scarf around her neck, might put down her Versace handbag and quite happily use a store-branded plastic bag to line the polypropylene garbage container that she purchased at Target—and not feel that she had squandered her money on the one hand, or compromised on the quality of her purchases on the other.

The fact that any given consumer has different jobs to do at different times of the week, and defines quality differently for each job, means that different business models need to be available to provide the quality she needs, in however way she chooses to define quality in a given circumstance.

The weighting of the functional, social, and emotional elements of a job can vary from one customer to the next. Our friend Helen, for example, would have been delighted with the quality of health care if her doctor had respected the diagnosis she'd made with her own otoscope and simply telephoned the prescription to the pharmacy: Helen had no need whatsoever for the social and emotional experience of personally seeing the doctor.[19] At the other extreme, another patient might highly value the sight of the doctor's degree from a leading medical school hanging on the wall while her earache is being diagnosed; and she might need a visit with the doctor just to talk about how things are going.

Quality should only be expressed relative to the job-to-be-done. That job differs by location on the disruption diagram. As a general rule, on the left side, performance and reliability tend to dominate the definition of quality. People in that situation often are willing to put up with all kinds of inconvenience and cost to get what they need. On the right side, functionality and reliability can be taken for granted, which means that emotional and social dimensions like speed, convenience, customization, and affordability become paramount measures of quality. We must be sure not to impose the wrong standard of quality in the wrong situation. We need to be certain we're measuring quality in the way customers measure quality, and beware of self-serving, defensive, or offensive claims that quality has the same meaning to everyone, for every disorder, in every location on the map of disruption.

DISRUPTING THE CARE OF CHRONICALLY ILL PATIENTS

The second set of activities that presently comprise the typical primary care physician's practice is overseeing the care of patients with chronic diseases. This is a vast topic that we'll explore deeply in the next chapter. Suffice it to say here that, within this vast category of chronic disease, very different jobs need to be cared for by very different business models of care delivery. Some can best be treated through the value-adding process business model of retail clinics. A few will actually fit handsomely within the solution shop business model of the primary care physician's future practice, provided its processes can be organized properly.

Most chronic diseases, however, should be cared for through facilitated network business models of the sort we'll describe more fully in the next chapter—a disease management network business model whose profit formula is based upon membership fees so providers profit from wellness, not sickness. The reason why this handoff is so crucial is that the current physician practice business model is structured in the opposite manner—to make money from sickness, not wellness. It was not designed to profitably oversee the day-to-day adherence to therapies that prevent the long-term costly complications of certain behavior-intensive chronic diseases. That is why these patients are so inadequately treated.

DISRUPTION OF SPECIALIST PHYSICIANS

After the care for routine, rules-based disorders has been transferred to retail clinics staffed with nurse practitioners on the one hand, and care for chronically ill patients has been shifted to disease management networks on the other, what will become of primary care physicians? Plenty. Their practices must become focused solution shops, and they must busily move up-market themselves to disrupt the specialists. They will pull into their practices the ability to diagnose and treat more and more diseases, which, because they are still in the realm of intuitive medicine, were previously referred to even more intuitively expert specialists.[20]

At least three types of technological innovation will help propel primary care physicians in their move up-market. The first is the disruption that brings analytical and imaging capabilities to the point of care. The second is the emergence of online decision tools—sometimes referred to as "expert system software"—that distill from the massive volume of published information algorithms that guide diagnosis. The third is telemedicine.

Decentralization of Testing and Imaging

Recall from Chapter 3 our assertion that because they aspired to be able to do anything for anybody, our hospitals are not meaningfully integrated. Their equipment and people must be organized in a disjointed and independent way that maximizes their flexibility to do nothing particularly well.

Physicians' practices suffer from this same problem extensively, because they incorporate three business models within a single organizational unit. In particular, the fact that most of them rely upon third-party providers of imaging and laboratory analysis means that few visits for the solution shop activities in a doctor's office can be conclusive. Typically, test results come back to the doctor several days later, only after which can the doctor interpret and apply the data. Occasionally, a nurse from the clinic will leave a phone message affirming that "everything is normal," but the patient rarely has the chance to talk with the doctor about what the results mean. If something in the test results warrants further investigation, the patient typically needs to return for another visit, doubling the time and expense from what would have been incurred had the test results been immediately available for review during the initial visit.

As we noted in the last chapter, in almost every instance where a radically new technology enables someone to do far more sophisticated work than was previously possible only through manual means, the technology is so expensive and expertise-intensive that the provision of the service must be centralized, and the work done by specialists. Once efficacy and reliability are assured, however, solutions once again become decentralized, as the basis of competition shifts toward convenience and other new metrics of performance.

The same pattern of centralization followed by disruptive decentralization has already taken place in certain segments of the health-care industry. Until the 1930s physicians and nurses typically went to where the people and problems were—in fact, in 1930, 40 percent of all doctor-patient interactions were through house calls.[21] But the complexity of modern medicine gradually concentrated care in major hospitals, where teams of specialists and sophisticated diagnostic equipment could be assembled to perform solution shop work. Disruptive innovators need to devise equipment that is simple and inexpensive enough so imaging and analysis can be dispersed again to the point of care—enabling physicians' practices to optimize their ability to get the job done on-the-spot in an elegantly integrated way.[22]

This already is happening in some instances. For example, early dialysis equipment was so complicated and expensive that the machines had to be housed in hospitals, and patients with kidney failure had to travel to the hospital for dialysis. The equipment subsequently became simpler and less expensive, enabling the construction of more conveniently located dialysis clinics where care is administered by technicians.[23] Pulmonary function testing equipment, portable electrocardiogram (EKG) machines, and infusion pumps have similarly moved care from hospitals into physician practices and clinics.

In several other areas of health care, however, things centralized more recently and have only just begun the decentralization phase of the cycle. For instance, through the 1960s many doctors examined blood, urine, and other tissue samples through microscopes in their offices. The advent of high-speed, complex, and capital-intensive multichannel blood analysis equipment drove doctors to outsource these services, resulting in a pervasive centralization of blood and tissue analysis. Now, courier vans regularly make the rounds of physicians' offices to pick up samples for analysis. They then drive or fly those samples to a central high-throughput testing facility. However, products like Piccolo xpress from Abaxis—a portable, shoe-box-size analyzer that can perform multiple types of routine chemistry panels—are enabling patient testing to decentralize once again.[24]

We will return to these concepts in Chapter 9, when we address the future of medical devices and diagnostic equipment.

Online Diagnostic Support Tools/Expert System Software

A second type of technology that promises to enable primary care physicians to disrupt the solution shop activities of specialists are online or software-based diagnostic support tools. One such tool is provided by SimulConsult, a Chestnut Hill, Massachusetts–based spin-out from Harvard Medical School. SimulConsult's founders integrated into their database the findings of tens of thousands of published studies of neurological conditions and syndromes—what the symptoms were, how symptoms differed across patients, how patients with various combinations of symptoms responded to various courses of therapy, and so on.[25]

SimulConsult's Web tool prompts the diagnosing physician to enter as much symptomatic information as is available. The system then generates hypotheses about which syndrome or disorder the patient might possibly have and expresses the probabilities that each one of these might be the correct diagnosis.[26] It would say, "There's a 65 percent chance that it is Condition A; 18 percent that it's syndrome B; 12 percent that it is Disease C; and then smaller percentages of probability that it could be one of these others." It would then ask the physician to collect a few additional pieces of information about the patient, either from observation, questioning, or testing. Then, on the basis of this additional information, the system could respond with a narrowed set of possibilities and revised probabilities. While SimulConsult started by building a diagnostic tool for neurological disorders, it is now expanding its facility for use in other fields as well.[27]

Our experience in talking with others about tools such as SimulConsult's is that specialists in the field often disparage it, because it cannot yet capture many of the subtleties that are still resident in the specialists' intuition. Primary care physicians, however, become genuinely excited. Like handheld ultrasound devices, it has one of the classic properties of disruption: in the hands of specialists it's not as good as the existing way of doing things, but in the hands of general practitioners, it helps *them* come much closer to a definitive diagnosis. In the hands of the former, the tools increase the chances of malpractice litigation. When used by the latter, however, such tools are likely to significantly *reduce* the chance of a lawsuit due to misdiagnosis.[28]

Telemedicine

As the ability to evaluate blood samples and generate clear images of the body's internal structures is brought closer to the point of care in the primary care physician's office, telecommunications will concurrently enable specialists in remote locations to examine the data as if they were in the same office as the patient and primary care physician. They can validate or revise the conclusions or hypotheses of the primary care physician—compensating for any initial deficiencies in relying on generalists to input information into tools such as SimulConsult.

Connectivity has dramatically transformed numerous industries, but like any technological enabler, it can be employed in either sustaining or disruptive ways. When telecommunications are used to help specialists essentially to extend their clinic hours, see more patients, and enhance their interaction with patients, it is an implementation meant to sustain the existing business model by helping specialists make money the way they've always made money. However, when global connectivity helps extend care into areas of nonconsumption, where the alternative is no health care at all, or when it helps primary care physicians, nurses, and physician assistants perform work that they normally would have referred to others, the business models that arise are truly disruptive.

For example, the University of New Mexico's Project ECHO uses telecommunication technologies to deliver specialty care for diseases like Hepatitis C and HIV to rural communities in New Mexico. But Project ECHO does this by using the collaboration between specialists and rural providers to constantly improve the skills and abilities of the local providers, which include nurse practitioners and physician assistants, so that they can become increasingly independent and capable of managing patients whom they previously had to refer.[29]

We believe that the confluence of these three types of tools (and surely others in the future—one of which is the electronic health record, which we'll discuss later in this chapter) will enable primary care physicians to optimally integrate processes to gradually disrupt the solution shop businesses of specialists and, ultimately, hospitals. In Chapter 3 we defined a "coherent solution shop" as an entity whose processes brought to bear the expertise of multiple relevant specialists in a patient-focused way, to more precisely diagnose intuitive diseases. We believe that over the next several decades, these tools discussed earlier will integrate the abilities of a coherent solution shop into the doctor's office. As with every disruption, this will begin in the simplest applications first. For many years to come, the more perplexing problems will still need to be referred to teams of specialists in coherent solution shops. The disruption will happen step by step, not overnight. And it will happen best in practices where the doctor uses these trends—point-of-care imaging and diagnostics, expert systems, telemedicine and personal health records—and integrates them to provide all of the experiences required to do the job that patients are hiring the doctor to do.

THE FUTURE OF NURSES, PRIMARY CARE PHYSICIANS, AND SPECIALISTS

Two of the most serious crises in America's health-care system today are the shortage of nurses and an acute shortage of primary care physicians. An alarming implication of this chapter's conclusions is that in the future we'll need even *more* of both types of professionals. And if the shifts in care indeed happen as we predict, we're certain to have a surplus of specialists.

The shortage of nurses seems to be the result of a confluence of factors. One is a shortage of training capacity in schools of nursing. Another is that the traditional career path for someone who chooses nursing has been quite limiting, relative to other career options open to someone who might be considering nursing as a career. We believe that the growth of retail clinics, and disruptively handing off to nurse practitioners and physician assistants more and more of the activities that doctors have heretofore performed, will alleviate the problem of career path constraints.

On the other hand, the shortage of primary care physicians is so severe that 43.7 percent of the 21,885 residency positions in internal medicine in 2005 were filled by graduates of foreign medical schools[30]—because most of those coming out of American medical schools opt for training as specialists. This is largely a distorted artifact of the mechanism by which the Medicare system and private insurers determine the prices they will pay for various services. They overpay specialists and underpay the very primary care physicians who will play such a key role in the disruptions described here. We will address the very complex issue of reimbursement and its unintended consequences in Chapter 7, and in Chapter 10 we'll dive more deeply into the challenges of training the caregivers that we'll need.

Role of Gatekeeper

A key reason why primary care has become financially and professionally less attractive to many students is that primary care doctors have been cast in the role of "gatekeepers" in the healthcare system. This has burdened their practices with overhead costs driven by the complexity of practicing some medicine that is inherently solution shop (fee-for-service), other medicine that is value-adding process work (fee-for-outcome), and providing yet other care that is the work of disease management network (fee-for-membership) businesses.

We have concluded that a personal advisor of some sort truly needs to be available to direct patients who may not know where to go, so they can find the care they need, and receive that care through the appropriate business models. Many of those who write and speak about reforming health care have called this advisor an *Accountable Care Organization*—one whose perspective enables it to orchestrate the health care that individuals consume. Dr. Elliott Fisher and his colleagues at Dartmouth College have played a leading role in promoting the concept of the Accountable Care Organization.[31] It is an entity that can guide each patient to the right provider at the right time, given the job he or she needs to get done, linking the more focused and specialized care providers together with personal electronic health records. Some have likened this advisor to a "medical OnStar button," referring to the button in General Motors cars that motorists can press whenever they get lost or need help.

Still others have encouraged the notion of a patient-centered medical home, a model of care in which a single individual—most often a physician—serves as the first point of contact for the patient, coordinates the entire team of providers, and integrates care across all institutions to ensure quality and safety.[32] We have concluded, however, that assigning this role to an independent primary care physician's practice is a bad choice. It forces those practices into commingling business models, with the result that they are integrated inadequately for the jobs patients need to do, and imposes accountability for areas of care that are often beyond the coordinator's control. Furthermore, the information, skills, and perspective required to play the role of an effective advisor are not uniquely instilled in physicians. With this burden placed on others, primary care doctors can practice medicine, which for most is the career they thought they had chosen in the first place. As we'll discuss in Chapters 6 and 7, responsibility for coordination and integration needs to occur at a higher level of care.

ROLE OF INFORMATION TECHNOLOGY IN COORDINATING CARE

We noted previously that the value proposition offered through most primary care physicians' business models essentially has been, "Whatever is wrong, bring it here. Either we'll solve the problem for you or we'll send you to someone who can."

For all of the problems with this model, the one compelling justification for its "we'll do everything for you" proposition is that, in theory at least, there is one person, our primary care physician, who has the perspective to ensure that each aspect of our care is knitted together as seamlessly and coherently as possible. Our primary care physician is the one who can monitor the overall picture of our care so we don't fall through a crack between two providers, and can ensure that contradictions and adverse interactions don't arise when care for different disorders is being provided by different specialists and institutions. When the system works as it was originally intended, our doctor's memory and the files in her office in many ways have been the locations in which our medical history is stored.

For most of us, however, those halcyon days when we really did have a doctor who was able to coordinate our care have long since passed. Indeed, studies such as *To Err is Human*, from the Institute of Medicine,[33] have revealed that the lack of coordination today results in significant, previously unacknowledged patient harm. It's not because today's doctors fail to take the Hippocratic Oath seriously, or don't *want* to carefully oversee and coordinate our care. Rather, in our distorted fee-for-service world, the work to coordinate and oversee care just isn't as profitable as other activities.[34] And there certainly is a lot to coordinate. One-quarter of Medicare beneficiaries has five or more chronic conditions, sees an average of 13 physicians each year, and fills 50 prescriptions per year.[35] In 2007 there were over 13,000 different drugs being sold in the United States that a physician might prescribe—16 times the number available 50 years ago.[36] Because of the nearly infinite number of possible combinations of diseases, providers, and treatments, predicting and monitoring patients for adverse interactions—much less optimal health outcomes— has simply scaled beyond the capacity of the human mind.

In light of this poor historic track record in coordinating care, it is disconcerting that the disruptive value network we see emerging is a *more* fragmented system than the one we have today. Instead of a generalist physician and a general hospital being "responsible" for all our care, we foresee nurse practitioners working in retail clinics caring for our everyday, rules-based disorders; facilitated networks helping us with the care for our behavior-dependent chronic ailments; coherent solution shops to sort out disorders that are still in the realm of intuitive medicine should they arise; and value-adding process clinics for procedures that need to be performed after definitive diagnosis. Given that the coordination of care is already being handled in a hit-and-miss fashion, when we receive care from so many independent, focused providers, won't the problems of coordination be exacerbated?

We hope not, and with reason. As we've depicted in Figure 4.3, personal electronic health records (EHR),[37] if implemented properly, can provide the connective tissue that draws and holds together the individual elements of our care. This central coordinating role simply cannot be played by a doctor, nor can patients do it, unless assisted by information technology.

Millions of units of airtime in legislative hearings and health-care conferences have been spent discussing the need for electronic health records. Already, billions of dollars have been spent developing and deploying various forms of EHR systems. There is no dispute that they are needed to address problems in the quality of care and the cost of administration—in our *current* system, let alone the new one. Yet despite the widespread pleas for medical record technology to be developed and deployed in a format that is standardized so providers anywhere in any health-care system can access patients' medical histories at the click of a mouse, electronic records still seem to be a distant dream.

It is seductively simplistic to attribute this sluggishness to some sort of "dinosaur" syndrome to which doctors are uniquely vulnerable; many of these same doctors and hospital administrators have harnessed the Internet with aplomb, bringing the wisdom

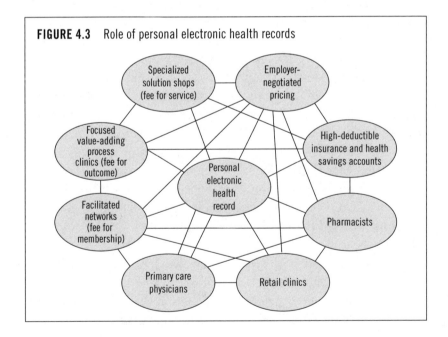

FIGURE 4.3   Role of personal electronic health records

of the world's finest specialist physicians in an organized way to caregivers and patients alike, anywhere in the world. Today's physicians check the latest clinical guidelines from UpToDate,[38] catch up on professional journal articles electronically, and maintain their licensing requirements by participating in Continuing Medical Education (CME) online. Instead of carrying reference books and charts, they refer to their handheld devices to make quick references and calculations. On the other end of the spectrum, they use powerful computers to synthesize from an array of X-ray "slices" three-dimensional images of internal body structures whose clarity is remarkable. So we clearly need to refine the question: why is it that so many professionals who so eagerly snap up leading-edge technologies in the provision of care seem so diffident to a leading edge information technology like electronic health records?

As has proven to be the case in most of our other studies of innovation, there are predictable, rational reasons why good people aren't doing what the rest of us feel they ought to be doing—and equally rational reasons explain why, for more than a decade, EHRs have always seemed to be just a few years away. The first reason, discussed next, is rooted in the concept of "jobs-to-be-done" that we introduced in our discussion about business models in Chapter 1. We'll then describe the second factor underlying this delay, which we've given a horrifically complicated but perfectly descriptive name: "the Problem of Mutual Accommodation of Interdependent Systems."

The Job-to-Be-Done of a Physician's Practice

The job that an EHR is designed to do is a *systemic* job, not a local one. It is designed to enable different providers in different locations to see what kinds of care other doctors and institutions have given or are rendering to a patient. It would be an extraordinarily selfless act for the independent physicians' practices that care for over 60 percent of America's population to invest in and adopt the EHR systems that would make it easier for other caregivers to care more effectively for *their* patients.[39] For many providers, patient records can even serve as a strategic asset, since paper records increase switching costs for patients.[40] Helping the *system* function more effectively simply isn't a job that most individual physicians or competing hospitals need to do. We revisit the refrain: it's hard to build a practice around activities for which you're not paid.

But still—wouldn't you think that doctors would adopt electronic health records to help themselves? Not in this case. Sometimes, in what we call "new market disruption," the customers' alternative to buying a disruptive product is to have nothing at all. This is why Ford's Model T, Sony's pocket transistor radio, and Black & Decker's cheap plastic $9.99 hand drill were so successful. For sure, they were disruptive to the competition, so competitors didn't attack. But just as important, from the customers' point of view, these simple products were infinitely better than nothing—which had been their prior alternative.

When there is no nonconsumption of a product, however—when everyone can buy something familiar to get the job done—then the height of the hurdle to success is a lot higher. The only way a disruptive product can succeed in this case is when it does the job better than what the customer already is using. Until it is better, or until it is "as good" and a lot cheaper, the customers simply won't buy it.

A great illustration is the emergence of electronic books in the late 1990s as a disruptive innovation relative to bound paper books from major publishing houses. Even though they were disruptive to the traditional publishing houses, electronic books never took off because everyone had access to traditional books. In both overt and subtle ways, electronic books just didn't do the job as well as bound paper books did. Finally, over a decade later, the Amazon Kindle seems to be getting substantial traction. Why? Because it's as good as a book in most dimensions of importance, and a lot better in others. So now, and only now, can the disruption of the traditional book publishing business begin in earnest.

For the average doctor who gets paid on a per-transaction basis, writing paper prescriptions and keeping paper records still cost less, and are a lot more convenient, than adopting an electronic health record. The key point of financial leverage in a physician's practice is the number of patients seen, not the efficiency of back-office record-keeping. Because doctors can always turn to paper records as an alternative, vendors of electronic medical records haven't gotten traction with independent physicians' practices—and won't get traction until their systems, like the Kindle, finally do the job better, *as the doctor defines the job*, than the pad in her pocket and the forms on her clipboard.

In our estimation, these jobs for electronic health records would include:

1. Help me organize, compare, and think through the data I've collected today and in past visits.
2. Store the data so that I and others can easily retrieve them in the future.
3. Satisfy requirements for documentation in order to justify my billing to insurers.
4. Protect me legally by recording my actions and decisions.
5. Do not impede my normal interactions with the patient, and do not obstruct the normal flow of work.

For many physicians, writing with pen and paper still accomplishes these jobs better than electronic systems. And while providers are often expected to bear the cost of implementing an electronic health records system, many of the benefits—such as improved patient safety, data security, care coordination, and disease prevention—accrue to patients, insurers, and payers, but often not to the providers. With little incentive or support to solve these "macro" problems, most physicians decide to simply keep their heads above water by doing what they've always done.

The Problem of Mutual Accommodation of Interdependent Systems

Not surprisingly, given their perspectives as *systems*, large provider organizations such as Partners, Mayo, Intermountain, the

Veterans Administration, MinuteClinic, and Kaiser Permanente have had more success in implementing electronic health records. The frustration that advocates of *personal* electronic health records have expressed about the way these institutions have implemented the technology, however, is that the records are not *personal*—in that they are not portable, interoperable, standard-format records patients can take with them and use wherever they go. These entities have implemented electronic health record systems that are *proprietary*. The records can be accessed instantly from any point *within* their systems, but generally not from points outside the system.

Why have they ignored everyone's urging that they build these records in a common format? There is a logical explanation. When there is a stage in an industry's value chain whose product or process architecture must be interdependent in order to be optimized, it cannot conform to anything else. Rather, the products or processes in the steps in the value chain adjacent to the optimized step need to be modular and conformable, in order to enable the optimization.

For example, the Intel microprocessor in personal computers has a proprietary, interdependent architecture, because it largely determines how well the computer performs. It must be optimized. This means that the computer in which it is used must have a modular architecture—engineers must design the rest of the machine to conform to the architecture necessitated by the processor, because the processor cannot be compromised. In the RIM BlackBerry, in contrast, engineers are still trying to optimize the performance of the entire device to meet the performance demands of the market—and as a result its architecture is proprietary and interdependent. This means, however, that the processor within it cannot be a one-size-fits-all, nonconformable Intel processor. Rather, it must be a custom-designed, *modular* processor. It must have all of the functionality that the BlackBerry needs, and none of the functionality that the BlackBerry doesn't need. In this case the processor must accommodate, because the BlackBerry's overall design cannot be compromised.

In other words, one side or the other must be modular and conformable, so that what is not yet good enough can be interdependent and optimized.[41]

When executives try to force two proprietary, interdependent products against each other in a value chain, the result is vast expense and excruciating pain, because neither side wants to accommodate the other. An example is the implementation of an enterprise resource planning software system from a company like SAP. The architecture of SAP's product is extraordinarily interdependent—if you change one element of the system, you have to change every other element. The economics of interdependence mandates standardization. Yet the production, technical, procurement, sales, and administrative processes of an operating company are themselves extraordinarily interdependent—if you change one thing, you have to change everything. So when executives undertake an "SAP implementation," they're forcing one immovable object into another immovable object. Companies often pay firms like Accenture or Deloitte over $100 million to help them implement the SAP system. In the end, the company's processes must give way and conform themselves to SAP. Few people have physically and emotionally survived more than one SAP implementation project.[42] It is very, very difficult!

The reason why the integrated health systems have all implemented proprietary electronic medical record systems is that their processes of care, compensation, costing, procurement, and management are interdependent—in unique and proprietary ways. Rather than force their processes to conform to a standard-format electronic medical record system, it is much more natural and cost effective for them to develop a system that conforms itself to their own organization's established processes, not the other way around.[43]

In addition, just as doctors are individual actors within a larger system, so are these hospital systems—they're subsystems within a larger system. It is simply not in their interest to force-fit their operating processes into a standard format so providers in other systems can easily care for *their* patients. In other words, we cannot expect entities whose scope is that of individuals within a subsystem, or subsystems within a system, voluntarily to invest to solve higher-level systemic problems. We have gotten exactly what we could expect.

THE WAY FORWARD

The history of the emergence of technical standards suggests that there are generically three paths by which personal health records can emerge to play their crucial role in tying together the elements of the disruptive health-care value network. The first occurs before an industry is established, where the entities planning to enter a market get together and agree on standards. The Europeans did this in wireless telephony, for example. Before they designed the handsets, built their towers, or installed base stations, they agreed to the GSM (Groupe Spécial Mobile) standard. They could then conform all of the products in their systems to this standard.

In health care, the emerging disruptive players could agree on a standard record format much more readily than Kaiser Permanente could agree with Mayo. A major orchestrator could assemble these disruptive entrants, much as IBM did for the PC industry. Then as this disruptive system coalesces and grows, any new entities that joined it could mold their emerging operating processes to conform to the existing personal health record system. We're not in this situation, unfortunately, because the existing players—especially the integrated health systems—need to play crucial roles in the disruptive process.

Because it is very hard to get standards accepted after major, competing proprietary systems have been established, the second route forward is virtualization—essentially a technology for translating "foreign languages" into a common one that allows previously incompatible formats to work seamlessly together. This is now happening at the interface of computer hardware and operating systems. A "virtualization layer" from companies such as VM Ware (a unit of EMC Corp.) enables computers with

CISC or RISC processors and UNIX, Windows, Apple, or Linux operating systems to work together seamlessly.[44] A technology called "software-defined radio" from companies like Vanu, Inc. has similarly emerged to provide this sort of virtualization between incompatible wireless telephony standards like GSM (AT&T), CDMA (Verizon and Sprint), and IDEN (Nextel).

The third possibility is coercion. The government could stipulate that funding only goes to entities whose IT systems conform to a standard. We suspect that even if the government did this, however, a sequence of the first two possibilities would still be the mechanism by which PHRs materialize to meet the government's mandate. A set of disruptive players will coalesce around and build their systems upon a platform (something like Facebook is a real possibility[45]). As it grows as the standard among entrants, virtualization software will emerge to render the major integrated providers' proprietary systems transparent—as if they were compatible.

We see something like this beginning to emerge from a group centered at Children's Hospital Boston, called the Indivo system.[46] It is grounded in the same philosophy that Toyota followed in the 1970s and 1980s when designing the information flows in its vaunted production system.[47]

When mainframe computers became widely available in the 1960s and 1970s, American manufacturers of automobiles, tractors, refrigerators, and comparably complex products essentially said, "We have a complicated problem, and it requires a complicated solution." So they developed Materials Requirements Planning (MRP) software systems, many of which cost tens of millions of dollars to design and deploy. They were built in a hierarchical arrangement—one that continuously collected information from each of the thousands of workers and work stations in the factory into a central computer. The computer then dispensed information back to each of those workers and work stations about what they should do next, when and how they should do it, and how long they should take. MRP systems almost never worked—because if one of the thousands of workers in the plant provided the wrong information, didn't receive the right information at the right time, or had a problem with his machine, what the computer system thought was happening wasn't what was actually happening. Workers quickly learned to ignore the computer system, and instead developed informal methods for exchanging the data required to get their work done.

Toyota took a very different approach: "We have a complicated problem, so we'd better simplify the problem so we can develop a simple solution." The company was guided in part by its unique philosophy, and in part by the fact that it lacked the capital to spend on MRP systems and mainframe computers. Rather than a hierarchical, centralized system that collected and dispensed information, Toyota decided that all information required to tell workers what to do, and how and when to do it, should always travel with the product as the product went through a plant and between plants. The information had to be visible to all who needed to see it, in a standard, immediately recognizable format. This was an infinitely simpler system that actually worked better—because the information was never separated from the product, and therefore was always there when workers needed to add value to the product. This information system has become a key element in Toyota's capability to build high-quality products with such extraordinary efficiency.[48]

The Indivo system is organized around similar principles. The data always travels, at least in a virtual sense, *with* the patient. The records are called *personal* health records (PHRs) because the patients decide what data they want to put in their records. While one health system has no legal right to demand data from another health system, patients have full rights to all data about themselves, from all providers. As depicted at the bottom of Figure 4.4, individuals can request that the data from hospitals, pharmacies, physicians, payers, and analytical laboratories be deposited in their record. The information is kept there in an open-source format, accessible only to those entities with whom the individuals choose to share it. Patients can request that data from each provider they visit be automatically deposited into their records, or they can import the data into their record on a case-by-case basis.

As depicted at the top of Figure 4.4, an ecosystem comprised of companies and research organizations can sit atop this system.[49] These can create proprietary applications for the data stored in the PHRs. For example, an entrepreneur might choose to develop an application to help patients with asthma better live with their disease. Patients who wanted to use that application could make their PHR available and receive whatever benefits the application promised. The application could also be a research project, and individuals wishing to participate in the project could make their PHR available to the researchers. The concept is akin to the organizing paradigm of social networking sites like Facebook. Only those whom you allow can see your information.

Though the data will probably be stored on a server rather than literally carried around in the patient's pocket in a storage

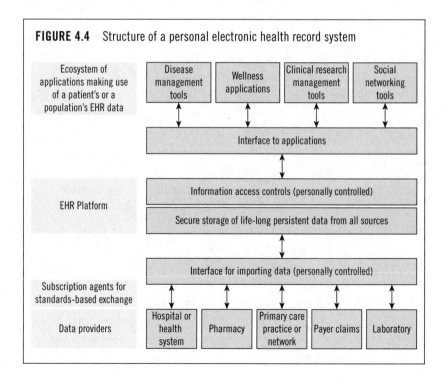

FIGURE 4.4   Structure of a personal electronic health record system

device, this system is very similar to Toyota's concept—the fundamental organizing principle is that the data can essentially travel with the person. It promises to yield remarkable benefits—not just for patient safety, but also in clinical research. As an example, in a clinical trial patients are often carefully selected to have no comorbidities, to simplify analysis of the direct effect of taking the drug in question. However, the real-world use of the drug involves a *very* different population, in which patients do indeed have more than the one illness of concern and are taking multiple medications that can interact with the new drug. Postmarketing surveillance for adverse interactions among all this noise becomes impossible. However, with PHRs in a structure like Figure 4.4, researchers can continue to monitor their drugs even after they're released into the rough-and-tumble world.

The Indivo system resolves the Problem of Mutual Accommodation of Interdependent Systems summarized earlier by inserting a layer of virtualization between two interdependent structures. It makes the data open, modular, and conformable, so that the applications using the data can be optimized. By being modular (open source), the data in PHRs are commoditized—it is no longer a strategic asset, nor where money can be made. Instead, profit in the industry will be made by firms that build applications that use the data. Some information technology companies whose strategies are to build businesses in this sector seem intent to keep the data proprietary—hoping that controlling access to the data will be their source of profit. This is a bad bet. As the data become commoditized, the applications that use them will become decommoditized—and *this* is where money will be made.

To date, a number of major employers—including Wal-Mart and Intel—have adopted the Indivo standard. We suspect that over time the data providers in the bottom boxes of Figure 4.4 will begin advertising the compatibility of their records with the Indivo system—and competition will force others to build or buy into a virtualization of the interface between their systems and the Indivo database.

We cannot overstate how important PHRs are to the efficient functioning of a low-cost, high-quality health-care system. We hope that our discussion of this topic will give impetus to a major, powerful potential orchestrator to step up, as IBM did with personal computer disruption, to define these PHR standards. We think that the Indivo system, or something like it, is a good place to start.

NOTES

1. These categories are not mutually exclusive. Many conditions are treated under more than one category of care.
2. McQueen, M. P., "Look Who's Watching Your Health Expenses: Employers Increasingly Turn to 'Care Managers' to Control Medical Costs, but Some Wonder If Patients Always Benefit," *Wall Street Journal*, September 25, 2007, D1.
3. PatientsLikeMe is a Cambridge, Massachusetts–based social networking Web site focused initially on communities of patients with multiple sclerosis, amyotrophic lateral sclerosis (Lou Gehrig's disease), Parkinson's disease, and HIV. We thank Graham Pallett of Carol. com for bringing our attention to this company. Also see Goetz, Thomas, "Practicing Patients," *New York Times Magazine*, March 23, 2008.
4. O'Meara, Sean, "Diabetes Education Goes Multimedia," *Nurses World*, April/May 2007.
5. For many primary care physicians, near-patient testing still needs to meet common expectations of performance and reliability before they will be used disruptively. Also, the unit cost of near-patient testing is not currently lower than centralized testing, but we suspect that the added convenience will actually command a price premium. Furthermore, if the cost of time delays and additional physician visits are included, then the overall cost of near-patient testing will likely be lower compared to centralized testing. Also, it is important to note that patients may carry lower expectations of performance and reliability than physicians, in which case a consumer-driven market may actually demand speed and convenience much earlier than physicians would be willing to provide it. For example, home testing kits, which many physicians and health experts have often been critical of due to poor performance and reliability (by their measures), have found markets among consumers across many conditions.
6. Some specialists have also integrated down-market to incorporate more primary care activities into their practices so patients don't have to return to see primary care physicians. However, we suspect that specialists will have little financial motivation to do this on a long-term and wide-scale basis.
7. We aren't the first to articulate this principle. Economists call this phenomenon "diminishing marginal utility." A maxim of microeconomics is that marginal price will gravitate to marginal utility—the increment in price that customers will pay for an improvement will equal the utility, or satisfaction, they receive from utilizing the improvement.
8. This customization was reflected in the much greater selection of hardware components, accessories, and software available to customers using the IBM-based PC architecture. In some industries the degree of customization and convenience becomes more than

adequate, in which case cost becomes the basis of competition. Price and cost are always important in every market, and because of this, price-based competition has never been the focus of our research on innovation. Rather, the salient question for innovators is, "What kinds of innovations will the customers value, and therefore be willing to pay a premium price to get?" For desktop personal computers, it appears that Dell might now be offering more than enough customization and convenience, in which case true cost-based competition, in which premium prices are impossible to sustain, might be expected to emerge—starting at the bottom of the market first, and then creeping up-market.

9. The American Medical Association's outlook on quality-of-care issues for retail clinics is summarized in Japson, Bruce, "Rise of Retail Clinics Giving Doctors a Chill," *Chicago Tribune*, June 12, 2006.

10. For a deeper discussion about how good theory is built, please see Christensen, Clayton M., and Michael E. Raynor, *The Innovator's Solution* (Boston, Massachusetts: Harvard Business School Press, 2003), 12–17.

11. We refer readers interested in studying this topic in more detail to Chapter 8 of Christensen, Clayton M., *The Innovator's Dilemma* (Boston, Massachusetts: Harvard Business School Press, 1997). This builds upon the buying hierarchy developed by Windermere Associates (San Francisco) and Chapters 4 and 5 of Christensen, Clayton M., and Michael E. Raynor, *The Innovator's Solution*, ibid.

12. MinuteClinic was acquired by CVS-Caremark in 2007. Clayton Christensen and his coauthors, John Kenagy and Richard Bohmer, first identified MinuteClinic as a disruptive business model in a September–October 2000 *Harvard Business Review* article, "Will Disruptive Innovations Cure Health Care?" when the fledgling company was called QuickMedx and operated only a few clinics in Minneapolis. CVS was aggressively incorporating MinuteClinics into its retail pharmacies as this book was being written.

13. The clinic in this case, MinuteClinic, was the largest chain of retail clinics in the United States at the time of this writing. It offers some of these services only to people in certain age brackets. For example, they do not offer care to children under the age of 18 months, and some types of care are not offered to the very elderly. The rationale for asking these patients to visit a regular doctor's office is that the likelihood of certain symptoms being a compound manifestation of multiple interdependent underlying disorders is high enough that they need to be seen in a business model attuned to the practice of intuitive medicine.

14. We thank Mary Kate Scott of Scott & Company, Inc. for sharing her research and insights with us. She categorizes the current offerings from retail clinics under seven common conditions: sinusitis, upper respiratory tract infection, pharyngitis, otitis media, bronchitis, urinary tract infection, and immunization. She described two types of technologies that will contribute greatly to expanding the scope of retail clinics: telemedicine and devices for diagnosis and treatment that are simple and cheap enough for this setting. If this scope expands as predicted, 15 to 30 percent of all emergency department and urgent care visits could also shift to retail clinics.

15. This reflects the savings to insurance carriers. The percentage savings for uninsured individuals who would otherwise pay out-of-pocket is likely much greater.

16. This refers to meritorious malpractice claims. A large number of nonmeritorious claims are attributed to poor communication between the physician and patient.

17. In most instances of disruptive innovation, a bubble has grown and then popped—setting the industry on a more realistic but resolute trajectory of growth. Bubbles swelled and

then popped in automobiles, telephones, personal computers, disk drives, discount retailing, and the Internet. In each case, journalists with limited historical perspective seized upon the popping to proclaim that everything had been built on hype. The journalists are then proven wrong within a few years, as a more rational and right-sized set of companies begin their resolute and disruptive march up-market. Mary Kate Scott of Scott & Company, Inc. estimates that the United States will need approximately 2,000 retail clinics (roughly one clinic for every 100,000 to 150,000 people), but by 2012 we may have 5,000 to 6,000 clinics in the marketplace (there are currently 1,020 in operation). This oversaturation and overcapacity is already seen in markets like Atlanta, Georgia. And if history is any guide, we can expect that the bubble will pop, a shake-out will occur, and journalists will proclaim that the excitement over retail clinics was all overblown. But the industry will then march forward in a steady way, disruptively drawing more and more disorders away from physicians' practices, as the ability to treat those disorders is brought closer to the realm of precision medicine and value-adding process business models.

18. Mehrotra, A., et al., "Retail Clinics, Primary Care Physicians, and Emergency Departments: A Comparison of Patients' Visits," *Health Affairs* 2008; 27:1272–82.

19. We suspect many clinicians will shudder at the notion of a mother diagnosing her own child's ear infection with an otoscope—whether she can interpret anatomical landmarks and signs of infection properly, whether this will lead to overuse of antibiotics and hence antimicrobial resistance, and even whether it will result in a loss of income for pediatricians from what are relatively simple cases. And yet we already ask patients to self-diagnose and self-treat for many conditions: adjusting insulin regimens depending on dietary intake and glucose measurements; adjusting diuretic doses, depending on weight changes and oxygenation levels. In fact, any PRN (*pro re nata*, a term used in medicine to mean "as needed") prescription is essentially asking the patient herself to make some kind of judgment call, and this practice often involves medications much more dangerous than antibiotics. In terms of reliably making a diagnosis using an otoscope, one could argue that a mother who has seen her child's normal eardrums many times over might be better able than the doctor to determine when something appears abnormal. The primary point of this discussion, however, is not whether all mothers should go out and buy otoscopes, but the acknowledgment that the diagnosis and treatment of a growing set of conditions, enabled by disruptive technologies, is shifting away from the physician's practice.

20. As would be expected for any market undergoing disruption, incumbent specialists will undoubtedly try to block this move up-market by primary care physicians by raising concerns about patient safety and lobbying for regulatory hurdles such as modification of reimbursement policies, instituting stricter licensure and training standards, and devising new standard protocols of care that block participation by disruptive entrants.

21. Jauhar, S., "House Calls," *New England Journal of Medicine*, vol. 351, no. 21:2149–51.

22. One of the pioneers in this effort was Sonosite, a Seattle-area maker of handheld ultrasound equipment. In a stunning achievement that shows how well-informed managers of an industry-leading firm can become the industry leaders in a disruptive technology, General Electric Medical Systems (now GE HealthCare) has taken the lead in handheld ultrasound, even while it maintains its industry-leading positions in MRI, CT, and PET scanning equipment.

23. We expect dialysis to decentralize even further, to the point where more people can perform it in their homes. It should be noted that home peritoneal dialysis actually preceded outpatient hemodialysis centers, but in terms of the disruption diagram, PD

was not good enough for older patients or for the many patients who could not handle the technical complexity. We will discuss the topic of home hemodialysis in Chapter 11.

24. See http://www.abaxis.com/medical/piccolo.html for more information. We thank Steve Wunker of Innosight LLC for this example.

25. Cases diagnosed through SimulConsult include adrenoleukodystrophy in Eig, Jonathan, "The Doctor, the Father, the Movie and the Medicine," *Wall Street Journal*, October 8, 2005; and Rett syndrome in Dreifus, Claudia, "Researchers Toil with Genes on the Fringe of a Cure," *New York Times*, March 22, 2005.

26. Other popular online and electronic tools, such as MD Consult and UpToDate, have traditionally served as one-way repositories of information, essentially replacing hard copies of textbooks and journals and hastening the search for information. They are often less elegant to use when the physician's job is, "Help me generate a differential diagnosis based on my patient's medical history, signs, and symptoms." However, they are extraordinarily helpful when the physician's job is, "Help me learn more about a particular disease" or, "Help me create slides for a presentation."

27. In using SimulConsult's system for this illustration, we're not endorsing this particular product or predicting its commercial success. Indeed, there are several additional systems with similar promise under development. Kaiser Permanente is among users of the Isabel system: once symptoms are entered into a computer, Isabel typically presents 10 diagnoses on the first Web page, and an additional five to 10 on subsequent pages, up to a total of 30, in no particular order. In Landro, Laura, "Preventing the Tragedy of Misdiagnosis," *Wall Street Journal*, November 29, 2006, D1. Another system is Aetna's Smart-Source: using a medical search engine developed by Healthline, SmartSource contains medical profiles based on records of each insured member's illnesses and diagnostic tests, and also assumptions about their health concerns as reflected in their search topics. In Freudenheim, Milt, "Aetna to Offer an Online Service that Helps Patients Link Records and Research," *New York Times*, March 12, 2008. Finally, Dr. Lewis Hassell pointed out a product for pathologists called Immunoquery/PathIQ (http://immunoquery.pathiq.com/PathIQ/), where the user can enter results from stains, and the system will offer a list of likely diagnoses and references to supportive literature. Also, one can enter several diagnoses under consideration for a tumor, and the system will suggest a panel of stains that will help confirm the diagnosis.

28. Of course, a primary care physician can be sued for *not* referring a patient when appropriate, but that is already the status quo. Armed with a decision tool based on clinical evidence reduces the likelihood of failing to refer when appropriate. Meanwhile, a specialist who uses the same tool might be reprimanded for substituting the device in place of the knowledge and experience for which he is paid.

29. Project ECHO (Extension for Community Health Care Outcomes) was founded by Dr. Sanjeev Arora, a hepatologist at the University of New Mexico Hospital, who wanted to find a solution for the large number of New Mexicans who had hepatitis C but either could not afford to see a specialist or did not live near one of the few hepatologists in the state. Project ECHO has since expanded its clinics to include cardiovascular risk reduction, child obesity, child and adolescent care, child adolescent family telepsychiatry, chronic pain, high risk pregnancy, integrated addiction and psychiatry, psychotherapy, pulmonary medicine, and rheumatology. See http://echo.unm.edu/ for more information.

30. Brotherton, Sarah E., and Sylvia I. Etzel, "Graduate Medical Education, 2005-2006," *Journal of the American Medical Association*, 2006, 296(9):1154–69.

31. Fisher, Elliott S., Staiger, D. O., et al., "Creating Accountable Care Organizations: The Extended Hospital Medical Staff," *Health Affairs*, vol. 26, no. 1 (2007):w44–w57.

32. For more information, see the Patient-Centered Primary Care Collaborative Web site at http://www.pcpcc.net/, a coalition of employers, consumers, and physician organizations.

33. Kohn, Linda T., et. al., *To Err is Human: Building a Safer Health System*. (Washington, D.C.: National Academies Press, 2000).

34. It's a somewhat different story for salaried doctors working for integrated providers or for the few patients whose employers have hired their own providers. When physicians are salaried and have an incentive to keep patients healthy, as opposed to primarily helping them only when they're sick, the original oversight model of primary care works much better. We refer interested readers to Chapter 6 for a discussion about the effect that status as an employee—rather than as an independent businessperson—can have on the role of primary care physicians in coordinating care.

35. Anderson, Gerard F., "Medicare and Chronic Conditions," *New England Journal of Medicine*, vol. 353(3):305.

36. United States Office of Personnel Management, Federal Employees Health Benefits Program, "Frequently Asked Questions," accessed at www.opm.gov/insure/health/qa/qa.asp?rx, September 6, 2008.

37. For our purposes, the term "electronic health record" is meant to include the category of traditional electronic medical records (EMRs), which are basically electronic versions of traditional medical records. We intentionally use the "personal" term to acknowledge the fact that data not typically kept in medical records in the past will likely be included in EMRs in the future. Adding the qualifier "personal" also identifies the growing movement to have records owned and controlled by the individual patient, rather than the institutions that provide care. We will further refine this concept later in the chapter.

38. UpToDate, at http://www.uptodate.com, is an aggregator of clinical data and information written by expert clinicians.

39. According to Wassenaar, J. D., and S. L. Thran, *Physician Socioeconomic Statistics* (Chicago: American Medical Association, 2001). In 1999, 38.2 percent of physicians were employed by a group practice, managed-care organization, or other organization; 28.4 percent were in solo practice; and 33.4 percent were in self-employed group practice. More recent data from the AMA indicates that 75 percent of physicians still practice in groups of eight or fewer physicians. See American Medical Association, "Health Care Trends 2006," accessed at http://www.ama-assn.org/ama1/pub/upload/mm/409/2006trends.pdf.

40. Anyone who has tried to obtain copies of their own medical records can attest to the switching costs involved. Lack of interoperability across electronic health record systems creates a similar barrier to switching. This lack of communication and data exchange also leads to significant duplication of tests, since it is often easier and quicker to redo a test rather than try to obtain records from an outside provider.

41. We thank our friend Chris Rowen, CEO of Tensilica Corporation, for articulating this concept to us. Rowen's name for this phenomenon is the "Law of Conservation of Modularity," named in honor of Clayton Christensen's twelfth-grade physics teacher, Mr. Steed, who first propounded the principle. The law is, we think, more obscure in the

present than it will be in the future. Christensen and Raynor labeled this phenomenon the "Law of Conservation of Attractive Profits" in the appendix to Chapter 6 of *The Innovator's Solution*, because what becomes more modular becomes less profitable, and what becomes more interdependent and proprietary becomes more profitable. We recommend Chapters 5 and 6 of that book to readers with a deeper interest in this topic.

42. We extend our apologies to our friends at SAP for this characterization of the process of implementing their extraordinarily capable product. In the end, most customers are glad they did it. The latest new products to emerge from SAP attempt to be more modular and conformable to the company's processes.

43. Even a proprietary system developed in-house, however, does not ensure adequate conformity. One of the most notorious failed implementations of electronic medical records occurred at Cedars-Sinai Medical Center in Los Angeles, despite the fact that the software had been developed internally. However, the reasons for failure are the same—the software lacked sufficient design input from its physician users and therefore forced many of them to try to conform to unyielding software processes. Connolly, Ceci, "Cedars Sinai Doctors Cling to Pen and Paper," *Washington Post*, March 21, 2006, A01.

44. In terms of the Law of Conservation of Modularity, what virtualization does is to insert a "modular" layer between two proprietary, interdependent layers so they can virtually conform to each other.

45. This was suggested to us by Marc Benioff, CEO of Salesforce.com.

46. Indivo, developed by the Children's Hospital Informatics Program (CHIP) at Children's Hospital Boston, also serves as the platform used by Dossia, a large employer-led consortium that aims to introduce a PHR platform that accomplishes the virtualization we describe in this chapter. Members of the consortium include Intel, Children's Hospital Boston, Pitney Bowes, AT&T, Wal-Mart, Sanofi Aventis, Applied Materials, bp, and CardinalHealth. Our thanks to Colin Evans, president and CEO of Dossia, for introducing us to this enterprise.

47. We thank Dr. Kenneth Mandl, leader of the Medical Informatics unit at Children's Hospital Boston, for teaching us about this initiative.

48. We will revisit the lessons of Toyota's remarkable production system in Chapter 10 while discussing future medical education.

49. Mandl, K.D., and I.S. Keohane, "Tectonic Shifts in the Health Information Economy," *New England Journal of Medicine*, vol. 358, no. 16, April 17, 2008, 1732–37.

Chapter 5

Disruptive Solutions for the Care of Chronic Disease

The business model innovations that we described in Chapters 3 and 4 are important elements of a strategy to reduce the cost, increase the quality, and improve accessibility of health care. But the business model innovations for the treatment of chronic disease that we describe in this chapter are perhaps the most important innovations of all.

Ninety million Americans currently have chronic conditions such as diabetes, hypertension, arthritis, and dementia. More than one-third of young adults aged 18 to 34, two-thirds of adults aged 45 to 64, and nearly 90 percent of the elderly have at least one chronic disease.[1] Acute conditions like infectious diseases, trauma, and maternity care create real costs, of course. But chronic disorders account for three-quarters of direct medical care costs in the United States. And of the myriad chronic diseases, five of them—diabetes, congestive heart failure, coronary artery disease, asthma, and depression—account for most of these costs.[2] Many often have their genesis in two other chronic illnesses, obesity and tobacco addiction. A key reason why such a large share of our health-care dollars is spent during the last 18 months of life is that this is when the complications of chronic disease have finally set in with a vengeance.[3]

In sum: any program for resolving our runaway health-care costs that does not have a credible plan for changing the way we care for the chronically ill can't make more than a small dent in the total problem.

Chronic illness is a relatively new phenomenon, because only recently has technological progress transformed many once-fatal diseases into chronic ones. Before the 1920s, for example, childhood-onset diabetes was an acute disease: those diagnosed with it died within a few months. But the ability to inject animal and now biosynthetic insulin has transformed Type I diabetes from an acute, fatal disease into a chronic condition. Coronary artery disease was largely an acute illness until the 1970s. It went largely undiagnosed until patients experienced, and often died from, a heart attack. Bypasses, stents, and statins have now transformed heart disease into a chronic condition. AIDS and some cancers have been transformed into chronic conditions in just the past decade. New drugs and devices are changing multiple sclerosis and cystic fibrosis from recurring, ultimately fatal episodes of acute illness into diseases whose victims can experience a better quality of life.

Though these triumphs are a cause for celebration, the number of patients who live with a chronic disease, the growth rate of that number, and the cost of their ongoing health maintenance over ever-longer periods of time are staggering.[4] A key contributor to this costliness, however, is that the primary business models being used to care for these patients—physicians' practices and hospitals—were primarily set up to deal with acute diseases. They make money when people are sick, not by keeping them well. There are more than 9,000 billing codes for individual procedures and units of care. But there is not a single billing code for patient adherence or improvement, or for helping patients stay well.[5]

Rather than hoping that improving the efficiency of caregivers working within these business models will solve these problems, a more robust solution must be found by creating new business models for managing chronic disease. Exploring these possibilities is the focus of this chapter.

CATEGORIES OF CHRONIC DISEASE

The task in building any valid theory is to define the categories correctly. In the preliminary or *descriptive* stage of theory building, researchers typically define the categories in their theory according to the characteristics of the phenomena they are studying. They then correlate the presence or absence of those characteristics with the outcomes of interest. A very typical study in business research, for example, would entail categorizing businesses as entrepreneur-funded or venture-capital-backed, and then compare the success rates of the companies in the two groups.

But descriptive theories that emerge from studies such as these can only indicate average tendencies. The predictive power of theory takes a huge leap forward when a researcher moves beyond such descriptive categories and correlations, and discovers the causal mechanisms that underlie the outcomes of interest. This understanding allows a scholar to make precise and predictably effective *prescriptions* about the actions that will and will not lead to the desired results in the different situations in which people might find themselves.[6]

The theories that have guided medical practice follow this pattern exactly. Early on, diseases are classified by their characteristics—by their physical symptoms. If the patient is wheezing, we'll call it asthma; if she has elevated levels of blood glucose, we'll call it diabetes; and so on. When medical theory is in this *descriptive* stage, the practice of medicine must be intuitive or empirical, and outcomes typically can only be expressed in probabilistic terms.

Medical theory takes a giant step forward, however, when scientists can categorize a disease by the different mechanisms that cause sickness or permit wellness. The ability to diagnose by cause rather than characteristics takes the theory about a disease from the descriptive to the *prescriptive* stage. This is the essence of the transition to precision medicine. In our example above, it can make a life-and-death difference to know if the patient is wheezing because of an allergic reaction, an inflammation of the airways, a foreign body in the airway, or fluid buildup because of a heart problem. Effective treatment hinges on precise definition.

One of the most common categorizations in health care is the distinction between chronic and acute disease: one group of diseases lasts for a long time, the other doesn't. This is a descriptive categorization, however; it tells us little about how to treat these diseases. Chronic diseases differ fundamentally among themselves, and before we can recommend which types of business models can be effective, we first need to define the different groups of chronic diseases that will require different business models.

In the treatment of many acute diseases, because of their relatively brief duration, the same business model can be used for both diagnosis and treatment. This is not the case with chronic diseases, however. The type of business model that is good at diagnosing the disease and prescribing a course of therapy must be different from the model that can most effectively help patients adhere to the therapy and make the behavioral adjustments necessary to live free from the complications of the disease. These are two fundamentally different tasks. In the following discussion, therefore, we'll note how business model innovation can improve the effectiveness and cost of diagnosis and treatment. We'll then explore what kinds of business models should be used to help people adhere to the treatments that have been prescribed. One of our conclusions is that despite the enormity of cost and suffering associated with chronic disease, there actually are very few business models in health care today whose design is optimized to diagnose and prescribe, and to encourage adherence to therapy.

Business Models for Diagnosing and Prescribing Treatment for Chronic Disease

In Figure 5.1 we've grouped a sampling of chronic diseases according to the precision of scientific understanding that underlies the disease, as well as the breadth of subspecialties whose perspectives need to be brought to bear to diagnose the problem and devise an effective therapy. Though experts may disagree with us in the placement of certain diseases, we ask our readers simply to regard these groupings as illustrative only.

We call the diseases on the left side of Figure 5.1 Intuitive Chronic Diseases. We don't know enough about them—because insufficient research has been done to date, often due to lack of

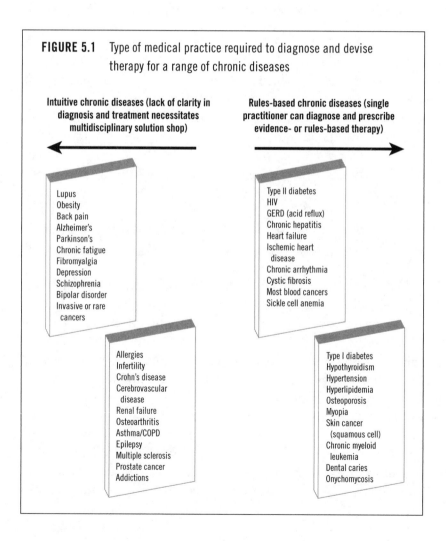

FIGURE 5.1 Type of medical practice required to diagnose and devise therapy for a range of chronic diseases

Intuitive chronic diseases (lack of clarity in diagnosis and treatment necessitates multidisciplinary solution shop)

Rules-based chronic diseases (single practitioner can diagnose and prescribe evidence- or rules-based therapy)

Lupus
Obesity
Back pain
Alzheimer's
Parkinson's
Chronic fatigue
Fibromyalgia
Depression
Schizophrenia
Bipolar disorder
Invasive or rare
cancers

Type II diabetes
HIV
GERD (acid reflux)
Chronic hepatitis
Heart failure
Ischemic heart
disease
Chronic arrhythmia
Cystic fibrosis
Most blood cancers
Sickle cell anemia

Allergies
Infertility
Crohn's disease
Cerebrovascular
disease
Renal failure
Osteoarthritis
Asthma/COPD
Epilepsy
Multiple sclerosis
Prostate cancer
Addictions

Type I diabetes
Hypothyroidism
Hypertension
Hyperlipidemia
Osteoporosis
Myopia
Skin cancer
(squamous cell)
Chronic myeloid
leukemia
Dental caries
Onychomycosis

funding or awareness, and/or the diseases are inherently complex and require multiple areas of expertise to fully understand.[7] We do know two important things, however. First, we know that science will ultimately teach us that each of these "diseases" in truth is a symptom—a broad manifestation of one or more different underlying causal mechanisms. Second, we know that these different causes probably involve multiple organ systems through interdependent molecular pathways, complicated by individual genetic differences and environmental factors. These combine to make diagnosis and treatment extremely complex, limiting the movement toward rules-based care.

Therefore, to effectively diagnose and prescribe the best course of therapy possible for these intuitive diseases, professionals from multiple medical subspecialties need to interact with each other and, using any available data, intuitively iterate toward the best possible prescription. At the outset, these physicians cannot know which disease truly underlies the presenting symptom, nor can they yet prescribe a predictably effective therapy. Rather, they must synthesize from the data and their multiple perspectives a "differential diagnosis": a hypothesis that is tested by prescribing an experimental course of therapy and seeing what happens. Then they must revise the diagnosis and therapy iteratively, when necessary, until the most effective course of action possible has emerged.

We call the diseases on the right side of Figure 5.1 Rules-Based Chronic Diseases because treatment is in the realm of empirical or precision medicine. The diagnosis and prescription of an effective therapy for rules-based chronic diseases, in contrast to the task with intuitive ones, usually can be competently managed by an individual caregiver. Most of these are not yet in the realm of precision medicine, in that we're not sure of the cause of the symptoms, but most of them ultimately will be sorted into more precisely defined types. For now, however, nearly all of these rules-based diseases are squarely in the empirical mode. Unambiguous measures of the disease-defining symptoms are readily available, and there is clear statistical evidence that if a particular course of therapy is followed, the undesirable symptoms and long-term complications will be minimized, on average, when compared to other therapeutic alternatives. Standardized protocols based on clinical evidence are commonplace for conditions like heart disease (chronic stable angina), diabetes, and congestive heart failure.

The business model to diagnose and arrive at a course of therapy for rules-based diseases exists: it is the traditional physician's practice. In fact, the rules for many of these diseases are now so widely accepted that diagnosis and prescription can be handed off to nurse practitioners without any compromise in outcomes.

There are two costly problems in the way we historically have treated chronic disease. The first is that while effectively treating the diseases on the left side requires the perspectives of multiple specialities, the business models we typically utilize to do this job almost always deploy single practitioners. Recall, for illustration, the account of our friend's struggle with asthma in Chapter 3. It wasn't until he visited the National Jewish Medical and Research Center that a set of practitioners was able to solve his problem by working in an integrated manner. Prior to that visit, our friend had been treated by a plethora of individual physicians in separate specialties. Most were staff members at reputable teaching hospitals. But they cared for him *individually*. There was no practiced *process*. And they had never converged upon him in an integrated way before. Although the hospitals *thought* of themselves as being integrated caregivers, in reality they were simply collections of individual practitioners who had passed our friend from one doctor to the next.

Our coauthor, Jerry Grossman, recounted a similar experience when he visited the Mayo Clinic for a heart problem while we were writing this book. After running him through a series of tests, a team of subspecialists converged in the same room, examined the data together, and told Jerry that he had a cancerous tumor in his heart—a rare condition that ultimately took his life. Despite the bad news he had received, Jerry was absolutely bubbly about the "exquisite experience these guys took me through" in our first meeting after he returned to Boston. "They have a process!" he said. "It's not a one-size-fits-all process. Every patient has a different disease, but they have a practiced way to treat every patient uniquely." National Jewish and Mayo Clinic are *coherent* solution shops, as opposed to disjointed ones.

The Cleveland Clinic has recently reorganized itself into solution shops. Where most hospitals are divided into departments of medicine, surgery, pediatrics, and other general areas of practice, CEO Toby Cosgrove has directed the restructuring of the clinic into "institutes"—coherent solution shops within the hospital. Its Neurological Institute, for example, employs neurologists, oncologists, radiologists, neurosurgeons, psychiatrists, and psychologists who can converge, as appropriate, in a coordinated way to diagnose as accurately as possible the cause of behavior changes, source of epilepsy, or type of brain tumor in each patient.

There are precious few coherent solution shops like National Jewish, Mayo, and Cleveland Clinic that have reliable processes for integrating the multiple relevant disciplines required to diagnose and recommend solutions for the intuitive chronic diseases in the left side of Figure 5.1. In general, the system in which most chronically ill patients are treated is comprised of individual caregivers. Even if they work in departments and groups, most doctors practice as individuals, and patients are routed from one individual physician to the next. In most of our hospitals there are few proven, practiced pathways through which physicians knit their expertise together in a way that could surface the uniqueness of our friend's type of asthma, or Jerry's heart tumor. Many physicians we've consulted while writing this book have reflected that doctors are trained to work alone, and not together. Other observers have remarked that health care remains the last great cottage industry in America.

The Economics of Diagnosis

Isn't it too expensive, one might ask, for millions of everyday folks to fly to these coherent solution shops that are seemingly staffed by the elite for the elite? There was a time, when the basic structure of our modern health-care industry was put into place a century ago, when it probably was too expensive. But our friend's trip to Denver was actually cheap when compared to the cost to him, his insurer, and his employer of seeing doctor after doctor and taking drug after drug. The diseases on the left side of Figure 5.1 are among the most pervasive and costly conditions in America. They represent markets that would support scores of coherent solution shop clinics around the country and the rest of the world.

The need for coherent solution shops for intuitive chronic diseases constitutes an extraordinary entrepreneurial opportunity to create new business models for the diagnosis and prescription of care for patients with intuitive chronic diseases. A few studies—we expect many more to come—have demonstrated that a significant portion of the cost of chronic care is wasted, because the prescribed therapy solves the wrong problem for the wrong patient.[8] The value of solving a correctly defined problem is immense, in every industry.

A core reason why more coherent solution shops for intuitive chronic diseases don't exist is that the reimbursement formulas of Medicare and private insurers make the provision of therapy much more profitable than diagnosis. Essentially, this is because these formulas are based upon activities, not the value created. As we'll see in Chapters 6, 7, and 11, one way to work around this distortion of value creation is for major integrated provider systems, which operate both insurance and care delivery organizations, to establish these coherent solution shops internally. These integrated systems have a perspective that is unique in our largely dis-integrated health-care system, because they can spend more money at one point in the value chain in order to capture greater savings elsewhere. Their insights about the economics of correct diagnosis can then inform the rest of the industry.

ASSURING ADHERENCE TO THERAPY

For many acute diseases, the job at this point would be complete: the problem diagnosed and a therapy devised and applied. But for chronic illnesses, diagnosis and prescription is only the start. Patients then need to adhere to the recommended therapy—hourly, daily, monthly, and often for the rest of their lives. Sometimes the prescription entails extensive and unpleasant behavioral changes. The business models that can profitably and effectively help patients succeed with these challenges are very different from those designed to diagnose and devise the original treatment plan. The general absence of such business models is the second major problem in the current care of chronic disease.

As above, the validity of the theory that underlies our business model recommendations is predicated on defining the categories or situations correctly. The chart in Figure 5.2 asserts that the job to be done by these business models varies along two dimensions.

The vertical axis measures the intrinsic motivation of patients to avoid the complications or symptoms of the disease by adhering to the prescribed therapy. What largely drives this motivation is the intensity and immediacy with which patients feel the complications. For example, even though wearing eyeglasses or contact lenses is a bother, nearly everyone for whom they have been prescribed wears them—because if they didn't, they instantly can't see clearly. Patients with chronic back pain religiously take their pills—because they immediately feel the consequences if they don't. At the other end of the spectrum, patients with high cholesterol feel the same on a day-to-day basis whether or not they take their medications and follow the dietary guidelines they've been given. Losing weight, foregoing unhealthy foods, and quitting tobacco are far less pleasant than the other option, which is to continue those habits for one more day. While acknowledging that many of the other patients with these diseases die of lung cancer, go blind, have their extremities amputated, and suffer kidney and heart failure, too many patients with diseases positioned near the bottom of Figure 5.2 intend to begin adhering "tomorrow," or they cling to a conviction that God will exempt them from the fate that so predictably befalls the others. All of this happens because of the deferred consequences for failing to heed therapeutic advice.

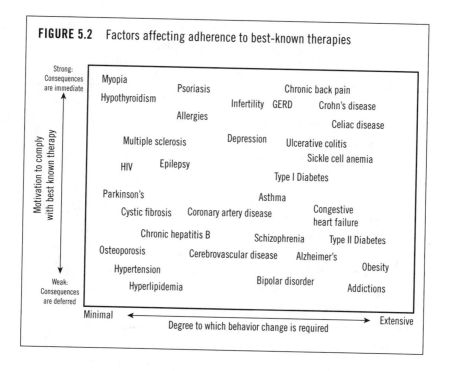

FIGURE 5.2   Factors affecting adherence to best-known therapies

Note that we've positioned asthma near the middle of this vertical spectrum. We'll highlight our reasoning for this particular placement to help explain the positioning of the others. When the complications of asthma have set in (wheezing and shortness of breath), patients are very motivated to breathe, and they badly wish they had taken the steps required in the days and hours leading up to the episode that might have prevented the attack—just like smokers who have been diagnosed with lung cancer wish they'd stopped smoking years earlier. The positioning on the vertical axis of Figure 5.2 is our assessment of patients' motivation, *before the onset of complications*, to take the actions that would have prevented the symptoms or complications from ever arising.

The horizontal axis of Figure 5.2 maps the second determinant of the appropriate business model: the extent to which the prescribed therapy entails behavioral change.[9] At the far left are diseases where simply taking a pill is all that is required.[10] Keeping at bay the symptoms and complications of diseases on the right side of the spectrum, in contrast, requires extensive behavioral change on the part of patients and their families. Methods of living with disease and adhering to the required new behaviors often need to be worked out intuitively by patients and their families.

Most of these diseases can be *diagnosed* by the physician, but following that diagnosis and prescription, in many instances physicians can't add much additional value beyond teaching patients broad categories of do's and don'ts. The patients and their families typically must distill from their own experiences algorithms of diet and activity that minimize the severity of their symptoms. When trained to do so, particularly when there is a closed-loop capability to feed back to patients the short-term results of their actions, patients with these behavior-intensive diseases can generally formulate better algorithms of care through trial and error than their physicians can. These rules of thumb can be learned but often are hard to teach because they vary from patient to patient.

As we've suggested in Figure 5.3, the diseases on the right side might be characterized as "behavior dependent," for which there is no simple way to ameliorate the symptoms or escape the consequences of the disease. Regular exercise, weight loss, dietary changes, and vigilant monitoring of symptoms are typical key ingredients—along with drugs in most cases—to living with the disease and avoiding complications. And we'll call those on the left side of Figure 5.3 "technology-dependent chronic diseases." Now let's slice the matrix horizontally. We call the diseases at the top those with Immediate Consequences. We can count on patients with these diseases to search for some combination of behaviors and medications that work and then to dutifully adhere to that regimen, because the immediate and unpleasant consequences of not doing so provide ample motivation to follow the rules. We term the diseases at the bottom as those with Deferred Consequences. Some patients with these diseases have a long enough view that spurs them to take the medication and adopt the

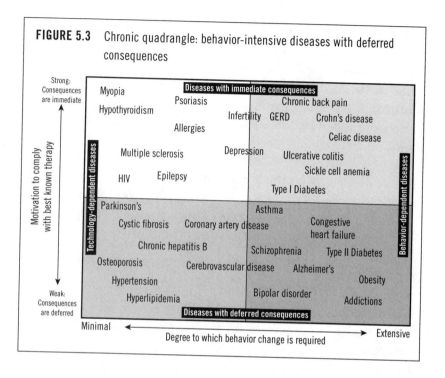

FIGURE 5.3 Chronic quadrangle: behavior-intensive diseases with deferred consequences

prescribed behaviors—but many do not. Many of these patients agree with their caregivers' recommendations, and fully intend to adhere to them—starting tomorrow.

The crushing costs of caring for chronically ill patients are largely attributable to diseases in the lower-right box in Figure 5.3. Obesity, tobacco and alcohol addictions, diabetes, asthma, and congestive heart failure are behavior-dependent diseases with deferred consequences affecting tens of millions of people each. We'll term this box the "Chronic Quadrangle."

TECHNOLOGICAL PROGRESS AND THE DYNAMICS OF CHRONIC DISEASE

Before we discuss the business models required to promote adherence to therapy in the four sections of Figure 5.3, we'd like to discuss the impact of technological progress on chronic diseases—because in many ways it is both the cause of chronic disease and the cure. The position of the chronic conditions in the figures above is our estimate of where they are *today*. But many of them are on the move. Historically, many of these were once acute diseases, in that patients often died from them within short time frames. Others were debilitating, lifelong diseases, and technological progress made it possible for patients to live more normal lives. Continued technological progress can transform intuitive chronic diseases from the left side of Figure 5.1 into diseases that are rules-based and require only a straightforward intervention.

Ultimately, scientific progress can transform chronic diseases into "acute" ones again—diseases that can be cured, and sometimes even prevented. The care of most stomach ulcers has undergone this transformation. A century ago severe stomach ulcers often resulted in bleeding and death. Living with ulcers required extensive behavioral and dietary modifications. Believing that the cause of most ulcers was excess production of stomach acid, providers offered medications like Tagamet to block the production of acid. Patients who avoided stress, shunned spicy foods, and faithfully took their medications then could live with this disease reasonably well.

In 1982, however, Dr. Robert Warren, an Australian pathologist who knew little about clinical gastroenterology, identified a strain of bacteria called *Helicobacter pylori* living in ulcerated human stomach tissue. This was a shocking discovery, because scientists previously had been convinced that such bacteria could not survive the hydrochloric acidity of the stomach. Warren asserted it was infection by this bacterium that was the genesis of most ulcers, meaning they could be cured with antibiotics. In a test reminiscent of Walter Reed's team allowing mosquitoes to bite them in order to prove that Yellow Fever was a mosquito-borne virus,[11] Warren's colleague Barry Marshall swallowed a cocktail containing the *H. pylori* bacterium. Within a few weeks he was diagnosed with stomach ulcers; and following a course of antibiotics, he was cured.[12] Subsequent research has revealed that this bacterium causes 90 percent of intestinal ulcers and 80 percent of stomach ulcers—and for most patients, what once was a chronic disease is now managed as an acute disease that can be cured. In a similar vein, technological progress seems to be shifting the position of Crohn's disease on the map of Figure 5.3. What are typically thought of as two different chronic diseases—multiple sclerosis and Crohn's disease—are actually different symptomatic manifestations that share a common cause: destructive inflammation caused by the influx of white blood cells. The drug Tysabri, which addresses the underlying inflammation by blocking signals to white blood cells, seems to ameliorate the symptoms of both "diseases." This holds the ultimate promise of shifting Crohn's to the left side of the map, where therapy is less behavior-intensive.[13] Indeed, "statin" drugs such as Lipitor have already moved the management of high cholesterol from the lower right to the lower left of Figure 5.3.[14]

Massive resources were mobilized in a relatively short period of time to transform AIDS—which is a significant disease in the United States and Europe but is a horrific epidemic in Africa— from being an acute to a chronic disease. Efforts continue in order to transform it further into an acute disease again—one that can be cured.[15]

There is some possibility that addictions to alcohol and tobacco can be shifted toward the lower left as well, as drugs are emerging that make the treatment of these diseases less behavior-intensive. There is even hope that some forms of obesity and diabetes likewise can be shifted toward the bottom-left of the map and ultimately transformed into curable diseases, as the different underlying disorders that manifest themselves through the symptoms of obesity and elevated blood glucose become better understood.[16]

BUSINESS MODELS FOR THE CARE OF CHRONIC DISEASE

What we've asserted to this point is that the care of chronic disease needs to be divided into two different "businesses." The first is a business of diagnosis and prescription, the second is a type of business that can help patients adhere to the prescribed therapy. And there's a handoff between the two that needs to be managed as well, as we'll discuss below. The business models we've historically relied upon to do this job weren't designed to do it—and that's why the diseases in the Chronic Quadrangle are causing such costly complications.

Problems with Historical Business Models in Assuring Adherence

The resources, processes, and profit formulas of doctors' offices and hospitals are optimized to manage acute crises or episodes, yet our health-care system has expected professionals working in these businesses also to be the caregivers during the adherence stage for nearly all chronic diseases. Doctors can be paid for diagnosing the chronic disease, evaluate its progression, and remediating the complications (when possible). But most health plans are really sickness plans, in that they will not pay for the cost that a doctor's office or hospital might incur to call patients between scheduled visits to monitor and encourage their adherence to the prescribed therapy. Insurance, for example, will pay for the amputation of a limb to treat diabetes-related gangrene, but not for the conscientious follow-through that can lessen the probability of needing such costly and tragic remediation. This is not the fault of physicians or insurers. The fault is in the misapplication of a business model that was designed for the practice of acute medicine long ago. As they are now organized, there simply is no way physicians' practices and hospitals can afford to help chronically ill patients during the period of adherence.

Consider the economics of caring for patients with asthma, one of the costliest chronic diseases, as summarized by George Halvorson, chairman and CEO of Kaiser Foundation Health Plan and Hospitals:

Run the numbers and look at the contrasts. Patients might pay a doctor $100 for an asthma prevention visit and another $200 for their inhaler prescription. An E.R. visit, on the other hand, can generate $2,000 to $4,000 in provider revenue, and a full-boat hospitalization could generate $10,000 to $40,000 in caregiver revenue. If money incents behavior, where are we as a society putting our money today? It's not in preventing asthma attacks—even though America is in an asthma epidemic.[17]

We need disease-appropriate business models to treat patients in the four situations depicted in Figure 5.3. The upper-left quadrant, comprised of technology-dependent diseases for which nonadherence to therapy has immediate consequences, has an easy answer. After diagnosis and prescription, doctors can be confident that patients will take their medication.[18] They simply must schedule periodic follow-up examinations to monitor patients' progress. They can get paid for this, as it fits the structure of a physician's practice, and they can do this job well. It is the patients in the other three quadrants who need new business models.

Patient Networks for Behavior-Dependent Diseases

A primary vehicle for care of patients with behavior-dependent diseases such as those on the right side of Figure 5.3 must be a facilitated network business model. As we described in Chapter 1, the essence of a facilitated network is that its participants exchange information or things with each other. Sometimes those things are bought and sold, as occurs in the networks facilitated by eBay and craigslist. In other instances, user-generated content is the material of exchange, as in YouTube's network. As a general rule, the companies that facilitate the networks make the money in this business model, while the users of these networks typically participate for other reasons.

Employing facilitated network business models to cost-effectively address behavior-dependent chronic diseases is not a new insight. Alcoholics Anonymous, for example, is a patient network within which the participants essentially exchange user-generated content. They teach each other how to overcome the disease of alcoholism, and they provide support for each other while doing so. Although most physicians have treated patients with acute symptoms of alcohol withdrawal, alcoholic liver disease, or alcohol poisoning, those same physicians often have little to add in the treatment of the underlying chronic disease. Another example is the host of weight loss networks. Though only modestly successful,[19] they are nonetheless focused on the challenge of bringing together people with the chronic disease of obesity and facilitating their interaction.

Many facilitated networks are organized by not-for-profit associations comprised of patients and their families, offering in-person and online support groups in which patients can help each other deal with the disease and find the best possible treatments. One example is the Web site dLife, a network of people with diabetes and their families. Through a weekly CNBC television program and an easy-to-navigate Web site, dLife enables community members to teach each other the "tricks of the trade"—helping and inspiring each other to do better.[20]—The Restless Legs Syndrome (RLS) Foundation, as another example, exists to help patients "learn about the latest treatments, and to arm themselves with information to *educate health care providers about RLS.*"[21] Funny, there was a time when the providers educated the patients! These networks are stepping into the breach where solution shops and value-adding process business models just can't viably provide care.[22]

We can expect patients in the upper-right quadrant—those who have behavior-dependent diseases with immediate consequences to nonadherence—to participate in these facilitated networks at their own volition. They are motivated to figure out better ways to live with their diseases. Not long ago, patients and their families networked as best they could, relying on doctors, friends, and family to introduce them to others with the same disease. Today, the Internet makes it much easier for patients with these diseases to find and connect with others in similar situations. Doctors still need to follow through periodically with these patients, of course, but until technological progress shifts the location of these diseases toward the left and bottom of the matrix, the objective should be to give patients the tools to care for themselves. Herodotus, the Greek historian who wrote *The History of the Persian Wars* in the fifth century BC (ca. 484 BC to 425 BC), observed what appears to have been a precursor to these sorts of networks during his travels through Babylonia:

The following custom seems to me the wisest of their institutions . . . They have no physicians, but when a man is ill, they lay him in the public square, and the passersby come up to him, and if they have ever had his disease themselves or have known anyone who has suffered from it, they give him advice, recommending him to do whatever they found good in their own case, or in the case known to them; and no one is allowed to pass the sick man in silence without asking him what his ailment is.[23]

Treating Diseases with Deferred Consequences

Care for chronically ill patients in the two bottom quadrants of Figure 5.3 needs to be overseen by entities that can profit from their patients' wellness, rather than profit from their sickness. This basically rules out all providers who work on a fee-for-service basis, because, as we noted earlier, there are no billing codes for wellness.

The entities that can profit by keeping patients well are those that provide all of the health care their members need, in exchange for a fixed annual fee. This insurance mechanism has acquired the unfortunate rubric of "capitation," because caregivers charge a fixed per capita annual fee. Capitation hasn't worked well in the nonintegrated health systems that provide care to 95 percent of all Americans,[24] because, as we'll discuss in greater detail in Chapter 7, it pits independent caregivers into a zero-sum, I-win-only-if-you-lose game. These independent providers aren't able to take a systemwide perspective on cost effectiveness. Capitation only can work in an integrated system where the insurer is also the provider.

There are two types of caregiving entities in which this insurance mechanism of capitation works. The first, which we'll call a "disease management network," is typified by Nashville, Tennessee–based Healthways, Inc., and by OptumHealth, a unit of UnitedHealth Group. Healthways and Optum take responsibility for the health of a "population" of patients with chronic diseases such as asthma, diabetes, obesity, and congestive heart failure.

Healthways employs nurse practitioners, who connect with each patient by phone at least weekly. The nurses collect data from the patients in order to monitor their progress in following the prescribed therapy. They teach patients how to care for and monitor themselves, and they work to tailor the therapy to each patient's situation. The data and details of each interaction are noted in Healthways' patient record system, so that the next week another nurse practitioner, if necessary, can call and interact with the patient and be fully informed, as if she had always been the one on the other end of the line. Major self-insured employers such as General Electric, Hewlett Packard, Caterpillar, and Federal Express have been primary drivers of the growth of disease management networks. They pay the network a fixed annual fee for the care of all of their patients who have certain costly, chronic diseases. To the extent that its oversight improves patients' health by helping and motivating them to adhere to their prescribed therapies, Healthways makes money. The company claims that its costs are significantly lower, and the outcomes much better, than for patients who are cared for in a fee-for-service world where money cannot be made by keeping people well. Healthways has been growing at 35 percent annually and now collects nearly $750 million in revenues, while covering 28.9 million lives.[25]

The other caregivers that can profit from patient wellness are integrated fixed-fee providers like Kaiser Permanente and Geisinger Health System. Providers like these own their own hospitals and clinics, employ their own doctors, and operate their own insurance companies.[26] Kaiser, for example, charges its members a fixed up-front monthly or annual fee for all of the care they might need—so it profits by keeping its members well. These integrated providers also profit by retaining members within their systems, which gives them the incentive to save costs by keeping their members well and satisfied with their care, not by restricting their access to care. Incidentally, Kaiser members are far less likely to switch plans than members of other health plans.[27]

In order for this business model to work effectively in keeping chronically ill patients free from the complications of their diseases, patients must be able to self-monitor (and often self-treat) their diseases using technological enablers. The potential for doing this is probably best developed for Type I diabetes care. Well-informed, proactive patients carry pocket-size blood glucose meters wherever they go; inject their own insulin, while adjusting the dose according to their recent glucose measurements; control the size and timing of their meals; and track their level of physical activity. All this monitoring and self-care allows them to develop individualized algorithms for controlling the levels of glucose in their blood. The interactions among diet, activity, and medication with patients' unique physical characteristics are not nearly understood well enough for physicians to articulate a rules-based regimen that will work for each individual patient—instead, the patients work it out for themselves.

Hypertension, hyperlipidemia, and congestive heart failure are other diseases in which affordable, convenient measurement equipment can be designed and made so patients can become their own primary caregivers, assisted and overseen by professionals in the disease management network business models described earlier.

We sense that the problem of adherence to prescribed therapy for disorders with deferred consequences will be mitigated, though not completely resolved, by putting care in the hands of providers whose economic model profits from wellness. The patients themselves need to be able to profit from wellness as well.

THE PERSONAL DRIVE TO ADHERE TO THERAPY

Nearly all health-care decisions that affect chronically ill patients are made by the patients themselves—out of the eyesight and earshot of their doctors. For example, doctors spend about two hours each year with their diabetic patients, but the patients spend 8,758 hours managing the disease on their own.[28] Even for those technology-dependent diseases in the lower left of Figure 5.2, the decision to take or not take prescribed medication is made by the patient. After all the caregivers can do, the efficacy of therapies for chronic diseases and the costliness of the complications from these diseases depends, in the end, on patients' motivation to adhere to courses of therapy that will prevent or delay the complications stemming from the disease.

For each of the major public health concerns in the Chronic Quadrangle at the lower right of Figure 5.3, we often know *what* needs to be done to reduce the cost and improve the care of patients with these diseases. Quit smoking. Lose weight. Maintain levels of blood glucose between 90 and 130 mg/dl. Keep LDL ("bad") cholesterol at or below 100 mg/dl. Use your steroid inhaler for asthma even on days when your breathing seems normal.[29] The question is: how can we help these patients become motivated to do what they know they should do?

Our research on the value of understanding the job that customers are trying to do, which we introduced in the discussion of business models in Chapter 1, offers some clues. To predict what actions people will prioritize, we need to watch what they *do*, because we are often misled when we listen to what they *say*.

Recall, for illustration, what life was like before digital photography. We took our roll of film to a store to be developed. Most of us chose to get double prints because the second one was almost free, and in case one of the prints turned out to be especially good, we wanted to be able to send that extra one to Grandma. When you picked the prints up, what did you do with them? You flipped through them and then put them back in the envelope, which you then put in a box or drawer. Ninety-eight percent of all photos that were taken have only ever been looked at *once*. Only the most conscientious people took the trouble to mount the most memorable photos in an album to look at again. The rest of us knew that we should, but we just didn't—

or we planned to start tomorrow. Market researchers learned from speaking with consumers that many of them *wanted* to start keeping photo albums. But if you watched what people *did*, it was very different than what they *said* they wanted to do.

When digital cameras emerged to disrupt film photography, companies offered several value propositions to camera users, based on this market research. One was, "You can click 'attach' and e-mail photos to friends and family whenever something interesting or important happens!" Another was: "If you'll just take the time to learn how to upload these photos, you can edit the red eye out of all those pictures that you used to look at only once!" A third proposition was: "You can keep all those images in this online scrapbook that makes it easy to sort, search, and print from your gallery of thousands of photos!"

If you watch what most digital camera users actually do, *very few of them* have learned to use photo editing software; and even fewer keep online photo albums. Why? These just weren't things that had been priorities in their lives before the new technology arrived. The feature that most digital camera users actually use is the facility for e-mailing images to family and friends. Why? Because that is the same job we were trying to do when we ordered double prints. An innovation that makes it easier and cheaper for people to do what they're already *trying* to do is called a "killer app."[30] An innovation that makes it easier and cheaper for people to do what they're *not* trying to do, in contrast, faces a struggle for success akin to an uphill death march through knee-deep mud—and then it typically fails.

People who don't *want* to do something that they know they *should* do have marvelously inventive abilities to ignore what they know. They resolve to start tomorrow, or conclude that it's okay if they just don't do it. We rationalize the rules to comply with our desired behavior. Marketers in *every* industry confront this reality: consumers demonstrate daily the propensity to prioritize what they *want* to accomplish, not what they are told they *should* accomplish. College students *should* be motivated to expand their learning by delving into the online expansions of their textbooks.

Drivers *should* obey speed limits, for their own good. But they don't. It's human behavior, not the behavior of diabetics, smokers, and the obese, that we're dealing with. Most of us are frightfully guilty of believing we don't need to follow certain rules that are demonstrably important for everyone else to follow.

One of the reasons why the jobs-to-be-done concept is proving so powerful in directing successful innovation within so many companies is that it gets directly at the *cause* of action. The fact that someone is in a particular demographic segment is often *correlated* with a propensity to buy certain products and not others, but what *causes* the purchase is that the customer has a job that needs to be done. Similarly, the fact that someone has Type II diabetes and is overweight might be *correlated* with tendencies to adhere or not adhere to recommended therapies. But what *causes* adherence is the need to do a job.

So what is the job that most noncompliant patients who suffer from obesity, Type II diabetes, heart disease, and tobacco addiction are really trying to do? They just don't want to have the disease. "I feel fine today and I'll feel fine tomorrow, so I just don't want to think about it." *Maintaining* health is a job that only a minority of people prioritize in their lives. *For the rest, becoming healthy only becomes a priority job after they become sick.* This is a key observation. In some ways it is tautological. Most patients for whom the "I want to become and remain healthy" job is important have kept themselves *out* of these chronic diseases. Or if they got the disease, they quit smoking, lost weight, and got the requisite cardiovascular exercise. Even when the genetic endowment of some of these patients makes it impossible to lose the weight that might put Type II diabetes into remission, for example, the patients who have the "become and remain healthy" job assiduously monitor and control their blood glucose so that complications don't happen.

Employees' Job-to-Be-Done

It turns out that for most people who have chronic diseases with deferred consequences, "improve my financial health" is a much more pervasively experienced job than "maintain my physical health."

An executive of one of America's largest companies reflected with us a short time ago about her frustrations in reigning in her company's health-care costs. "We set up several different wellness programs offering fitness club memberships to our employees at a 50 percent discount to give them an incentive to lose weight and become and remain fit. A couple of years into the program, we looked at which employees were using the benefit. Less than 15 percent of the total had enrolled, and *almost all of these were people who already were in good physical condition.* Few of those we had targeted—those with or at risk of developing diabetes and heart disease—took advantage of the benefit."

This company offered a 401(k) retirement plan as another benefit. The company matched employees' contributions to their 401(k) account dollar-for-dollar. We asked this executive what portion of her employees were enrolled in and actively contributing to their 401(k) savings plans. "Over 70 percent," was her reply. "It sure seems like people care a lot more about their financial health than their physical health."

This executive's observations are typical. Many of those with or at risk of developing obesity, Type II diabetes, tobacco addiction, and heart disease are actively working to assure their long-range financial prosperity. Seventy-two percent of Americans contribute to a 401(k) account.[31] A large and growing number of people monitor and proactively manage their FICO,[32] or credit scores. They pay their bills on time, constrain their debts, and manage the other variables in the equation that determines this score, in order to preserve the option of borrowing affordably in the future.

An important implication of this behavior is that for diseases with deferred consequences, a system that makes adherence to therapies a vehicle for getting the "financial health" job done will be more successful in reducing the costs and tragic complications of these diseases than traditional "wellness" programs. Systems such as health savings accounts (HSAs) make the pursuit of health a mechanism for accomplishing the pursuit of wealth.[33]

The present systems of Medicare and employer-paid health care actually *decouple* patients' health from the job of ensuring long-range financial prosperity. For example, patients with diabetes are supposed to test their blood glucose regularly. At a price of over a dollar for each test strip, this self-monitoring can cost up to $1,500 per year. It actually costs less than ten cents apiece to make these strips.[34] The major retailers of diabetes supplies such as CVS, Wal-Mart, and Liberty years ago began selling their own brand of glucose meters, with test strips priced at less than half those of name-brand strips.[35] But the store-brand tests have gained only modest traction in the market because patients covered by conventional reimbursement plans experience little cost difference.

Currently, when patients fail to adhere to prescribed therapy for diseases in the Chronic Quadrangle of Figure 5.3, there are no immediate consequences for physical *or* financial health. In the short term, nonadherence in this category has little effect on physical well-being, nor does the rigor by which patients strive to cure themselves or manage their diseases more cost-effectively impact their short-term trajectory of asset accumulation. And the long-term trajectory isn't affected either, because insurance and Medicare will step in to cover the very high costs of complications that result from nonadherence.

At present, a range of regulations forbid employers or insurers from differentially pricing the cost of health coverage for those employees who, because of genetic predisposition or behavioral choices, have these diseases and are not complying with pre-scribed therapy. Interestingly, we allow life insurers to price dif-ferently, based upon risks associated with various diseases their customers have. Disability insurance can also be differentially priced. We price loans differently, as well, based upon customers' financial behaviors, fortunes, and misfortunes. As we'll describe in Chapter 11, we need to change these regulations so that improving adherence improves *financial* health, not just *physical* health.[36]

Here's one possible mechanism for doing this: just as several companies are constantly keeping our credit scores up to date by collecting data on all of our debts and the extent to which we pay our bills on time, other companies, like Ingenix, have been calculating a *health score* for each of us.[37] They reach into the databases of pharmacy benefit managers and compile a complete record of all the prescriptions each of us gets filled. They therefore have a very good sense about most of the acute and chronic diseases we've had, and, using those profiles, they've developed algorithms to predict the costs of insuring each of us and our families in the future.

Until now, Ingenix has only made our health scores available to insurers like Blue Cross/Blue Shield, which then use those scores to price the health insurance policies they sell to employers. It would be a small step for Ingenix to begin sending each of us our updated health score every six months. They could send this score through the same firm, such as Fidelity, that is already handling our 401(k) and health savings accounts. Such a statement could include predictions of what our HSA account balances will be in the future if we maintain our current health scores and if we and our employers continue to contribute to our HSAs at historical rates. The statement could also estimate for us how the projected balance in our HSAs could be increased if we improved our health scores—and it could show us which behaviors and components of our health scores will have the greatest leverage.

Each employee HSA will have an insurance policy against catastrophic illness packaged with it.[38] Because health scores are used today to calculate the costs of reimbursement and insurance coverage for each of us, a system such as this would simply make the calculations explicit. If a person's health score is low enough so the projected future cost of catastrophic insurance will increase, the employer's contribution to the employee's HSA might drop and be diverted to pay for insuring against the increased cost of long-term complications.

A system such as this—one that aligns physical health with financial health—is essential to developing viable business models to care for the chronically ill. In the past, some have objected to such propositions on fairness grounds. The argument essentially is that because to some degree our health might be determined by things beyond our control, those who became sick through no fault of their own should not have to pay a higher price for their health coverage. We would argue in return that with literally every other type of insurance—life, disability, home, and auto—society already has agreed that people can and should pay different rates based upon their experience—whether it was their fault or that of others. We predict that despite all of the predictable, self-protecting rhetoric around this issue, people will actually adjust to this policy quite readily.

Employers' Job-to-Be-Done: Managing the Handoff Between Diagnosis and Adherence

A key tenet of this chapter is that the business of diagnosing the disease and recommending a therapy is very different than the business of assuring day-to-day adherence to the behavior and medications that were prescribed. Because the business models are so different, different caregivers must provide each piece of the complete package of care for chronic disease—which means there is a big handoff between the two. Some entity needs to be sure that patients don't fall through this crack.

Though we treat this topic more thoroughly in the next chapter, we'll note here that employers are critical players to enroll in the fight against chronic disease, and need to play an active role to ensure that their employees don't fall into the chasm between these providers. A critical job that employers always need to do is attract and retain the best possible employees, and make those employees as productive as possible.

When you listen to what employers *say*, most sound eager to get out of the business of funding health care for employees and their families. But if you watch what employers *do*, they spend thousands of dollars per employee every year, and invest an extraordinary amount of managerial attention to attract, train, improve, and retain their employees. We expect, as a result, that employers will take an increasingly active role in managing the quality and cost of employee health care—especially chronic diseases—because they profit from productive employees. In the past, because they haven't known what else to do, many employers have simply been shifting costs to their employees. We hope to show through this book that health-care cost isn't a variable determined exogenously to our system. It is caused by our system; and as the next chapter shows, proactive executives can profoundly influence those costs and service quality.

We hope that the sections above have laid bare the basic parameters for how care for chronic disease must change. Diagnosing these diseases and defining the most effective therapy possible is a very different business than ensuring day-to-day adherence to the recommended course of action. The same chronically ill patient needs to be served by two fundamentally different business models.

A significant portion of the cost of caring for chronic disease arises because the patients have been misdiagnosed and treated with medications that are not effective for them. Although some of these misdiagnoses can be traced to actual medical error, for many others the culprit is *business model error*. Because so many of these diseases arise at a multiavenue intersection of several different systems of the body in the realm of intuitive medicine, a single specialist often will not have the perspective required to get the right answer. Simply passing the patient off to another subspecialist with a comparably specialized perspective doesn't solve the problem of interdependencies. It's not the doctors' fault. It's the fault of the business models in which they've been asked to work. Many more need to do what a few of our leading medical centers already have done: create coherent (as opposed to disjointed) solution shops whose job is to diagnose and devise effective therapy for patients with intuitive chronic diseases.

Patients whose therapy is behavior-dependent need help to figure out what to do and how to do it. From at least as early as Herodotus, to Alcoholics Anonymous in our day, network business models have a proven track record as the best of the three types in getting this job done. The Internet makes it infinitely easier for patients with these diseases to find "someone like me," who can inspire and coach others from personal experience.

In the past, the physicians' practices that by default were the ones we've counted on to police adherence to prescribed therapy weren't motivated to do it, because they simply couldn't make money doing it—and professionals cannot survive doing what they don't get paid to do. We know of two business models that can make money by keeping patients healthy: disease management companies like OptumHealth and Healthways, and integrated fixed-fee provider companies like Kaiser Permanente and Geisinger.

The fact that these (and the few others like them) care for only a fraction of patients with diseases whose consequences are deferred means there is an extraordinary opportunity for employers and insurers to guide more of their employees and members who need this type of oversight into the reach of the businesses that can provide it. And the fact that many of those with behavior-dependent diseases, whose consequences are deferred, care more about financial than physical health, merits addressing, not denial, by those who would do good among the massive population of patients with these diseases.

NOTES

1. While some who study these problems make a distinction between chronic diseases and chronic conditions, for purposes of brevity we'll refer to both conditions and diseases as diseases.
2. Halvorson, George, *Health Care Reform Now! A Prescription for Change* (San Francisco: Jossey Bass, 2007), 4.
3. This means, of course, that the aging populations in most economically developed countries will cause health-care costs to balloon even more in the future.
4. Indeed, while much of modern health care is lifesaving and life-prolonging, it often is not yet a complete cure—making lifelong treatment necessary. But the technological progress that makes this possible, which is so welcome in the developed world, creates huge new problems in impoverished nations. There, the technologies that transform acute, fatal diseases into chronic ones, while welcome at the personal level, can spell financial disaster to government health ministries that simply do not have the resources to prolong the lives of so many more sick people.

5. See Centers for Medicare and Medicaid Services, "HCPCS Release and Code Sets Overview;" American Medical Association, "CPT (Current Procedural Terminology);" and "Relative Value Units and Related Information Used for Medicare Billing," Federal Register, Nov. 15, 2004.

6. See Christensen, Clayton, and Paul Carlile, "The Cycles of Theory Building in Management Research," Harvard Business School Working Paper Series, no. 05-057, 2005.

7. Some diseases, like depression and schizophrenia, have lagged behind most other chronic diseases in research funding, for example, and in many aspects are still poorly understood. Other conditions, like chronic back pain and dementia, remain quite imprecisely defined with fuzzy diagnostic criteria, and therefore demand a more intuitive approach than a simple chronic disease like myopia (nearsightedness). Other diseases, like prostate cancer, may be simpler to diagnose, but involve competing treatment options. Finally, some diseases, like lupus, are inherently complex because they can affect multiple organ systems at different times.

8. The Institute of Medicine estimated that $17 to $29 billion annually is spent unnecessarily, and between 44,000 and 90,000 people are killed each year as a result of misdiagnosis and preventable medical errors. These figures include diagnostic errors for acute care as well, but do not include the substantial malpractice costs involved in many cases.

9. The extent of behavioral change required, and the degree to which the intuition of patients and family members needs to guide those behavioral changes, in theory are two different variables. We feel that the correlation of the two constructs is close enough that, for simplicity, we've chosen to map them on the same axis, as if they were one variable constructed from two highly correlated ones.

10. Interventions can also include surgical procedures and devices, probably the best examples of "set it and forget it" treatments for chronic disease. However, the scope of these interventions has been limited primarily to conditions rooted in anatomical and mechanical defects. In addition, there are other chronic diseases for which treatment options are extremely limited and behavior changes have little impact, such as Huntington's disease or Amyotrophic Lateral Sclerosis (Lou Gehrig's disease). Our discussion in this chapter will focus on the management of chronic diseases through medications.

11. A Cuban doctor, Juan Carlos Finlay, seems to have been the first to assert that mosquitoes were the perpetrators of yellow fever. To test this idea, several members of Walter Reed's team, based near Havana, allowed themselves to be bitten—and one of Reed's top deputies, Jesse W. Lazear, actually fell sick and died. Further research convinced Reed that the disease was spread by mosquitoes sucking the blood of people victimized by yellow fever and then biting others. These brave volunteers were essential to Reed's work. Major Reed took what was then the unusual step of securing each man's informed consent— the volunteers understood that by participating in his research they risked contracting yellow fever. To advance science, they flirted with death. Mortality rates fluctuated from outbreak to outbreak, but generally about 20 percent of those who contracted yellow fever could expect to die from it. The volunteers' courage is perhaps best embodied in the words of Private William Dean of Lucas, Ohio, who insisted that he wasn't "afraid of any little old gnat." Dean became the first man to let an infected mosquito bite him. He developed yellow fever and recovered.

12. Dr. Warren and his colleague Dr. Barry Marshall were awarded a Nobel Prize in 2005 for this discovery. As an aside, their initial announcement was greeted with disdain by the

world community of gastrointestinal specialists. Thomas Kuhn chronicled in his 1962 classic, *The Structure of Scientific Revolutions*, 1st ed. (Chicago: University of Chicago Press) that the insights that lead to the toppling of incorrect or incomplete scientific paradigms rarely come from within the discipline of most experts in the reigning theory. Almost always, insights leading to the breakthrough come from an outsider, because typically you need to view an old problem from a new angle in order to see different things. In the case of ulcers, it took well over a decade after Warren and Marshall's discovery before the mainstream gastrointestinal community accepted these findings and began treating ulcers with antibiotics. In terms of our model in Chapter 1, the diagnosis and treatment of duodenal and gastric ulcers has advanced significantly along the spectrum from intuitive to precision medicine. We will return to Kuhn's insights about scientific research in Chapter 11.

13. Because these diseases are defined historically by symptom rather than cause, Tysabri (developed at Elan Pharmaceuticals and marketed in the United States by Biogen-Idec) was tested in clinical trials and approved initially as a multiple sclerosis drug. FDA rules required an entirely new set of trials for Tysabri to be approved for on-label treatment of Crohn's. See Honey, K., "The Comeback Kid: TYSABRI Now FDA Approved for Crohn disease," *Journal of Clinical Investigation*, March 2008; 118(3):825–26. With continued scientific progress, we can expect that not all patients diagnosed with multiple sclerosis and Crohn's will respond to Tysabri, and that still more precise diagnostics will need to emerge.

14. In many ways, cholesterol-lowering drugs are a disruptive innovation relative to angioplasty, just as angioplasty was a disruptive innovation relative to open heart surgery.

15. One reason so much progress was made so rapidly in AIDS is that it was quickly found to be an infectious disease. A history of successful innovations in the world of infectious diseases has given us processes, paradigms, and an entire infrastructure that could be leveraged in the AIDS effort. A key reason why AIDS and malaria—another horrific disease—have defied curative solutions is that the organisms that cause the diseases mutate and evolve faster than science can keep up with them. If history is any guide (as was the case with ulcers), it is quite likely that the resolution to these problems will come from outside the discipline of infectious diseases and immunology.

16. Indeed, some would argue that bariatric surgery has the potential to transform some diseases that we now lump under the rubric of obesity and diabetes into a disorder whose primary symptom can be made to disappear.

17. Halvorson, George, *Health Care Reform Now! A Prescription for Change* (San Francisco: Jossey Bass, 2007), 109.

18. Of course, there are still socioeconomic and educational barriers that can impede therapy, in which case facilitated networks can play a more important role. We will again address some of these barriers that disproportionately affect the uninsured poor in our chapters on reimbursement and regulation.

19. Dansinger, Michael L., et al., "Comparison of the Atkins, Ornish, Weight Watchers, and Zone Diets for Weight Loss and Heart Disease Risk Reduction," *Journal of the American Medical Association*, 2005; 293:43–53. Although overall patient adherence rates to dietary recommendations were low, each diet program in the study demonstrated modest reductions in body weight and cardiac risk factors after one year.

20. O'Meara, Sean, "Diabetes Education Goes Multimedia," *Nurses World*, April/May 2007. Newsletters, recipes, forums, a national weekly television show and radio station, and

online educator-customized interactive tools for providers and patients can be accessed at http://www.dlife.com.

21. Quote taken from the Restless Legs Syndrome Foundation home page, accessed at http://www.rls.org on March 24, 2008.

22. To be sure, not all of these emerging networks are created equal. Whether their recommendations are in the tradition of mainstream medical science or rooted in alternative medicine, some of these Web sites advocate solutions that have no grounding in well-designed research. In every industry at the outset, great value is created by entrepreneurs who create a "portal," with an assurance that once you walk through that portal, what you find inside will be of a quality that you can trust. For example, Sears, Roebuck and Company did this for mass-produced goods as those products first emerged. There were few product brands that people knew and could trust, but you knew if it passed muster in the Sears purchasing process, it had to be good: Sears guaranteed it. For this reason, we would expect that "portals" such as WebMD will play critical roles in validating the trustworthiness of these networks. Over time, some of the Web sites and networks will develop adequate brand reputations of their own so that they can stand alone.

23. Herodotus, *The Histories* (c.430 BC), I:197.

24. Estimate from Lawrence, David, "Gatekeeping Reconsidered," *New England Journal of Medicine*, vol. 345 (18):1342–43.

25. This information comes from Clayton Christensen's personal interviews with company executives, as well as Healthways Investor Presentation, June 19, 2008, accessed at http://media.corporate-ir.net/media_files/irol/91/91592/HWAYInvestor_Presentation_06_19_08(1).pdf.

26. There can be multiple entities involved due to regulations. For example, Kaiser Permanente is actually comprised of several organizations, including Kaiser Foundation Health Plan, Kaiser Foundation Hospitals, and a for-profit Medical Group—however, they are tightly aligned and cooperate within a "closed network."

27. See Rainwater, J; P. S. Romano; and J. S. Garcia, "Switching Health Plans and the Role of Perceived Quality of Care, *Abstr AcademyHealth Meet.*, 2005; 22: abstract no. 4232. The switching rate of Kaiser members was 1.0 percent, versus 11.1 percent for members of other HMOs.

28. Demchak, Cyanne, "Choice in Medical Care: When Should the Consumer Decide?" AcademyHealth issue brief, October 2007. Accessed at http://www.academyhealth.org/issues/ConsumerDecide.pdf.

29. These recommendations can differ, of course, depending on the chronic disease involved and its severity.

30. Killer App is a term popularized by Downes, Larry, and Chunka Mui, *Unleashing the Killer App* (Boston, Massachusetts: Harvard Business School Press, 2000).

31. See "American Express National Survey Finds Multiple and Duplicate Retirement Accounts Pervasive; Benefits of Consolidation, Real Diversification Not Understood by Most Americans," *Business Wire*, Feb. 9, 2004.

32. FICO is a credit score calculated according to a formula devised by Fair Isaac Corporation.

33. Covel, Simona, "High Deductible Policies Offer Savings to Firm and Its Workers," *Wall Street Journal*, April 9, 2007, B4.

34. "Test Strip Reveals a Big Profit Motive," *Los Angeles Times*, November 7, 2007.

35. Mendosa, Rick, "Stripping Down the Cost of Testing," *DiabetesHealth*, June 1, 2004.

36. As we'll discuss in Chapters 6 and 7, some creative employers and insurers have started to employ this concept already, often testing the legal system in the process. In September 2008 the state of Alabama announced that it would begin charging additional premiums to employees who failed to undergo screenings for health risk factors and, for those found to be at higher risk, failed to see a doctor free of charge to discuss those risk factors. See http://www.cnn.com/2008/HEALTH/diet.fitness/09/19/alabama.obesity.insurance/index.html.

37. Ingenix is a unit of UnitedHealth Group.

38. As we will discuss in Chapter 7, HSAs are required by law to be paired with high-deductible, catastrophic insurance.

Chapter 6

Integrating to Make It Happen

"At the end of the day, the only reasonable conclusion is that
we waste a huge amount of money on the most nuttily
cumbersome administrative system in the world."

— Henry Aaron, Brookings Institution economist,
writing about the U.S. health-care system.[1]

As we've wrestled in our research with the challenges of making health care higher in quality, lower in cost, and more conveniently accessible, it has become quite clear what needs to be done. The basic problem is not unique to health care: improving quality, cost, and accessibility has been an issue in the history of many industries. In each of these other cases, it was disruptive innovation that transformed expensive, complicated products and services into simple and affordable ones. This has consistently required three enablers—technological, business model, and a value network—which is the case in health care too.

The technological enabler is the ability to diagnose diseases more precisely by cause—an achievement that generally is a prerequisite to developing predictably effective, rules-based therapies. Then, as we discussed in Chapters 3, 4, and 5, we need disruptive business model innovations that can take the simplified solutions cost-effectively to market. Initially this will come from disaggregating the work of hospitals and physicians' practices into coherent solution shops and value-adding process clinics, and by relying on patient and disease management networks in which patients and providers can profit from wellness and the care of many chronic diseases. Disruption will then continue within each of these categories, as lower-cost venues of care and lower-cost caregivers become more capable.

These disruptive changes are no small order. Who in the world is going to pull all of this off? The answer lies in the third enabler of disruption, which we call a value network—the context in which new methods coalesce to govern interaction and coordination among the new disruptive actors in the system. What value networks are, how new ones emerge in industries that are being disrupted, and how to make it happen in health care are the topics of this chapter.

VALUE NETWORKS AND DISRUPTION

A value network is the context within which a firm establishes its business model, and how it works with suppliers and channel partners or distributors so that together they can respond profitably to the common needs of a class of customers.[2] The business models of each of the firms in a value network tend to be consistent with those of the other firms in the system—firms from whom they buy and to whom they sell. Together, their business models determine their perceptions of the economic value of various innovations, shaping the rewards and threats they expect to experience through disruptive and sustaining innovations.

An example we mentioned briefly in Chapter 1 that illustrates the role of value networks in disruption occurred in the consumer electronics industry between 1955 and 1975. Until the early

1970s, most radios and televisions were made with expensive and power-hungry devices called vacuum tubes, which were about as big as a child's fist. These products were made by the giants of the electronics industry at the time—including Radio Corporation of America (RCA), General Electric, Westinghouse, Motorola, Zenith, and Philco. Vacuum tube TVs and radios were bulky and expensive, and they were sold primarily through appliance stores—which made much of their money by sending repairmen into their customers' homes to replace burned-out vacuum tubes in the products they had sold in prior years. For most people, it seemed that a tube burned out and disabled their TVs once or twice each year.

As depicted in Figure 6.1, Sony began disrupting the vacuum tube TV and radio companies in the late 1950s and early 1960s when it introduced its transistor, or solid-state, pocket radios and small portable televisions. A classic example of disruption, Sony's products weren't nearly as good as RCA's vacuum-tube-based products. But they were so affordable that a whole new population of people, who in the past hadn't had big enough wallets or apartments to own big RCA products, now could have a radio and a TV. At the beginning, Sony tried to get distribution through appliance stores too—because that was the channel through which almost all of the industry's products were sold. But Sony couldn't get the time of day from appliance stores. Sony's price points, and the gross margin dollars that could be earned per unit sold, were far too low. What was worse, Sony's solid-state products contained no vacuum tubes that would burn out, so the appliance stores couldn't make money repairing them.

Luckily for Sony, however, discount retailers like Kmart and Wal-Mart were emerging at about the same time. These retailers hadn't been able to sell vacuum tube TVs because their price points were far above the range of other products sold in those stores at that time, and the discounters lacked the expertise to service them in the aftermarket. Sony's products were a great fit for discount retailers: low-cost products that needed little

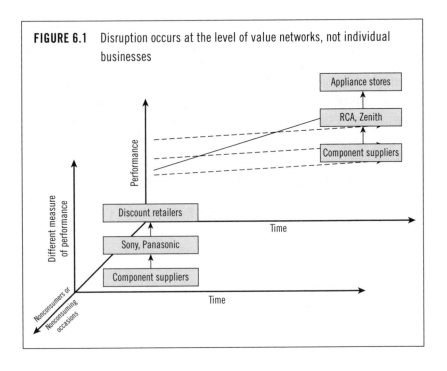

FIGURE 6.1 Disruption occurs at the level of value networks, not individual businesses

service, married with a low-cost channel that couldn't provide service. The disruptive competition at that time in the consumer electronics industry, in other words, wasn't simply between RCA and Sony.

By the late 1960s, when solid-state electronics had improved to the point at which large TVs could be made with transistors, it wasn't just Sony that disrupted RCA. An entire value network—ranging from component suppliers to the retailers who faced the customer—disrupted the entire old value network. Each of these value networks was internally coherent in terms of technologies and business models. You couldn't just do a single-point hot-swap of Sony for RCA into the original value network, because of the technological and economic interdependence that spanned the materials and components suppliers, designers, assemblers, distributors, and retailers in the original system.

The Co-opting Power of the Present Value Network in Health Care

When disruptive innovators attempt to commercialize their innovations within the established value network in their industry—essentially trying to cram it into the back plane of competition in Figure 6.1—that system will either reject it (as it did with Sony's transistorized products) or co-opt the potential disruption, forcing it to conform to the existing value network in order to survive.

To visualize this, imagine you are a member of Congress and you've developed a brilliant idea for a government program that will resolve a pressing social problem. You draft the proposal and introduce the bill into the legislative process. A few weeks later you get a letter from relevant labor unions putting you on notice that they will oppose your program unless you remove certain provisions and add others. Because their support is critical, you change your bill to win labor's support. A month later you get a letter from the senior senator from Texas, chairman of the committee that needs to approve your bill, asserting that unless you remove certain provisions and add others that make it economically attractive to his state, he won't even schedule hearings on your bill. So you change it to accommodate Texas. And then you get a visit from the Republican whip, who pledges to orchestrate a filibuster against your bill unless you remove certain provisions, and add others to make it attractive to business. Your bill ultimately becomes law—but the program that emerged from the legislative process was very different from the one you had conceived. In order to win the support of the powerful entities that could block your innovation, you had to shape and morph your idea to conform to what they needed. We're not saying that this is bad or good. It's just the way the process works.

The very same "legislative" process is at work within every company, and within the value networks in which each company is ensconced. Imagine that you get a compelling idea for an innovative new product that will address a pressing need for a large group of potential customers. To get it funded, you must draft a business plan for the new product and introduce it into your company's resource allocation process. Within a few weeks you get a call from the engineering manager, who says she likes the concept but objects to your plan to procure uniquely designed components from new suppliers. Unless you agree to use the design of several components that the company's existing suppliers already are providing for other products at high volumes and attractive prices, she says, she just can't support it. So you compromise, even though the product's performance will suffer.

Then you get a cryptic e-mail from the chief financial officer, which says, "You don't seem to be aware that our company has a five-year financial plan. This product idea of yours doesn't help us achieve the numbers in the plan. It's *got* to generate 45 percent gross margins. Then maybe I can support it. Otherwise, there are more important fish to fry." So you revisit the functions and features of the machine to sustain the pricing needed to yield the margins needed to sustain the plan, and the CFO then jumps aboard.

Finally, the sales manager stops by. "I got a copy of this business plan. This might be a great idea for somebody else—but not for us," he says. "The customers you're targeting? Our salespeople just don't have relationships with them, and you can't expect them to develop a set of completely different contacts to push this one product. And with the incentive compensation system we adopted last year, we just can't sell this product. Unless you refocus on what *our* customers need, and create more room in the pricing for special sales compensation, I just can't support this." Because nothing goes anywhere if the sales force isn't behind it, you make the changes in your plan.

Ultimately, your idea gets funded. What got approved, however, is a very different product than the one you conceived. The power of the entities whose support you needed in order to get funded is so strong that you had to shape and morph your product into something that *fits the business model of the company*, not *the market opportunity you had originally foreseen*. And therein lies the rub. If your idea doesn't fit the business model of the company, the system will either reject your idea or change your product until it fits the business model and the value network in which your company is ensconced. We're not saying this is bad or good. It's just the way the world works.

The executives of many companies stand at the end of the product development process, and, seeing me-too product after me-too product dribbling out the end of the "pipe" year after year, they shout out to the people at the beginning of the process, demanding, "Be creative! We need more creativity!" They don't realize that a lack of creative product ideas isn't the problem. The root of the problem is their *own* inability or disinclination to create new business models matching the needs in the market.

When introducing new products or services, it almost always seems less expensive to utilize the business models in the existing value network as the vehicle for commercialization, instead of creating new business models. For sustaining innovations, using the existing system is the right thing to do. But for disruptions, it spells suicide. The seeming savings in cost and time of reusing what you have are illusory.[3] These are "nested" systems. Creating an appropriate business model is essential to making disruptive innovations successful. And creating an appropriate value network is critical to making disruptive business models successful.

The Current Value Network in Health Care

A thorough description of today's dominant value network in health care would itself be a book-length undertaking. However, it has several core features. Most physicians are independent, for-profit businesspeople, working as solo practitioners or in partnerships. The hospitals at which doctors have "privileges" are managed independently of the doctors' businesses. Many are part of multihospital companies. Whether they are for-profit or not-for-profit is a salient distinction only for the tax authorities. Both need to earn a surplus of revenues over expenses. The doctors and nurses working in this value network are certified to do so by the professional associations to which they themselves belong. And they were trained in schools of medicine and nursing that are accredited by their own associations of medical and nursing schools. Third parties—employers, insurers, and the government—pay for the lion's share of the health care that we consume.

The mechanism that governs how these players act and interact is reimbursement. As we'll explore in greater depth in Chapter 7, the formulas that Medicare and health plans use to determine the prices they will pay, in essence determine which products and services are profitable and which are not. Providers cannot persist doing things that cannot make money, and will predictably do more of the things that will make them a lot of money. As a result, reimbursement ends up being an ever-present mechanism of regulation, by and large inadvertently—making it even more challenging for health-care reformers to deal with.

Employers generally establish blanket contracts—renewable annually—with one or two health plans from companies such as UnitedHealth and Blue Cross/Blue Shield (BCBS) to provide health coverage for their current (and often retired) employees and their families. In order to get the best pricing leverage, the health plans in turn negotiate blanket contracts with the major hospital operators in their regions, offering to route members of their plans to those hospitals in exchange for volume discounts for the full range of services that would be required by the covered members. The health plans also establish contracts with physicians' practices, in which physicians agree to refer patients to other physicians and hospitals within the health plan's network whenever possible—all in exchange for the most advantageous pricing possible.

Because most patients who do not otherwise qualify for government-sponsored programs like Medicare and Medicaid are covered by one of these plans, the effect is that health care offered to patients outside of these plans must be priced very high, in order for the plans to create economic benefit for employers who are paying for health care.

This system of blanket contracting throughout the supply chain creates an interdependent, mutually reinforcing bond among the actors in the existing value network, and it makes opportunities outside the network less attractive for all of them. Ironically, it funnels volume to the highest-cost business models—the general hospitals—because they have the scope to win blanket contracts. Rather than opening them up to disruption, the system sustains these hospitals, keeping them as full as possible. This tight inter-dependency is a characteristic of all value networks—which is a key reason why, when disruption occurs, it invariably entails creating a new value network.

Many disruptive technological enablers are emerging every year, so that care can shift from the realm of intuitive medicine toward the practice of empirical and precision medicine. And disruptive business models are emerging too—in the form of coherent solution shops, focused value-adding process clinics, personal health records, networks to assist in the care of chronic diseases, and health savings accounts (which we'll discuss in Chapter 7). But our sense is that the entrepreneurs behind these innovative business models typically have tried to plug them into the existing value network—and as a result their disruptive potential has largely been co-opted by the current system. Until a powerful player with sufficient scale and scope journeys up the waterway to create a new value network in which the disruptive entities can combine to form a new system, health care will remain expensive for all, and inaccessible to many, for a very long time.

INNOVATIVE INCAPACITIES OF NONINTEGRATED SYSTEMS

Who can pull this off? A good way to visualize what kinds of entities might and might not be able to create a new disruptive value network is to unscrew the cover of your desktop or notebook computer and look at the components from which it was built. Each part was made by a different company. In all likelihood, Microsoft built the operating system, and Intel made the processor. Seagate probably made the disk drive, and Samsung the flash memory. Nvidia likely made the graphics chip, while the DRAM chips came from Micron or Samsung. Sharp makes most flat-panel screens, and though the brand was likely supplied by

Dell, Hewlett-Packard or Lenovo, it was assembled in Asia by Quanta, Flextronics, or ASUSTeK.

The good news about an industry like personal computers, whose product architectures are mature and modular and whose companies are focused, is that each one of these companies can get very good at what it does. Little overhead cost is incurred coordinating among the companies that make the components, because coordination is accomplished through standardized interfaces. The bad news about an "open" architecture like this, however, is that if the fundamental architecture of the product needs to be reconceived, it cannot be done within the existing industry's structure. In computers, Microsoft can give us a better operating system, Intel can improve the processor, Seagate can give us more gigabytes on the disk drive, Sharp more mega-pixels on the screen, and Flextronics can assemble the parts more efficiently. But none of these companies today has the scope to design—and implement—a fundamentally different architecture of the common PC.[4]

Most of the health-care industry is as dis-integrated and spe-cialized as the personal computer industry—and this means that most of the current actors in the health-care industry lack the scale and scope to create a new system architecture.[5] Our hospitals can figure out how to maximize utilization of their operating suites, insurance companies can improve the efficiency with which they process claims, drug companies can minimize the cost and duration of their clinical trials for new drugs, and physicians can try to see more patients per hour. But often these actors are stymied in carrying out improvements because their actions work at cross-purposes. By and large, caregivers make more money by providing more services that elicit higher prices, but insurance companies make money by reducing medical loss ratios through discounting or denying payment. Drug companies make money with patented, proprietary drugs, but employers want more low-cost, generic drugs to be used. Only a few players in today's health-care industry have the scale and scope to restructure a dis-ruptive value network.

POTENTIAL INTEGRATORS

So if most of the current actors can't assemble a new disruptive value network, to whom might we turn? Let's look first at the criteria by which we should evaluate the candidates. The ideal entity that puts together the disruptive value network is one whose dominant profit formula makes money by keeping us healthy, not just by making us well. It must be one whose tenure with us is long enough that it would be willing to spend more now, when necessary, in order to save even higher costs down the road. It must be a system whose participants are motivated to spend what is needed—so that neither money nor health is wasted. And it must be capable of acting with considerable speed.

We've arrayed some potential change agents in Figure 6.2. For reasons we hope will be clear by the end of this chapter, we've concluded that waiting for a population of independent entrepreneurs to piece together the new system, or asking most gov-

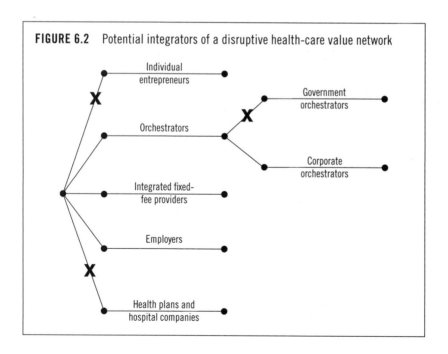

FIGURE 6.2   Potential integrators of a disruptive health-care value network

ernments to orchestrate the needed changes, will take too long and be too ineffective. Nonintegrated entities—even very large health plans and hospital chains—likewise cannot take a leadership role unless they become integrated fixed-fee providers. We've signified our lack of confidence in these solutions by marking an X in those pathways in Figure 6.2. We conclude that corporate orchestrators, integrated fixed-fee provider systems, and large employers are the entities most likely to get the ball of value network reform rolling.

Individual Entrepreneurs

We carefully chose our words in the previous story about Sony being *lucky* that Wal-Mart, Target, and Kmart emerged as channel partners in solid-state electronics. Had the discount retailers not emerged autonomously, and at just the right time, Sony's products would have taken off much more slowly, or not at all, because Sony needed a sales channel that was genuinely excited to sell its products. We welcome anyone willing to try, but in health-care reform we don't believe there is enough time to wait for each of the components of a new disruptive value network to emerge piece by piece from individual entrepreneurs. Nor can we bet on being so lucky that they will all emerge together. Most of our cities and towns will be bankrupt, many of our leading employers will have lost their international competitiveness, and millions upon millions of people will have received substandard care before our system heals itself. That's why proactive integration is so critical.

Government as Orchestrator

Democracy is not a tool of change. It's a good system of governance when the way things have been is the way they should remain. In democratic societies, those who profit from the status quo typically have many avenues of influence and appeal to manipulate regulation and policy to preserve the present system. Chapter 11 will use a model of these methods to examine the processes by which government regulatory policies can change in the face of disruptive opportunity. It will show that invariably, because of the strength of those entities whose interests are vested in the status quo, when policy changes it does so belatedly, in response to a fait accompli of innovation that already has taken root outside the reach of regulation. The model also shows that except for those few situations among developed nations where power is centralized (such as in Singapore), we cannot expect governments to have the power—let alone the will—to wield it, to orchestrate the emergence of a disruptive value network.

Most nationalized health systems are structured as fragmented fiefdoms just as America's private system is, and in Chapter 11 we will show that they're even less capable of disruptive change. There are a few instances in which governments act as integrated providers, in that the same powerful administrative entity manages the financial and payments side of the business, and also operates the hospitals and employs the doctors. In those instances, such as Singapore's health ministry and the Veterans Health Administration in the United States, we judge the government to be as capable as an integrated private sector provider to lead the creation of a disruptive value network.

Corporate Orchestrators

One method of integrating a disruptive value network is for a major, powerful company, or a group of companies, to step forward, declare what the architecture of the new system is going to look like, define how the pieces of the system will interface, and then—through financial and marketing muscle—spawn a set of companies and institutions that can fulfill each crucial role in the new system. These roles in health care would include the coherent solution shops, value-adding process clinics, disease management and patient-centric networks, and retail clinics discussed in Chapters 3, 4, and 5, as well as a new system of insurance and payment, which we will address in Chapter 7. Indeed, because this new value network will be comprised of a greater number of focused institutions and fewer general-purpose ones, the personal health record described in Chapter 4 must be the glue that holds the system together—facilitating institutional interactions, and ensuring that nobody falls through the cracks.

As we will discuss in Chapters 8 and 9, pharmaceutical and medical device companies need to be oriented to providing the technological fuel—much more of it diagnostic[6] and in the form of expert systems than in the past—to enable primary care physicians to disrupt specialists, nurses and technicians to disrupt doctors, and ambulatory clinics to disrupt hospitals. An orchestrator of a new value network will also need to lead changes in the way doctors and nurses are trained, to enable them to practice effectively in this new system—a topic we will cover in Chapter 10.

Orchestration of this sort is how IBM accelerated the development of the personal computer value network. IBM was a rarity in the annals of disruption, because it already had coped successfully with disruption once. In the early 1960s, Digital Equipment Corporation's minicomputer began its disruptive march against the mainframe computer market that IBM dominated. Without an orchestrator first setting the table, this disruption took about 30 years to complete. First, a range of start-up companies including Digital Equipment, Data General, Prime, Stratus, and Nixdorf—later joined by Wang Laboratories and Hewlett-Packard[7]—made the minicomputers. However, their growth was limited until other start-ups, such as Oracle, built software to run on their machines; and *their* growth was limited until another bunch of start-ups, like Priam and Quantum, began making eight-inch disk drives.

In 1969[8]—about 12 years after Digital Equipment initiated the minicomputer revolution—IBM created an autonomous minicomputer business unit in Rochester, Minnesota. IBM gave its new unit the charter to create a very different business model—one that made money by selling thousands of minicomputers with 45 percent gross profit margins, instead of the 60 percent margins that IBM needed to earn on the hundreds of mainframe machines it had been selling each year. This was a highly unusual move, but it allowed IBM to be the only mainframe maker that survived the minicomputer disruption. IBM was no doubt aided by the fact that the pace of disruption was so gradual.

Later, when the personal computer emerged to disrupt the minicomputer business, IBM was the only maker of minicomputers that subsequently became a leader in personal computers; the other minicomputer makers were all toppled. What's more, this disruption took only a decade to complete. How did IBM do it? First, it set up an autonomous business unit in Florida, and gave it the flexibility to create yet another different business model—one that could make money selling millions of units at 25 percent gross margins. But just as important, IBM orchestrated the creation of the entire value network in which its own PC business unit would operate.

Building a successful personal computer business required a completely different set of component suppliers than the minicomputer business had used. The logic circuit, for example, was a microprocessor, not a printed wiring board, and IBM made a major equity investment in a little Silicon Valley company called Intel to ensure an adequate supply. Similarly, the PC needed a 5.25-inch disk drive and a simple operating system. So IBM helped two fledgling companies, Seagate and Microsoft, launch themselves with generous, long-term supply agreements. The PCs could not be sold as mainframe and minicomputers had been—through factory salespeople who called directly on customers—so IBM created its own retail stores to get its products flowing into the market. They were later joined at this point in the value chain by independent companies like MicroAge, ComputerLand, and CompUSA.[9]

Because disruptive innovations are usually brought into their industries by start-ups, there are very few examples in which an industry leader like IBM was so determined to disrupt itself that it wielded its scope and power to orchestrate the assembly of a disruptive value network. Could this happen in health care?

It is conceivable that a giant like Johnson & Johnson could step into this breach. J&J is a powerful player in the pharmaceuticals, consumer health products, medical devices and diagnostics pieces of the business; and conceivably it could acquire or orchestrate action among providers and insurance companies. UnitedHealth Group is a dominant player on the insurance and information sides of the business, and could leverage those positions to orchestrate change. And General Electric conceivably could act as an orchestrator, using its massive medical systems business as a base. The conclusion, however, is there just aren't many companies in the world that could, or would want to, play the role of a corporate orchestrator.

INTEGRATED FIXED-FEE PROVIDERS

The second set of entities that could integrate a new value network are large providers that create and knit together underneath their corporate umbrellas all of the necessary elements of the new value network. There are several important characteristics of such integrated health systems.

First, they operate their own insurance and payments systems. Patients or purchasers in the system pay a fixed fee, typically yearly, that covers the cost of all care they might need. Second, the physicians are essentially employees of the system, not independent businesspeople. Third, the caregiving institutions in the system are apt to use focused business models, as described in Chapters 3 through 5. They can operate a limited number of general hospitals, while rationally siphoning work out to coherent solution shops and value-adding process clinics, outpatient clinics, and even retail clinics. And they have created and operate an information system that glues these different providers together to properly coordinate care. Finally, these firms are large employers themselves.

Note that we're expecting these integrated fixed-fee providers to operate the disruptees as well as the disruptors. This is a demanding but not an impossible expectation. Typically, we'd expect that the provider of a service, such as a hospital, would not disrupt itself by launching a chain of ambulatory and retail clinics, for example. But the unique structure of an integrated fixed-fee provider actually creates the incentive to shift care to the most cost effective venues possible—and to create those venues if they do not exist. The structure also encourages them to spend more money on a coherent solution shop diagnosis for a chronic illness, or to prevent that chronic illness in the first place, because it has the scope to realize savings elsewhere and over time. In general, most patients perceive higher switching costs across providers than across health assistance plans (our term for reimbursement and insurance plans). As a result, members of integrated fixed-fee provider systems tend to remain in these systems much longer than in a typical nonintegrated health plan. This gives the integrated system a much longer time horizon over which to evaluate the profitability of investments in members' long-term health.

It is easier for integrated providers such as these to create outpatient centers that disrupt hospitals, and to enable nurse practitioners to disrupt primary care physicians, who themselves can be encouraged to disrupt the specialists—because the executive teams at the center possess a systems view. They don't need to orchestrate a disruptive value network. They can create it. By fiat, they can declare the format by which electronic health records will be kept, so that these records are instantly accessible wherever the patient goes within the system. Some provider organizations—including most that arose during the surge of loosely defined integrated delivery networks of the late 1980s and 1990s—are *diversified* across all of these activities, but they are not managerially integrated, and thus each of their units operates with relative autonomy. It is unlikely that this latter type of organization is capable of putting all of these disruptive pieces together.

But in a truly integrated system, the incentives are in fact present to keep patients well, and these incentives often prove critical. For instance, thanks to sophisticated polymer technology, dentists can apply a sealant to children's teeth that nearly eliminates cavities and the subsequent necessity of dentists drilling and filling teeth; yet less than one-third of all dentists apply this sealant to the teeth of children seen in their practices. Why?

Dental fillings are a major source of revenue for most independent dentists. Interestingly, dentists who practice in prepaid dental plans, where providers are paid a fixed sum every year for all needed dental care, seal patients' teeth enthusiastically—because to them, drilling teeth is an expense, not a revenue opportunity.[10]

Some worry that when fixed-fee payments and the provision of care are linked within the same business entity such as the ones we've described, those organizations will be motivated to maximize profits by minimizing care. History has shown that this is rarely the case. Our economy is filled with examples of companies and not-for-profit organizations whose customers pay an annual fee that entitles them to receive services on an as-needed basis. Athletic clubs, the American Automobile Association, and the General Motors OnStar service are three examples. The main profit driver of these organizations is customer satisfaction and loyalty. They are strongly motivated, therefore, to figure out ways to delight their customers as cost effectively as possible.

Failed Attempts at Integration

We note that "integration" was attempted in at least two waves in the 1990s, with quite disastrous results. The first effort occurred as tertiary care hospitals acquired community hospitals and physicians' group practices. Though they owned these other institutions, the large hospitals made little attempt to truly integrate them as we describe here. Indeed, their objective was to build large "catchment" systems to feed as many patients as possible to the dinosaur—the general hospital. In contrast, the objective of the integration we advocate is to manage the orderly shifting of care *away* from costly venues and costly providers, and *toward* disruptive business models that can capitalize on technological enablers as they emerge.

The second aspect of "integration" that has been tried before is capitation—a system in which employers or individuals paid an annual per capita fee to the insurance company, which then contracted with primary care physicians to act as "gatekeepers" to the system, creating a strong financial incentive to ensure that the total cost of care for a covered population did not exceed the sum of the capitation revenue received. The reason capitation worked so poorly was that it was deployed into a system of nonintegrated providers—so one entity's gain was always another's loss. Those responsible for directing care had only the perspective of their own revenue and costs; they lacked a systems perspective. Further, actual usage and cost data was often unavailable or obscured to those providers who agreed to a specified capitation rate. And in a nonintegrated system, no single entity could be held responsible for a patient's care.[11] As with most policies and programs, the same thing that works well in one context is disastrous in another. Capitation has been shown to work very well in integrated systems and very poorly in fragmented ones.

Relative Abilities to Reduce Costs and Prices

Integrated fixed-fee providers aren't as captive to obsolete regulations as fragmented providers, in the following sense. We noted earlier that much of the certification that enables professionals to practice and operate is carried out by the trade associations of the existing players. These are guilds, essentially, and through a range of mechanisms the current members decide who else can join their guild. This system of certification-by-peer is given teeth in our present system by reimbursement—when Medicare or a private health plan declares that they will only reimburse for "licensed" procedures. This means that even when technology advances to the point at which a nurse can competently do what formerly required the training of a physician, the doctors can't hand the procedure off—because the practice can't get paid when the nurse isn't certified, and she isn't certified because the doctors' trade association does the certifying.

Integrated fixed-fee provider systems can, to some extent, circumvent the inertial blocking power of guild membership because reimbursement is not an issue. They can more easily make the decisions that are best for the overall system. If nurse practitioners can provide care for rules-based disorders, an integrated fixed-fee provider can devise a pricing system to direct patients to retail clinics, essentially creating internal transfer prices that optimize behavior across the system. This sort of disruption would hurt the business of independent physicians, but an integrated system can make this decision in a balanced way because its physicians are employees, not autonomous businesspeople—and because it can share some of the systemic cost savings with its physicians.

If specially trained physician assistants can competently perform colonoscopies, an integrated system can more readily turn that work over to them. A nonintegrated system can't do this, because independent insurers will only reimburse when a licensed physician does the work—and it would take years for the formal machinery to grant licenses, procedure by procedure, to physician assistants. When responsibilities are being shifted in ways that trade off the parochial interests of certain parties against the systemic benefits, integrated systems can resolve these inconsistencies with less of the paralysis that impedes reform elsewhere. They're basically set up to "optimize globally, not locally."

The mechanisms for determining reimbursement rates in the fragmented system in which most Americans receive care actually mitigate the motivation of those who pay for care to shift it to the most cost effective venues. The formulas that the Centers for Medicare and Medicaid Services use to determine reimbursement, and which most health plans tend to follow, generate cost estimates with a construct called relative value units (RVUs), which essentially try to capture the cost of the expertise, activities, and time required to perform a service or procedure. The weighted sum of these RVUs is then adjusted annually by a general estimate of cost inflation and by an index of geographic cost differences (it costs less to practice in Salina, Utah, than in San Francisco, California).[12]

There is no factor in Medicare's pricing formulas that adjusts for the business model of the provider, however. This means that if a value-adding process surgical center opens to perform hip and knee replacement surgeries, it is likely reimbursed the same amount as a nearby general hospital, which has much higher levels of overhead cost. So the surgical centers profit handsomely thanks to their lower overheads, and hospitals can continue to be paid at a rate that covers their costs. Basic examinations are reimbursed at rates that are profitable for physicians' offices—even if performing them at a lower-cost retail clinic is possible. The system, in other words, holds a price umbrella over the low-cost providers so the high-cost hospitals and doctors' offices can stay in business. In competitive industries, in contrast, if a low-cost provider moved into town, the high-cost providers would be forced to drop prices in order to remain competitive, or they would cede the low-priced business to disruptive competitors and move up-market. Integrated fixed-fee providers can make decisions based upon the costs in different business models, rather than having to guide their resource allocation decisions by administratively derived prices that do not differentiate across business models.

In addition to Kaiser Permanente in California[13]—Intermountain Healthcare in Utah, Geisinger Health System in Pennsylvania, Via Christi Health System in Kansas, and the massive Veterans Health Administration are among the institutions that have the scope to create within themselves a new disruptive value network.[14]

We urge scholars not to put our book down at this point and run off to see if the inflation of health-care costs has been better controlled in these companies than in the industry as a whole. We do not expect that these systems will have yet demonstrated the disruptive potential to dramatically reduce the costs of care. To date, they have generally used their integration to optimize the performance of the existing set of business models. However, we believe that integrated fixed-fee providers such as these are structured in a way *that gives them the capacity* to create a new disruptive value network. We would expect that if they do so, their dominance of the geographic markets in which they already serve will increase, and that they will have opportunities to expand their geographic scope. An implication of this is that the disruptive transformation of the health-care industry is likely to happen regionally, rather than in a uniform national wave.

The governing boards and executives of major nonintegrated hospital chains and health plans need to confront the reality that for the next decade or two health care will be in the circumstance where integration of the sort we've described is competitively critical. There seems to be a movement afoot for health assistance plans to merge and integrate with each other.[15] These firms will be integrating in the wrong direction. The objective of integration should not be size and overhead cost-sharing, but the creation of enterprises that can profit from wellness, rather than sickness. This would result in systems with disruptive business models for the practice of intuitive, empirical, and rules-based medicine, employing mechanisms that channel patients to appropriate providers.

Employers as Integrators

Major employers comprise the third group of entities that have the integrative scope to create an entirely new disruptive value network. At first blush the idea that employers might integrate into directing—and even providing—employees' health care might seem ridiculous. If you listen to what employers *say*, you might easily conclude that they want to get *out* of the business of paying for employees' health care. But if you watch what employers *do*, it indeed seems plausible that many of them will integrate into managing their employees' health care much more proactively than they have in the past. Employers profit by keeping their employees as healthy and productive as possible. Consequently, they spend thousands upon thousands of dollars each year attempting to attract, train, improve, and retain employees. Indeed, the fact that so many employers grouse about the cost of health care and yet are skittish about even minor changes in their health policies—for fear of alienating employees—is a testament to the role health coverage plays in many employers' human resource strategies.

As we hinted before, the ideal entity to be given responsibility for managing our health-care system would:

1. Have a long-term perspective, so it would be willing to spend on health care today, if necessary, in order to save more tomorrow.
2. Make money by keeping us well, not beginning when we become sick.
3. Know and care about us personally.
4. Be in a geographic position where care can be provided conveniently.
5. Be capable of implementing the needed changes with relative decisiveness.

It turns out that employers and integrated fixed-fee providers come closer to this ideal than any other entity—including insurance companies, independent physicians, and hospitals. Often they care more about our health than *we* do.

The karma from capitalist robber barons past and present leads some to suspect that corporate executives would take every opportunity to short-change workers and drop more money to the bottom line. We would of course be foolish to assert that all employers would be equitable and compassionate administrators of their health-care programs. But as a general rule, employers have a bigger stake in the health and productivity of their employees and employees' families than any other entity or institution in our society. This is the basis for our belief that certain major employers will become much more assertive in guiding and even providing care for their employees. They will thereby create an infrastructure that other, smaller employers can then utilize.

Figure 6.3 organizes our thoughts on this question. We've listed in the left column some candidates for taking on overall responsibility for managing care. This is not a complete list of the candidate entities, of course. Financial services companies like Fidelity, pharmacy benefit managers like Medco, and information technology companies like Intuit and Google also could be assessed. We have limited the number simply because we want this to be an illustrative, rather than exhaustive, exercise. At the top of the five columns to the right we've listed the criteria for the ideal entity. We borrowed the bubble methodology in the table from *Consumer Reports*.

Health plans don't fare well in this comparison, primarily because of their personal and geographic distance from the patients. They also suffer from short time horizons: the average length of time-in-plan for members of most plans is about five years,[16] giving some companies a financial incentive to skimp on spending for nearer-term preventive care—because the complications will likely arise on someone else's watch. We rate them below average in their ability to act decisively—not because they're poorly managed or don't want to, but because lack of integration hamstrings what they can and cannot do.

The reason for the empty bubbles on the rows for independent physicians and hospitals is that their business models are designed to make money when people become sick, not when they remain well. Governments suffer from impersonality, and while they must live with us for the rest of our lives, often the government's time horizon is defined by the next election and by other budgetary pressures outside the health-care arena.

Many employers, in contrast, find that investing in the health and productivity of employees pays off handsomely. The evidence: look at how much they're already spending to train their employees, because productive employees are profitable. Employers work to minimize employee absenteeism and turnover—they track these statistics, and if they see them inching upward, they launch problem-solving projects to figure out how to improve retention. Employers have a longer time perspective than the other candidates, because employees work for a company, on average, longer than they remain in a health plan.[17] In short, employers come closer to the "ideal" manager of our health programs than any of the candidates other than integrated fixed-fee providers. In many instances, employers rate better than the *patients*. The problem with leaving the patients in charge is that many of us have a very short time horizon, as we discussed in the last chapter. Many of us ignore the long-term consequences of unhealthy daily habits.

Employer-managed, integrated employee health programs would entail the following:

1. The employer is self-insured. The mechanisms for covering employees' health costs include high-deductible "true" insurance coupled with a health savings account. As we'll discuss in Chapter 7, HSAs must be marketed to employees as an additional tax-advantaged vehicle for retirement savings, not just another type of health insurance;

2. Salaried primary care physicians and nurse practitioners, on the payroll of the company or of a contractor firm like Whole Health Management, would be the primary care physicians to most employees and their family members.[18]

FIGURE 6.3   Assessment of candidate entities for managing our health care

	Long time horizon	Profits from wellness	Knows us individually	Con-venient	Able to act decisively
Health plans	Good	Good	Badly counterproductive	Badly counterproductive	Detracts
Independent physicians	Detracts	Badly counterproductive	Good	Good	Badly counterproductive
Independent hospitals	Badly counterproductive	Badly counterproductive	Badly counterproductive	Detracts	Badly counterproductive
Governments	Detracts	Good	Badly counterproductive	Neutral	Detracts
Employees	Neutral	Good	Excellent	Not applicable	Badly counterproductive
Employers	Good	Excellent	Good	Excellent	Good
Integrated providers	Good	Excellent	Neutral	Excellent	Excellent

Key: ● Excellent   ◗ Good   ◐ Neutral   ◖ Detracts   ○ Badly counter-productive

These salaried providers would oversee care decisions, and their performance must be measured and rewarded by employees' improved health.

3. Employers would contract directly with hospitals, outpatient clinics, and retail clinics. Whenever possible they would direct care for disorders still in the realm of intuitive medicine to coherent solution shops; and for those who have been precisely diagnosed, to value-adding process hospitals and clinics. They would encourage the use of retail clinics and even direct employees to low-cost "medical tourism" hospitals abroad when high-cost value-adding process procedures are needed. And they'd promote self-care when appropriate.

4. Employers would provide access to personally controlled electronic health records in an open-source format readily compatible with systems in use at the hospitals, clinics, and specialist physicians' practices that employees use. In fact, records compatibility would be a precondition in the negotiation the employer conducted with each potential provider.

5. They would contract with disease management network operators to manage the adherence of patients with behavior-dependent chronic diseases. Some of these networks might be operated by firms such as Healthways and OptumHealth, whose business models profit from health rather than sickness. Employers would carefully manage the handoffs between the coherent solution shops that diagnose and devise therapy for employees' chronic diseases and the networks that will help those with behavior-dependent diseases adhere to their therapy.

6. They would integrate into their HSA system financial rewards for behaviors such as weight loss, regular exercise, cessation of smoking, and compliance to prescribed therapies for chronic diseases.

To give you a sense of what we mean by employers integrating upstream into managing employee health, we'll recount here the experience of one company that has done this—Quad/Graphics—and then we'll couch what Quad has done in a generalized theory of integration.

Quad/Graphics: Vertical Integration into Health Management

Quad/Graphics, headquartered near Milwaukee, Wisconsin, is one of America's largest printing companies, with nearly $2 billion in annual revenues and 12,000 employees. Harry Quadracci started Quad as a print shop with 11 employees in 1971. As it developed into a major player in the industry, Quadracci still lunched with employees in the company cafeteria. They often brought up problems with medical claims or doctors' appointments. Meanwhile, the company's medical costs were surging. Quad built its own printing machinery, made its own ink, and did its own catering, the boss thought. Why not its own health care?[19]

Quad subsequently set up its first primary care clinic in 1990 as a way to bypass the middlemen of medicine and control costs. The company now operates four medical centers, offering family practice, internal medicine, pediatrics, obstetrics, gynecology, minor surgery, lab work, rehabilitation from injuries, and physical examinations. It's free to employees and their families. The emphasis is on wellness, not just on treating illnesses, and it therefore has programs to combat chronic diseases such as diabetes and obesity. Quad is fully self-insured and contracts directly with local hospitals and specialists for advanced care.

This system has slashed the company's health-care costs, reduced morbidity and absenteeism, and demonstrably increased employee wellness. Quad/Graphics spends about $6,500 per employee on health care, compared with its midwestern peers, which spend over $9,000 per employee on average. "Instead of trying to put a Band-Aid on a broken model, we wanted to build primary care from scratch," says Dr. Leonard Quadracci, brother of Quad's late founder, and head of its medical operations (QuadMed).[20]

About 80 percent of Quad employees and their families use the company's clinics as their main source of primary care and other common services such as prenatal and skin care. The other 20 percent of employees prefer going to outside doctors, even though that plan costs more. Together, the Quad clinics logged 60,500 patient visits in 2004.

Quad spends more on primary care than most companies—$715 for each person in 2003, compared with an average of $375 for other local employers. However, this investment helps keep employees and their families from requiring care in hospitals and the offices of higher-priced specialists. This is a system-optimizing trade-off that a nonintegrated system simply could not make. The bonuses of QuadMed's 26 doctors are tied to patient evaluations and health outcomes—not how many patients they can squeeze in every day. Quad doctors see only one patient every half hour, using the extra time to ask about other health problems and give advice on disease prevention. Employees pay just five dollars a visit. By 2005, Quad's employee health costs had risen less than 5 percent annually over the previous five years, versus 9.8 percent for the country as a whole.

Because Quad invested early in electronic medical records, it can easily analyze how well it's meeting national health standards. Of Quad employees with high blood pressure, 92 percent of those who go to QuadMed take regular medication to keep it in check. The U.S. average is 40 percent, according to data from health plans collected by the National Coalition on Quality Assurance. Nationally, 26 percent of mothers give birth by caesarean section, but only 12 percent of women who get prenatal care at Quad do.

Quad pays its doctors about $130,000 to $160,000 a year—comparable to what the average general practitioner makes in greater Milwaukee. Some doctors have an entrepreneurial bent—they want to run their own business—and they can't realize their dreams at QuadMed. But others studied medicine to care for patients—and they *like* corporate health. Ann Merkow, an internist who joined Quad 11 years ago, says: "When I interviewed, I said 'I don't want to just take care of sore throats.'" Merkow adds that she finds it rewarding to work with incentives built around patient health. In private practice, because doctors are reimbursed per visit but don't get paid for preventive care, "You almost get punished for taking time for patients."

"What we've learned here is that when primary care is done right, the results can be amazing," says John Neuberger, business manager of Quad's medical division. To preserve confidentiality, all medical staff must sign confidentiality agreements promising to keep patient details within the clinic—whose computer systems are separate from those of the printing business.

Quad is now selling health-care services to other companies—paralleling the process by which Henry J. Kaiser opened Permanente to the general population of southern California in the 1940s. Two other Wisconsin-based employers, Briggs & Stratton Corp. and Rockwell Automation Inc., have contracted with Quad to run full-service clinics for their employees.

For Briggs, a maker of small engines, the move came after its Milwaukee-area medical costs doubled between 2000 and 2003. "We'd done just about everything you can to tinker with the current system," said Jeffrey Mahloch, Briggs's vice president of human resources. Because of sometimes contentious relations between management and labor, Briggs turned to Quad instead of operating its own clinic directly.

The Briggs clinic, opened in 2003, logged 8,000 visits in its first year—more than the company expected—and shaved $500,000 in health and worker-compensation costs. Buoyed by the success, Briggs opened a second Quad-operated clinic last July at its Poplar Bluff, Missouri, plant. There, the clinic has been so popular that several other big employers are drawing up plans to build their own joint clinic, although the town of 17,000 already teems with dozens of medical practices and a two-campus hospital.

"There's only one way to avoid paying more and more for the health-care system," says John Shiely, Briggs's chief executive, "and that's for corporations to get back into the health-care business."

Companies such as CHD Meridian and Whole Health Management are emerging to operate integrated employee health

systems on a private-label basis for employers in situations similar to that of Briggs & Stratton that prefer not to build the capability themselves.[21] We've included at http:// Innovators Prescription. com a description of several other companies that have integrated into managing employees' health like Quad and Briggs & Stratton. These include Perdue Farms, Toyota, Safeway, Scott's, Pitney Bowes, the University of Vermont, Sprint, Qualcomm, and General Mills.

A History of Vertical Integration

Although a common mantra of management is that executives should "stick to their knitting" and focus on competencies that are "core," companies have long been driven to integrate upstream in their supply chain, into activities that were not their core competencies, whenever they could not assure themselves of a cost- and performance-effective supply of critical inputs into their production process.

For example, until the 1880s cattle had to be locally raised and butchered. The meat also had to be sold and consumed locally, because there was no way to transport it economically over any significant distance. This kept the beef industry from achieving significant economies of scale. Gustavus Franklin Swift then saw the opportunity to transform the beef industry into "an era of cheap beef" by centralizing stockyards and butchering operations in Kansas City on a massive scale. Cattle ranchers would drive their herds to Swift's stockyards, where Swift could process the beef at very low cost. But there wasn't any way to transport Swift's fresh beef to the large urban markets of the Midwest and Northeast—so Swift had to design and build the world's first practical ice-cooled railcars. And once the beef made its way to those urban markets, he needed to integrate into making and selling ice cabinets in which retail shops could prevent the meat from spoiling. Thanks to his willingness to integrate into competencies that hadn't been core but certainly were critical, the House of Swift for decades slaughtered as many as two million cattle, four million hogs, and two million sheep each year.[22]

As another illustration, when Henry Ford was building his disruptive Model T cars, he couldn't get steel from independent manufacturers that was low enough in cost and of consistent enough quality that parts stamped from the steel would be uniform in dimension and properties. So Ford built his own steel mill on the River Rouge, right next to his assembly plant in Dearborn, Michigan. Steelmaking hadn't been Ford's "core competence," but of necessity it became one.

Meanwhile, in our era of rampant outsourcing, more and more companies find themselves integrating into the training of their own managers by creating their own corporate universities. Because MBAs trained by the independent business schools are very expensive to hire, yet aren't being trained adequately for what these companies need, General Electric, Toyota, Motorola, McDonald's, IBM, Tata Consultancy Services, Black & Decker, Goldman Sachs, Perdue Farms, Intel, and thousands of other companies have established management universities or training programs of their own. Management training wasn't a "core competence" of General Electric or these other companies. But in order to assure themselves of a cost effective supply of a critical input to the production process—management—these companies have had to make the training of great managers a core competence.

The companies that have integrated into managing their employees' health care have made a similar decision. Just as management training was the core competence of Harvard Business School and not General Electric, health care was the core competence of independent physicians' practices and hospitals. But because they cannot assure themselves of a cost effective supply of a critical contributor to work-force productivity, these companies have decided health care needs to become a competence.

Swift and Ford ultimately got out of the railcar, refrigerated display, and steelmaking businesses when what they needed became specifiable, and external suppliers became competent and cost effective. We suspect that General Electric would follow suit if it could specify what sorts of training its managers needed, and if there was a business school that could deliver the training.

For the same reasons, we'd expect that Quad/Graphics won't be in the business of managing employees' health care forever.

What About Small Businesses?

Small businesses, of course, cannot vertically integrate to the extent that major employers can. But not all businesses invest equally in recruiting, developing, and retaining human capital, either—so we cannot expect all employers, covering all citizens, to flip to integrated employee health programs in unison. Even major companies for whom integrated employee health makes sense will need to roll it out experimentally, employee by employee, facility by facility, over the course of several years. Disruptions always arise where it is easiest for them to take root, and the disruptive transformation of industries is a process, not an event. The fact that all employees of small businesses may not be able to participate in the disruptive value network during the earliest years does not mean it won't happen.

Integration, Consumer-Driven Health Care, and Competition

Professor Regina Herzlinger, who, as noted earlier, was the first to have drawn on Wickham Skinner's measures of focus to advocate "focused factories" in health care, has more recently led in the call for consumer-driven health care.[23] Professors Porter and Teisberg have recently prescribed clear, market-based metrics of value as the enablers of competition, which promises to reduce the costs of health care.[24] Now Drs. Christensen, Grossman, and Hwang come along and assert that provider *integration* and the assembly of *market power*—characteristics often associated with uncompetitive markets—are the keys to making health care higher in quality, lower in cost, and more conveniently accessible. Isn't the specter we paint of larger, more powerful integrated fixed-fee providers, with employers becoming much more involved in health-care decisions, the antithesis of the sort of open-market competition that typically makes an industry consumer-driven?

We endorse the calls that Herzlinger, Porter, and Teisberg have issued. Integration is simply a key step in the creation of the new business models that will enable the eventual ends they envision. History speaks very strongly on the value of integration at points of fundamental architectural change in value networks.[25] This change is critical because it isn't just competition per se that drives cost down, but *disruptive* competition that brings affordability.

A business model is built around a value proposition that helps a group of customers do more effectively, affordably, and conveniently a job they have long been trying to do. Understanding the job is a prerequisite to integrating resources and processes in a coherent way that optimally gets it done. Then and only then can consumers truly be satisfied. The fact that hospitals and physicians' practices are *not* job-focused, but instead aspire to do anything for anybody, has caused them not to be integrated correctly. In their current configuration, they cannot be consumer-driven.

SUMMARY

We will close this chapter with some predictions, and make recommendations based upon those. We predict that in areas where an integrated fixed-fee (IFF) provider aggressively uses disruptive business models to provide better care at lower cost, they will prosper, and overall health-care costs will drop without a compromise in quality or convenience of care. This is because quality comes from correct integration, and lower costs come from low overheads that are enabled by focus. Within five years these improvements will be apparent, and in 10 years the differences in cost and customer satisfaction will be stunning. In these areas, many employers will not feel the urgency to integrate into directing and providing health care for their employees, because the IFF provider does it well. In these situations the IFF providers will gain an even larger share of their local markets. Hospital chains and health plans that do not integrate will cry foul as they lose share. Some will invoke antitrust arguments. If instead those other providers also adopt an IFF structure, so that three or more IFF providers compete in the same geographic area, competition within these clusters will cause business model innovation to accelerate.

A few of these IFF providers will expand geographically, replicating their integrated model in multiple markets. As employers shift volume to IFF providers, the nonintegrated providers with no disruptive business models will experience the financial crises and consolidations that befall all disruptees eventually.

The major health assistance plans from traditional health insurance companies will struggle to remain viable, because the fee-for-service model will be relegated to a shrinking portion of the market. As we'll discuss in Chapter 7, their comprehensive coverage products in the nonintegrated portion of the market that is not served by IFF providers will be overtaken by high-deductible "true" insurance coupled with health savings accounts. While these products will account for only 10 percent of the market in 2010, they will have half the market by 2013, and 90 percent by 2016—a scant eight years from now. The 401(k) administrators such as Fidelity Investments will have an inherent advantage in marketing and administering health savings accounts, because the two products will be hired by the same customers for the same job. Health insurance companies should seek to merge with those major hospital companies that are intent on becoming IFFs in order to create new disruptive business models.

Despite our vision, however, we predict that most strategic investments in health care will be made under the assumption that the business models of the past will remain the dominant ones of the future. For example, most major health assistance plans are likely to react to their loss of market share by merging with each other and consolidating even further—and as they increase their national scope they will find it even more difficult to combine with providers. They will integrate in the wrong direction.

Guided by well-intentioned members of their boards of trustees who are anxious to leave monuments to their communities, many hospital companies will build new state-of-the-art general hospitals in the belief that they are stepping boldly into the future. This actually will trap them in the past. Such massive capital investments and the heavy levels of fixed cost they entail will create inexorable pressures to utilize those hospitals fully—making it difficult to justify building value-adding process clinics or coherent solution shops—the new disruptive business models that are the true bold steps into the future.[26]

Because employers in most areas of the country won't have access to IFF providers for their employees, and because most provider and insurance systems will continue in their present modes, more and more employers will see no alternative than to actively provide and direct the provision of health care for their employees. Their stance will likely pull IFF providers into their communities from other areas in the country.

In many ways, the present system of contracting with providers through intermediary health insurance plans is limited to controlling costs by negotiating with providers in inherently high-cost business models. Because of this, more and more employers will step forward and contract with providers that can provide better care but through fundamentally low-cost business models. Direct contracting will help the value network escape the distorting grip of formulaically determined prices. They will cut health assistance plans—the middlemen in the system—out of the loop.

Major employers who choose not to integrate into the provision of first-level care for employees and their families nonetheless will take a significant role in orchestrating the emergence of a disruptive health-care value network—through a few high-impact policy changes. For example, if we are correct that a significant portion of the cost of chronic care is spent on therapy for misdiagnosed variations of intuitive chronic diseases, major employers that have the scope will send more patients with these conditions to coherent solution shops—thereby fostering their establishment and helping to define their economic value. They will increasingly contract with professional network companies such as Healthways or OptumHealth, who profit from keeping patients with behavior-dependent diseases chronically healthy. And more employers will encourage employees who need certain procedures to utilize value-adding process clinics, retail clinics, and medical tourism destinations whenever one of those disruptive delivery models offers the optimal route of care.

As the disruptive value network becomes established, employees of small businesses, the self-employed, and the uninsured poor—most of whom are largely neglected by the current value network—will then be able to avail themselves of this system, from which higher quality, lower cost, more conveniently accessible health care will be available.

We conclude that there are indeed entities that can pull this off. We hope they'll choose to do so.

NOTES

1. Wessel, David, Bernard Wysocki Jr., and Barbara Martinez, "As Health Middlemen Thrive, Employers Try to Tame Them," *Wall Street Journal*, December 29, 2006; A1.

2. Christensen, Clayton M., and Richard S. Rosenbloom, "Explaining the Attacker's Advantage: Technological Paradigms, Organizational Dynamics, and the Value Network," *Research Policy* (24), 1995, 233–57. We invite those readers who want to understand value networks more completely to read "Value Networks and the Impetus to Innovate," Chapter 2 in Christensen, Clayton M., *The Innovator's Dilemma: When New Technologies Cause Great Firms to Fail* (Boston, Massachusetts: Harvard Business School Press, 1997).

3. For more detail on how traditional methods of financial analysis distort sound decision making in innovation, see Christensen, Clayton, Steven Kaufman, and Willy Shih, "Innovation Killers," *Harvard Business Review*, January, 2008.

4. Enter the "One Laptop per Child" project, whose mission has been to design and manufacture computers at a price below $100 so every child in the world can own one. Doing this required an architectural reconception of what a computer is: a microprocessor that consumes very little power; use of the Linux operating system; elimination of the disk drive entirely; a complete redesign of the display screen and battery; and use of Internet-based software. The only companies that could develop a completely new computer system architecture like this were integrated firms whose scope enabled them to wrap their arms around all of the constituent components and technologies—maintaining full control over decisions to combine or eliminate components, create new ones, and redefine how they interact with each other. The two firms in the world that have the reach to do this are in Taiwan: Quanta and ASUSTeK. Together, they design and build almost 70 percent of all notebook computers in the world. Other computer companies—like Dell, Apple, and Hewlett-Packard—have outsourced so much of the design and manufacture of their computers to Quanta and ASUSTeK that they do not have the scope to succeed in this challenging project.

5. This is a recurrent theme in the work of Alfred D. Chandler, the great historian of business: at the beginning stages of every industry's history, when the value network needed to be put together, it required the "visible hand of managerial capitalism"—firms with the requisite scale and scope—to put these industries together. See, in particular, *Scale and Scope* (Cambridge, Massachusetts: The Belnap Press of Harvard University Press, 1991).

6. We assume in this statement, as well as throughout this book, that therapeutic innovations will follow the development of precise diagnostics. While this sometimes does not happen readily, we feel comfortable in asserting that the diagnostic technology lays much of the groundwork upon which a predictably effective therapy can be devised.

7. Wang Laboratories and Hewlett-Packard had previously been making other electronic equipment. Wang began by making electronic calculators, and HP by making oscilloscopes. The minicomputer was an "up-market" diversification to these firms, enabling them disruptively to leverage their existing business models into this new market. The other firms were start-ups.

8. Soltis, Frank G., *Fortress Rochester: The Inside Story of the IBM ISeries* (Loveland: Penton Technology Media, 2001).

9. When sufficient independent retailers had emerged, IBM shut down its own retail outlets.

10. Halvorson, George, *Health Care Reform Now: A Prescription for Change* (San Francisco: Jossey Bass, 2007), 27–28.

11. We thank our friend Professor Lewis Hassell of the University of Oklahoma Medical School for teaching us about this troubled history. For a historical view of capitation, see Ginsburg, Paul B., "Competition in Health Care: Its Evolution over the Past Decade," *Health Affairs* 24, no. 6 (2005): 1512–22.

12. For more details on this system, see Centers for Medicare and Medicaid Services, "Medicare Physician Fee Schedule," January 2008. ICN: 006814.

13. Some have asked why the "Kaiser model" seems not to have succeeded in other geographies where it has expanded, to the extent that it has in California. We believe the answer is that Kaiser hasn't replicated the full model in each geography and that there are strong scale economics within regions, rather than across regions. We suspect that Kaiser could achieve comparable success in other regions if it invested to implement its full model, and invested to achieve the requisite scale.

14. See, for example, Abelson, Jenn. "Shift in Health-Cost Focus Is Said to Show Promise," *New York Times*, July 12, 2007; and Agarwal, Madhulika, "Meeting the Challenges of Veterans with Chronic Illnesses," *Forum*, November 2005, 1–3.

15. Tanne, Janice Hopkins, "A Few Health Insurers Monopolise US Market," *BMJ*, 29 April 2006.

16. According to data from the Commonwealth Fund, the average annual turnover rate for health plans is 17 percent. See Brink, Susan, "Prevention Pays, But Not in the Short Term," *Los Angeles Times*, May 7, 2007, F-8.

17. In 2006, the median tenure that workers aged 35 and older in the United States spent working for their current employer was 7.8 years. Despite the popular perception that employee job-hopping is accelerating, this is down only by a few months from what it was in 1996. Younger workers, of course, have a significantly lower job tenure. We have focused on those aged 35 and older, however, because they and their families account for most health care costs. Source: *Statistical Abstract of the United States*, 127th Edition, 2008.

18. Whole Health was recently acquired by the major chain pharmacy, Walgreens.

19. Much of this account of the Quad Graphics integration into employee health care has been excerpted from Fuhrmans, Vanessa, "Radical Surgery—One Cure for High Health Costs: In-House Clinics at Companies," *Wall Street Journal*, Feb. 11, 2005, A1.

20. Quadrucci explained some of these details in a speech at the annual meeting of the American Association for Clinical Chemistry in Chicago on Tuesday, July 25, 2004.

21. Katz, Paula S., "Big Employers Bring Health Care In House," *ACP Observer*, January-February 2007.

22. Chandler, Alfred D., *Scale & Scope*, op.cit.

23. Professor Regina Herzlinger has published a stream of highly regarded pieces on consumer-driven health care. Her books include *Market-Driven Health Care* (New York: Basic Books, 1999), *Consumer-Driven Health Care: Implications for Providers, Payers & Policy Makers* (San Francisco: Jossey Bass, 2004), and *Who Killed Health Care? America's $2 Trillion Medical Problem and the Consumer-Driven Cure* (New York: McGraw-Hill, 2007). We thank her for all she has taught us.

24. Porter, Michael and Elizabeth Teisberg, *Redefining Health Care* (Boston, Massachusetts: Harvard Business School Press, 2007).

25. Chandler, op. cit., 1991. Chandler's earlier Bancroft Award–winning work, *The Visible Hand* (Cambridge, Massachuetts: The Belnap Press of Harvard University Press, 1977), focused on the same thing.

26. An example of this is playing itself out in Salt Lake City. Intermountain Healthcare, a portion of which is an integrated fixed-fee provider, has constructed a huge new general hospital in the south-central portion of the Salt Lake Valley. They reportedly are experiencing pressure to keep it full—which will likely preempt any proposals that emerge to create lower-cost value-adding process clinics and coherent solution shops.

Chapter 7

Disrupting the Reimbursement System

Some would say that doctors, once licensed, aren't subject to lots of traditional regulation. A review of the Federal Register[1] would in fact show that doctors face few explicit regulations governing:

- Patients they will and will not treat
- Therapies and protocols they use
- Where to administer treatment to their patients
- Whether and how to measure the results of their work

In many ways, however, doctors' choices on each of these four dimensions of practice are microscopically regulated—through the way they are paid for their services. Reimbursement has become the primary mechanism through which the regulation of doctors occurs in the United States.[2] To the extent that doctors cannot afford to do things they are not paid to do, and will gladly do more of those things they are paid handsomely to do, the decisions about whether, when, and how much to pay doctors for the various things they do has unwittingly become one of the most pervasive and powerful regulatory mechanisms ever devised.

Most discussions about reforming health care run into a dead end when the participants realize that the regulatory system that we call reimbursement will not allow it. The reimbursement system is structured to sustain the status quo. Caregivers who do things the way they've always been done, or who make improvements within the present architecture of care, can get paid for what they do. Those who wish to disrupt the system by changing the very architecture of care, however, often are stymied by the specter that there literally is no money to be made from doing it. This is because disruptive innovations, being new to the world, just don't fit within the existing categories of products for which prices have been set and approved for reimbursement.

Health-care reformers have made compelling cases that improving the value of health care can't happen unless those who receive health services know what they cost and bear at least a share of the cost burden.[3] At the same time, however, the belief that employers or the government are morally obligated to cover health-care costs has become a tenet accepted with near-religious fervor by most people in modern societies. We therefore seem bound in the tautologically tight paradox that employers, Medicaid, or Medicare must cover most health-care costs in ways that insulate providers and patients from the very market pressures that would normally force efficiencies, greater accountability, and the delivery of increased value.

What makes the encumbrance of reimbursement even more distortive and binding is that most prices insurers pay are not set by market forces. Rather, they are *administered prices* that reek of the pricing algorithms and backroom negotiations used in communist systems. Those who set or approve prices for medical products and procedures are typically physicians, health economists, and actuaries who are impaneled by Medicare and private insurers to tell them what they should pay.[4]

Not surprisingly, we reap the same inefficient results that characterized Communism. Hospitals aggressively pursue some types of procedures—like coronary bypass surgery, for example—that are highly profitable.[5] And they often shun money-losing services such as psychiatric and trauma care, as well as services like preventive and primary care, which could save costs in the long run.[6] Eventually, more and more people lose "access," as the services that aren't paid well or must be provided at a loss become harder to find. But the profits and losses aren't a reflection of value to their customers, society, or the forces of supply, demand, and competition: they are the phantom result of inaccurately set prices that are grossly out of line with costs. Yet as in the communist system, we muddle along because the prices that are set mistakenly high roughly offset those set mistakenly low, allowing most hospitals and physicians' practices to eke out a modest profit after all cross-subsidization is complete.

The purpose of this chapter is to define the changes that need to be made in reimbursement systems so they can efficiently facilitate disruptive innovation, and to describe how policy makers, insurers, and employers can successfully implement these changes. We'll do this in six sections. We begin by recounting the history of health insurance and reimbursement, to give our readers a sense of how we got to where we are today. Second, we'll review the systems commonly used throughout the world. Then, in the third section, we'll explore more deeply the problems that these reimbursement systems have created in the health-care industry. In the fourth and fifth sections we'll offer our recommendations for two reimbursement systems—integrated capitation and a pairing of high-deductible insurance and health savings accounts—that can overcome the problems created by existing products. The final section will offer additional suggestions for helping the uninsured poor access the right kind of health care.

A HISTORY OF HEALTH INSURANCE AND REIMBURSEMENT

Before the advent of modern medicine in the early 1900s, the cost of caring for serious illnesses wasn't financially devastating. It was affordable because family members cared for the patients at home, or charitable organizations brought them into community facilities. Because there wasn't much that doctors and hospitals could offer the gravely ill, life insurance—not health insurance—matched the reality of medicine. Health insurance policies that were sold in that era resembled what we now call disability insurance—protection against lost wages due to illness or serious injury rather than against the costs of medical care.

By the 1920s to 1940s, however, general hospitals had become capable enough that patients could recover from some diseases that were previously fatal—and this care was expensive enough to be financially devastating. In an era when families struggled to save five dollars per month, the average hospital bill of $140 in 1928 could send a family to financial ruin.[7] A health insurance industry therefore emerged to help people hedge against the costly event of catastrophic illness or accident.

During the Great Depression, a set of pioneering not-for-profit companies that became known as Blue Cross began selling prepaid insurance plans that guaranteed hospital services in exchange for a low annual fee. Another set of companies that became Blue Shield sold similar plans covering physician services.[8] Regulators forced the companies of Blue Cross and Blue Shield, because they were not-for-profit, to price by *community* rating, regardless of individuals' health condition. All people in a community were therefore charged the same price for the same coverage.

The health insurance market expanded rapidly when for-profit insurance companies got into the act. Not facing the same regulatory restrictions as the Blues and similar state-approved insurers of last resort, for-profit insurers were able to offer *experience*-rated plans, enabling them to "cherry pick" lower-cost younger and healthier customers with lower prices. This new type of health insurance was sold by individual agents, mirroring how home and life insurance were sold. The cost of all health insurance was paid by individuals. As reflected in Figure 7.1, the portion of people

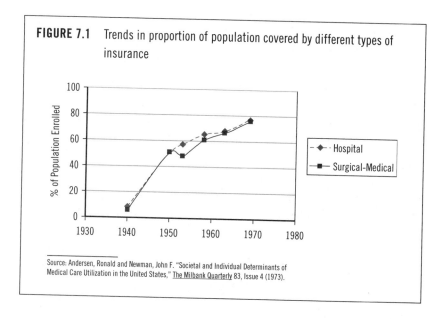

FIGURE 7.1 Trends in proportion of population covered by different types of insurance

Source: Andersen, Ronald and Newman, John F. "Societal and Individual Determinants of Medical Care Utilization in the United States," The Milbank Quarterly 83, Issue 4 (1973).

covered by these plans grew from less than 10 percent in 1940 to nearly 80 percent by the 1970s.[9]

Employer-Based Health Insurance Becomes the Norm

Even while this self-paid market for health insurance was in its infancy, a few industrialists in the 1930s, including Henry Kaiser in California, began covering the cost of health insurance as an employee benefit. Kaiser's employee health initiatives began in the Mojave Desert with the construction of the Colorado River Aqueduct during the Great Depression. Sidney Garfield, a physician who had begun treating Kaiser's construction workers at a small desert hospital, and Harold Hatch, an insurance agent, devised a new plan that didn't just insure against catastrophic costs, but involved prepayment for *all* medical care. At five cents per day, this was a bargain to Kaiser. It helped him recruit workers into that forbidding environment and to keep them healthy on the job.

Congress enacted pervasive price controls, in the Stabilization Act of 1942,[10] to keep inflation under control amidst the massive budgetary deficits during World War II. This law limited wage increases but permitted companies to provide employee insurance plans as a means for recruiting and compensating workers. Most employers offered pension plans and life insurance. But Henry Kaiser, with fresh memories of the impact that covering employees' health costs had in building the Colorado River Aqueduct, used this Act to recruit needed employees to his Long Beach, California, shipyards. His strategy was not just to pay for employees' health-care costs, but to *provide* the care as well through company-operated clinics—in hopes that this would help keep employees healthy and out of the hospital. Dubbed "Permanente," this was one of the nation's first health maintenance organizations (HMOs).[11] In 1944, Kaiser opened the Permanente Health Plan to the general public. It proved to be especially popular with union members, who were attracted by the affordability and comprehensiveness of coverage compared to the traditional insurance system.

After World War II, employers began to expand health insurance offerings into what became known as "major medical" plans, which covered a broader range of the costs of major illnesses or serious injuries that had not been covered by the basic hospital insurance plans introduced earlier. The first major medical policy was written by Liberty Mutual Insurance Company in 1949, and similar plans rapidly captured the private insurance market. By 1953, 1.2 million people (roughly 1 percent of all Americans) were covered by major medical plans.[12]

In the first complete overhaul of the federal income tax system since its establishment in 1913, the Internal Revenue Act of 1954 (P.L. 83-591) declared employer contributions to employee health plans to be deductible business expenses. Health insurance was now formally recognized as a tax-advantaged form of compensation, and employers began scrambling to offer health insurance in lieu of increasing wages. By 1962, 38.2 million people (25 percent of all workers) had employer-provided major medical insurance. This increased to 92.6 million by 1969, and, with the help of the HMO Act of 1973, to 117.3 million by 1977 (79 percent of all workers).[13]

To differentiate themselves in the markets for talent and for insurance, employers and health plans in the 1960s next began to promote "comprehensive" coverage, which included reimbursement for day-to-day health-care expenses. The best employers offered the most comprehensive plans—with the least amount of employee contribution—to attract and retain the best employees. Before long the two types of employer-provided health-care assistance—true insurance against catastrophic illness, and reimbursement for day-to-day health-care expenses—had been combined into single-package health plans. This unwittingly induced a pervasive sense of entitlement that today burdens employers who struggle to remain competitive in the global markets for their products. As we did in Chapter 6, we'll term this bundle of two very different products—insurance and reimbursement—as "health assistance."

TYPES OF REIMBURSEMENT

Fee-for-Service

The dominant form of assistance today is fee-for-service (FFS), which gives providers a clear path to revenue: the more services you render, the more you get paid. In America's system today, as a result, a lot of providers offer a lot of care. Studies concluding that up to half of all medical services performed in the United States are medically unnecessary pin much of the blame on the financial incentives embedded in fee-for-service.[14]

Medicare and Medicaid are government-sponsored programs for particular populations not covered by employer-offered insurance. These programs resulted from the deepening divide between coverage of the younger, healthier workforce and the indigent and elderly populations. The push for universal coverage had existed since the time of Roosevelt's New Deal, as the prospect of leaving the neediest and sickest patients without health care has long been unappealing to many Americans. Interest groups led by the American Medical Association, however, feared that a universal insurance system would harm the physician-patient relationship (which some would say was a smoke screen for harming their pocketbooks). They fought off attempts to create such an infrastructure until 1965, when, in a compromise, Medicare and Medicaid were established to provide coverage to the elderly and needy.[15]

Part of this compromise was a pledge to build these programs around fee-for-service payments. This seemingly innocuous decision has been a key driver of the unsustainable growth in spending over the following decades as health-care costs continued to rise and the number of elderly enrollees increased.

Capitation

By the 1980s it became clear that medical costs had spiraled out of control. The fee-for-service model of reimbursing physicians and hospitals received much of the blame. Capitation was a mechanism designed to solve this problem. For a fixed fee set annually, Health Maintenance Organizations like Kaiser Permanente agreed to provide all the care that each of their covered patients needed.

Capitation continues to thrive today as a fruitful health assistance mechanism used in managerially integrated provider organizations such as Kaiser. It eliminates the incentive that fee-for-service reimbursement creates for providers to give more care than is needed, and ostensibly gives providers an incentive to engage in wellness care and preventive services to keep their patients healthy. Capitation actually encourages the development of disruptive business models within these integrated provider organizations, in that using lower-cost venues of care and lower-cost caregivers such as nurse practitioners and physician assistants drives greater surplus or profitability.[16] We term this type of capitation, which is practiced within integrated provider organizations, as *integrated capitation*.

What caused capitation to come off the rails was when non-HMO insurers co-opted the concept by knitting together networks of independent primary care physicians, specialists, and hospitals to replicate the cost control mechanisms of HMOs, without limiting patients' choice of a personal physician. Primary care physicians were given stewardship over a fixed fee per capita (hence the rubric *capitation*), and they became "gatekeepers" who granted or denied access to more expensive levels of specialist and hospital care.

Nonintegrated capitation generally fell into disfavor for three reasons, the first of which is that because employees change jobs, and employers often change the health plans they offer employees, the average tenure of a person in a particular health plan through the 1980s and 1990s was only three years.[17] Thus, it was not in the economic interest of insurers or providers to incur the cost of care that could prevent costlier, more serious problems that had an impact beyond the three year horizon. Rather, the incentive was to minimize spending on those diseases in the short term, because the statistical odds were that the bill for those patients' more serious problems would arise on someone else's watch—often that of Medicare.

The second problem was that capitation restricted freedom of choice. Some consumers were comfortable choosing a health-care system, such as an HMO, rather than choosing a doctor. But others had grown accustomed to the freedom to choose their own doctors and hospitals at every level. They bristled aggressively when their gatekeepers refused access to second opinions or to reputable specialists because they were deemed unnecessary or were outside the network. Because a key reason why employers began offering health coverage in the first place was to attract and retain the right employees, most employers decided that the potential savings weren't worth jeopardizing employee goodwill.

The third problem arose because of the nonintegrated structure in which capitation was used. Capitation works well in integrated systems like Kaiser. But gatekeeper physicians, as independent businesspeople, found themselves playing a zero-sum game with specialists, who were themselves independent business-people.[18] If the gatekeepers referred a patient to a more expensive specialist, they made less money; if the gatekeepers tried to restrict referrals, the specialists complained that they were making less money. Neither had been equipped with the perspective of systemwide costs and benefits of the decisions they were asked to make. When they denied access to more expensive care, gatekeeper physicians faced acrimonious confrontations with their patients, with whom trusting relationships were important. And when they made access to expensive care too easy, gatekeeper physicians had their judgment questioned by the insurance carriers, who were in search of opportunities to squeeze down costs even further. Hence, many independent physicians as business owners came to dislike capitation intensely. Salaried physicians working in integrated provider organizations didn't feel this Catch-22 as much, because such referrals did not significantly affect their income.[19]

By 1998 a backlash by employees and providers in nonintegrated systems led most employers to return to more traditional fee-for-service plans, and health-care inflation resumed its rapid rise, returning once again to double digits in 2003. From this point on, the strategy of many employers has been to shift more of these costs to employees. But cost-shifting is not cost-reduction.

DISTORTIONS CREATED BY THE PRESENT HEALTH ASSISTANCE SYSTEMS

Today's methods of health assistance—which have reverted strongly back to fee-for-service for the reasons described above—create three major distortions to the efficacy and efficiency of health care. First, they preserve costly providers rather than enabling disruptive ones to emerge. Second, they dictate the price of services, and as a result create artificial bubbles of profitability and unprofitability in different sectors of the industry—thereby misdirecting the flow of investment in new products and services. And third, their contracting practices actually drive hospitals' costs up, not down. We'll consider each of these distortions below.

Trapping Care in a High-Cost Business Model

The first problem that the present assistance system creates is that fee-for-service traps health care in high-cost institutions, to the exclusion of disruptive models. There is no better way to illustrate this perversion than through the history of payment for dialysis patients.[20]

Dr. Willem Kolff created the first drum dialyzer in 1943.[21] Its widespread use in the Korean War cut mortality from acute renal failure in half. After this success, hospitals quickly built inpatient dialysis units for their acute renal failure patients, to tide them over until the cause of temporary kidney failure could be addressed. A handful of hospitals opened wards for patients with chronic renal failure, but this was impractical because it essentially entailed permanent hospitalization.

This changed in 1960, when Belding Scribner developed the first arteriovenous, or AV, shunt—a Teflon-coated, U-shaped tube that offered long-term, convenient access to a patient's blood vessels for dialysis. Once the Scribner Shunt was inserted, no further surgery was necessary. While patients still needed dialysis for the rest of their lives (or at least until transplant), they could now come and go as they pleased between dialysis sessions. Recognizing the potential for his invention, Scribner founded the world's first outpatient dialysis center in 1962, and the field of nephrology grew tremendously to handle the burgeoning number of chronic renal failure patients whose life expectancies were suddenly extended through dialysis. In the language of Chapter 5, renal failure was transformed from an acute to a largely chronic disease.

Scribner's AV shunt enabled a truly disruptive business model. Today, there are 4,200 dialysis centers in the United States. Patients can travel far from home by scheduling treatments at dialysis centers around the country. Dialysis nurses, rather than nephrologists, and clinics, rather than hospitals, could provide most of the care. While dialysis continues to prolong the lives of 350,000 Americans today, the cost of care has been tremendous: $32.5 billion was spent on care for end-stage renal disease patients in 2004, and this amount is expected to grow at 9 to 10 percent each year.[22]

But the story does not end there. Just as outpatient dialysis centers disruptively drove hospitals from this market, in-home dialysis has tremendous potential for disrupting the dialysis centers. The first in-home machines of the 1960s weren't pretty—they were typically converted washing machines that required costly modifications to the home electrical and plumbing systems. The machinery was complex and difficult to operate. But as the technology for home dialysis improved, the added convenience and privacy it offered generated strong demand. By 1972, 40 percent of the 11,000 dialysis patients in the United States were on home hemodialysis.[23] Today, machines like System One from Lawrence, Massachusetts–based NxStage are just the size of a microwave, enabling portability within the house and away from home. There is no need to modify electrical and plumbing systems. Patients follow simple rules to operate the device.[24] *Home hemodialysis is about 40 percent less costly than clinic-based dialysis.*[25] Adopting this disruptive technology would have saved Medicare $3.9 billion in 2005[26]—chump change for some, but for those of us who work for a living, that's *a lot* of money. What's more, in-home dialysis typically is done daily, compared to the thrice-weekly regimen offered in clinics—better matching normal human physiology and very possibly leading to improved health outcomes.

Despite the advantages in cost and convenience that disruptive home hemodialysis offers, however, the market is moving *away* from it, not into it. Over the past 14 years, in-center hemodialysis has grown 7.25 percent annually.[27] Only 0.6 percent of all patients—fewer than 2,000, compared to 11,000 in 1972, when the technology wasn't nearly as good—are on home hemodialysis today.[28]

What derailed the disruption? Fee-for-service reimbursement. In 1972, as renal care clinics were rolling out, Congress created the End-Stage Renal Disease (ESRD) program to guarantee fully reimbursed dialysis to anyone with kidney failure. ESRD remains the only medical condition that has ever been given a legislated guarantee of access to reimbursed care for everyone.

Because of their fixed cost investments, owners of dialysis clinics like Fresenius and DaVita profit by keeping their clinics full. Further, nephrologists often have a financial stake in the clinics in which they work, and are cited by patients as the most influential factor in determining whether they are dialyzed in the clinic or at home. They comprise a value network that has been very successful to date, having helped millions of patients with kidney failure. But can we expect them to urge patients toward home dialysis? Not when they profit so handsomely from guaranteed fees for high-cost service.

As evidence that reimbursement reform would facilitate disruptive business models in the absence of such fee-for-service, NxStage reports that 30 to 40 percent of its patients are private-pay.[29] And in New Zealand, where consumers are much more engaged in determining when and how to start dialysis, over 25 percent of hemodialysis candidates are treated at home.[30]

How can we be so concerned with exploding health-care costs and be pouring fee-for-service fuel on the fire? The reason is that, given the present independent structure of hospitals and physicians' practices, there is no alternative. That's why separation of the different business models that are now conflated within hospitals and doctors' offices is such an important initial step, and why integrated entities—employers and integrated fixed-fee providers—need to emerge to wrap their arms around this problem. Then and only then will we discover that FFS is *not* the only way, let alone the best way, to transact business in health care. FFS will persist in solution shops. But we'll be able to bill, guarantee, and pay for work done in value-adding process businesses on a price-for-outcome basis, and gain the benefits of network services on a fee-for-membership or fee-for-transaction basis.

Dr. Robert Nesse of Mayo Clinic described the present condition with this query: "What would the cost of [a] hamburger at TGI Fridays be if, instead of paying for the outcome of good food delivered in a congenial location by friendly service, we actually just paid for the number of cooks . . . and how many wait staff that went by . . . What would happen to the price of a hamburger?"[31]

Distortions Created by Administered Pricing

The second of the three involuntary evils created by today's health assistance industry is the system by which Medicare and insurance companies' formulas and appellate processes determine the prices of various health-care products and services. Medical fees were initially reimbursed by insurers based on "usual, customary, and reasonable" (UCR) charges determined by the hospitals and physicians that provided the care. As we described in Chapter 3, however, the conflated business models and the almost limitless number of pathways that patients can take through hospitals makes it literally impossible for the typical hospital to allocate its massive bucket of overhead costs to individual patients and procedures with any degree of accuracy. What's worse, the fees are based on costs, not the value created by a procedure. Except for the focused operators of value-adding process hospitals and clinics, neither the providers nor the insurers have an accurate sense of what real costs and real value are for most services offered.

As Medicare, Medicaid, and private health assistance companies pervasively inserted themselves between patients and providers, the market ultimately evolved toward what economists call *monopsony*—where a few huge, powerful buyers essentially determine the prices they will pay to their more fragmented suppliers. As market power shifted, health assistance firms essentially decided that while the charges from hospitals and physicians might be usual and customary, they almost certainly were *not* reasonable. They therefore devised formulas of the genre of the cost-based time-and-motion studies that characterized the work of Frederick Taylor in manufacturing a century ago.

The insurers' algorithms incorporated physician labor, indirect expenses, equipment costs, geographic location, and many other factors in calculating amounts for reimbursement. Because many of these formulas are based upon methods and technologies commonly used 20 years ago, the pace of change has rendered the resulting fee schedule hopelessly inaccurate. Although the fee schedule is constantly updated, having undergone thousands of corrections since its inception, the reimbursement payments it dictates often bear little relation to the value of the services rendered. As a result, health assistance companies and providers often find it easier to simply pass cost increases on to the employers, rather than argue with each other about prices.[32] "They're spending my money as if it were my money," the CEO of a major manufacturing company lamented to us.

The result is that some medical services—particularly those that are procedure-based—have remained or become wildly profitable, while others, including office visits and out-of-office care, are undercompensated and therefore undesirable. Because profits attract investment, the de facto but pervasive economic regulation through this pricing mechanism has transformed America's health-care economy into a centrally planned one. The difference between a communist central planning system and this one, however, is that those who were pulling the strings in the Kremlin, for instance, were consciously empowered to do so. In America it is inadvertent central planning.

And it gets worse. In the present system of administered pricing, Medicare, Medicaid, and the health assistance companies simply cannot establish unique pricing algorithms for each nuanced improvement in drugs, devices, or services. Instead, they have created major groupings of these things, and they analyze and administer pricing by these categories—each of which is known by its Current Procedural Terminology (CPT) code under a system administered by the American Medical Association (AMA). A drug or device might have the disruptive potential to solve a problem in a cost effective but unique way, but the cost of getting a unique CPT code established for this new product is so high, and the probability that the AMA—the organization representing those who will be disrupted—will approve a disruptively positioned product is so low, that even the most determined disruptors can become disheartened. It is far easier instead to force-fit potentially disruptive innovations into existing CPT categories. That act, however, typically juxtaposes the disruptive technology head-on, on a sustaining basis, against the price and performance of established technologies in the existing market. In a world of fee-for-service and passed-through costs, the decision makers simply have no incentive to adopt disruptions.

Market Distortions from Blanket Contracting

The third way in which today's health assistance programs impede the efficiency of the health-care industry is through the practice of insurance companies negotiating volume discounts with hospitals through blanket contracting. This badly distorts the signal and amplifies the noise to providers and investors about where the opportunities for improving health care actually are. These discounts are an illusion—they are achieved by hospitals raising prices on patients who aren't covered by the blanket contracts with major insurers.

The competitive structure of most other industries causes companies to differentiate themselves—to find products or services that they can provide better than any competitors, and then to focus their resources on what they're best at providing. The process of winning contracts from the insurance companies, in contrast, compels general hospitals to offer the full breadth of services the insured population might need—to offer every service that every other hospital is offering. This exacerbates the complexity of general hospitals, driving up their overhead costs. It pits one-size-fits-all businesses into competition with other one-size-fits-all businesses, where every hospital aspires to be the best in everything. No manager would predict that such strategies will lead to efficiency and quality. Because disruptive care delivery institutions will be more focused, these contracting practices continue to funnel most patient volume to high-cost general hospital business models, preserving their prosperity despite their high costs, rather than directing patient volume to the disruptive providers.

Health assistance companies assert that they're creating value by bundling the volumes from multiple employers to negotiate lower prices from hospitals. But this sort of negotiation-for-discounts only creates lower costs if the suppliers are earning excess profit, or if suppliers' competitive markets are so lax that they have lost control of their costs. Neither of these situations characterizes today's hospitals. In a good year, the typical hospital's profit will be 2 percent of revenues.[33] The high cost of hospitalization isn't driven by the excess profits of general hospitals. The costs are simply inherent to the one-size-fits-all value proposition they offer. Squeezing the prices paid to hospitals won't cause them to become markedly more efficient—any more than the corporate bean counters could squeeze more cost out of Noelle Allen's Pontiac plant at Michigan Manufacturing Corporation. The cost in hospitals is created by the conflation of multiple business models, and the complexity of service offerings within each of those models, all under one institutional roof. The contracting practices of health assistance companies exacerbate this practice and continue to drive costs up, not down.

In the remainder of this chapter we'll advocate that we need two types of payments products in tomorrow's health-care system. When employers begin directly managing employees' health care to ensure that they find providers whose business models best suit the nature of each problem, a combination product of high-deductible insurance with health savings accounts will help our system become better. And in cases where integrated entities are providing care, capitation is the best answer.

DISAGGREGATING DISSIMILAR PRODUCTS

High-Deductible Insurance

Insurance creates value by hedging against low-probability events that have financially devastating results. Insurance is an important component of our financial plans to build and protect our prosperity: it protects us and our families from the financial consequences of death, disability, fires, and accidents. Hedging against devastating hospital costs was the genesis of health insurance as well—it emerged in the 1920s when hospital care became a viable but unaffordable pathway to recovery. We call products like these "true insurance."

Ever since medical expenses began to rise dramatically in the 1920s, the need to insure against the cost of financially cata-strophic illness has been remarkably unchanged. Figure 7.2 compares the distribution of medical costs across the U.S. population in 1928 and 2002. In both years, Pareto's law was apparent: 20 percent of the population accounted for 80 percent of health-care costs, and 5 percent of the population accounted for 50 percent of all costs. Yet because it is so difficult to predict exactly who will fall into that 5 percent, insurance is necessary for all but the very rich, to protect ourselves from this financial risk.

But insurance makes little sense for events that have a high probability of occurrence and recurrence and which are not

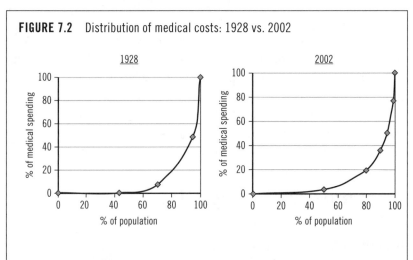

FIGURE 7.2   Distribution of medical costs: 1928 vs. 2002

Sources: Falk, IS, et. al. "The Costs of Medical Care," Publications of the Committee on the Costs of Medical Care: No. 27. The University of Chicago Press, 1933; Conwell, L. J. and Cohen, J. W. Characteristics of Persons with High Medical Expenditures in the U.S. Civilian Noninstitutionalized Population, 2002. Statistical Brief #73. March 2005. Agency for Healthcare Research and Quality, Rockville, Md.

financially devastating. One would not purchase insurance against the possibility of needing to pay for clothing and electricity, for example. To profitably cover the sales and administration costs of providing such insurance, premiums would need to be priced above the ongoing costs of those predictable events—meaning it is cheaper for people simply to pay those costs out of pocket rather than route the money through a third-party claims processor.

When employers began to pay for low-priced, predictable, recurrent health-care events, it was a tax-advantaged form of employee compensation. When insurance companies lumped that benefit together with true insurance in "comprehensive health plans," however, they lumped a sensible, value-creating insurance product with a reimbursement service that actually destroys economic value because of its administrative overhead.[34]

Just as mutually incompatible business models within hospitals need to be teased apart in order to appropriately price the services of solution shops and value-adding process businesses, these mutually incompatible health insurance and reimbursement products need to be separated so they create rather than destroy economic value. This is the rationale behind the unbundled pairing of high-deductible insurance (HDI) and Health Savings Accounts (HSA) that more and more companies are offering their employees. Unbundling comprehensive health plans into these constituent parts is, in our view, one of the most important reforms to be made in health care. Where employers cannot or choose not to link their employees into an integrated health system that uses capitation and is aggressively implementing disruption, an HDI-HSA plan will be a necessary element of the new disruptive value network that major employers will need to orchestrate.

Health Savings Accounts

Health savings accounts were formally enabled by the Medicare Prescription Drug, Improvement, and Modernization Act signed by President George W. Bush in 2003. These accounts offer a tax-free, portable savings vehicle to help people pay for low-ticket, relatively predictable and recurrent medical expenses. As such, HSAs typically are offered with a high-deductible insurance product. Though the concepts underlying HSAs had already existed for at least 20 years, the Medicare Modernization Act relaxed a number of restrictions on eligibility for enrollees.

Briefly, here's how health savings accounts work. Our employer says to us, "It's costing us $10,000 per year to provide health assistance to your family—and you're contributing an additional $3,000 per year to your health-care costs in the form of copayments and other expenses we don't cover. From now on we're going to spend $5,000 per year to purchase a true umbrella insurance policy for you—a high-deductible health plan—to protect your assets and cover the cost of unpredictable high-cost medical events that arise. But we're going to put the other $5,000 into an account at a firm like Fidelity Investments.[35] It will be linked to the 401(k) retirement account you already have there.

"Just like our expenditures to cover your health-care costs in the past, this amount that we deposit into your HSA account will be a before-tax expense to us. And just like you can make before-tax contributions to your 401(k) account, you can contribute additional money, before it is taxed, to your HSA to maximize your savings beyond the $5,000 we'll be putting in for you.[36] You should invest this money just as you do in your 401(k), and the earnings will compound tax-free. In other words, this can be a *huge* enhancement to your retirement package.[37]

"Until you hit the level of spending on health-care costs at which the high-deductible insurance kicks in, you'll need to pay for those costs from your HSA. This means that the more frugally you manage your health-care costs, the more will accumulate, tax-free, in your HSA account. When you retire, this money and the money in your 401(k) are yours to use in any way you wish.

"And one more thing. Our costs of insuring your family have been increasing at about 10 percent per year. If we keep shelling money out for health-care costs, our company will go under—and none of us will have jobs. So we're not going to increase this HSA contribution beyond $5,000 per year. But you'll be okay. The typical mutual fund in which you're likely to invest your HSA

balance historically appreciates at a compounded annual rate
of about 8 to 10 percent—so you'll be able to keep up with the
inflating costs of your health care.[38] And if the disruptive business
models that Christensen, Grossman, and Hwang recommended
in their book come to fruition, you'll be *much* better off than you
are today. You'll have better care for serious problems. Access to
the day-to-day stuff will be much more convenient. And you'll
have a significantly larger retirement nest egg."

Figure 7.3 diagrams how health savings accounts will fit with
high-deductible insurance. HSAs will be used for lower-cost,
recurrent health-care expenses. Insurance will kick in after an
annual deductible has been incurred. Whether there is a gap
between the amount that could be covered by the HSA and the
point at which insurance would kick in will vary by employers'
plans and the propensity of individuals to economize their health-
related spending.

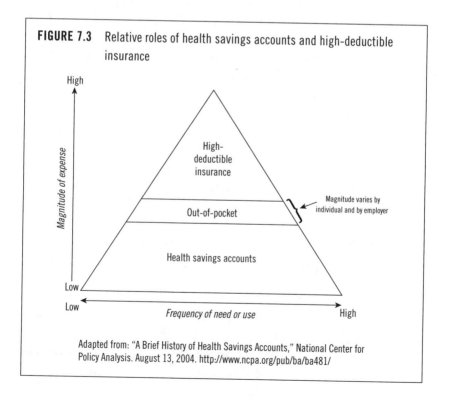

FIGURE 7.3   Relative roles of health savings accounts and high-deductible insurance

Adapted from: "A Brief History of Health Savings Accounts," National Center for Policy Analysis. August 13, 2004. http://www.ncpa.org/pub/ba/ba481/

In short, HSAs are meant to encourage users to spend wisely by giving them control of their health-care dollars. It removes the drawbacks and restraints of the reimbursement system and gives price-sensitive consumers the motivation to seek value as they have defined value for themselves. At the same time, the pursuit of health also becomes a mechanism for increasing wealth. Individuals who practice healthy behaviors will generally see their long-term savings increase by a greater margin.

WHAT JOBS ARE REIMBURSEMENT AND INSURANCE HIRED TO DO?

The jobs-to-be-done model that we presented in Chapter 1 (remember the milkshake?) helps us evaluate the strengths and weaknesses of various forms of health assistance. Two specific implications of the model merit special attention.

First, the process of paying for health care isn't a job to be done—it is an *experience* that customers go through as they hire a provider to do the fundamental jobs of becoming or remaining healthy. More convenient methods of payment will typically be preferred over less convenient ones. Similarly, *cost* isn't a job either. It's a characteristic of each of the competing products and services that might be hired to do the job.

And second, if we want to reform the present reimbursement system, the reform has to get the job done for employers, providers, politicians, patients, *and* insurers. Each has veto power. If one presents an insurmountable hurdle, then that group needs to be cut out of the new system—or the reform will sputter and fail.

Jobs that Patients, Providers, Suppliers, Politicians, Employers, and Insurers Need to Do

While we would welcome others' attempts to delve deeply into this question, we suggest that among patients, providers, suppliers (such as pharmaceutical, biotechnology, and device companies), politicians, employers, and health assistance companies, there are eight jobs that need to be done that impact insurance and reimbursement. We'll describe each briefly here, and then summarize in Figure 7.4 how well various insurance and reimbursement products do these particular jobs.[39]

Patient Jobs

1. **Help me and my family to become healthy.** Almost universally, becoming well gets top priority when people become sick.

2. **Help us to remain healthy.** One needs only to stand along running trails, or study sales figures for natural foods and nutriceutical products, to see that this is an important job that many (but not all) people are trying to do. Many of those with illnesses like obesity, diabetes, heart disease, asthma, and nicotine addiction either don't feel the urgent need to do this job on a daily basis or find the challenge simply too daunting to overcome.

3. **Help us achieve financial ability.** Financial ability means different things to different people at different stages of life. For the young, it often means acquiring the ability to afford things they want, such as cars, homes, and high-definition flat screen televisions. For the middle-aged, it means saving enough to provide for a comfortable retirement. And so on. One frustrated physician once vented to us that some of his patients seemed "to care more about their wallets than about their health." This is often true. Until poor health arrives, many people feel the need to achieve financial ability more intensely than they feel the need to be healthy.

4. **Protect my assets from being taken or destroyed.** This is the raison d'être of most types of insurance. We hire property and casualty insurance, mortgage insurance, and auto insurance to protect the value of important assets from being taken or destroyed in the event of theft, accident, or disaster.

Provider and Supplier Jobs

5. **Help me get paid fairly for products and services rendered.** Getting paid at a profitable level is essential to the financial viability of hospitals, physicians, and networks.

Providers of solution shop services need to receive fee-for-service payment; those providing value-adding process services can be paid for outcomes; and network facilitators need membership fees. All providers want to be paid in ways that account not just for costs, but for the value of the outcomes achieved—and to be paid promptly with minimal harassment. Similarly, makers of diagnostics, therapeutics, equipment, and other supplies need to remain sufficiently profitable to continue innovating new solutions.

Employer Jobs

6. **Help me cost-effectively attract and retain the best possible employees, and make them as productive as possible.** This job-to-be-done was the primary rationale for putting employers in the business of covering employees' health-care costs in the first place. This job persists today—and is experienced more urgently, in many companies, than in the past.

Insurance Company Jobs

7. **Help me avoid paying for unnecessary services.**[40] Health assistance companies, whether for-profit (e.g., Aetna, UnitedHealth), not-for-profit (BCBS), or government (Medicare and Medicaid in the U.S., national systems elsewhere), need to remain financially viable. A key lever for doing this is to pay only for medically appropriate services. This often pits insurers in an adversarial role against providers, whose job is also to make a profit and who submit claims at what they believe are fair prices. A key point of cost control for insurance companies is to deny, delay, or make partial payments—engaging in a costly tit-for-tat with providers that adds significant costs to health care.

Politicians' Jobs

8. **Help me to win votes.** One way politicians stay in office is by plausibly promising more, while still balancing the budget. But if balancing governmental budgets is hard now,

we haven't seen anything yet. As we noted earlier, the trajectory of health-care cost inflation already has rendered nearly every local government technically bankrupt. And the cost of health coverage for the burgeoning population of the elderly will balloon America's Medicare costs to the point that 20 years hence there will be no room in the federal budget for anything except defense, Medicaid, and Medicare. Yet it seems that every significant attempt to reign in these exploding costs unleashes a maelstrom of electoral malice, intimidating even the most courageous politicians, thereby preventing this job from getting done.

THE SCORECARD: HOW WELL DO DIFFERENT SYSTEMS GET THESE JOBS DONE?

In Figure 7.4 we've arrayed our assessment of how well the available alternative payment mechanisms do each of these jobs. We've again used *Consumer Reports* style of circles to rate the performance of each product (where a filled-in circle signifies that the product does that job excellently, and an empty circle depicts the product performing poorly). These ratings represent our synthesis of information gathered from hundreds of hours spent in interviews, industry meetings, and study of published reports.

Note that none of the systems does the first job excellently: "Help me to become healthy." The reason is that the payments mechanism doesn't heal. At best it constitutes no barrier to access. In our calculus, therefore, the best rating that can be given to a payments program for this job is a neutral one. Capitation in a nonintegrated system does this the worst, because it restricts access. We also rate national health plans as neutral. In many of these plans, entry-level care is more readily available than in the United States. But access to specialist care is often tightly rationed. Integrated capitation and the HDI-HSA combination score best on "help me to maintain my health" because they embody financial motivation to do this job.

FIGURE 7.4 Assessment of how well alternative systems get the job done

		Fee for service	National health plans	Capitation in independent systems	Capitation in integrated systems	HSAs and HDI
Patient jobs	Help me to become healthy	Neutral	Neutral	Detracts	Good	Neutral
	Help me to maintain my health	Neutral	Neutral	Detracts	Good	Good
	Help me achieve financial security	Neutral	Neutral	Neutral	Neutral	Good
	Protect my assets from being taken or destroyed	Neutral	Good	Excellent	Excellent	Excellent
Provider jobs	Pay me for services rendered.	Good	Detracts	Neutral	Excellent	Good
Employer jobs	Help me cost-effectively attract and retain the best possible employees.	Good	Badly counter-productive	Detracts	Good	Excellent
Insurer jobs	Help me avoid paying for unnecessary services	Badly counter-productive	Detracts	Excellent	Excellent	Neutral
Politicians' jobs	Help me stay in office while I balance the budget	Badly counter-productive	Badly counter-productive	Badly counter-productive	Good	Good

Key: Excellent, Good, Neutral, Detracts, Badly counter-productive

Fee-for-service, capitation, and nationalized health plans pay for health costs, but only the combination of HDI and HSAs has a mechanism to help consumers build financial ability. We rate nationalized health systems poorly for the "pay me for services rendered" job. The reason is that while collecting a paycheck from the national health service is simple, caregivers are typically paid at modest levels, compared to those in private practice.

The table in Figure 7.4 suggests that the three historically dominant forms of health coverage—fee-for-service (which includes Medicare and Medicaid), capitation in nonintegrated health systems, and nationalized health systems—each suffer from fatal flaws, in that they do one or more crucial jobs very poorly. FFS, in particular, rates badly on the jobs that politicians and insurance companies need to do, because they put no brake on the unbridled escalation of health-care costs. In contrast, the combination of Health Savings Accounts (HSAs) and High-

Deductible Insurance (HDI) seems to offer a set of experiences and features that, while not perfect, do more jobs better than traditional alternatives.[41] Capitation within integrated providers (integrated capitation) gets the best overall score.

Why Haven't Integrated Capitation and HSAs Taken Off?

If integrated capitation and the HSA-HDI combination rate so strongly, why has the switch to these new mechanisms been so sluggish? The answer for integrated capitation is obvious: capitation only works in an integrated provider system, and integrated providers currently account for about 5 percent of people covered in America.[42] When capitation is attempted in a nonintegrated system, it places independent businesspeople in a zero-sum game, where one doctor's gain becomes another's loss. As the advantages of integrated providers become apparent among firms attempting to build a disruptive value network in health care, we would expect integrated capitation to grow in popularity.

There are two reasons why the uptake on the HDI-HSA cocktail has been slower than some reformers envisioned.

First, they have typically been offered in isolation—ignoring the mandate for creating a new disruptive value network that we discussed in Chapter 6, and without the business model innovations discussed in Chapters 3 through 5 that make week-to-week access to caregivers convenient and affordable. Comprehensive health plans have long shielded us from the real costs of health-care services. When the copayment is only $10, most of us have been willing to put up with the inefficiencies and poor service that the typical physician's practice offers. For $10, after all, what more could you expect? But when patients suddenly have to pay the doctor the full $150 cost of the visit out of their HSAs, they become very conscious of the value and convenience of what they're buying. And they rarely like what they see. For this reason, simultaneous innovations like retail clinics are crucial to satisfaction with HSAs. If we're going to ask people to start paying for their health care, we'd better make it affordable and convenient.

The second reason the rate of adoption has been more modest than anticipated is related to the first. One rule in launching disruptive innovations is that the initial customers should be non-consumers rather than users of the traditional products—because the only way the new will unseat the old among the original customer set is if the new performs better along the metrics of performance valued by those who use the old product.[43] Many companies have simply offered HSAs as one option on a menu of health plans open to employees. In doing this, they pit HSAs head-on against sustaining competition from existing products—and history has shown that such strategies rarely succeed. When invited to compare HSAs versus comprehensive fee-for-service plans on a feature-by-feature basis, HSAs don't stack up well to the untrained eye. Employees compare the copays levied by their comprehensive plans, versus the risk that HSAs might entail an "out-of-pocket gap" of the sort depicted as the middle band in Figure 7.3. Many have consequently opted to "play it safe"—and stick with conventional comprehensive coverage.

Where paired HDI and HSAs have disruptively taken root is in small and start-up companies that can't afford the luxury of traditional comprehensive insurance. There is a direct analogy between this and the pattern by which 401(k) retirement investment plans disrupted traditional pension plans in the 1980s. Pension plans first appeared on the American benefits landscape in the early 1950s. For the first three decades, most workers' retirement benefits such as pensions and Social Security were structured as *defined benefit* plans. These plans defined the benefits retirees would receive upon retirement—a stream of payments after retirement that, in theory at least, would flow from cash being stockpiled during the employee's working life by the company or the government in a pension investment fund. Most small and start-up companies could not offer pension plans—their employees were left to save for retirement as best they could.

Beginning in the 1980s, Individual Retirement Accounts and 401(k) plans emerged. In these *defined contribution* plans, employers that had not been able to offer generous pension plans defined how much money they would contribute—which typically was much less than major companies were paying into their employee pension plans at the time. Because employees could contribute pretax money into these plans too, some employers offered to match employee contributions, and employees working in smaller companies could still save for retirement in a tax-advantaged way.

In contrast to defined benefit plans, in defined contribution schemes the employees are responsible for investing their retirement funds as they accumulate. The benefits that ultimately flow from the accounts depend on how frugally and well the employees contribute to and manage these accounts. When measured by the metrics of "quality" in the world of defined-benefit pension plans, 401(k) accounts don't stack up. But like all disruptions, these plans have proven to be enormously popular among nonconsumers of traditional pension benefits—because the 401(k) is infinitely better than nothing.[44] Fewer and fewer companies now offer traditional pension plans as a result of this disruption.

Traditional comprehensive health plans—whether fee-for-service (including Medicare), capitation, or nationalized medicine—are defined *benefit* plans similar to pension plans. They focus on what employees and their families get *out* of the plan; and the assumption has been that employers and the government will put whatever is required *into* these plans in order to get the defined benefits out. Health savings accounts are defined *contribution* plans. The focus is on what employers and employees put *into* the plans and keep there. The benefits that participants are able to take out depend on how conscientiously they contribute, how carefully they manage what is put in, and how judiciously they use health-care services. We expect that, because of their disruptive character, these plans will take root first among companies and individuals that have struggled to pay the full cost of traditional comprehensive plans—small businesses, start-ups, and the self-employed—and then move disruptively up-market.

The perception today of many observers that the HDI-HSA combination will never gain enough traction to sweep the health-care world is caused by the S-curve pattern by which nearly all new technologies substitute for the old. When a new approach substitutes for an old one because it has a technological or economic advantage, the pattern of substitution almost always follows an S-curve,[45] as depicted on the left side of Figure 7.5. The vertical axis measures the percent of the market for which the new approach accounts. The S-curves are sometimes steep, at other times gradual. But almost always disruptions follow this pattern: the initial substitution pace is slow, then it steepens dramatically, and finally asymptotically saturates 100 percent of the market.

A persistent problem emerges for the incumbent industry leaders when one of these substitutions occurs, however. When the nascent technology accounts for only a tiny fraction of the total market (they're on the flat part at the bottom of the S-curve), the incumbent leaders project linearly into the future and conclude that there is no need to worry about the new approach because it will not be important for a long time. But then the world flips suddenly, crippling the established companies. For example, after a decade of incubation on the curve's flat portion, digital photography flipped on the film companies very rapidly. The result? Polaroid is gone. Agfa is gone. Fuji is seriously struggling. Kodak alone caught the wave—and it's been a rough ride.[46]

You might think that companies would learn from this experience, but the S-curve pattern of adoption begs a vexing question: if I'm on the initial flat portion of the curve, how can I know whether my world will flip to the new approach next year or in 10 years? It turns out there is a way to forecast the flip. First, as shown on the right side of Figure 7.5, one must plot on the vertical axis the *ratio* of percentage market share held by the new, divided by the percentage share held by the old (if each has 50 percent share, this ratio will be 1.0). Second, the vertical axis needs to be arrayed on a logarithmic scale—so that .0001, .001,

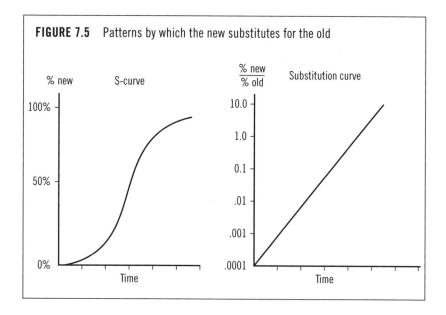

FIGURE 7.5 Patterns by which the new substitutes for the old

.01, 0.1, 1.0, and 10.0 are all equidistant, as can be seen in the graph. When plotted in this way, the data always falls on a straight line. Sometimes the line slopes upward steeply, and sometimes it is more gradual. But it is always straight. The reason is that the mathematics "linearizes" the S-curve.

As a result, you get a pretty good sense of the slope of the linearized curve, even when the new approach accounts for only 2 to 3 percent of the total. That makes it easy to extend the line into the future to obtain a general sense of when the new innovation will account for 25 percent, 50 percent, and 90 percent of the total. We call this line a "substitution curve."

Figure 7.6 shows the pace of substitution of HSAs and HDI, versus conventional private health plans.[47] The new instruments now account for about 3.1 percent of the total number of individuals covered through private insurance.[48] This suggests, however, that by 2010, HDI-HSAs will account for 10 percent

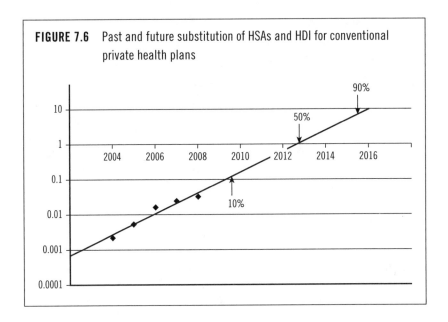

FIGURE 7.6 Past and future substitution of HSAs and HDI for conventional private health plans

of the market. The 50 percent mark will be hit in about 2013. They will asymptotically approach 90 percent by about 2016 or so. In other words, we've been on the flat part of the S-curve for several years, but we seem to be approaching the steep portion of the ramp quite quickly.

Note that even after HDI-HSAs supplant today's comprehensive health coverage, solution shops will need to be paid on a fee-for-service basis; value-adding process providers can be compensated on a fee-for-outcome basis; and patient management and patient network providers can be paid on a fee-for-membership basis. They can adopt appropriate profit formulas, independent of the insurance-reimbursement method in use.

Different Products Competing for the Same Job Will Eventually Integrate

When different products compete for the same job, those products often converge—and as a consequence we expect that 401(k) and HSA plans will converge into two different pages on the account statements that we receive from financial management companies like Fidelity Investments.

By way of illustration, the BlackBerry, made by Research In Motion, Ltd., has been highly successful because it was designed to do a job that *lots* of people needed to do—to be productive in small snippets of time. The BlackBerry actually competes for this job against the cellular telephone in the mind of many customers—because placing a phone call is another way to be productive in a small snippet of time. We predicted in an article written in 2001 that as a result, the BlackBerry and the cellular telephone would merge into a single product—because at that time customers had to carry both products and choose between them whenever they had that job of "help me be productive in this small snippet of time."[49] The BlackBerry subsequently has incorporated voice capabilities, and most cellular phones now offer wireless messaging, games, and personal organizer functions.

The principle is: when two different products are being hired for two different jobs that arise at different points in time and space in the lives of customers, we expect those products to remain independent of each other. Companies that offer both will not have an advantage over companies that focus on one or the other. But if the job(s) that different products are being hired to do arises at the same point in time and space in the life of a customer, then we expect companies that offer both products to build a competitive advantage. This is why, for example, companies that seek to become "financial supermarkets" by offering the full range of products customers could possible need—including checking accounts, savings accounts, credit cards, brokerage services, life insurance, consumer loans, and mortgage loans—typically fail. The jobs that each of these are hired to do arise at different points in a customer's life. In contrast, the reason why gasoline stations and convenience stores have converged is that the desire to fill up on junk food and the need to fill up with gasoline arise at the same time for many customers.

What this suggests is that companies like Fidelity Investments, whose 401(k) management services are positioned on the job of "help me achieve financial ability," as it was put in Figure 7.4, are likely to begin offering HSAs and market them to customers as fulfilling the same job as the 401(k). They will begin reporting their status in the same monthly statement to their customers. Since Fidelity's business model relies on a percentage fee of assets under management, they have an interest in helping customers maintain their health and keep long-term medical expenses low through appropriate preventive care. This type of integration between financial services and health care will accelerate as companies realize the interdependence of these products and continue to merge their features.

Indeed, in order to minimize administrative costs for HSAs, some HSA account holders are already given debit cards to use when purchasing health-care products and services—so that with no reimbursement paperwork required, owners simply swipe their HSA card, and special bar codes will verify the eligibility of the product or service to be purchased with HSA funds.[50]

Just as the FDIC, Federal Reserve Bank, and Securities and Exchange Commission oversee the operations of commercial and investment banks, a "Federal Health Assistance Commission" will need to set standards for financial health and customer service. Policies must be portable—so that as we change employers we can take our coverage and accounts with us. Different employers can choose to contribute different portions to the cost of our HDI and HSA accounts, but the accounts themselves must be personal and portable.

THE UNINSURED AND THE POOR: COVERAGE WITHOUT CARE?

When politicians, advocacy groups, and emergency department administrators huddle to discuss the growing cost of health care, the increasing number of Americans who lack insurance coverage for catastrophic care is frequently fingered both as a culprit and a result. Some states, such as Massachusetts, have recently enacted rules requiring that *everyone* be covered by health insurance.[51] Employers above a minimum size are required to purchase insurance for their employees. Smaller employers that cannot afford to purchase such insurance can receive government assistance in doing so; and low-income individuals can apply for assistance in purchasing their own insurance. To make these insurance products affordable, they typically have very high deductibles—creating the rather silly situation where the poor are forced to be "covered" by paying for mandated catastrophic insurance whose threshold is so high that the vast majority of them will be unable to use it.

The medical expenses foremost on the minds of most of the uninsured are not those resulting from catastrophic hospitalization. Rather, they are the costs of day-to-day care for acute infectious diseases and routine medications. When we mandate high-deductible insurance coverage and yet allow physicians' groups to block the licensing of affordable retail clinics in poor neighborhoods, those we are hoping to help have little access to the noncatastrophic care so essential to their daily well-being. Dr. Marcia Angell, former executive editor of the *New England Journal of Medicine*, calls this situation universal "coverage without care."[52]

There is a solution, however. Just as certain employers have created incentives for accumulating retirement savings by matching, dollar-for-dollar, employees' contributions to their 401(k) accounts, governments could do the same with HSAs—matching by formula contributions that low-income citizens make to their HSAs. In addition, by fostering low-cost disruptive business models such as retail clinics and patient networks that can be paired with payment mechanisms such as joint-contribution HSAs, governments can make a significant dent in the persistent problem called the "uninsured poor." The solution for the uninsured poor isn't just to help them afford health care. It must also make care affordable.

NOTES

1. The Federal Register is a federal government publication that includes official transactions of the U.S. Congress, as well as all federal agencies.

2. We will return to the topic of regulations in health care in Chapter 11.

3. Two important recent works make the case for consumer value. See Herzlinger, Regina, *Consumer-Driven Health Care: Implications for Providers, Payers, and Policy-Makers* (San Francisco: Jossey-Bass, 2004); and Porter, Michael, and Elizabeth Teisberg, *Redefining Health Care: Creating Value-Based Competition on Results* (Boston, Massachusetts: Harvard Business School Press, 2006). Both thoroughly explore the issues of creating value that can be measured. We recommend their work to all serious students of these problems.

4. Medicare rates must also fit within the federal budget, and therefore often have little to do with the value delivered in return. Typically, commercial insurers will use Medicare rates as a baseline for setting their own payment schedules, thereby compounding the problem.

5. The motivation can even lead to questionable care, as evident by the investigation in 2002 of Redding Medical Center in California, where doctors were accused of performing unnecessary tests and surgeries. See Eichenwald, Kurt, "Operating Profits: Mining Medicare; How One Hospital Benefited from Questionable Surgery," *New York Times*, August 12, 2003; and Gaul, Gilbert M., "At California Hospital, Red Flags and an FBI Raid," *Washington Post*, July 25, 2005, A09.

6. Horwitz, Jill R., "Making Profits and Providing Care: Comparing Nonprofit, For-Profit, and Government Hospitals," *Health Affairs*, vol. 24, no. 3 (2005): 790–801.

7. Falk, Isadore S., et al., *The Cost of Medical Care* (Chicago: University of Chicago Press, 1933).

8. The first incarnation of Blue Cross was in 1929 at Baylor University, which offered a health plan to Dallas area teachers that guaranteed 21 days of hospital care for six dollars per year. The origin of Blue Shield was the California Physicians' Service, which in 1939 began offering physician services for $1.70 per month to low-wage employees. These prepaid plans were also a response to a contemporary push to adopt compulsory health insurance nationwide.

9. Thomasson, Melissa, "Health Insurance in the United States," EH.Net Encyclopedia, edited by Robert Whaples, April 18, 2003. Accessed from http://eh.net/encyclopedia/article/thomasson.insurance.health.us.

10. Stabilization Act of 1942. Title 50, Appendix—"War and National Defense," October 2, 1942.

11. The history of HMOs can be traced back much earlier, though Kaiser's predecessors were more limited in scope. In 1930, Dr. George M. Mackenzie of the Mary Imogene Bassett Hospital (now part of Bassett Health Care) implemented a program in which full medical coverage was provided in exchange for an annual premium of $25 per individual. See http://www.bassett.org/history.cfm for more information.

12. Johnson, Harry M., "Major Medical Expense Insurance," *The Journal of Risk and Insurance*, 32, no. 2 (1965), 211–36.

13. See Follmann, Joseph F., "The Growth of Group Health Insurance," *Journal of Risk and Insurance*, vol. 32, no. 1 (March 1965), 105–12; Johnson, Harry M., "Major Medical Expense Insurance," *Journal of Risk and Insurance*, vol. 32, no. 2 (June 1965), 211–36; Hallman, G. Victor, "True Catastrophe Medical Expense Insurance," *Journal of Risk and Insurance*, vol. 39, no. 1 (March 1972), 1–16; and Wilensky, Gail R., et al., "Variations in Health Insurance Coverage: Benefits vs. Premiums," *Milbank Memorial Fund Quarterly. Health and Society*, vol. 62, no. 1 (Winter 1984), 53–81. More information on the HMO

Act can be found at http://www.hpolicy.duke.edu/cyberexchange/Regulate/CHSR/ PDFs/I-1-HMO%20Act%20of%201973.pdf.

14. John Wennberg, Elliott Fisher, and their colleagues at Dartmouth University pioneered this research on the drivers of health-care spending. See also Pearlstein, Steven, "A Better Way to Spread the Health—and the Wealth," *Washington Post*, February 8, 2006, D01.

15. This opposition from the AMA led to the compromise in which physician services were carved out of medical coverage that would be provided by Medicare. Therefore, Medicare would only cover hospital services, funded by payroll deductions, made available to all Social Security beneficiaries, and which later came to be known as Part A of Medicare. Eventually, physician and outpatient services were incorporated through new legislation that created Part B, which was funded by monthly premiums and had optional enrollment.

16. Our readers will note that we loosely use the term "profits" instead of the term "surplus" that is more commonly associated with "nonprofit" organizations. We deliberately do this out of a belief that the categorization scheme of for-profit vs. nonprofit is relevant only for tax purposes. From a managerial point of view, executives of both types of organizations strive to generate sufficient surplus revenue beyond expenses so they can sustain the health of their enterprise as they try to satisfy the needs of their multiple stakeholders.

17. "A Conversation with Matthew Holt," *Managed Care*, July 2004.

18. It is interesting to note that Kaiser has had poor results historically when trying to expand its business model elsewhere, even though it remains popular in California. In part, this may be due to Kaiser's difficulty in creating a truly integrated capitation system in communities where providers have largely been independent businesspeople.

19. Though many integrated organizations still tied physician salaries (typically bonuses) to referrals, for example, most of the risk in managing capitation fell upon the organization rather than the independent provider.

20. We thank Dr. John Hsieh for sharing with us his insights and clinical expertise in nephrology.

21. "The History of Dialysis," DaVita Web site. Accessed from http://www.davita.com/ dialysis/motivational/a/197.

22. JPMorgan North America Equity Research, October 23, 2006. Much of the background history and data for this case comes from JPMorgan's NxStage analyst report.

23. Blagg, Christopher, "Having Options: Home Hemodialysis," *RENALIFE* 18, no. 5 (2003); and Blagg, Christopher, "A Brief History of Home Hemodialysis," *Adv Ren Replace Ther*, 1996 Apr:3(2):99–105.

24. NxStage Web site, accessed from http://www.nxstage.com/acute_renal_care/Products/ index.cfm.

25. Lee, Helen, "Cost Analysis of Ongoing Care of Patients with End-Stage Renal Disease: The Impact of Dialysis Modality and Dialysis Access," *Am J Kidney Dis* 2002;40(3):611–22; and McFarlane, P. A., et al., "The Quality of Life and Cost Utility of Home Nocturnal and Conventional In-Center Hemodialysis," *Kidney International*, Sep. 2003, 64(3):1004–11.

26. This estimate is based on the U.S. Renal Data System (USRDS) 2007 Annual Data Report. Accessed from http://www.usrds.org/adr.htm. Calculation was made by combining the total Medicare costs for outpatient hemodialysis and for dialysis capitation paid to physicians and suppliers in 2005 (excluding inpatient dialysis). Actual savings

would be lower due to some patients being unable to manage home hemodialysis, while savings would be higher after including cost savings of non-Medicare programs as well as possible improvement in clinical outcomes.

27. Based on data from USRDS 2007 Annual Data Report, comparing the total outpatient hemodialysis costs paid by Medicare in 1991 versus 2005.

28. USRDS 2006 Annual Data Report.

29. JPMorgan North America Equity Research, op. cit.

30. See Roake, J., "Withholding and Withdrawing Therapy: Humanity, Human Rights and Access to Renal Dialysis," *New Zealand Medical Journal*, June 6, 2003, vol. 116, no. 1175; and Busko, M., "Home Hemodialysis Prevalence Varies Greatly by County, Could Be Much Higher," *Medscape Medical News*, August 14, 2006. Accessed from http://www.medscape.com/viewarticle/542738.

31. Mayo Clinic National Symposium on Health Care Reform. Rochester, Minnesota, May 21–23, 2006.

32. In 1989, Medicare adopted a payment schedule based on the Resource-Based Relative Value Scale, a system that hoped to give rationality to payments based on value delivered. Created at Harvard University by William Hsiao and a multidisciplinary group of researchers, the RVS payment schedule determined appropriate reimbursement levels based on the relative value of each procedure and service. However, the RVS system was heavily politicized and distorted, and ultimately unsuccessful in tying reimbursement to actual value.

33. Median operating margins (which exclude investment income) of hospitals were 2 percent in 2004, according to Appleby, Julie, "Hospitals' Profit Margin Hits 6-Year High in 2004," *USA Today*, Jan. 4, 2006, 3B. According to the American Hospital Association, profit margins at hospitals recently moved from negative 16 to 2 percent. Medicare Payment Advisory Commission Public Meeting, Washington, DC: MEDPac, March 11, 2005, accessed from http://www.aha.org/aha/content/2005/pdf/050311medpactranscript.pdf on August 31, 2008.

34. This decision was certainly not malicious, however, and in fact was rooted in good intentions. Insurers reasoned that encouraging their customers to see their physicians earlier for low-cost, routine visits could possibly prevent higher-cost, downstream events like hospitalization. Yet, in retrospect, this was also the start to moving patients further from having to make any real trade-offs in their health purchasing decisions, as "first-dollar coverage" increasingly became the norm.

35. Some employers will find the cost of a high-deductible plan to be even less, in which case they would have the option of keeping some of the cost savings or returning some of it to employees in the form of higher wages or other benefits.

36. The maximum contribution for family coverage in 2008 was $5,800. This is adjusted yearly to keep pace with inflation, and employers may choose to increase their contribution levels accordingly. The HSA is the only employee benefit account that has a "triple tax advantage"—money deposited into HSAs is prestate, -federal, and -FICA tax, grows tax-free, and can be spent tax-free on health-care-related expenses.

37. Although the HSA-HDI combination in this scenario may not be advantageous for the chronically ill and for families with high medical expenses if their yearly health-care costs already exceed $5,000 annually *and* the HDI carries a deductible of greater than $5,000. However, if the deductible is less than $5,000, they would also be better off under this plan. The minimum deductible to qualify as HDI in 2007 was $2,200.

38. Year-to-year fluctuations in growth rate can occur of course. However, savings vehicles like health savings accounts and retirement accounts rely on a much longer time horizon, as well as appropriate diversification. We encourage readers to base their decisions upon the historical compound annual growth rate of well-diversified, market-based investments, in which case our estimate of 8 to 10 percent growth will hold.

39. We thank Mr. John Kaegi, chief marketing officer of Blue Cross and Blue Shield of Florida, for sharing with us his very capable body of research whose aim has been to identify what these jobs-to-be-done are.

40. This includes medically inappropriate services that are supply-sensitive (as the Dartmouth Institute for Health Policy & Clinical Practice would describe it), so-called "never events," and fraud.

41. Note that HSAs fulfill some of these jobs better than its contemporary insurance vehicle, the Health Reimbursement Account. HRAs are not portable, meaning that funds remain with the employers when employees change jobs, and thus they fail to help consumers achieve financial stability by remaining healthy. It also does not always fulfill the jobs of (1) cost effectiveness for employers and (2) avoiding paying for unnecessary services for insurers. Some employers choose not to rollover unused HRA funds from year to year, creating a perverse incentive for employees to use up all their remaining HRA dollars before they go to "waste" at the end of each year. The same incentive exists when employees plan to leave the company.

42. *State Regulatory Experience with Provider-Sponsored Organizations*, Falls Church: The Lewin Group, Inc., June 27, 1997.

43. The findings on this are summarized in Chapter 3 of Christensen, Clayton, *The Innovator's Dilemma* (Boston, Massachusetts: Harvard Business School Press, 1997); and Chapter 4 of Christensen, Clayton, and Michael E. Raynor, *The Innovator's Solution* (Harvard Business School Press, 2003). In addition, a book co-written by our colleagues at Innosight LLC discusses how to spot nonconsumption and what to do about it; see Anthony, Scott D., et al, *The Innovator's Guide to Growth* (Harvard Business School Press, 2008).

44. One other advantage is that 401(k)s and HSAs are both portable. Under traditional pension plans, employees were typically tied to an employer for five to 10 years before their pension funds were vested.

45. Everett Rogers, *Diffusion of Innovations* (New York: Free Press, 1962). Richard Foster of McKinsey has also studied this phenomenon thoroughly. See *The Attacker's Advantage* (New York: Summit Books, 1986).

46. Another example is AT&T, which relied on a McKinsey study that in 1984 advised them there would be fewer than 1 million wireless phone units by 2000. There were 740 million—reminiscent of IBM CEO Thomas Watson's forecast that the world would not need very many computers.

47. Data for HSA enrollment are from the AHIP (America's Health Insurance Plans) Center for Policy and Research (http://www.ahipresearch.org/). There were 438,000 enrollees in HSA plans in September 2004; 1,031,000 in March 2005; 3,168,000 in January 2006; 4,532,000 in January 2007; and 6,118,000 in January 2008. These figures do not include individuals with HDI but no HSA. Data for Private Health Insurance coverage are from the U.S. Census Bureau Current Population Survey Annual Social and Economic Supplement (http://www.census.gov/hhes/www/cpstc/cps_table_creator.html). There were

199,870,585 lives covered by private insurance in 2004; 200,923,910 in 2005; 201,167,391 in 2006; 201,690,112 in 2007; and 201,990,660 in 2008.

48. Some individuals are simultaneously covered by other insurers, such as Medicare and the Veterans Health Administration.

49. This was incorporated into Chapter 3 of Christensen, Clayton M., and Michael E. Raynor, *The Innovator's Solution: Creating and Sustaining Successful Growth* (Boston, Massachusetts: Harvard Business School Press, 2003).

50. Rubenstein, Sarah, "Patients Become Consumers," *Wall Street Journal*, December 28, 2005.

51. "Health Care Access and Affordability Conference Committee Report," Commonwealth of Massachusetts, April 3, 2006. Accessed from http://www.mass.gov/legis/summary.pdf.

52. Kuttner, Robert, "A Health Law with Holes," *Boston.com*, January 28, 2008. Boston.com is an online product of the *Boston Globe*.

Chapter 8

The Future of the Pharmaceutical Industry

Are drugs, which comprise about 10 percent of overall health-care costs,[1] part of the health-care cost problem? Or are they part of the solution? Critics of the pharmaceutical industry often point to the rise in spending on pharmaceuticals—which doubled between 1995 and 2002—as a major culprit in the unsustainable increase in health-care spending during these years.[2] Others assert that while they are expensive on a per-ounce basis, pharmaceutical solutions are much cheaper than other alternatives for care.

Both views have merit. Some drugs have helped to transform historically fatal acute diseases into chronic ones, allowing us to live longer with reasonable qualities of life. While extending both the length and quality of our lives, these drugs have played a major role in driving up the world's health-care bill—not just through the cost of the drugs themselves, but through the cost of complications that arise as patients live with, rather than succumb to, these diseases.

Other drugs drive down the cost of care, however, because they're the technological enablers of disruption.[3] Little by little and layer by layer, scientists and physicians are peeling away the shrouds that have masked true understanding of diseases, leading us toward greater precision. Many of those who lead this transformation of knowledge are academic scientists ensconced in or adjacent to our best medical schools, funded through grants from our National Institutes of Health. However, much of the applied science and nearly all of the commercialization technology in this transformation is being developed and implemented in pharmaceutical and medical device companies. Indeed, the most recent victories in the march toward precision medicine have emerged from firms like Novartis (Gleevec), AstraZeneca (Iressa),[4] Genentech (Herceptin), and others. The pharmaceutical and medical device industries must play a pivotal role in the disruptive transformation of health care, because they supply the technological enablers that allow lower cost venues of care, and lower cost caregivers, to do more and more remarkable things. In this chapter we'll consider the role that pharmaceutical companies will need to play in transforming health care, and then turn toward devices in Chapter 9.

The disruptive transformations in health care will profoundly affect the structure of the pharmaceutical industry itself—posing extraordinary managerial challenges to the leaders of these companies. The disruption that threatens today's "big pharma" companies is of a different sort than was mounted by steel minimills, personal computer makers, Wal-Mart, and Toyota. Those disruptors started with simple, affordable products that were sold to the least-demanding customers. They then marched up-market, market tier by market tier. We call the disruptive threat to pharmaceutical companies a "supply chain disruption," and it is already under way in the industry. Its form: many of the vertically integrated pharmaceutical companies that have long dominated the business began actively outsourcing many of their functions to specialist companies, ranging from the discovery and development of new drugs, to the administration of clinical trials, to manufacturing. Those to whom this work is being outsourced are integrating to add more and more value to their offerings, even as the pharmaceutical companies are shedding activity after activity, seeking to do less and less.

The driver of this disruption is the same as the one that drives "market tier" disruption. The leaders improve their profitability by getting out of the least profitable of their activities, while focusing investments on the most profitable. The disruptive entrants, by inheriting the activities cast off by the incumbent leaders, improve their profitability by taking on more and more of the value-adding activities the leaders are "outsourcing."

Unless they reverse course, many of today's major pharmaceutical companies will find a decade from now that they have inadvertently leveled the playing field in their industry, so that entrants can overcome what historically had been high barriers to entry. They will find that they outsourced to suppliers those activities they will wish had become their core competencies. And the activities that the majors in the past have considered to be their core competences—especially sales and marketing—will in the future prove to have lost much of their competitive relevance. After this disruption occurs, the pharmaceutical industry will be much more efficient and effective in leading health care toward precision medicine. Whether today's major companies lead in this transition or become victims of it will depend on how adroitly their executives navigate their corporate ships through these disruptive shoals.

DISRUPTION IN THE PHARMACEUTICAL SUPPLY CHAIN

To illustrate how and why disruption up the supply chain occurs, we'll recount the interaction between a supplier—a small (initially, at least) Taiwanese electronics manufacturer called ASUSTeK , and its customer, Dell Computer. We have chosen this pair because the interaction we typify below is common to all companies that find themselves experiencing this phenomenon of supply chain disruption.

ASUSTeK started out making the simplest of the circuit boards within a Dell computer. Then ASUSTeK came to Dell with an interesting value proposition: "We've been doing a good job making these little boards. Why don't you let us make the motherboard for you? Circuit manufacturing isn't your core competence anyway, and we could do it for 20 percent lower cost."

Dell's analysts examined the proposal and realized, "Gosh, they could! And if we hand off the motherboard to them, we can also get all those circuit manufacturing assets off our balance sheet!" So they transferred the making of the motherboard to ASUSTeK. Dell's revenues were unaffected, but its profits improved significantly. ASUSTeK's revenues improved, and *its* profits improved—because it was utilizing its assets more efficiently. In other words, it felt good for Dell to get *out* of motherboards, and good for ASUSTeK to get *into* motherboards.

Then ASUSTeK came back. "You know, we've been doing a good job making these motherboards for you. Come to think of it, the motherboard is really the guts of the machine. You shouldn't have to bother to assemble the rest of the computer. Let us do it for you. Assembly isn't your core competence anyway, and we'll do it for 20 percent lower cost."

Dell's analysts examined the proposal and realized, "Gosh, they could! And if we hand off assembly to them, we can also get these manufacturing assets off our balance sheet!" So they transferred responsibility for computer assembly to ASUSTeK. Dell's revenues were unaffected, but its profits improved significantly. ASUSTeK's revenues improved, and *its* profits improved—because again it was utilizing its assets more efficiently. It felt good for Dell to get *out* of assembly, and good for ASUSTeK to get *into* assembly.

Then ASUSTeK came back. "You know, we've been doing a good job assembling your computers for you. Come to think of it, you shouldn't have to bother to manage your supply chain—dealing with all those component suppliers, working out all those logistics headaches, and shipping those computers to your customers. Logistics isn't your core competence anyway. Why don't you let us take on the management of your supply chain? We could do it for 20 percent lower cost."

Dell's analysts examined the proposal and realized, "Gosh, they could! And if we give the supply chain to them, we can not only reduce costs, but also get all the *current* assets off our balance sheet!" So they transferred responsibility for the supply chain to ASUSTeK. Dell's revenues were unaffected, and this time its profits improved even more than before—especially return on assets, because they had no assets. (As you may have noticed, Wall Street *loves* asset-light companies.) ASUSTeK's revenues improved again too, and *its* profits improved—because it was getting into value-added services. (As you may have noticed, Wall Street *loves* value-added services companies.) It felt good for Dell to get out of managing the supply chain, and good for ASUSTeK to begin managing the supply chain.

Then ASUSTeK came back. "You know, we've been doing a good job managing your supply chain. Come to think of it, you shouldn't have to bother to design those computers, because design is little more than component selection—and we have *all* those relationships. Why don't you let us design your computers for you? We could do it for 20 percent less."

Dell's analysts examined the proposal and realized, "Gosh, they could! And if we hand off design to them, we can fire our engineers and drive our costs even lower! Besides, it's our *brand* that's our core competence." So they transferred responsibility for computer design to ASUSTeK. Dell's revenues were unaffected, but its profits improved again. And ASUSTeK's revenues and profits improved. It felt good for Dell to get out of design, and good for ASUSTeK to get into it.

As we write this book, ASUSTeK is in the process of coming back one more time. But this time they aren't coming back to Dell, but to the giant electronics retailers like Best Buy. And they're saying, "You know, we design and manufacture some of the best computers in the world. Why should you have to bother stocking those Compaq, Hewlett-Packard, and Dell brands on your shelves? We'll give you your brand, our brand—*any* brand—at 20 percent lower cost."

Bingo. One company is gone, another has taken its place. How did it happen? There's no stupidity in the story. The managers in both companies did exactly what business school professors and the best management consultants would tell them to do—improve profitability by focusing on those activities that are most profitable, and by getting out of activities that are less profitable. Just like the types of disruption where an entrant company comes into the bottom tier of a market and then eats its way up-market, tier by tier, the causal mechanism of supply chain disruption is the pursuit of profitability. The pursuit of profits is what causes the customer to keep handing off the lowest of the value-adding activities that remain in the company. And it is the pursuit of profitability that causes the supplier to seek offering ever higher value-adding activities to its customers.

The reason why disruption is such a predictable phenomenon is that the pursuit of profit causes the industry's incumbent leaders essentially to flee from the entrant attackers—when the attackers enter into the least profitable tier of the market, or the lowest value portion of the supply chain. And it is the pursuit of profit that so predictably propels the attackers to try to capture the next tier of the market, or the next stage in the value chain. To the disruptee, these are the least profitable of their remaining activities; to the disruptor, these are the most profitable of their activities.

When Is Supply Chain Disruption Possible?

In our studies of strategy and innovation, one constant is that when there are unpredictable interdependencies among pieces of a product system, a company's span of integration must encompass those interdependencies in order to be successful—and the type of supply chain disruption described above is impossible. The period in an industry's history when these conditions seem most prevalent is depicted in Figure 8.1. It occurs in the early years of an industry, when the technology is immature and the best products don't perform well enough that companies need interdependent, optimized solutions to optimize performance. For example, in the early years of mainframe computing, a company could not have existed as a stand-alone provider of operating systems, logic circuitry, memory systems, or applications software. The design of each of these elements of the system depended at that time on the design of each of the other elements. Hence, a computer company had to do *everything* if it hoped to do *anything*, and a significant competitive advantage accrued to companies that were vertically integrated.

The advent of advanced digital radiology services was characterized by similar interdependence. There were no standards to define how CT scanners, computer image stations, storage systems, and transmission services could interface—so giant, integrated systems providers were the only entities that could play in this game.

If a company wished to assemble a computer or a digital imaging system in that era (the upper-left portion of the disruption diagram) from modular components, it would have had to specify how each piece of the system interfaced with each other piece of the system. However, even *specifying* those interfaces, let alone standardizing them, would have required far more technological understanding than existed in the early years of either of these industries. It also would have taken so many degrees of design freedom away from the engineers that they would have had to back off the frontier of what was technologically possible—and during the stage of an industry's history when product performance and reliability aren't yet sufficient, that would be competitive suicide. When products don't perform well enough or reliably enough, competitive advantage goes to those firms that compete with proprietary, optimized product or process architectures.

Interdependence—the requirement to create everything at once—raises the fixed cost of participating in an industry. This then creates steep economies of scale—conferring cost advantages on larger companies. Interdependence also creates many opportunities for competitive differentiation. The result of these factors is that vertically integrated giants grow to dominate nearly every industry in its early years. AT&T, U.S. Steel, Alcoa, Swift, General Motors, Ford, IBM, Digital Equipment,

DuPont, Goldman Sachs, Citibank, United Aircraft,[5] and Harvard Business School are just a few examples of institutions that came to industry leadership by taking advantage of vertical integration.[6]

Incidentally, this is why (as of this writing) Apple's iPod portable music player has so quickly grown to dominate its industry. Other companies' attempts to assemble systems from modular components resulted in difficult-to-use, unreliable products. But by optimizing end-to-end the integration of its iTunes music store with the formatting and technology for downloading music and the design of its iPod player, Apple created an elegantly simple system against which companies with nonoptimized, industry standard architectures cannot now compete.[7]

During this early era in an industry's history supply chain disruption generally cannot occur—because for the industry leaders, outsourcing is not technologically feasible or competitively desirable.

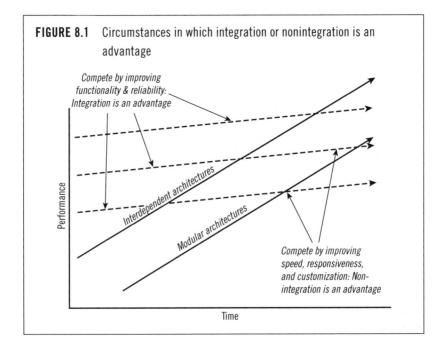

FIGURE 8.1 Circumstances in which integration or nonintegration is an advantage

Compete by improving functionality & reliability: Integration is an advantage

Interdependent architectures

Modular architectures

Performance

Compete by improving speed, responsiveness, and customization: Nonintegration is an advantage

Time

When an industry's technology matures and its products begin performing well enough, however, the architecture of an industry's products or services can become *modular*—meaning that the standards by which the different components must interface can be specified with sufficient clarity and comprehensiveness so independent companies can supply individual components. And when the components are all "snapped" together, the product performs sufficiently well. Under these conditions, industries formerly dominated by vertically integrated behemoths come to be structured as a horizontally stratified collection of specialist companies.[8]

We've illustrated in Figure 8.2 how this happened in the computer industry, by listing on the left side the stages in the value chain of building and servicing a computer. During the industry's first two decades, it was dominated by vertically integrated companies such as IBM, Control Data, and Digital Equipment—because they *had* to be integrated, given the nature of the technology and the basis of competition at the time. But as part of its orchestration of the disruptive personal computer value network, IBM defined what the components of a personal computer would be, and established clear standards by which those components would interface in the product's architecture. As a result, the industry *dis-integrated*, as shown on the right side of the diagram. It came to be comprised of a horizontally stratified group of focused, independent makers of each component—including Microsoft, Intel, Seagate, and so on.[9]

Dis-Integration Has Already Begun in Pharmaceuticals

Merck, Pfizer, and most of the other major pharmaceutical companies can trace their beginnings to specialized chemical factories that manufactured and supplied compounds for the pharmacy industry. Over time, they integrated into adjacent activities, such as researching and developing new drugs, distributing products to pharmacies and hospitals, and marketing the drugs to various consumers and institutions. Just like IBM, General Motors, U.S. Steel, AT&T, and the other companies listed previously,

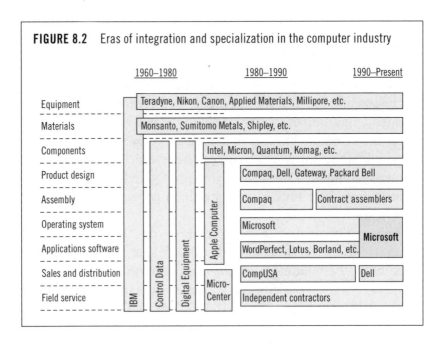

FIGURE 8.2 Eras of integration and specialization in the computer industry

vertical integration across the spectrum from researching new compounds to the sale and advertising of their products has been a competitive strength to the major pharmaceutical companies. The differentiation and steep scale economics stemming from this enabled the leading pharmaceutical companies to extract enormous profits for many years.

Little by little, however, the pharmaceutical industry has been dis-integrating. Companies like Myriad Genetics are focusing primarily on diagnostics development. Many of the major companies are increasingly relying upon contract discovery companies like WuXi PharmaTech, or upon in-licensing drugs from smaller firms in order to offload the risk associated with drug discovery. These in-licensed products already represent 30 percent of "Big Pharma" sales today.[10]

Meanwhile, other portions of the drug development process are also being outsourced. As the process of running clinical trials became better defined—and more complex, due to FDA regulations—Quintiles, ICON, PAREXEL, PPD, Covance, and other contract research organizations have offered to take on the burden of managing trials for pharmaceutical firms. Clinical trials have become extraordinarily costly because of the number of patients needed, the number of geographic sites involved, the complex regulatory hurdles in place, and the potential need to engage multiple areas of medical expertise. Converting the fixed costs of managing these trials year-round into variable costs better suited for an unpredictable product pipeline has relieved some of the cost pressures on the leading pharmaceutical companies. Not surprisingly, however, some CROs have gradually integrated—as did ASUSTeK in computers—across the spectrum of activities in the value chain from discovery to formulation and product development, to contract manufacturing, marketing, and detailing. Some have even begun competing against their customers.[11] For example, Covance announced in August 2008 that it would acquire an early drug development site from Eli Lilly. As part of its 10-year service agreement with Covance, Lilly was also expected to close the Lilly Center for Medical Science at Indiana University Medical Center, as Covance uses its own clinic in Evansville to conduct Phase I clinical trials.[12]

Likewise, specialized manufacturing and marketing organizations have also sprung up to help the major pharmaceutical companies transform fixed costs into variable ones. Codexis in the United States, Hovione in Portugal, Cadila Health Care in India, and Shanghai Pharmaceutical Group in China are a few of thousands of contract manufacturers worldwide that are expected to comprise a $145 billion market by 2009.[13] Contract sales and marketing firms such as Ventiv Health and Professional Detailing, Inc. can assemble and train large sales forces that make in-house salespeople superfluous.

This progressive dis-integration has been a powerful leveler of the playing field in the pharmaceutical industry. Whereas the cost of integration posed a nearly insurmountable barrier to entry in the past, the business model of the "virtual" pharmaceutical company has become a viable option for new entrants—even while some of our largest and historically most powerful pharmaceutical companies have been outsourcing their way toward becoming little more than product portfolio managers.[14] We'll see below that when this happens in an industry, the playing field doesn't stay level—it tilts away from the old leaders, in favor of a new set of companies.

Differences in Scale as a Driver of Dis-Integration

An important driver of pharmaceutical industry dis-integration has been the mismatch of scale economics at different points in its value chain. In some elements of this chain the scale required to compete successfully has been *huge*. At other points small companies can compete very effectively against large ones because scale economies are essentially flat.

To illustrate how a mismatch in scale economics can drive industry dis-integration, we'll draw upon a case study that chronicles the emergence of the Big Idea Group.[15] BIG began by holding "Big Idea Hunts" in which it searched for innovative ideas for toys in communities around the country. Through advertisements in hobbyist magazines, BIG's founder, Mike Collins, would invite people who had invented new toys or games to come to a hotel conference room to present their idea to Mike and a panel of his colleagues who had a demonstrated intuition for spotting successful new toy products. When they spotted one with high potential, they'd sign a licensing arrangement with the inventor, shape the idea into an appealing prototype and business plan, and then license it to any one of 70 toy makers or retailers whose business model and reach into the marketplace seemed to best fit the idea. Who brought their inventions to these Big Idea Hunts? An extraordinary collection of unlikely people—including retail clerks, homemakers, office managers, Ph.D. physicists, and lawyers.

When Collins decided not to license an inventor's idea, he was always careful to feed back to the inventor what it was about the idea that made it less appealing—in hopes that he could maintain a close relationship with each inventor and help them get better at inventing. Little by little BIG developed a network of thousands of inventors who just got better and better at inventing. Collins's database showed the types of inventions that each of these people had demonstrated an instinct for developing. Companies not in the toy industry soon began asking Collins if he could conduct Big Idea Hunts for them. These included makers of household utensils, office products, lawn and garden tools, and even medical devices. As he broadened his scope, Collins gradually found that instead of advertising broadly for inventors to bring their ideas to his hunts, he simply could parse his database of inventors who in the past had demonstrated an intuition for inventing the sort of new product BIG's client was searching for. He could then solicit entries in a more targeted and efficient way—with great success. It turned out that even multi-billion-dollar companies could not afford to assemble an R&D staff that could compete against Collins, who had at his fingertips access to a network of thousands of proven inventors.[16]

There is a clear pattern in the types of industries where the BIG model of outsourcing new product development can work, and where it cannot. There are certain industries—which include toys, office products, household utensils, gardening tools, and medical devices—where you don't have to be big at all in order to develop a new product. The minimum efficient scale is two people. You come up with an idea, and then as long as you have a mechanical engineer in the family or the neighborhood who can help fabricate a prototype, you're in business. When you sum up the innovative power of all these people, it just overwhelms the R&D capabilities of even the largest companies in these industries. Most of these inventors don't have a prayer of building a successful company around their inventions, however, because the scale required to take them to market through Staples, Toys 'R' Us, Wal-Mart, Home Depot, and hospital association buying groups is huge. The mismatch of scale intensiveness at the different stages in the value chain causes companies in these industries to dis-integrate at the interface between development and commercialization. Henry Chesbrough has labeled this "open innovation."[17]

There is a type of industry where this sort of open innovation is not possible, however. It is where the minimum efficient scale of product development is large, and where there are unpredictable interdependencies between what happens in the commercialization stages of the value chain and what needs to happen in the invention and development stages. Historically, the microprocessor business was one of these. The scale required to be competitive in the development, manufacturing, and marketing stages of the value chain was huge—and there were powerful interdependencies between the way you manufactured the product and the way it could and could not be designed; and so on.[18]

The mismatch in minimum efficient scale explains, at least partially, why the world of drug discovery and development has become so crowded with start-up biotechnology companies, and why the traditional pharmaceutical companies, try as they might, have not succeeded in dominating the science of biotechnology in the way they had come to dominate the small-molecule chemistry of traditional pharmaceuticals. The nature of understanding in molecular biology, and the scale of an enterprise required to push that understanding forward, are such that small companies can compete with big ones in the discovery and development of biotech products. Open innovation wasn't possible in the pharmaceutical industry of the past, but it is now.

There is a compounding factor favoring dis-integration, in addition to the newfound technological feasibility of open innovation. We might term this factor a "predictability mismatch" across the stages in the value chain. Since its inception, the essentially random process of discovering successful new products has been a constant and fundamental plague that pestered the pharmaceutical industry. Discovering new molecular entities, identifying their sites of action, investigating their potential efficacy against human diseases, and determining their safety profiles remain for the most part matters of costly trial and error. Recent advances such as combinatorial chemistry and high-throughput screening do not solve the underlying problem of inherent randomness, which stems from the fact that our understanding of how the body works is still frighteningly limited. Rather, these technologies primarily serve to automate this process of random discovery.[19]

When pharmaceutical companies like Lilly and Pfizer serendipitously find themselves with new drugs like Prozac and Viagra,[20] they must build a commercial business to take that drug to a segment of patients and their caregivers. However, when those commercial organizations are in place and their managers are held accountable for growing their business, they find themselves asking their random discovery process to somehow predictably deliver next-generation drugs that even more effectively address the unmet needs of patients and doctors in the same field. The result is that, increasingly, the marketing mass of the pharmaceutical companies forces them to in-license drugs that fit with their marketing presence. This is another driver of disintegration in the industry.[21]

"SKATING TO WHERE THE MONEY WILL BE" IN THE PHARMACEUTICAL INDUSTRY

The fact that their industry is dis-integrating poses the hazard that at each stage in their value chain, the integrated companies increasingly face competition from focused firms. The pharmaceutical giants face war on all fronts, while the focused attackers face war on just one.

Possibly the more serious threat that the major players face, however, is that they will choose to win the wrong war. They are very likely to focus on winning at the stage in the value chain that was profitable in their past, and will flee from the fight for the territory in the value chain where attractive profits will be made in the future. Therapeutics is where most of the money was made in the past, and the majors will fight to win that battle. Yet diagnostics is where the most attractive profits will be made in the future.

We have termed this challenge as "skating to where the money will be," in honor of the great Canadian ice hockey player, Wayne Gretzky. When asked once why he had become such a dominant player, Gretzky is said to have responded, "I skate to where the puck is going to be, not to where it has been."[22] At times of disruptive transition such as the one facing the pharmaceutical industry, we can expect most players in the industry to "skate" toward, or invest at, the points in the value chain where the money has been made in the past. If history is any guide, when they get there, it's likely they discover that the money has moved to another point in the chain.

The diagnostics industry in the United States is presently comprised of over 200 companies accounting for $28.6 billion in sales.[23] To date, the numbers logged by diagnostics makers have been dwarfed by the $300 to $400 billion pharmaceutical market.[24] Diagnostics products historically have been less valued than businesses in the pharmaceutical industry. Diagnostic tests have often been perceived as adding limited value to clinical decision making: tests are defensive, directional, or confirmatory in nature, and meant to guide and reinforce the intuition of the physician rather than supplant it. As a result, diagnostics have been assigned low value by the reimbursement schedule established by Medicare. Diagnostics comprise only 1.6 percent of Medicare payments—though the savings resulting from precise diagnosis, and the costs that stem from inaccurate diagnosis—dwarf this number.[25]

With this heritage as baggage, new precision diagnostics are often reimbursed at the same rate as their predecessors. This tendency is exacerbated when firms seek reimbursement for new diagnostics within existing CPT codes[26] rather than attempting to establish a new code with the American Medical Association. This practice rewards diagnostic tests that lower testing costs, but not necessarily those that deliver more value per dollar by enabling lower-cost caregivers such as nurses to deliver predictably effective therapies. This impedes the development and use of genetic and molecular diagnostics that may be costlier, but offer savings in other parts of the health-care system—a key reason why the perspective that stems from integration is so crucial in implementing disruption in this industry. When the cost of diagnosis comes out of one organizational pocket, and the savings it enables are put into another, the system can't be expected to make decisions that are optimal for the system. We believe the pricing that reflects the true value of precise diagnoses will emerge from the contracting between diagnostics providers and integrated fixed-fee providers.[27]

The accurate diagnosis of a disease and its predictably effective treatment are akin to a lock and key, both of which are necessary to open the doors to new business models of health-care delivery that we have described. Just as the technological enablers of disruption in the computer industry—the microprocessor and the Windows operating system—captured a significant portion of the profits as the personal computer disrupted larger machines, the attractive money in the pharmaceutical industry will be made at the interface of diagnostics and therapeutics, because it will fuel the growth of care provided in lower-cost business models.

The Danger of Outsourcing the Wrong Thing

The "Five Forces" framework propounded by strategy scholar Michael Porter has explained for a generation of analysts why particular elements of an industry's value chain seem to have the ability to capture a disproportionate share of an industry's profits.[28] Porter's is a *static* model, in that it explains why things occur as they do at a given point in time. The model of disruption adds a dynamic dimension to his model, showing how the impact of these Five Forces shifts in predictable ways to different portions of the value chain over time. It shows when, how, and why the stage in the value chain where the Five Forces have historically concentrated the ability to earn attractive profits are likely to become lackluster and commoditized, and allows one to predict when stages in the chain that historically had languished in marginal profits are likely to become very attractive.[29]

To illustrate why understanding the dynamic dimensions of the Five Forces is so critical for today's pharmaceutical industry executives, consider the massive strategic mistake that executives in IBM's personal computer business made when they were in an analogous situation to where pharmaceutical companies are today.

In the world of mainframe computers, performance was determined at the level of the *system architecture*. IBM computers were built from thousands of different components, none of which substantially determined how well the machine would perform. Rather, performance was determined at the level of the system, through the artistry employed by the system engineers who knitted these components together. By some reports, 95 percent of the industry's profits were earned by IBM. Its components suppliers, in contrast, lived a miserable, profit-free existence year after year—because no individual component impacted the performance of the computers in a significant way.

When IBM set up its separate personal computer business unit in Florida, it possessed better microprocessor technology than Intel, and better operating system technology than Microsoft. But it chose to outsource those components, so it could focus on the design and assembly of computers. What happened, of course, was that IBM put into business the two companies that subsequently made the lion's share of the industry's profits, while it stayed at the stage in the value chain—in system design and assembly—where no company subsequently was able to make attractive profits.

Why did IBM do this? Because in its *past*, components weren't the place where attractive profits were made. But in the disruptive personal computer system, as well as in almost all disruptions, *it is the technological enablers inside the product* that determine the product's performance—and that is where the money is made in the new disruptive industry. As a general rule, money is made at the stage(s) in the value chain where the performance of the overall system is determined. In the early stages, performance tends to be determined through the proprietary design of the product itself. As disruption proceeds and the architecture of the product becomes more standardized and modular, however, more of the product's performance is determined by the performance of the components inside the product. Hence, in the prior example, the ability to make money shifted to certain components because it was Microsoft and Intel inside that drove the computer's performance. There was little proprietary artistry through which engineers knit those components together.

Major automobile manufacturers have done the same thing as IBM's executives: they walked away from the right war, in order to win the wrong one. Because historically components businesses weren't as profitable as the business of designing and assembling cars, through the 1990s consultants, financial engineers, and investment bankers prodded the major auto companies to divest their auto parts businesses and begin procuring major subsystems from "Tier One" suppliers. Those executives were reacting to the auto manufacturers' *past*, not their *future*— because as the architecture of the car became more standardized, the subsystems *inside* the car would become most profitable and increasingly proprietary, since they determine the performance of the automobile. Though we warned of this more than a decade ago,[30] the outsourcing of tomorrow's critical competencies has proceeded apace in the auto industry. The leading Tier One suppliers are now significantly more profitable, and their stock market earnings multiples significantly higher, than the auto assemblers.[31]

In pharmaceuticals, in general, the key technological enabler limiting therapeutic efficacy is diagnostics.[32] Yet (and not surprisingly), a parallel pattern of the divestiture of tomorrow's attractive businesses has begun in the pharmaceutical industry. For example, Bayer recently sold its diagnostic unit for $5.3 billion. In 2007, Abbott Laboratories negotiated to sell much of its diagnostics business for $8.13 billion.[33] These companies, following the tradition established by IBM and General Motors, are reacting to the past rather than preparing for the future. A warning to all who contemplate these deals is that the investment bankers who urge them on have been prone to peer into the future through a rearview mirror.

At the same time, molecular diagnostics firms like Celera Genomics and Applied Biosystems,[34] sensing the strong technological interdependence between diagnostics and therapeutics in the future, have already begun to acquire pharmaceutical companies. Other players, like Millennium Pharmaceuticals, have worked in diagnostics and pharmaceuticals from the start, while Roche has a long history of impact in both industries. As the systemic value created by precision diagnostics and predictably effective therapeutics becomes more apparent, we expect that the Five Forces determining attractive profitability will shift to this point in the industry's value chain.

Indeed, as the biomarkers that render a more precise signal of a specific disease are identified for more and more drugs, the threats of malpractice litigation will increasingly center on those who prescribed inappropriate drugs or dosages because they did not utilize available diagnostic tools.[35] The recent push to incorporate genetic testing into the protocol for administering the blood thinner warfarin (also known as a nomogram), an example we discussed in Chapter 2, indicates a willingness and desire of the system to improve clinical care by combining testing and treatment.[36]

The value created by precision diagnosis can be significant. One study, for example, measured that the breast cancer therapeutic Herceptin cost $79,181 per patient cured if the diagnostic test to identify the overexpression of the HER2 protein was not done first. When the diagnostic test was performed at the outset, the cost per patient cured was $54,738. The reason? Without the precise diagnosis, the drug was given to some patients who could not benefit from it. The test, by the way, costs $366 to perform, and yielded nearly $24,000 in savings per patient.[37]

Repurposing the Clinical Trials Process

In recent years the stages in the pharmaceutical value chain have become "modular" enough that focused companies have emerged, as noted above, to perform each of these steps in relative independence from the other specialists up- and downstream in the chain. As a result and in particular, pharmaceutical companies have begun to outsource more of their clinical trials to focused contract research organizations such as Quintiles. The CROs are developing superior competencies in designing and managing these trials.

To capitalize on the promise that precise diagnosis brings for precision medicine, however, the steps in the industry's value chain will need to become more interdependent in the future—and much of the interdependence will center around the clinical trials process. This means today's industry leaders that have begun outsourcing the management of these trials are also outsourcing tomorrow's core competence. And it means that tomorrow's pharmaceutical giants will be operationally integrated differently than are those of today.

The process that drug companies historically have followed to win approval to manufacture and market a drug has been comprised of four steps. First, the safety and efficacy of the drug must be "modeled" in animals that can mimic the human disease of interest as closely as possible. The next step, called Phase I, tests the drug's safety on human volunteers, some of whom might not even have the disease in question. When safety is established, a preliminary sense of efficacy in humans is then explored in Phase II trials by administering the drug to a relatively small group of volunteers who have been diagnosed with the disease in question. If the drug is found to be effective in a sufficient portion of those patients, it is then tested in a Phase III trial, using a much larger group of diagnosed patients for a much longer period of time. In most cases the trials are conducted on a "double blind" basis: neither the patients nor the researchers are aware of whether the new drug or a placebo (occasionally a control drug) has been administered until the study has concluded.

The result of most Phase III trials is that only a portion of those who received the drug respond favorably to it. In most cases a fraction of patients report undesirable side effects as well. If the group of physicians advising the FDA feels that the treatment success rate is sufficient (typically greater than 30 percent), and if the side effects aren't severe or can somehow be mitigated, the advisory panel typically recommends approval.[38] The company then prepares a carefully worded "insert" placed in each drug package that details how, by whom, and to whom the drug should be administered; what fraction of diagnosed patients receiving the drug can be expected to respond to the therapy; and what portion can be expected to experience side effects.

The four-stage clinical trials process inherently assumes that all patients with the same symptoms have the disease in question— an assumption that molecular biology has shown is often false, as we discussed in Chapter 2. When the designers of a clinical trial assume that the diagnosis has been made accurately and that everyone in the trial has the same disease, the trial is essentially framed as a *test* to see whether the drug helps patients or not. The fact that some portion of the patients do not respond is treated as probabilistic noise from which statistically significant signals of efficacy must be isolated. As a result, little is learned from the trial beyond the probabilistic profile of side effects and the proportion of patients for whom the therapy is effective. In other words, most clinical trials, by design, keep therapy safely within the realm of intuitive medicine.

To accelerate the movement of more diseases toward precision medicine and its intrinsic improvements in affordability and quality, the pharmaceutical industry and its regulators need to begin framing clinical trials as an interwoven part of the research process, rather than simply as "tests" that occur at the end of the process. When a portion of patients respond to a therapy while others with the same symptom do not, it is evidence that there's more going on than meets the eye. Either there are multiple diseases sharing that symptom—and the drug being tested happened to be effective in treating at least one of those underlying diseases—or there are genetically based differences in the way patients with the same disease respond to the therapy—or both. This should trigger molecular- and genetic-level studies to explore what is different about those who respond, versus those who don't. Drugmakers can then develop biomarkers to identify the factors critical to disease-patient interaction and help guide therapeutic decision making.[39]

Reframing clinical trials as "research trials" in this way could greatly assist those who are working to precisely diagnose specific diseases that today only fall under broad umbrellas of commonly shared symptoms. These trials must become part and parcel of the process of drug discovery and development. The development of diagnostics and therapeutics must be skillfully interwoven with these research trials in new ways. The appendix to this chapter provides some preliminary guesses about how this process might work.

Companies that outsource these activities will simply be unable to play in this league. In contrast, we expect that companies whose core competence is first to extract precision diagnostic biomarkers out of research trials, and then to couple them with therapeutics that will be predictably effective, will prosper. They will continue to build their businesses forward from that core, disruptively taking on more and more value-added services from their customers, who are the major pharmaceutical companies—just as ASUSTeK has with Dell. Ultimately they will take on the marketing of their products because—as we'll show at the end of this chapter—the very definition of the market for many drugs will have completely changed as well.

Future Cost of Clinical Trials

Armies of tort lawyers in America circulate among patients receiving approved drugs, hoping to find one who experiences a side effect that was not presaged in the insert. They then file a barrage of costly lawsuits against the drugmaker. These potential costs have pressured the drugmakers and their regulators to expand the scope and prolong the duration of Phase III trials, in order to surface as many potential problems as possible so that dangerous drugs can be kept from the market and protective language can be included on the insert. The scale of these clinical trials is driving drug development costs toward $1 billion and beyond.[40] This in turn has driven many of yesterday's pharmaceutical companies to merge, creating mammoth organizations with the resources to finance these trials.

Initially, transforming clinical trials into research trials won't save money because precise diagnosis won't be possible for most classes of disease—meaning that for some time, people with different diseases will continue to be enrolled in most trials.[41] Indeed, there may actually be a period of increased costs as diagnostics and pharmacogenomics come on board. This is due in part to the advent of new genetic targets. In the past, by the time pharmaceutical companies started developing a drug against a particular target, there were several dozen publications about that target—how it worked, what it did, etc. After diagnostics and drugs for those well-studied targets had been developed, however, by the early 2000s the average number of publications per genomic target had dropped to *eight*. To the extent that there is a higher failure rate of more novel targets, it could cause genomic-based drugs initially to become more expensive to develop, rather than less. This lends impetus to projects that develop "me too" products out of existing, well-understood targets, as they are much less risky.[42]

As pharmacogenomics leads us further toward precision medicine, however, the scope, duration, and cost of many clinical trials will drop significantly. When we can precisely diagnose a disease, every patient enrolled in a trial will have the same disease. With diagnostic ambiguity removed, most drugs will be shown more conclusively to work or not work, in less time, and in smaller trials.[43] This will mean that the scale advantages huge pharmaceutical companies enjoy today in financing clinical trials will be rendered less relevant in the future—the playing field will be more level for large and small companies alike. We emphasize again that this will happen not in one fell swoop, but disease by disease, research trial by research trial.

For example, instead of including patients diagnosed as having "breast cancer" in its trial for the drug Herceptin, Genentech used the HER2/neu test to include in its trial only those whose tumors could be characterized by an overexpression of the HER2 protein. Genentech enrolled only 470 patients in the trial, compared to an estimated 2,200 that would have been required in a typical cancer trial. It was able to reduce the duration of the trial from the usual five to 10 years to *two*. It pulled in an additional $2.5 *billion* in accelerated income by getting to market earlier. And 120,000 patients were able to get access to this therapy who otherwise would have been denied it while a typically structured clinical trial dragged on and on.[44] It is hard to conclude that the costs of clinical trials will continue to increase monotonically. Despite the winding and bumpy road, costs ultimately will trend downward.

So how should today's leading pharmaceutical companies deal with these changes? One option, of course, is to argue that disintegration and a shift in where attractive money can be made won't happen. But the reason we predict that they will indeed happen is because the causal mechanism is the rational pursuit of profit. This pattern already has played itself out in dozens of industries, and in fact already is under way in earnest in pharmaceuticals. The other option—if we were managing one of the leading drug companies—is to own the best company that is operating at the core of future diagnostics technologies, but manage it separately so it can provide these services for many of the industry leaders, not just our own company.

The challenges facing the pharmaceutical industry that we've described to this point are indeed formidable. But we haven't finished chronicling the changes in store for pharmaceutical companies. As we'll see next, their markets will fragment. Opportunities for developing blockbuster drugs that find a huge market by targeting symptomatically defined diseases will diminish under the attack of precision medicine. New types of blockbuster drugs will emerge, but the market for these products will cut across medical specialties—fundamentally changing the value of the sales prowess of today's companies.

HOW THE INDUSTRY WILL FRAGMENT

Product Markets and the Firms Serving Them Will Be Smaller

The pursuit of profit is creating another disruptive headache for major pharmaceutical companies, beyond those described above. Big companies need big markets in order to grow. It is hard for them to allocate resources toward products that target small markets, because not one of them brings the promise of sufficient revenues to keep the top line of a global giant growing. Yet the market for pharmaceutical products will fragment in the future.

Despite a combined R&D budget nearly double that of the National Institutes of Health, the pharmaceutical industry faces troubling data about its recent innovation track record (summarized in Table 8.1). Pharmaceutical companies far outspend all other industries in R&D. Spending has soared from $2 billion in 1980 and $8.4 billion in 1990, to $55.2 billion in 2006; yet the industry has been introducing fewer successful drugs into the market. With spending going up and results going down, the cost per new drug is skyrocketing. And to make matters worse, of those drugs approved for sale over this period, 75 percent could be classed as "me too" products: only a quarter of them offered real improvement over existing products.[45] Why is this happening?

Table 8.1 Trends in R&D Costs[46]

Year	Number of New Molecular Entities approved by FDA[1]	Number of NME's Given Priority Review[2]	R&D Spending by PhRMA Members ($ billions)	Cost per successful drug ($ millions in Year 2000 Dollars)
2006	18	6	43.4	$1500*
2005	18	13	39.9	$1300*
2004	31	17	37.0	$1200*
2000	27	9	26.0	$800
1990	23	12	8.4	$300
1980	12	**	2.0	$150

*Denotes authors' projections; **priority review process did not exist

---

[1] Does not include Biologic License Application approvals.

[2] "Priority Review" by the FDA is reserved for new molecular entities that offer significant improvement over existing products in the treatment, diagnosis, or prevention of a disease. Standard Review is offered to drugs which possess therapeutic qualities similar to those of one or more existing drugs.

The lack of innovative success in the face of such increased spending is not due to the exhaustion of science and technology that typically characterizes the end stage of a technology curve.[47] With modern technology and equipment, scientists have never been as capable of developing new molecules as they are today. More likely, the problem resides in the resource allocation process, in the expectations derived from a long history of success and industry growth.[48] Recently, pharmaceutical companies have primarily grown via mergers—with at least 20 involving targets valued at $2 billion and higher between 1994 and 2004.[49] The common rationale for these mergers was typically to build up the product pipeline by absorbing existing products, amass the scale required to increase the discovery of new compounds, and fund the cost of their clinical trials. While these firms indeed beefed up their scale and scope, they also raised the threshold for the market size a particular drug needs to create in order to be "interesting" enough to merit aggressive funding in the resource allocation process.

Here's a way to visualize how this is happening: A company's share price represents in some way the discounted present value of a future stream of cash flows that investors foresee. If something causes investors to expect that a company's cash flow will grow more slowly than they previously thought, the mathematics of discounting will cause its share price to fall to the point where the new price represents the discounted present value of the newly foreseen flow of cash. As a result, good managers feel compelled to grow—and more specifically, to grow at a constant or increasing rate—in order to maintain or grow their company's share price. If investors expect a company with $1 billion in revenues to grow 10 percent annually, its managers need to find $100 million in new product revenues the next year. The rub is, if that company achieves $50 billion in revenues and still hopes to grow by 10 percent, it must now somehow produce $5 *billion* in new product revenues the next year. The bittersweet reward of success is that the larger and more successful a company becomes, it actually loses its ability to prioritize new products whose markets might be small at the outset. A market that at one point represented an exciting growth opportunity might not be big enough later on to attract the resources required for development.

It wasn't too many years ago that most pharmaceutical companies considered a $100 million-a-year drug an exciting growth opportunity. As they grew, however, $100 million opportunities lost their luster—and $1 billion-a-year drugs defined "blockbuster" status. Today, the leading companies are so large that even billion-dollar drugs don't solve their growth problem. Huge product markets are like heroin to executives of these companies. In the end, products with small markets or inadequate reimbursement get ignored, while "me too" products that can be developed at lower cost for broader markets hold the most appeal. It is for this reason that we have six statins available, but only two manufacturers willing to supply the entire nation's flu vaccines.[50]

The danger with the drugmakers' addiction to large markets is that most of today's blockbuster product markets are comprised of drugs targeting broad, symptomatically defined diseases. For example, Lilly's Prozac and Zyprexa achieved blockbuster status by targeting depression and schizophrenia, respectively. We suspect we'll learn in the coming years, however, that both of these major diseases are in fact families of many different disorders that share common signs and symptoms. And we might learn as well that Prozac and Zyprexa are predictably effective in treating just one (or a few) of these diseases.

The same can be said for lipid-lowering blockbusters such as Lipitor. We'll likely discover that elevated levels of blood cholesterol is a "symptom"[51] shared by several different diseases— and that Lipitor is effective only in treating one or a few of these diseases. We'll learn that many of the patients taking these medications had a disease for which these drugs are not particularly effective. The advent of precision medicine will fragment most of these markets—there will be many more diseases, many more products, and significantly lower revenues per product. These markets will be very visible and very exciting to smaller drug companies. But to the mega-merged pharmaceutical giants, these markets simply won't solve their pressing needs for huge chunks of instant revenue growth. Their business models just aren't made for developing and selling products to smaller markets.

How, you ask, can companies afford even to roll the dice in a game where the cost of developing a single new drug approaches $1 billion? The answer is that while today's drug companies are *spending* this amount per drug developed, it doesn't *cost* $1 billion to launch a successful product. It is trial and error that are expensive. A significant portion of that cost is spent sifting through drugs whose markets are too small, in order to find those that are large. A lot of innovation gets tossed aside in that filtering process. Another portion is spent on testing the drugs in clinical trials that ultimately prove to be ineffective for a large majority of patients with the symptomatically defined disease. As we move toward the realm of precision medicine, we will find that development of successful new products will cost substantially less than it does today.

In the face of this fragmentation of pharmaceutical markets, new blockbusters will arise *because* of diagnostic precision, rather than its absence. We've previously mentioned one example of this—the case of Elan Pharmaceutical's Tysabri (natalizumab). Elan's scientists discovered that multiple sclerosis is but one of several symptomatic expressions that result from a common underlying disease pathway. In the case of multiple sclerosis, this molecular pathway promotes excessive entry of white blood cells into the central nervous system, leading to inflammation and nerve cell damage. Interestingly, the same molecular pathway was found in other patients, but the disease manifested in them as an inflammatory bowel disorder called Crohn's disease. It's quite possible that the same underlying disease might be manifesting itself with symptoms now identified as ulcerative colitis and rheumatoid arthritis. Another example of this new type of blockbuster is the Novartis drug Gleevec, which is used in treating not just a particular type of leukemia called chronic myeloid leukemia, but gastrointestinal stromal tumors as well. Both of these tumors propagate through similar molecular pathways.

Because it alleviates the underlying molecular disease, Tysabri is a potential blockbuster—a treatment for all these various symptomatic expressions of the underlying disease. Frustratingly, of course, the FDA still defines the diseases by symptom, requiring Elan to conduct separate clinical trials for each. However, as scientific research continues to push toward precision medicine, it is still quite possible to find blockbusters of this new genre.

Such new blockbusters already appear to be emerging in cancer treatment. In a provocative presentation at an Innosight Institute conference in 2008, Dr. Mara Aspinall asserted that if you are diagnosed with cancer, you should never seek treatment at a hospital that is structured according to body organs—with departmental specialties in breast cancer, bone cancer, brain cancer, and so on. The reason is that, by definition, the institution will have diagnosed your disease incorrectly. Whether you respond to the therapy they offer will truly be a matter of chance. The cancer institute you can trust, she asserted, will be structured around the different molecular pathways by which tumors have been found to propagate. While there will no longer be blockbuster drugs to fight leukemia (which has been shown to comprise 51 different types of cancers), there will be blockbusters (or "niche busters") that fight diseases defined by molecular pathway rather than geographic location.

We have replicated Dr. Aspinall's illustration of this contrast in Figure 8.3. As suggested in the diagram of the hospital on the left, in the past, when we classified patients and their diseases by location, we were applying the same therapy across multiple diseases. In the future, as suggested by the hospital on the right that classifies patients by the type of tumor growing within them, we will be able to treat specific diseases that arise in multiple locations in the body with a predictably effective therapy for each of them.

How Should Today's Drug Giants Respond?

What does this mean for major drug companies like Pfizer and GSK? In all probability, they are too large for today's competitive conditions, and much too large for the fragmented product markets they will confront in 10 years. Aside from divesting themselves of the companies they acquired to become so large, another possibility is for them to structure themselves internally as Johnson & Johnson has. J&J's $61 billion in revenues comes from over 250 operating companies, each of which has its own management board.[52] Some of these, like Ortho-McNeil, Janssen, and Centocor, have themselves become massive multi-billion-dollar enterprises, while others are much smaller. The guiding principle that today's huge pharmaceutical companies need to follow is that the growth markets of tomorrow will primarily be small ones. Corporations that are comprised of many small companies will see these opportunities with much greater acuity than a large monolithic company ever could.

Fortunately, there are a few early indications that at least some of the major pharmaceutical companies—particularly Novartis—are seeing this future quite clearly. They have chosen to segment their R&D into divisions based on molecular pathways, rather

---

FIGURE 8.3 The definition of disease drives the structure of the organizations that treat the disease

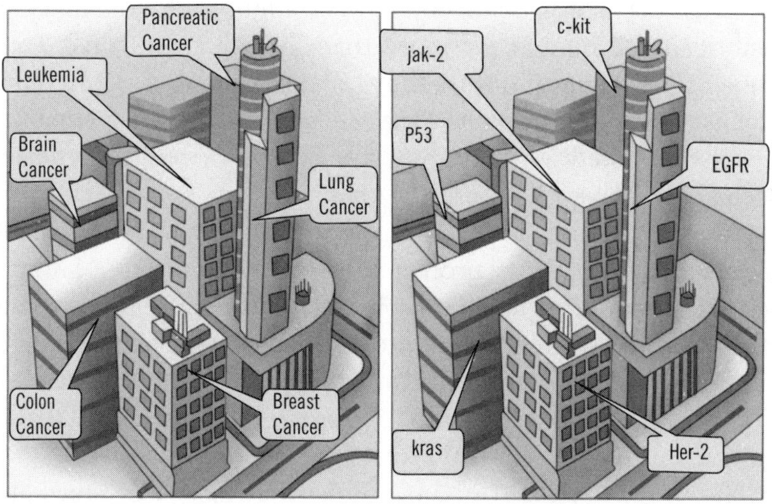

The typical structure for providing care in the past centered on the location in the body where the disease arose.

The structure of the future, in order to provide appropriate care, should center on the type of disease.

Source: Mara Aspinall, of Genzyme Corporation and the Dana Farber Cancer Institute, June 2008.

than by anatomically defined organ system or symptomatically defined disease. One benefit to matching drug development to properly defined diseases is the likely reduction in the number of patients susceptible to being harmed by treatment. This not only reduces potential liability from patient lawsuits, but can also lead to the rescue of dozens of drugs that were denied FDA approval because they proved effective on too small a portion of the population, or had been pulled from the market due to previously unpredictable side effects. The clinical trials involving Iressa (gefitinib) and Herceptin (trastuzumab) have already demonstrated the value of molecular testing in identifying the value of drugs that would otherwise have failed to garner FDA approval because they were effective in only a minority of patients.

CHANGES IN THE MARKETING OF PHARMACEUTICAL PRODUCTS

Historically, "detailing" was the primary sales mechanism for drugs. Pharmaceutical company salespeople called on physicians to give them the detail they needed about new drugs they could prescribe for their patients. As shown in Figure 8.4, drug detailing historically accounted for more than 70 percent of drug companies' total selling and marketing expenses. It constituted a major expense investment not just for the pharmaceutical companies, but also entailed a major opportunity cost for the physicians. Both sides, however, found it in their interest to spend this time together, explaining and learning about drugs that were available to prescribe for patients' problems. Strong relationships of mutual trust often developed between physicians and those that detailed drugs to them. This, in turn, created yet another barrier against the entry of new companies into the pharmaceutical business. Creating a sales force with the requisite reach represented a huge investment that few companies had the resources to muster.

The heavy fixed cost of a detailing sales force also steepened the scale economics in the industry by creating a strong drive for volume—driving the thirst for blockbuster drugs and for acquisitions that brought the ability to push more volume through the sales force. Detailing doesn't work well anymore, however—and that's a big problem, because in many respects companies' profit models and competitive advantages are structured around the reach and relationships their direct sales forces have had with doctors. Doctors today are under such pressure to see more patients that they simply don't have the time to spend with drug company salespeople. And doctors are much less dependent upon detailers to learn about drugs: there are alternatives. The Internet enables physicians to search for the right drug, and to refresh their knowledge of its side effect profile and possible interactions with other drugs, even while the patient is in the office.

In reaction to the obsolescence of their sales model, the pharmaceutical firms have increasingly aimed their marketing efforts at patients, helping them to "self-diagnose" and then "pull" the drugs through their physicians. Since the FDA began allowing in August 1997, brand-specific direct-to-consumer (DTC) television advertising has been an increasingly important segment of the marketing budget. As we've shown in Figure 8.4, DTC had grown to account for over one-third of drug companies' total marketing and sales budgets by 2005.[53] DTC spending was $4.2 billion in 2005, compared to about $1 billion in 1996, outpacing the growth in total promotional spending.[54]

Almost every disruption involves a story like this. When products are complicated and expensive, they typically must be sold by expert, company-employed salespeople who sell to expert users on the customer side. Hence, for example, mainframe and minicomputers were sold directly to users. The reach and reputation of IBM's sales organization was a forceful presence no competitor could beat. But the personal computer couldn't be sold that way. They had to be marketed direct to end users, who then pulled the products through the distribution channels. The marketing methods for photocopiers, mutual funds, customer relationship management software, cameras, and many others followed a similar pattern. Instead of relying upon company salespeople to push their products into the market, the economics of disruption changed the marketing model to one of mass marketing to customers, who then pulled the products through the distribution and retail channels.

In the first stages of disruption of the sales model, there still are fairly steep scale economies in sales and distribution. Direct-to-consumer television advertising and getting space on retailers' shelves requires scale, scope, and capital. In many of these instances, however, the Internet has flattened those scale barriers so that small companies can advertise with broad reach, and customers can find products without needing to go to brick-and-mortar retailers.

For patient safety advocates and for those who worry about unwarranted consumption of health-care products and services, DTC advertising of drugs is one of the most worrisome dimensions of the disruption of health care. Here's our sense as to why this change is worrisome. Recall the effect that capitation had when it was imposed in the system of independent practitioners and providers. When responsibility for constraining spending

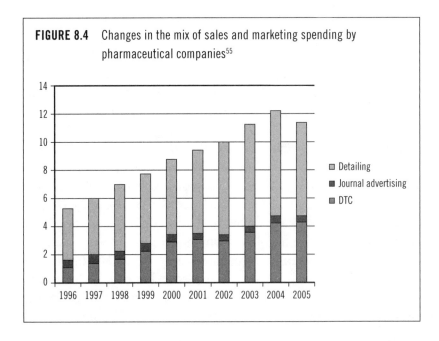

FIGURE 8.4 Changes in the mix of sales and marketing spending by pharmaceutical companies[55]

was placed upon the shoulders of primary care physicians as gate-keepers, it imposed upon them the role of saying no to patients' requests for access to specialists and for second opinions when those were not warranted. Doctors complained that saying no strained their relationship with patients. Direct-to-consumer advertising again imposes upon physicians the responsibility of saying no in those occasions when patients haven't self-diagnosed correctly—and again puts doctors in an uncomfortable and unaccustomed role. It is unpopular because life was much simpler when patients' abilities to know what to ask for were so limited that they simply accepted what doctors offered.

In making these assertions, we are not being critical of physicians and the negative reaction many of them have to DTC advertising. Every parent has experienced the same feelings. When money is not a constraint, it is infinitely easier (in the short term) to accede to our children's requests than to deny them. Similarly, when money is not a constraint (as is the case under fee-for-service), life is a lot easier for physicians when they do not have to say no.

A better way to address the change of marketing direct to consumers is simply to accept that this transition in marketing is here to stay in health care—and in the end it will be a good thing. When an industry is in the realm of intuition—whether it is intuitive computing, construction, printing, or investing—experts tend to sell to experts. But as things evolve toward the realms of pattern-recognition and then rules-based decision making, we transition toward selling to the end user. Direct-to-consumer advertising of drugs may have jumped the gun in circumstances where the disease in question hasn't moved toward pattern-recognition or rules-based diagnosis and therapy. But our approach to dealing with this problem should be to give consumers ever more accurate tools for self-diagnosis, and transition toward payments systems such as health savings accounts, which create incentives not to consume what is not needed. And the doctors who need to write these prescriptions will, unfortunately, need to get comfortable with saying no on occasion.

At present, the disruption of the selling system for pharmaceuticals is still in its first phase, in that it is expensive and scale-intensive to advertise on national television and in national print media. This creates barriers for smaller entrants. But the use of online diagnostic tools will become more prevalent as primary care physicians (PCPs) disrupt specialists, as nurse practitioners disrupt PCPs, and as self-diagnosis disrupts professional care. We expect those sites to become the locus for DTC advertising of drugs in the future, again flattening the barriers against entry that have historically been in place.

THE IMPACT OF GENERIC DRUGS

The generic drug sector has been depicted as both savior and wrongdoer when it comes to the pharmaceutical industry's uncertain future. By simply waiting for drugs to go off patent before reverse-engineering their own bioequivalent molecules, generic manufacturers don't incur the significant clinical trial costs that inflate the expensive drug development figures in Table 8.1. They can often piggyback onto the extensive, decade-long marketing efforts of the branded pharmaceutical companies.[56] Throw in allegations of bribing and unethical conduct,[57] and it's not surprising that the generic manufacturers are often likened to vultures, who exist only as long as they are able to feed on the unwanted remains of once viable products.

On the other hand, competition among generic manufacturers is particularly intense, as the loss of patent protection essentially turns the drug molecule into a commodity that any drugmaker in the world can try to produce. This competition, particularly from overseas companies like Teva, Dr. Reddy's, and Ranbaxy (recently acquired by Daiichi Sankyo), drives prices down significantly. And when patients, insurers, and payers alike see four dollar prescriptions available from Wal-Mart,[58] it's not hard to understand why they expect generic drugs to help bring down some of the costs of a much maligned pharmaceutical industry.

In cooperation with health plans and employers, many hospitals have developed "tiered formularies," which list not just the drugs within each category that physicians can prescribe, but rank order them by tier. The generic equivalent, if available, always is the first tier therapy. If it isn't appropriate or isn't available, then the formulary shows the next allowable choice, and so on.

We would agree that generic manufacturers can begin to disrupt the larger, branded manufacturers—but not for any of the reasons listed above. If generic manufacturers were to begin competing directly against branded manufacturers by initiating their own R&D for new molecules, the technological enabler— the drug molecule—would basically be the same for both. The question therefore becomes whether generic manufacturers have built or are capable of building a disruptive business model with which to carry out the necessary R&D and postdevelopment marketing to compete effectively.

However, until recently there hasn't been a pressing need to do this. The health-care reimbursement system in the United States has effectively ensconced a cost-plus system of pricing that guarantees a sufficient amount of revenue to cover the R&D and marketing costs of branded pharmaceutical companies. It is a practice reminiscent of some of the most egregious U.S. Department of Defense contracts: when prices can be negotiated so costs are always recouped, why would anyone care what things *should* cost? This pricing system even balances the lost revenues from foreign markets, where branded drugs are often sold at far lower prices than in the United States. Prices are so much lower elsewhere that many intrepid entrepreneurs and lawmakers are trying to reimport branded drugs. But this price differential exists not because other countries and single-payer systems are so much better at negotiating prices; it exists because cost-plus reimbursement has inadvertently made the United States the primary financier for the world's pharmaceutical R&D.

So what's the *true* cost of drug development? Generic manufacturers, which did not arise in an environment of cost-plus contracts but rather from the ashes of vigorous competition and low pricing, would likely have developed business models that come much closer to reflecting real, rational costs. But comparing the business models of generic and branded manufacturers has been difficult in the past. Generic manufacturers had rarely forayed into developing new molecules, and therefore were offering a very different value proposition. They were quite content to continue earning acceptable profits based on their more modest R&D and marketing expenses, without having to place the risky bets of their larger brethren.

For years the administered pricing scheme created a détente, with branded and generic manufacturers standing on either side of a battle line defined by a patent expiration date. But frustrated with the slow pipeline of drugs from branded manufacturers upon which they are dependent, a few generic manufacturers like Teva began to venture into drug development for themselves. Already, 20 percent of Teva's revenues are derived from patented products. R&D and marketing costs of new molecules developed by generic manufacturers in India and Israel seem to be 30 to 40 percent below the average drug development costs of branded manufacturers in the United States and Europe.[59] This will fit quite nicely into a disruptive value network of cost-conscious patients, providers, insurers, and payers looking for more four dollar drugs. Ultimately, much like the situation with IBM and Digital Equipment in the era of microprocessors, both generic and branded manufacturers will have access to the same technological enablers. But disruption prevails when the technological enabler is implanted into a business model that can make money at lower margins, while still delivering the quality its customers demand.

SUMMARY

We foresee significant redirections in the seas ahead through which the pharmaceutical industry's chief navigators will need to steer their companies. For reasons of technological and commercial interdependence, vertical integration typically plays a key role in the early growth of most industries, and in the rise to dominance by their leading companies. The processes of disruption then reverse the factors that had necessitated integration, causing industries to dis-integrate—to become populated by a horizontally stratified value network of specialist companies. The pharmaceutical industry, long led by large, powerfully integrated companies, is now moving inexorably toward dis-integration.

The driver of dis-integration is outsourcing, which results in "supply chain disruption." The industry's leading integrated competitors, in the pursuit of greater profitability, begin by out-sourcing their most peripheral, lowest value-adding activities to lower-cost suppliers. With this done, the next step toward enhancing profitability is to outsource the lowest value-adding activity of those that remain; and so on. The companies that receive these outsourcing contracts have the opposite motivations. In the pursuit of greater profitability, they are eager to take on the progressively higher value-adding activities their customers are eager to shed. Little by little the industry-leading companies do less and less, and their suppliers do more and more—until the leaders have liquidated their business models. This process is well under way in pharmaceuticals. Companies that initially specialized as recipients of outsourcing contracts for drug dis-covery and development, contract manufacturing, and managing clinical trials, have expanded their scope to encompass most of the industry's value chain.

Once dis-integration has occurred, the stage in the value chain where attractive profits can be earned shifts. The ability to make attractive profits typically centers at the stage in an industry's value chain whose technology determines overall system performance. As disruption occurs, this stage typically is the enabling tech-nology *inside* the product.

In pharmaceuticals, this suggests that in the future, activities that link precise diagnostics with predictably effective thera-peutics will become the center of industry profitability. At the core of this will be the management of clinical trials—which need to be framed as *research* trials, rather than end-of-the-process tests of whether drugs work. The development of diagnostics and therapeutics will be intertwined through these research trials. For reasons that seem (to them) to be perfectly rational and profit-maximizing, most leading pharmaceutical companies are walking away from these activities, which will coalesce as the critical core competencies of tomorrow. The leaders would be wise to reverse course.

The market for drugs will fragment. Instead of being dominated by multi-billion-dollar blockbuster products, pharmaceutical companies' revenue streams will generally come from a much wider variety of products, with much lower revenues per product. The cost structure and investment models of today's mega-merged global pharmaceutical companies, which have become addicted to blockbuster drugs, will therefore need to be unwound and rewritten.

New types of blockbuster drugs will emerge, but these will require a significant restructuring of these companies' sales and marketing capabilities. As we learn what these diseases are, we'll realize that most companies' sales forces are organized incorrectly, because medical specialties themselves have been defined incorrectly.

In most industries, the early products are so complicated and expensive that they must be sold direct—by experts, to experts. As disruption gains momentum, the economics of these disruptive products force direct selling to give way to a model of marketing to the end user, who then turns around and pulls the product through distribution. The boom in direct-to-consumer advertising of pharmaceuticals fits this pattern precisely. There are significant commercial opportunities to companies whose products and services make self-diagnosis ever more straightforward. The question isn't whether this will become the dominant mode of marketing. The question is who will make this system work effectively.

At the same time, generic manufacturers will begin to work their way up-market by adapting their business model to the changing health-care environment. Whether traditional, branded manufacturers can adapt as quickly and easily to the new value chain is yet to be determined.

We see, in other words, extraordinary changes sweeping through the pharmaceutical industry. There is a well-established pattern by which these changes arise, which we've seen in industry after industry. They always have loomed as threats to some, and opportunities to others—and whether it is one or the other is a *choice*. We hope this chapter will help pharmaceutical executives choose the perspective that spells opportunity.

APPENDIX

Clinical Research Trials that Supplant Clinical Test Trials

The budding science of pharmacogenomics holds the promise that one day health care can be specifically tailored to each individual patient, selecting an optimal treatment by taking into account the patient's unique genetic makeup. This concept of subdividing patient populations into subsets defined by molecular testing encourages researchers to drill down to the root causes of disease. In the future, the pathway of drug development and disease treatment might look like the schematic in Figure 8.5.[60]

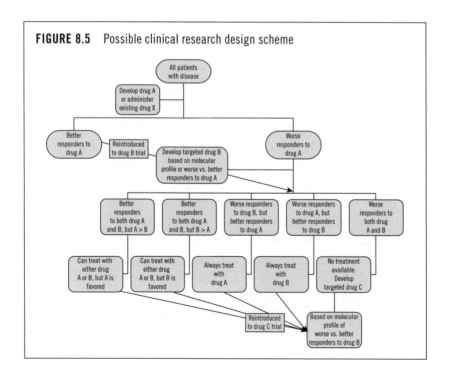

FIGURE 8.5 Possible clinical research design scheme

With multiple detailed outcomes, these large trials result in optimal decision making for each possible category of patients. However, this process also raises a number of concerns.

Using the traditional approach, each drug requires another large, lengthy trial to demonstrate its value. Furthermore, the multiple subgroups of patients involved make subject recruitment and data analysis difficult. Understandably, with no cost savings and added complexity, pharmaceutical companies with incumbent products might be reluctant to develop additional drugs that more than likely have smaller target markets than those that already exist.

At the same time, the process also results in the development of "me too" drugs that offer only marginal improvement over existing therapies. However, since existing markets tend to be larger and already well-defined by past marketing and sales efforts, the left-hand side of the chart in Figure 8.5 would probably appear more attractive to incumbent players. Under this drug development model, sustaining products almost always make the most sense to these companies.

In seeking to disrupt the existing drug development model, we argue that the groups of patients who we call "Worse Responders" are in fact underserved consumers or nonconsumers. What modern science allows us to do with increasing frequency is to parse out those individuals for whom existing therapies just aren't good enough. As the technological enabler, molecular diagnostics can therefore create new target markets ripe for disruption by newcomers who are willing to focus their operations on these nonconsumers.[61]

In the way we have diagrammed the drug development process above, these nonconsumers tend to fall on the right side of Figure 8.5. Those patients who end up on the left side already have a drug that is good enough. Any attempt to further improve their outcome is of only marginal benefit. Of course, these patients could always be included in later clinical trials. Our point is that they should not be the focus of further large-scale trials, unless there is reason to believe that a new treatment will advance their care enough to warrant retesting.

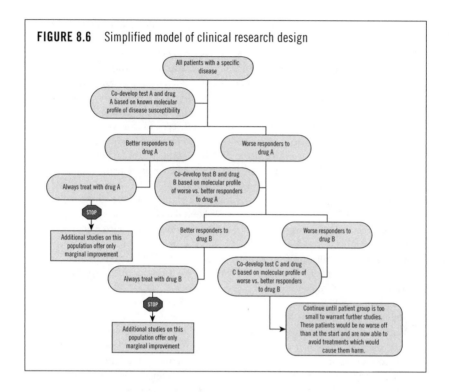

FIGURE 8.6   Simplified model of clinical research design

We propose a modified drug development process, outlined in Figure 8.6, which results in a more cost-effective approach that focuses on patients for whom nothing works. This model is somewhat oversimplified, since pharmacogenomic testing typically extracts an overlapping segment of the population that may contain some existing responders and may not contain all nonresponders. Within each generation of the tree, we would expect to see more than one test/drug combination. However, the principle of focusing on those who do not respond to existing therapies still applies.

NOTES

1. *Prescription Drug Trends* (Menlo Park: Henry J. Kaiser Family Foundation, May 2007).
2. Avorn, Jerry, *Powerful Medicines: The Benefits, Risks, and Costs of Prescription Drugs* (New York: Knopf, 2005), 217.

3. Dr. Lewis Thomas described the same phenomenon in 1977, differentiating between "halfway technologies" and curative ones. See Thomas, L., "The Technology of Medicine," *New England Journal of Medicine*, vol. 285 (24):1366–68.

4. The story of Iressa is a favorite of Personalized Medicine advocates. Initially, Iressa (gefitinib) actually failed to demonstrate a survival advantage in a large randomized trial of non-small-cell lung cancer patients in 2004, after which AstraZeneca withdrew the drug from the market. However, by late 2005, Genzyme had made available a test that could distinguish patients with a particular EGFR (epidermal growth factor receptor) mutation that was predicted to be much more responsive to a drug like Iressa, which was in a class of drugs called "tyrosine kinase inhibitors." More recent studies that incorporate testing for such markers in advance have demonstrated great potential. A presentation in June 2007 at a meeting of the American Society of Clinical Oncology revealed that 73 percent of 31 patients who received Iressa in a small study were alive at 12 months, compared to 15 percent of those who received traditional chemotherapy. The advent of precise diagnostic tests may one day "rescue" other drugs from failed clinical trials in a similar fashion. See also Aspinall, Mara G., and Hamermesh, Richard G., "Realizing the Promise of Personalized Medicine," *Harvard Business Review*, October 2007.

5. United Aircraft subsequently decoupled into United Airlines and United Technologies, with its Pratt & Whitney aircraft engine business.

6. Chandler, Alfred D., *The Visible Hand* (Cambridge, Massachusetts: The Belknap Press of Harvard University Press, 1977).

7. We have carefully chosen the words used here: "cannot now compete." The reason is that when the iPod's performance and reliability become more than good enough, we can expect lower-cost, not-as-good modular solutions to emerge at the low end. Indeed, it already has begun to happen as cell phones come equipped with ever larger amounts of memory, onto which music can be downloaded via industry standard interfaces from Amazon music.

8. The "unwinding" of Chandlerian vertical integration was first explained in Christensen, Clayton M., "The Rigid Disk Drive Industry: A History of Commercial and Techno-logical Turbulence," *Business History Review*, vol. 67, no. 4 (Winter 1993), 531–88.

9. In this section we have simply illustrated the underlying management theory with the example of the dis-integration of the computer industry. We invite readers who have a deeper interest in the theory itself to read Christensen, Clayton M., et al., "Disruption, Dis-Integration, and the Dissipation of Differentiability," *Industry and Corporate Change*, vol. 11, no. 5 (November 2002), 955–93.

10. According to Research and Markets, "The Licensing Agreement in Pharmaceutical Business Development." 3rd ed. According to the Adis International R&D Insight Database, about half of the 2,000 compounds being tracked were developed through alliances. Lou, Kasper and Mark de Rond, "The 'not invented here' myth," *Nature Reviews Drug Discovery*, vol. 5, 451–52. Simons, John, "Is Outsourcing the Prescription for Pfizer?" *Fortune*, December 6, 2006.

11. "Contract Research Organization (CRO)," Emissary Web site, accessed at http://emissary.com on June 16, 2008.

12. "Lilly Sells Its Greenfield, Indiana, Operations to Covance; Expands Existing Collaboration Between the Two Companies," PR Newswire press release, August 6, 2008. Accessed at http://www.forbes.com/prnewswire/feeds/prnewswire/2008/06/prnews

wire200808060900PR_NEWS_USPR____CLW032.html. This is a very difficult call for companies like Lilly to make. Our friend Steve Wunker of Innosight LLC has pointed out that the understanding of the high-potential "targets" toward which drugs need to be developed is so broadly understood and diffused that it has created an unprecedented commonality in the portfolios of development projects under way at most drug companies. With fewer proprietary insights about high-potential targets, discovery to a significant extent seems to have become commoditized.

13. Frost & Sullivan's Study on Contract Research and Manufacturing (CRAM), Health Care Practice, Frost & Sullivan 2006. McDonald, Matt, "The Niche: Filling Syringes; Biotech Firm Hyaluron Enters Contract Manufacturing," *Boston Globe*, March 3, 2005, 14.

14. In our experience, when pharmaceutical company representatives are asked what their company's core competence is, the most common response is "marketing."

15. Christensen, Clayton M., and Scott Anthony, "What's the BIG Idea?" Harvard Business School case #9-602-105, 2001.

16. Big Idea Group currently boasts a network of 13,000 inventors (http://www.bigidea group.net) as of Sept. 2008. The global marketing behemoth WPP recently purchased a 30 percent stake in Big Idea Group, headquartered in Manchester, New Hampshire, as part of WPP's bid to become a one-stop marketing house for its clients.

17. Professor Henry Chesbrough of the University of California, Berkeley, and Harvard Business School coined the term "open innovation," and has written extensively on this topic. We recommend that interested readers study his work—beginning with Chesbrough, Henry W., *Open Innovation: The New Imperative for Creating and Profiting from Technology* (Boston, Massachusetts: Harvard Business School Press, 2005).

18. To be sure our friends at Intel and AMD do not lose their paranoia, we warn that this era in the microprocessor industry is drawing to a close. The architecture of the processor itself is becoming modular, so smaller companies such as Santa Clara, California–based Tensilica and United Kingdom–based Advanced Risc Machines can cost-effectively design microprocessors. They can be manufactured by third-party, large-scale manufacturers such as Taiwan Semiconductor Manufacturing Company.

19. Professor Gary Pisano of Harvard Business School has written an extraordinarily thorough book on the history of the biotechnology industry (Pisano, Gary, *Science Business: The Promise, the Reality, and the Future of Biotech*, Harvard Business School Press, 2006). One of his key insights is that the net present value of drug discovery and development is actually *negative*—much more venture capital has been poured into the industry than has come out—especially when the impact on the averages of the very few winners from Genentech, Amgen, and Genzyme are removed from the data. It is akin to gambling in Las Vegas. On average, the population as a whole and any individuals within it should rationally expect to lose money—and a *lot* of it—when they undertake to gamble in the city. But they still gamble, in hopes that they might beat the odds and hit a big jackpot.

20. Indeed, Viagra was an accidental discovery, as the compound was initially tested as a potential treatment for hypertension or angina.

21. Of course, the pharmaceutical industry has tried to combat and adapt to the forces described here. To improve the yield of the discovery process, pharmaceutical companies (and some retail software providers) attempt to identify specific molecular targets ahead of time using rational drug design tools such as computer-assisted modeling. Although the process is still far from perfect, this technology gives scientists a better idea of what

they should be looking for and whether something might already exist in the company's library of molecules.

22. The initial source of this quotation is unknown to us, but it has been attributed repeatedly to Wayne Gretzky for many years, including Herrmann, Mark, "Gretzky Thriving in an Unlikely Setting," *Los Angeles Times*, October 15, 1990, 14.

23. See Gorman, E. G., "The *Slowly* Emerging Future of Diagnostic Testing," *Medical & Health Care Marketplace Guide*, 19th Edition, Dorland Health Care Information, 2004; and "The Value of Diagnostics Innovation, Adoption and Diffusion into Health Care," July 2005, the Lewin Group.

24. Taken from Hermann, L., et al., "Pharmaceuticals for Beginners: A Guide to the Pharmaceutical Industry," March 12, 2003, Deutsche Bank AG Global Equity Research; and "Pharmaceutical Industry Profile 2006," March 2006. Pharmaceutical Research and Manufacturers of America (PhRMA), http://www.phrma.org/files/2006%20Industry%20 Profile.pdf, accessed January 2007.

25. "The Value of Diagnostics Innovation, Adoption and Diffusion into Health Care," July 2005, the Lewin Group.

26. The Current Procedural Terminology (CPT) is a coding system maintained by the American Medical Association and is used by physicians and other health-care professionals to identify services and procedures for billing purposes. We will return to discuss the unintended side effects of the CPT system in Chapter 9.

27. As we would have predicted, however, the rate of investment has only recently started to increase dramatically among companies that are producing exactly the precision diagnostics we espouse in this chapter.

28. See Porter, Michael, *Competitive Strategy* (New York: The Free Press, 1980); and Porter, Michael, *Competitive Advantage* (New York: The Free Press, 1985).

29. The most widely read article on this topic is Christensen, Clayton; Michael Raynor; and Matt Verlinden, "Skate to Where the Money Will Be," *Harvard Business Review*, Nov.–Dec. 2001. In pharmaceuticals the "puck of profitability" has been therapeutics. Diagnostics, often inextricably linked with a therapy, is where that puck will be in the future. For a deeper description of why transitions such as this occur, see Chapters 5 and 6 of Christensen, Clayton M., and Michael Raynor, *The Innovator's Solution* (Boston, Massachusetts: Harvard Business School Press, 2003).

30. Our first Harvard Business School working papers on this topic were published in 1996. These were ultimately summarized in Christensen, Clayton M., Michael E. Raynor, and Matt Verlinden, "Skate to Where the Money Will Be," *Harvard Business Review*, November/December 2001.

31. Notable exceptions are Delphi and Visteon, which have been plagued by the same pension and health-care liabilities as their parent companies. In addition, their customer base has been heavily weighted toward General Motors and Ford, whose sales have been shrinking in response to disruption by Toyota, Honda, Nissan, Hyundai, and Kia.

32. We thank Arshad Ahmed of Scientia Advisors in Cambridge, Massachusetts, for his input and guidance regarding the future of molecular diagnostics.

33. Kranhold, K., and Johnson, A., "GE's Deal with Abbot Labs Displays Immelt's New Strategy," *Wall Street Journal*, Jan. 19, 2007, C3. This deal was eventually called off in July 2007.

34. Applied Biosystems was acquired by Invitrogen in June 2008 for $6.7 billion. Pollack, Andrew, "Invitrogen to Buy Applied Biosystems for $6.7 Billion," *New York Times*, June 13, 2008, accessed at http://www.nytimes.com/2008/06/13/business/13drug.html.

35. This was the subject of a presentation by Dr. Mara Aspinall, of Genzyme and the Dana Farber Cancer Institute, at a meeting sponsored by the Innosight Institute on July 10, 2008.

36. AEI-Brookings has estimated a potential $1.1 billion savings with routine genetic testing in combination with warfarin treatment. For more on this project see Dr. Samuel Goldhaber's work at Harvard Medical School and Brigham and Women's Hospital at http://facultyresearch.bwh.harvard.edu/cgi-bin/search.cgi?id=19.

37. Elkin. et al., "HER-2 Testing and Trastuzumab Therapy for Metastatic Breast Cancer: A Cost-Effectiveness Analysis," *Journal of Clinical Oncology* (2004) 22:854-63. The data in this study was further analyzed by Dr. Mara Aspinall of Genzyme and the Dana Farber Cancer Institute. The value of such testing would be even greater after accounting for the pain and suffering of patients treated with drugs that are futile or even toxic. Another question is to whom these savings should accrue. Our argument in this chapter is that a significant portion ought to flow to the provider of the diagnostic test, but some will also need to flow to those making decisions to create the proper incentives for testing and therapy. These additional parties could include insurers, patients, and providers, all of whom can influence the process.

38. The 30 percent benchmark isn't a randomly selected one. The placebo effect in many trials can be as high as 30 percent. This will, of course, compound the difficulty of sorting out why some patients in these trials respond to the therapy and others do not.

39. Our pathologist friend Dr. Lewis Hassell of the University of Oklahoma offered a great way for the nonscientists among us to visualize the two different reasons why patients who are symptomatically diagnosed with a disease might not respond to the drug being tested. One reason is that they might have different diseases. But two patients could have exactly the same disease, and yet the therapy that is efficacious for one patient doesn't work as effectively in another. It is akin to a fastball pitcher throwing a strike at belt level over the inside of the plate against the Boston Red Sox slugger David Ortiz. Ortiz is "wired" to hit pitches like that out of the ballpark. Another batter could have the same pitch thrown at him, in exactly the same place, and he can't hit it, because given the way he learned to swing the bat, that spot is a "hole" out of which he can at best punch back weak ground balls.

40. Tucker, Leslie, *Pharmacogenomics: A Primer for Policymakers* (Washington, DC: National Center for Policy Analysis, George Washington University, Jan. 28, 2008). Joseph A. DiMasi of the Tufts Center for the Study of Drug Development estimated that pharmaceutical manufacturers could save $129 million per drug (of a total development cost of $802 million) if clinical trials could be shortened by 25 percent, and $235 million per drug if they could be shortened by 50 percent.

41. A problem that has simply been inherent in drug development is that diagnostic capability of some sort necessarily precedes the creation of the drug and enrollment of patients in the trial—let alone the completion of the trial. As our abilities to diagnose improve and the categories of disease change, we still will be organizing therapeutic trials with the schema of earlier years. This invites a deeper rethinking of the clinical trials process than we have been able to do at this point. We invite our readers to share their thoughts on how to deal with this problem.

42. We thank our friend Dr. Keith Dionne for sharing this insight and data with us.

43. This certainly was the case in Genentech's trials to approve the cancer drug Herceptin. Where the trials for many cancer drugs stretch for five and often 10 years, the unambiguous efficacy of Herceptin for patients with tumors characterized by an overexpression of the HER2 protein was conclusively apparent after only two years. It remains

to be seen how much more efficient trials can become, given that the degree of precision needed is still lacking for most diseases outside of oncology and infectious diseases. Other enabling technologies, however, including computer-assisted predictive modeling such as Archimedes (http://archimedesmodel.com), will help hasten this progression to precision trials.

44. Source: Presentation by Dr. Mara Aspinall, Genzyme and the Dana Farber Cancer Institute, at the Innosight Institute Health Care Conference, Cambridge, Massachusetts, July 10, 2008.

45. Avorn, J., *Powerful Medicines: The Benefits, Risks, and Costs of Prescription Drugs*, 217.

46. Data used in constructing this table were taken from the following sources: "NDAs Approved in Calendar Years 1990–2004 by Therapeutic Potentials and Chemical Types," U.S. Food and Drug Administration Center for Drug Evaluation and Research, last updated Dec. 31, 2004, accessed at http://www.fda.gov/cder/rdmt/pstable.htm; "Pharmaceutical Industry Profile 2006," Pharmaceutical Research and Manufacturers of America (PhRMA), March 2006, accessed at http://www.phrma.org/files/2006%20Industry%20 Profile.pdf; "R&D Spending by U.S. Biopharmaceutical Companies Reaches a Record $55.2 Billion in 2006," PhRMA, Feb. 12, 2007 press release, accessed at http://www. phrma.org/news_room/press_releases/r&d_spending_by_u.s._biopharmaceutical_ companies_reaches_a_record_$55.2_billion_in_2006; DiMasi, J. A.: R. W. Hansen, and H. G. Grabowski, "The Price of Innovation: New Estimates of Drug Development Costs," Oct. 28, 2002, *Journal of Health Economics*, 22 (2003): 151–85; Tufts Center for the Study of Drug Development, "Total Cost to Develop a New Prescription Drug, Including Cost of Post-Approval Research, Is $897 Million," press release from May 13, 2003 (accessed at http://csdd.tufts.edu/NewsEvents/NewsArticle.asp?newsid=29) and "Average Cost to Develop a New Biotechnology Product Is $1.2 Billion, According to the Tufts Center for the Study of Drug Development," press release from Nov. 9, 2006 (accessed at http://csdd.tufts.edu/NewsEvents/NewsArticle.asp?newsid=69); "Pharmaceutical Industry Profile 2008," PhRMA, March 2008, accessed at http://www. phrma.org/files/2008%20Profile.pdf; and "R&D Spending by U.S. Biopharmaceutical Companies Reaches a Record $55.2 Billion in 2006," PhRMA, Feb. 12, 2007 press release, accessed at http://www.phrma.org/news_room/press_releases/r&d _spending_ by_u.s._biopharmaceutical_companies_reaches_a_record_$55.2_billion_in_2006. These data are meant for guidance only; estimates are widely debated. For example, Bain & Co. has estimated drug development costs to be $1.7 billion when factoring in the cost of 12 months of sales and marketing.

47. See Foster, Richard, *Innovation: The Attacker's Advantage* (New York: Summit Books, 1986).

48. We refer readers with a deeper interest in how the resource allocation process can affect drug companies' new product success rate to Bower, Joseph L., and Clark Gilbert, "A Revised Model of the Resource Allocation Process," Harvard Business School Working Paper Series, No. 05-078, 2005.

49. Hermann, L., et al., "Pharmaceuticals for Beginners: A guide to the pharmaceutical industry," March 12, 2003, Deutsche Bank AG Global Equity Research.

50. Avorn, Jerry, *Powerful Medicines: The Benefits, Risks, and Costs of Prescription Drugs* (New York, Knopf, 2005), xix.

51. As in Chapter 2, we will use the term "symptom" loosely here to represent any of the observable characteristics of disease. In practice, medical terminology separates these characteristics into "signs" (evidence of disease that is discovered through examination and testing) and "symptoms" (descriptive sensations of diseases expressed by the patient). However, we have chosen to combine these facets of diagnosis into a single term, as neither typically provides the precise diagnosis necessary for many of the innovations we describe in this book.

52. *Johnson & Johnson 2007 Investor Fact Sheet* (New Brunswick: Johnson & Johnson, June 2008), http://www.investor.jnj.com/investor-facts.cfm.

53. We have elected to exclude the cost of free samples as part of the standard sales and marketing budget, but include those costs as part of "total promotional" spending. The annual cost of free samples actually exceeds the yearly sum of all the sales and marketing expenses listed in Figure 8.4.

54. Thomaselli, Rich, "Record year: Pharma outlay could reach $5B; Support for Lunesta and Ambien drives spending up 9% in first half of 2006," *Advertising Age*, 23 Oct. 2006, vol. 77, no. 4.

55. Donohue, Julie M.; Marisa Cevasco; and Meredith B. Rosenthal, "A Decade of Direct-to-Consumer Advertising of Prescription Drugs," *New England Journal of Medicine*, vol. 357(7):673–81.

56. This is one of the primary reasons why pharmaceutical companies will tend to choose a simple brand name, but a complicated generic name.

57. "Hospital Stops Using Generic Drugs," *New York Times*, Oct. 17, 1989.

58. Wal-Mart's four dollar Prescriptions Program offers over 1,000 over-the-counter drugs and hundreds of prescription drugs at four dollars for a 30-day supply, and some at $10 for a 90-day supply. Accessed at http://www.walmart.com/catalog/catalog.gsp?cat=546834.

59. Langer, Eric S., *Advances in Biopharmaceutical Technology in India* (Rockville, Maryland: BioPlan Associates, Inc, 2008), 668. This estimate is from Utkarsh Palnitkar, director and head of Life Sciences Practice at Ernst & Young India.

60. We thank Steven Fransblow of Innosight LLC for helping us develop this framework.

61. We thank Dr. Bern Shen, Chief Medical Officer of Adjuvo Health and a Board member of Innosight Institute, for pointing out the parallels to the "long tail" problem found in many other industries. We would theorize that a facilitated network model, similar to what Amazon and eBay have done in their respective markets, might be most capable of aggregating these nonconsumers and coordinating drug development in the proper direction.

Chapter 9

Future Directions for Medical Devices and Diagnostic Equipment

Doctors using products from the medical device and diagnostic equipment (MDDE) industry have wrought unimagined blessings in the lives of millions of people. Implantable pacemakers and defibrillators enable people with otherwise debilitating heart irregularities to live normal lives. Angioplasty has alleviated symptoms of recurring chest pain in millions of people. Artificial hips and knees have permitted more active and independent lifestyles for millions who would otherwise be invalid. Portable blood glucose monitors enable diligent patients with diabetes to live long and normal lives, escaping the devastating complications of their disease. Where conventional surgery entailed weeks of recuperation, minimally invasive surgical equipment allows serious surgery to be done on an outpatient basis—with recovery completed in a matter of days. Electrical micropulses from deeply implanted neural stimulators in the brain can cause the tremors of Parkinson's disease to disappear—and even, in other patients, to mitigate the symptoms of depression.

A generation ago X-ray was the only imaging technology, and it could only provide images of bones. Because there was no way to capture images of soft tissues, many surgeries were "exploratory" in nature: doctors had to cut us open to see what was going on. Today, thanks to scanners using computer-aided tomography (CT) and positron emission tomography (PET), magnetic resonance imaging (MRI) machines and ultrasonic and fluoroscopic "movies" of organs as they function, doctors can see with remarkable clarity what is going on inside of us. Most surgeries today occur *after* imaging technologies have given a definitive diagnosis of the problem to be repaired.[1] In fact, the clarity with which doctors can see into the body has given rise to a new medical discipline, *interventional radiology*—where radiologists whose skill is in imaging are actually performing the minimally invasive surgery too.

We have become so accustomed to these miraculous technologies that most people don't even stop to think that 40 years ago, none of these existed.

Some would complain, of course, that these unimagined blessings have brought unimagined cost to health care as well. The blessings indeed have been costly—but they need not continue to be so. In this chapter we will outline a path for innovators in the MDDE industry to make their miracles affordable and even more broadly accessible. We propose that executives in this industry can use two "growth compasses" to find their way to the next waves of growth in their markets. While these compasses are good guides to future growth in many industries, we believe they point to future growth in MDDE with particular accuracy. The first compass points to decentralization in the technological terrain of the MDDE industry; the second points toward products that commoditize professional expertise. The more these two waves of growth converge in the same market opportunity, the more growth there will be.

GROWTH WAVES OF CENTRALIZATION AND DECENTRALIZATION

A recurrent theme in this book is that in the beginning stages of nearly every advanced industry, the initial products and services are complicated and expensive. Disruption then "democratizes" these, by making products and services that are simpler and more affordable. We will also use that theme in this chapter, but frame it using sustaining and disruptive innovations that democratize products and services in a geographical sense.

Before most modern industries emerged, during a period we'll call "Stage Zero," things were almost always done by hand. We wrote letters, calculated with slide rules, made copies with carbon paper, and so on. Activities during Stage Zero in these industries are diffused and local. When "modern" technology comes to an industry, it often brings quantum improvements in quality, cost, and speed. But the equipment that accomplishes this typically is so complicated and expensive that only people or institutions with a lot of skill and a lot of money can own and use that equipment. To economize on the scarcity of money and skills, activity in the industry becomes *centralized*—meaning we must take the problems we're trying to resolve to a central location, where people with the requisite expertise and equipment can solve them. Ultimately, however, the cost and inconvenience of these centralized solutions creates the impetus for disruptive innovators to find ways that *decentralize* the ability to solve these problems. When this is accomplished, rather than taking our problems to the center to be addressed, technologically advanced solutions go to where the problems are.

As an example, during Stage Zero of the "distance communication" industry we wrote letters that were delivered by railroad, stagecoach, or boat. When the telegraph emerged, it was much faster than the mail. But we had to take our message to the nearest telegraph office, where a skilled operator sent the message in Morse code. Eventually, the wire-line telephone brought the capability of distance communication to our homes. We no longer had to go to a central location where an expert did the job for us; we just had to go home and do it for ourselves. Today, wireless mobile phones have brought the ability to communicate to *us*, wherever we are—so we no longer have to go to the phone.

In industries ranging from entertainment to education, from telecommunications to banking, and from printing to retailing, the initial implementations of technology were expensive and complicated, and therefore needed to be centralized. However, the improved performance and reliability of these centralized products and services led to a surge in growth which we'll call *Wave One*. These solutions were then decentralized through successive stages of disruption, which we'll arbitrarily label *Wave Two* and *Wave Three*—though there are often more, as the technology becomes more ubiquitous, affordable, and convenient. In Table 9.1 we summarize a sampling of some of these industries whose histories can be characterized by this pattern of Wave One growth through centralization, followed by growth through decentralization in subsequent waves.

By drawing on your own memory, note how the disruptive technological enablers of this decentralization affected these industries. The customers, in general, are much better off. Because of greater convenience and lower costs, many more people have access to and consume a lot more of these products and services—and their quality is better than what was available in Wave One. The companies whose products and business models created Wave Two and then Wave Three became even bigger "growth stories" for investors than the companies in the first wave—as innovators disrupted their industries through decentralization.

Note that we've listed health-care delivery institutions such as hospitals in the bottom row of Table 9.1, because they're going through this same cycle. During Stage Zero, care was provided in the patients' homes by doctors and nurses making house calls. During the first growth wave, the industry centralized around general hospitals; they were so expensive to build that we had to take our sicknesses to the place where the experts were. But gradually the hospital industry is decentralizing again. The growth waves of the future are ambulatory clinics, where they do the simplest of the things that previously had to be done in a hospital, and in doctors' offices, where they begin doing the simplest of the things that previously required an ambulatory

Table 9.1: Patterns in the centralization and decentralization of access to technology

Industry	Stage Zero	Growth Wave One	Growth Wave Two	Growth Wave Three, etc.
Communication	Letters were the only way to communicate over a distance.	We went to the telegraph office, where an operator transmitted our message in Morse code.	With wireline phones we just had to go to the next room to have a distance conversation.	Mobile phones allow us to have distance conversations *from* any place, *to* any place.
Calculation	We calculated on our slide rules.	We took our computational problems, as punched cards, to the mainframe center where an expert ran the job for us.	The desktop computer and calculator allowed us to calculate and compute in our homes and offices.	We can now compute anywhere on notebook computers and handheld devices.
Shopping	We went from shop to shop to get what we needed.	Downtown department stores like Macy's brought the goods to a central place. We went there to get what we needed.	Suburban shopping malls brought the goods closer to our homes.	Instead of our having to travel to where the goods are, Internet retailing brings the goods to us.
Printing	Secretaries made carbon copies as they typed, or ran off mimeograph copies.	We took our original to the photocopy center. A technician made copies on a high-speed Xerox machine.	Canon's tabletop copier put the ability to make copies just around the corner.	Inkjet printers now can make quality copies on our desks.
Education	Learning occurred informally from anyone who could teach us.	We went to universities, where professors dispensed their knowledge.	Online universities bring courses to our homes.	Students listen to lectures on handheld devices while they commute and exercise.
Entertainment	We entertained each other.	We went to where the movies were—in big downtown theaters and drive-ins.	We could watch movies in our homes, on VCRs, DVD players, and premium cable television networks.	We can watch movies anywhere on portable DVD players or by downloading or streaming them onto handheld devices and mobile phones.

Table 9.1:*(continued)*

Industry	Stage Zero	Growth Wave One	Growth Wave Two	Growth Wave Three, etc.
Music	We listened to the village fiddler, if there was one.	We had to travel to concert halls to hear quality music.	Record players allowed us to listen to music at home.	We carry our collections of music wherever we go, on our iPods.
Banking/Money management	We hid our money in a jar at home.	We kept our money in a downtown bank, which was open during "bankers' hours": 9:00 A.M. to 3:00 P.M.	ATMs allow us to access cash at any time, anywhere in the world.	With credit cards and online banking, we need to go to ATMs and handle cash less and less often.
Stock Investment	Few people owned stock.	We visited a broker whose firm had a seat on the NYSE, where traders personally negotiated prices and executed trades. A single trade typically cost $300.	We would call a broker, who could execute trades over the NASDAQ computer system, at $70 / trade.	We buy and sell stocks online with minimal fees. Trades are executed through electronic communication networks.
Medical Care	Doctors, nurses, and family took care of the sick in the patients' homes.	We take our patients to the general hospital, where doctors and nurses provide care.	Procedures that once required hospitalization can be performed in ambulatory clinics and surgery centers.	Procedures that once required going to an ambulatory clinic or surgery center can be done in doctors' offices.

clinic. Then they will get better and better, drawing patient after patient into the next wave of growth.

In Table 9.2 we've listed a few examples of this pattern of waves of growth in the MDDE industry. This is illustrative and isn't meant to be a statistical sample, but it seems consistent with the pattern we have seen in other industries: the economics and logistics of the first implementation of modern technology that created the initial wave of growth have required centralization. The boxes with **Bold** type represent mainstream markets today. Those in regular font are markets that are just emerging. Those in *italics* are our conjectures for what the future will look like.

Table 9.2 Cycles of centralization and decentralization in medical procedures

Stage Zero	Wave One	Wave Two	Wave Three, etc.
Doctors examined blood samples through microscopes in their offices.	**Blood samples are sent to central labs, where high-speed multi-channel machines run the required tests. Results are then sent back to the doctor.**	Tabletop and hand-held diagnostic devices such as Istat brought testing to the physician's office.	*Home testing equipment and mail-order services enable patients to monitor their own blood chemistries without having to see a doctor.*
Patients have heart attacks, seemingly at random. They recover or die.	**Cardiac surgeons perform bypass surgeries in academic medical centers, and later, general hospitals.**	**Cardiologists perform angioplasty in hospitals, but a cardiac surgeon must be waiting in the wings in case something goes wrong.**	*Equipment enables cardiologists to safely perform these procedures in ambulatory clinics, without needing a surgeon-in-waiting.*
Many doctors' offices had basic X-ray machines.	**Patients go to general hospitals' radiology departments, where experts use CT, MRI, and PET scanners to look inside our bodies.**	Stand-alone imaging centers bring these machines closer to the neighborhoods in which we live. Trucks even take this equipment into areas that cannot support a permanent center.	*Portable, affordable CT and MRI machines are in VAP clinics, operated by surgeons, and integrated into the patient process flow.*
Doctors intuited problems by listening through stethoscopes and feeling for lumps.	**Ultrasound machines installed in radiology departments of hospitals enabled radiologists to see soft tissues in motion.**	**Smaller, cart-based ultrasound machines became available in many obstetrics and cardiology practices.**	Hand-held ultrasound devices are allowing doctors in intensive care units, emergency departments and primary care clinics to take a "quick look" to help guide diagnoses.
Patients died of kidney failure.	**Patients with renal failure were hospitalized, where they underwent dialysis on massive machines.**	**Ambulatory dialysis centers closer to home are staffed by nurses and technicians.**	Small in-home dialysis machines can be operated by patients and family members.

Table 9.2 *(continued)*

Stage Zero	Wave One	Wave Two	Wave Three, etc.
Doctors diagnosed diabetes by tasting whether patients' urine was sweet.	Machines in hospital labs could measure the amount of glucose in a patient's blood. Nurses drew the blood, orderlies carried it to the lab, and technicians operated the machine.	Chemical reagent strips were developed for use in endocrinologists' offices. Nurses drew the blood and compared the color on the strip against a template to estimate glucose levels.	Patients take portable meters—the size of pocket calculators—with them wherever they go. They prick their own fingers and apply a drop of blood onto a reagent strip.
Surgical skill depended on dexterity, among other things. Patients often travel long distances to find the best surgeon.	Surgical robots enable surgeons to perform intricate, minimally invasive procedures with much better outcomes. Only the largest hospitals can typically afford these million-dollar robots.	Remote surgery, in which surgeons control robots from a different site, allows patients to access some of the best surgeons closer to home.	*Some surgical robots, such as modern LASIK machines, have become self-contained operating rooms.*

*The strong possibility exists for medications to disrupt devices in many instances, since drugs permit greater decentralization of both location (most drugs can be taken at home) and expertise (unlike many devices, drugs do not require skill to administer—even complex intravenous drugs can be implemented with minimal training). In any case, studies like COURAGE (Clinical Outcomes Utilizing Revascularization and Aggressive Drug Evaluation) will continue to help elucidate when the next disruptive wave is looming.

For example, at Stage Zero a generation ago, analysis of blood was done in doctors' offices by the practitioners themselves, looking through microscopes for little bugs swimming in samples of blood and urine. A few crude chemical reagent strips were also available for use in the office. Then companies like Metropolitan Pathological Laboratory (MetPath), operating extraordinarily sophisticated high-speed, multichannel analytical machines the size of an IBM System 360 mainframe computer, lifted the industry's analytical capability to unimagined heights. These machines[2] give doctors precise measures of electrolytes, blood cell counts, and levels of enzymes, hormones, antibodies, and other proteins.

Most doctors' offices don't even have microscopes today, and fewer and fewer hospitals operate their own laboratories.[3] The testing industry has been centralized. Several times every day, drivers collect blood samples placed in collection boxes outside doctors' offices. They transport them to the central laboratory, where technicians process thousands of liters of blood, tube by tube, performing whichever tests the doctors have selected from long lists of possibilities. Results are then sent back to the doctors. The explosion in the number of possible tests has been so breathtaking that most of the industry's technological energy is still focused on sustaining innovations that make these centralized, expertise-intensive machines even faster, more accurate, and able to do even more tests.

The explosion in device and equipment technology has been so recent that most of the MDDE industry's technological energy until now is still focused on innovations that sustain the industry's first wave of growth, as in the example of blood testing. These innovations help skilled clinicians working in solution shop hospitals and physician practices to see and do even more remarkable things.

Only in a few cases has there been enough time and entrepreneurial impetus to create the next waves of growth that would complete a full cycle of centralization-decentralization. Point-of-care diagnostic companies like Inverness, Quidel, and Abaxis have begun to decentralize the diagnostics industry.[4] General Electric Health Care and Sonosite have together created a $1 billion market in handheld and hand-carried ultrasound equipment in less than a decade.[5] The technology for home dialysis exists, as we noted in Chapter 7, but has been trapped in dialysis centers by reimbursement. Blood glucose monitoring for patients with diabetes is one of the few categories of MDDE products that has run the full cycle. But in most other cases, the MDDE industry has been in a sustaining innovation mode for the centralized business models that characterize the first wave of growth.

In Figure 9.1 we reproduced the multiplane diagram of disruption from Chapter 3 (Figure 3.3)—in which we asserted that

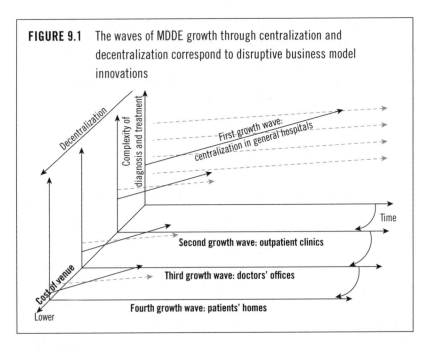

FIGURE 9.1 The waves of MDDE growth through centralization and decentralization correspond to disruptive business model innovations

bringing capability to progressively lower-cost venues of care, and then enabling caregivers in those places to do progressively more remarkable things, was the primary mechanism by which health care can become affordable. Note how closely the labels for these successively disruptive venues of care correspond to the stages of growth we're predicting for the MDDE industry. That's because the technology that enables these lower-cost venues of care to pull activity out of higher-cost ones is to a great extent embodied in medical devices and diagnostic equipment. The first wave of growth arises through centralizing sophisticated expertise and equipment in hospitals. The next waves are enabled by rapid in vitro assays, imaging diagnostics, and medical devices that shift the point of care to clinics, offices, and ultimately homes.

THE COMMODITIZATION OF EXPERTISE

The second of the growth compasses for MDDE companies points toward opportunities to commoditize professional expertise. It might sound harsh to call for the commoditization of doctors, but that is exactly what is needed—and what many device and equipment makers can do. We will get growth and affordability in health care not by replicating the expertise of today's physicians in the form of new physicians. We will get it by embodying their expertise in devices and equipment, so expertise becomes widely available, more affordable, and much easier to obtain. This is what we mean by the commoditization of expertise.

Recall that in our discussion in Chapter 2 on the technological enablers of disruption we summarized the history of scientific progress in the chemistry business. As understanding of chemistry and quantum theory coalesced, this knowledge transformed the "art" of building molecules into a science—whose rules were so well understood that they could be embodied in software. This, in turn, enabled chemical engineers with much less training and intuition to design better molecules, faster, and at lower cost, than the world's best scientists of the previous generation. The expertise of building organic molecules had been commoditized—packaged up and broadly distributed at affordable prices to hundreds of fiber and chemical companies worldwide—to the great benefit of mankind.[6]

Let us summarize three examples of how MDDE companies can create disruptive growth by commoditizing expertise. Each summer, Clayton Christensen and a colleague, Elizabeth Armstrong, lead a course at Harvard Medical School on managing change in medical education. Those who attend the course typically are the deans and associate deans of medical schools around the world. Christensen recounted the history of plastic molecule-building technology in this course a couple of years ago and then asserted, "At any point today if you will just stand and turn around 360 degrees, you'll be able to see or touch about 20 plastics and fibers that have proven to be an extraordinary blessing to mankind, because of their cost, durability, and appearance. But this blessing did not come by *replicating* the expertise of DuPont's scientists. It came from scientific and technological progress that *commoditized* their expertise."

At that point the dean of a major medical school raised her hand and asked, "Why are you telling us this story? We're not *chemists*. We're *doctors*, and we train *doctors*. Are you somehow suggesting that doctors will be commoditized?"

Christensen then did what all case method teachers have been trained to do: he turned her question to the class by asking, "What do the rest of you think? Will physicians become commoditized?" The question elicited a hailstorm of criticisms toward Christensen, of course—all expressed with a conviction that medicine is different than all those other less complex industries in which Christensen had studied the phenomenon of disruption.

The teaching tide was turned, however, when another dean—a reputable and experienced orthopedic surgeon—raised his hand and then stood to ask for quiet in the classroom. He began, "You don't think that doctors can be commoditized? Look at *me. I've* been commoditized. Twenty-five years ago there were only a few of us who could perform those pioneering hip and knee replacement surgeries, and we had to do them in the best academic medical centers. Successful outcomes were highly dependent upon the intuition and skill of the surgeon—and as a result, we, the surgeons, typically were paid more than half of the nonhospital portion of the bill."

Then, mimicking Christensen's language, he continued, "But do you know what those device makers have done? Every year, as they keep improving their products, they've made the implants ever more foolproof and idiot-simple—so that today almost any orthopedic surgeon, operating in an average community hospital, can do a perfect implant every time. I've been commoditized." As evidence to support his statement, he noted that in the prior year for the first time, the implant makers had begun to capture over 50 percent of the nonhospital portion of the bill. "And we poor surgeons are getting only 30 percent."

An emerging medical specialty called interventional radiology is having a similar impact of "commoditizing" what formerly had been unique expertise.[7] Imaging technologies are now so good that physicians trained primarily as radiologists can perform surgeries or preempt other ones that would otherwise require years of specialized surgical training to treat.[8] At a meeting of the department heads of a major Boston-area teaching hospital that one of us attended recently, a physician was showing the audience a movie taken with an endoscopic camera, demonstrating the removal of a growth in the patient's abdomen. You could see the surgeon's tools had been inserted through a minimally invasive portal to do the work of the surgery as clearly as you can see your fingers on the keyboard of your computer. At the conclusion of the movie, the physician said, "And the great thing about this technique is that it makes it so simple, *anybody* can do it!"

She then put her hand over her mouth and apologized, "Oh! I'm sorry. I didn't mean to say that!"

By fundamentally changing the nature of the skill required to perform certain procedures, interventional radiology has the potential for enabling the shift of many surgical procedures into value-adding process business models. The physicians' understanding of all the anatomical landmarks, the variations from patient to patient, and all their potential aberrancies could be less important, in the future, than the mastery of real-time radiology required to see what is being done.

Laser-assisted in situ keratomileusis (LASIK), a vision-correction surgery, is a third illustration of how MDDE companies can commoditize professional expertise, thereby making quality care broadly available and affordable. LASIK went through initial clinical trials in 1995, and approximately 1.4 million people underwent the procedure in 2007, making it the most common elective surgery in the United States.[9] Compared to previous vision-correction procedures, LASIK is straightforward.[10] The entire surgery lasts only 10 to 15 minutes for each eye; a topical anesthetic is applied with an eyedropper, and computer-guided lasers do most of the work. Compared to the previous option of radial keratotomy, LASIK does not require the same level of skill and experience to achieve quality results. Instead, those skills are effectively embedded in the machine. It has increasingly commoditized the ophthalmologists offering the procedure, so that it is in the making of the equipment, rather than the execution of the procedure, where the attractive profits in the industry's value chain are made.[11]

BARRIERS TO DISRUPTIVE GROWTH IN MEDICAL DEVICES & DIAGNOSTIC EQUIPMENT

In most industries the factors that create the "innovator's dilemma"—the drive to increase gross profit margins and the need to address the demands of current customers whose orders support the business—are the reason established companies don't lead the charge to create disruptive markets. In the MDDE business this doesn't seem to be the case, however. Executives at Johnson & Johnson and GE Health Care, in particular, have studied—and in some instances mastered—the methods of targeting products at jobs to be done, of shaping their business plans to be disruptive relative to competitors, and of managing them, as appropriate, in separate business units. Indeed, it seems that start-up companies in this industry have been slower to disrupt than the established companies. Synthesizing across the successes and failures of both types of companies, however, we have identified three factors or barriers that have constrained the disruptive decentralization of medical devices and diagnostic equipment.

The first barrier is simply technological immaturity. Making a formerly complicated device simple, affordable, and yet adequately powerful so people with less training can own and use it effectively is a tough problem. As we discussed in Chapter 2, the emergence of technological enablers in infectious diseases transpired over a period of 250 years! It just takes time to understand and solve a problem, and the timeline can be unpredictable, particularly when the goal is to find nonincremental, *disruptive* enablers.

Our review of many examples of centralization and decentralization suggests that a 20- to 25-year time course is typical for disruption to materialize. We offer these examples not to feign statistical precision, but rather, to illustrate that it typically takes a couple of decades, not a couple of years, for technological enablers of disruptive decentralization to fall into place.

For example, the first IBM personal computer appeared in 1981—about 25 years after IBM initiated Stage One centralization by producing mainframe digital computers in volume.[12] Henry Ford's Model T, the disruptive innovation that began putting a car in every driveway, was introduced in 1908—20 years after Karl Benz began modern production of automobiles.[13] The Sears catalog, which began the century-long disruptive decentralization of retailing, was introduced in 1893—26 years after the first downtown department store was organized.[14] Xerox pulled the copying industry out of the Stage Zero era of typing with carbon paper and mimeograph masters in 1959, when it introduced its model 914 high-speed plain paper photocopier,[15] which centralized copying in corporate photocopy centers. The industry remained a centralized Stage One industry for 20 years, until Canon and Ricoh introduced their first tabletop copiers in the late 1970s.[16] It just takes time.

The same 20- to 25-year cycle seems to characterize the MDDE industry as well. Stage One centralization of the diagnostic testing industry, for example, began in earnest in 1967, with the founding of MetPath in New York City. (MetPath subsequently was acquired by Corning Glass Works[17] and then was divested into what is now Quest Diagnostics.) It was 25 years later, in 1992, that i-STAT Corporation of Princeton, New Jersey introduced the world's first handheld blood diagnostic device, which could perform the six most common tests on a sample of blood.

The first linear-array real-time (LART) ultrasound scanner,[18] which produced images of moving soft tissues within the body whose clarity was sufficient to be clinically useful, was launched in 1973 by Advanced Diagnostic Research Corporation.[19] It was 25 years after LART machines began to be produced in volume that the first handheld ultrasound devices were developed by Sonosite Corporation, which was quickly joined by GE Health Care.[20]

Although the time frames may seem frustratingly long for many who wish to see disruption in health care occur sooner, our sense is that in many branches and product categories of the MDDE industry, the basic technology has been maturing for a couple of decades. Disruptive decentralization can now accelerate.

Is this a Job the Customer Is Trying to Do?

The second barrier to bringing self-testing and self-diagnostics technologies ever closer to the patient and to their homes is marketers' pervasive habit of segmenting markets by product or customer category. Innovators need to understand the jobs that customers are and are not trying to accomplish. We discussed this in Chapter 5: all of us, when we feel sick, want to become well. But only a subset of patients feel the daily need to *maintain* health. Maintaining *financial* health, in fact, is a more regularly perceived job than maintaining physical health. Innovative companies that plan to introduce self-testing and self-monitoring technologies for home use must keep in mind that, in general, people will buy and use these tests only if:

1. There is an impetus to do so. This might come from the specter of the weekly call from a nurse practitioner working for a disease management network. It might come from a wish to avoid adverse symptoms of a disease, or be financial in nature, if and when the magnitude of employers' contributions to HSAs depends upon health scores, as discussed in Chapter 5.
2. The results are reasonably conclusive (customers don't like to be inconvenienced only to experience even more uncertainty).
3. The results are actionable.

The market for self-testing devices has been limited thus far to only a few big hits such as pregnancy testing, glucose testing, and ovulation prediction, all of which tend to elicit multiple uses.[21] However, we believe that a decentralized, consumer-focused market is not an inherently difficult one, and there are indeed signs that other devices will continue to push testing, monitoring, and follow-on care into patients' homes. INR meters help patients on blood thinners monitor their clotting levels at home, rather than having to regularly visit a Coumadin clinic. Vests that detect the hyperactive movements of a bipolar patient progressing into a manic phase help families take care of their loved ones before a crisis occurs. And paired with facilitated networks of patients sharing information and experiences, even simpler, long-established devices such as peak flow meters for asthma may experience a resurgence.

Regulatory and Reimbursement Barriers

The third barrier to decentralization of the MDDE industry is regulation. When technology is immature and its correct use requires extensive training and intuition, regulations that constrain who can use it and where it can be used are important. The Clinical Laboratory Improvement Act of 1988 (CLIA) had exactly this purpose for the clinical laboratories industry that we described earlier. Implemented in 1992, CLIA set standards that significantly improved the consistency with which quality standards in testing were met. The standards raised testing costs significantly.[22] But almost always such regulation is necessary for complex, intuitive activities where judgment can affect outcomes in a significant way.

However, regulations that made sense for the treatment of a disorder in an era of intuitive medicine often inhibit disruptive innovation after technological progress has shifted treatment toward the realm of precision medicine—because technological progress enables caregivers who would not have been qualified to practice intuitive medicine previously to start providing care with great competence. To tackle such regulations while a MDDE market is still in Wave One, innovators typically must be willing to invest in full clinical trials in order to demonstrate that performance of their disruptive products are equivalent to existing solutions, and to prove that regulation is no longer necessary. Although a cumbersome hurdle, obviating the need for obsolete regulation that blocks disruption constitutes a significant growth opportunity for MDDE innovators, because technologies that commoditize expertise are often found to have better outcomes, more consistently, than when care was in the realm of intuitive medicine. We will explore the topic of disruption and regulation in greater depth in Chapter 11.

We noted in Chapter 7 that the reimbursement policies and practices of Medicare and private insurers constitute powerful regulatory forces. These often inhibit disruption if would-be disruptive innovators adhere to the reimbursement logic of the first-wave centralized market. Typically for the entities in the world of centralized equipment and specialists, providing the service is the core value proposition, and profitable survival entails charging a fee for each service.

For example, Western Union charged for each word in a telegram.[23] Photocopy centers charge by the page. Mainframe computer centers allocated their costs to the other departments in the company based upon usage. And so on. The entities that operate centralized health-care services typically make their money the same way—by charging a fee each time they provide a service. Companies supplying equipment to these operators consequently must succeed in high-stakes negotiations with Medicare and private insurers to secure a profitable reimbursement rate for the use of their equipment before launching their products. The operators of the equipment then bill for each MRI scan performed, for each X-ray or ultrasound scan, and for each test run on each sample of blood. This is the revenue formula by which these centers operate profitably, and the equipment makers consequently are driven to secure the highest reimbursement rates possible to encourage uptake by the providers.

When an industry decentralizes during the second and third waves of growth, however, the technology often simply becomes a mechanism through which users become more efficient at their core profit-making activity, enabling them to make more money the way they're structured to make money. A danger to which some would-be disruptive innovators have succumbed as they strategize the launch of products that could potentially decentralize an industry is they think that the new disruptive product will make money in the second and third wave in the same way it was made in the first—on a fee-per-use basis. They therefore seek to minimize time- and cost-to-market by getting reimbursement approval under the same Current Procedural Terminology (CPT) code under which the centralized providers in Wave One were paid. "Fitting" a potentially disruptive product into an existing CPT code forces the innovators to make their product conform as much as possible, and be used in ways similar to, the standards set by products in the centralized core business. "Current Procedure" means just what it says: *current* procedure, not disruptive procedure. Cramming disruptive devices and equipment into current procedures often significantly impairs their disruptiveness and competitive advantages.

To illustrate how the profit logic needs to change with decentralization, let's pose a hypothetical situation for point-of-care diagnostics and handheld ultrasound equipment. As used in hospital radiology departments and Ob/Gyn practices, ultrasound images are reimbursed on a fee-per-test or a fee-per-patient basis. When an emergency department staff needs to acquire an ultrasound image, they must wheel the patient to the radiology department, or wheel an ultrasound equipment cart to the emergency department. The insurance company will then be billed separately for the ultrasound imaging services performed for the patient, at prenegotiated CPT rates. The same is true for blood analyses. Each test is reimbursed at a prenegotiated rate—and the hospital needs to be sure it bills the insurance company for each test performed. So the bill for a visit to the emergency department is the sum of a long list of specific activities for which reimbursement has been approved.

But now, take off your Wave One thinking cap and watch what's going on in most emergency departments. The vast majority of the time patients spend in these facilities is spent waiting. They lay on beds waiting for lab results to come in. Or they occupy a bed, waiting to be wheeled to Radiology for an image to be taken, or for the image to be interpreted. And worse, they sit in the waiting room, waiting for a bed or room to become available.

What drives the performance and profitability of an emergency department? They don't make their money marking up or passing through the cost-per-test. Emergency care, like much of traditional health-care delivery, is a fixed-cost-intensive business—one that makes money on patient turnover and throughput. For a given number of beds and a given staffing level, emergency departments make money (or more realistically, lose less money) by getting patients in and out as fast and as effectively as possible. If a disruptive innovator would bring to an emergency department portable point-of-care testing capabilities and provide its physicians the imaging studies they need to accurately diagnose their patients' problems on the spot, image-by-image and test-by-test, reimbursement would no longer be necessary—because testing and imaging equipment become ancillary productivity enhancing investments that improve the emergency department's ability to make money in the way it is structured to make money.[24]

It's fallacious for the hospital and the equipment maker to think that the profit from the disruptive products will still be generated by negotiating reimbursement rates that substantially exceed costs. We would have many, many more stand-alone emergency and urgent care centers that are unattached to hospitals if the MDDE equipment vendors would get busy making the equipment that will enable the second wave. We would reach similar conclusions for the use of MDDE in many other decentralized settings.

CONVENIENCE, COST, AND THE CONSUMPTION OF HEALTH CARE

When the second and third waves of disruptive decentralization make products and services more convenient and affordable, people always consume more—a lot more, in most cases. Now that most offices have high-speed photocopy machines within a 20-second walk, and computers on every desk, we consume many more copies, create many more spreadsheets, and send many more e-mails than when we had to take our originals to the photocopy center, put our punched cards in the job queue at the mainframe center, or drive to the post office to send handwritten letters by first-class mail. We (especially teen-age girls) consume much, much more telephony and data messaging now that there is a wireless phone in every purse, than when the wire-line phone required us to sit in one place that was quiet enough to use our voices to communicate. We listen to more music and watch more movies than we used to, because Stage-Two and -Three innovators have made consumption convenient and affordable. And in general we consider the fact that we can consume more of these things as good news. It is an important means of measuring the improvement in our standard of living. Indeed, we happily pay out of our own pockets in order to consume more of these products and services.

Some health-care observers have voiced concern, however, that convenient access to lower-cost diagnostic and imaging equipment during the industry's second and third waves of growth might not be good news—because it could entice people to consume more tests and images than they do through today's costly centralized entities. If half of our health-care dollars are spent on services that are medically unnecessary,[25] shouldn't we be concerned that people will consume more health care? It depends upon your perspective.

To insurance companies that negotiate annual contracts with employers, and to employers and governments who face the escalating costs of these coverage contracts year after year, increased consumption is bad news. Indeed, a major driver of cost escalation in our past has been the expensive, centralized imaging and diagnostic services in a fee-for-service world. But to consumers in the new disruptive value network described in Chapter 5—consumers who will be paying for noncatastrophic care through their health savings accounts—affordable, convenient access to these products and services will be unambiguous good news. Most of us have an important job to do: we just want to be sure there isn't anything serious going on inside of us, which is for now unseen and unfelt, but might be a harbinger for death or difficulty in the near future. Or when we are sick, we just want to get onto a course to recovery as fast and as conveniently as possible. Right now there aren't affordable, conveniently accessible services to hire to do these jobs—and we're left feeling unfulfilled by a health-care system that seems unable or unwilling to do these jobs well.

The Centers for Medicare and Medicaid Services (CMS), which almost always leads the decision making about which medical devices and equipment will and will not be covered, faces the impossible task of weighing its budgetary constraints against the jobs of its enrollees. But confronted with skyrocketing expenditures, Medicare will be under increasing pressure to consider cost effectiveness when determining what technologies truly are "reasonable and necessary." The controversy over recent, high-profile coverage decisions, like those for implantable cardioverter-defibrillators (ICDs) and left ventricular assist devices (LVADs), demonstrate that things likely will only get tougher, not easier, for both insurers and MDDE makers working under the traditional system of negotiated reimbursement fees.[26] And despite its long history of innovation, the MDDE industry has also been complicit in trapping health care in a high-cost, centralized state by thwarting previous efforts to adopt new criteria for coverage decisions by CMS.[27] As a result, CMS still does not explicitly consider cost effectiveness in its coverage decisions, and at least until now, MDDE makers have done quite well by generating a lot of sustaining innovation in the first wave of growth.

But our bet is that if innovators in the medical devices and diagnostic equipment industries aggressively pursue the second and third waves of growth in their industries by transforming products and services that are now expensive and centralized into ones that are progressively more affordable, portable, and "idiot-simple" (borrowing the words of the orthopedic surgeon/ dean), consumers will happily pay out of their own pockets to monitor their own health; self-diagnose when things go wrong; and receive an ever larger portion of their care from nurses and primary care physicians, in venues that are closer and closer to home.

NOTES

1. As discussed in Chapter 3, the need for exploratory surgery has declined with improvements in diagnostic imaging.

2. Makers of these pieces of analytical equipment now include Johnson & Johnson, Eastman Kodak, Miles Inc., Abbott Laboratories, Nova Pharmaceutical, and Baxter International.

3. "SIC 8071 Medical Laboratories," Encyclopedia of American Industries, 2005.

4. The first such device was sold by the i-STAT Corporation of Princeton, New Jersey. About the size of a cellular telephone and weighing only 16 ounces, the i-STAT system performed six tests—sodium, glucose, potassium, chloride, blood urea nitrogen and hematocrit, and calculated hemoglobin—in about 90 seconds. It cost $3,000 per machine, used whole unprocessed blood, and could be operated by a doctor or nurse. I-Test was later sold to Abbott Laboratories. Source: Calem, Robert E., "Technology; Moving the Common Blood Test Closer to the Patient," *New York Times*, June 21, 1992.

5. Romano, Benjamin J., "Ultrasound on the Move," *Seattle Times*, Jan. 8, 2006; "SonoSite Revenue Rises 25% Net Income Rises 48% in Second Quarter," SonoSite press release, July 24, 2008.

6. As is so often the case, this ultimately caused DuPont to exit much of the synthetic fibers business. Unthinkable as it seems, DuPont no longer makes nylon, polyester, or acetate fibers—a disruption of comparable scope to IBM being disruptively driven from the computer business, AT&T from the telephony business (only its brand has survived), and Kodak from photographic film.

7. Several of Clayton Christensen's MD-MBA students have targeted interventional radiology in papers they have written for his course at Harvard Business School. We thank, in particular, Chirag Shah and Max Laurans for teaching us about this phenomenon.

8. Initially relegated to tissue biopsies, fluid drainage, and other basic surgeries, interventional radiology has dramatically expanded its capability in treating a variety of conditions that previously warranted major surgery. A recent study at Dartmouth Medical School, for example, found that endovascular repair led to better outcomes than surgery in treating blunt trauma injuries. (See Hoffer, Eric K., A. R. Rorauer, et al., "Endovascular Stent-Graft or Open Surgical Repair for Blunt Thoracic Aortic Trauma: Systematic Review," *Journal of Vascular and Interventional Radiology*, vol. 19, no. 8:1153–64). Other interventional radiology procedures preclude the need for surgery altogether, such as uterine fibroid embolization, which can treat uterine bleeding that is more commonly treated with hysterectomy.

9. According to research data from Market Scope, LLC, accessed Sept. 5, 2008 at http://dev.market-scope.com/practice_information/market_information.html. Worldwide, 27 million laser vision correction procedures on 15 million patients have been performed through the end of 2007, although this figure includes procedures other than, but similar to, LASIK.

10. Tu, H. T., and J. H. May, "Self-Pay Markets in Health Care: Consumer Nirvana or Caveat Emptor?" *Health Affairs*, Feb. 6, 2007. Although this article expresses some concern that consumer shopping may not occur as vigorously as previously thought, the price trend remains consistent with the theories of disruptive innovation.

11. Nunneley, J., "Has LASIK Price-Cutting Lost its Luster?" *Review of Ophthalmology*, March 2001, 39–43.

12. IBM Archives, accessed online at http://www-03.ibm.com/ibm/history/history/year_1964.html and http://www-03.ibm.com/ibm/history/history/year_1981.html on Aug. 1, 2008.

13. "The Model T Put the World on Wheels, Ford Motor Company," accessed online at http://www.ford.com/about-ford/heritage/vehicles/modelt/672-model-t on Aug. 1, 2008.

14. By most accounts the first department store, Zions Cooperative Mercantile Institution (ZCMI) was founded in 1867 by Brigham Young in Salt Lake City. Marshall Field opened his landmark department store on State Street in downtown Chicago in several stages between 1868 and 1878—each of the stages interrupted or redirected by fire. Sources: Bradley, Martha Sonntag, *ZCMI: America's First Department Store* (Salt Lake City, Utah: ZCMI, 1991); and Tedlow, Richard S., *New and Improved: The Story of Mass Marketing in America* (Boston, Massachusetts: Harvard Business School Press, 1996).

15. Lest we lose perspective, the high-speed Xerox 914 weighed 648 pounds and produced seven copies per minute.

16. Ricoh initially produced machines that were branded as Savin and Pitney Bowes in U.S. markets. It introduced its own brand in about 1984. For more details, see Boulton, William R., "The Plain Paper copier Industry," working paper, 1995. Accessed online at http://www.auburn.edu/~boultwr/copiers.pdf, July 21, 2008.

17. The rationale for Corning's initial investment into MetPath, which was followed by outright acquisition, was that in many ways it was innovations in the properties of the glass containers used in performing high-speed tests that enabled the growth of this industry. Corning's technology, not just its cash, proved crucial to the growth of MetPath.

18. Like the computer, the automobile, and most other products, the invention of ultrasonic imaging looked more like a process, rather than a discrete historical event. The first ultrasonic image of the human body was published in the British medical journal *Lancet* in 1958. The Vidoson, introduced by Siemens in 1965, was the first commercial medical ultrasound machine. It was unwieldy and expensive, however, and produced images of marginal quality. The linear-array, real-time architecture for ultrasonic scanners became the "dominant design" for this class of machines. The concept of a dominant design was first articulated by William Abernathy and James Utterback in "A Dynamic Model of Product and Process Innovation," *Omega* (3), June 1975; and "Patterns of Industrial Innovation," *Technology Review*, June–July 1978, 40–47.

19. Advanced Diagnostic Research Corporation was later acquired by Advanced Technology Laboratories, or ATL Corporation. ATL, in turn, was subsequently acquired by Philips.

20. For a history of handheld ultrasound, see Christensen, Clayton, and Jeremy Dann, "SonoSite: A View Inside," Harvard Business School case # 9-602-056. A few companies have entered this market, including General Electric Health Care. Long the leader in the market for mammoth X-ray, CT, MRI, PET, and cart-based ultrasound machines, a few years ago GE Health Care executives decided to decentralize ultrasound. A Bothell, Washington start-up called SonoSite had spotted this potential earlier, and developed the first low-cost, handheld ultrasound devices. GE then threw its muscle behind the opportunity. Recognizing its disruptiveness, its executives followed a rule that the handheld business would be managed completely separate from the mainstream imaging businesses—and that they would not ask or allow it to share or utilize any of the resources

of the old business. The result: by our estimate, it has built a $300 million business in five years, and the market has yet to truly take off. GE's primary customers are caregivers such as primary care physicians, who in the past had no access to ultrasound within their offices or clinics. Now, rather than being limited to listening for internal problems through a stethoscope, or feeling for lumps and enlargements with their fingers as they examine their patients, these physicians can see inside their patients' bodies and come much closer to making definitive diagnoses at the point of care.

21. The economic value of diagnostic tests, even in the retail market, is such that one-off tests are typically difficult to support with business models that focus on high-cost consumer marketing. We thank our colleagues at Innosight LLC, Steve Wunker and Matt Eyring, for sharing their deep knowledge of the device industry with us.

22. "SIC 8071 Medical Laboratories," Encyclopedia of American Industries, 2005.

23. Not many of our readers will remember having sent or read a telegram—but because each word cost money, telegrams gave meaning to the term "terse." In fact, because punctuation cost extra while a four character word was free, people adopted the common practice of using the word "stop" rather than periods to end their sentences. See "Telegram Passes Into History," Associated Press, Feb. 2, 2006. Accessed from http://www.wired.com/science/discoveries/news/2006/02/70147 on Sept. 4, 2008.

24. Of course, the productivity gains would still have to be sufficient to offset the fixed cost of the equipment. Electronic medical records, for example, undoubtedly improve efficiency and outcomes, but the cost of implementation for many physician practices outweighs the gains (which typically accrue to the payer and patient but not the provider). Fortunately, many decentralizing devices tend to be smaller, portable, and more affordable, which should enhance the probability of uptake in disruptive models of care delivery.

25. Wennberg, John E., "Variation in Use of Medicare Services among Regions and Selected Academic Medical Centers: Is More Better?" New York: The Commonwealth Fund, 2005. Wennberg states that more than 50 percent of Medicare spending is used to buy "supply sensitive" health care—visits to physicians, diagnostic tests, and hospitalizations, mostly for patients with chronic illnesses. Here the most important problem is overuse—more is not necessarily better, and patients are exposed to the burdens and risks of treatment that are unnecessary or counterproductive.

26. Gillick, Muriel R., "Medicare Coverage for Technological Innovations—Time for New Criteria?" New England Journal of Medicine, vol. 350, no. 21:2199–203; and Tunis, Sean R., "Why Medicare Has Not Established Criteria for Coverage Decisions," New England Journal of Medicine, vol. 350, no. 21:196-98. The coverage decisions for implantable cardioverter-defibrillators (ICDs) and left ventricular assist devices (LVADs) in 2003 were especially scrutinized due to the extremely high cost of these devices and (at the time) their unclear benefits. In the end, CMS decided to cover both devices, but only for restricted sets of patients for whom clinical trials had demonstrated proven benefits. In addition, CMS actually set the reimbursement rate for LVADs below market cost—$70,000 reimbursement for a $65,000 device and a procedure that increases the overall cost to greater than $200,000. The total cost of the additional coverage was $350 million to $3 billion for 10,000 to 90,000 ICD patients each year, and $350 million to $7 billion for up to 100,000 LVAD patients each year.

27. Foote, Susan B., "Why Medicare Cannot Promulgate a National Coverage Rule: A Case of Regula Mortis," Journal of Health Politics, Policy and Law, 2002, vol. 27(5):707–30. As

Chapter 10

The Future of Medical Education

America's medical education system is generally viewed as the best in the world. Despite the decline in physician salaries over the past 10 years[1] and a corresponding increase in the bureaucratic oversight of health-care delivery, many of the brightest students in the world compete for the opportunity to enroll in one of America's 129 medical schools, with an average of two to three applicants for each of the 15,000 to 16,000 available seats.[2] After investing four years to earn their medical degrees, these newly minted physicians move on to three to five additional years of residency training, where 24,000 positions await them.[3] Those seeking careers as specialists then undergo one to five additional years of training in a fellowship.

The graduates of this remarkable system of medical education comprise a group of highly trained, highly motivated individuals eager to deliver the best care possible. Counting college, tomorrow's doctors will have spent 10 to 18 of the most productive years of their lives just *training* for their careers. Will those careers be what they've hoped for? Many finish this training with well over \$100,000 in debt.[4] Will their income give them an appropriate return for this investment?

Our medical schools have inspiring missions, seeking to train "people committed to leadership in alleviating human suffering caused by disease."[5] But it is an expensive vision—and not just for students. In 2007 the Centers for Medicare and Medicaid Services alone spent \$8 billion on Graduate Medical Education.[6] Is society getting an appropriate return on this investment?

We fear that society at large, and tomorrow's doctors in particular, will be disappointed. The basic architecture of our medical schools' curriculum was designed nearly 100 years ago. The content of the building blocks within this architecture has changed substantially, of course, but the fundamental design of the experience is a century old. The result of our medical schools being stuck in this rut is that it takes much longer to educate tomorrow's doctors than other curricular architectures would require. And despite the time and cost invested, some of our best medical providers find that new doctors still are not ready to work, needing as much as two additional years of on-the-job training before they can practice profitably within their systems.[7]

Our medical schools face two crises. The first relates to what the model of disruption terms the *sustaining* trajectory of performance improvement—helping the existing system perform better, according to the measures of goodness broadly accepted among the existing schools. The need to improve the existing system is vast and urgent. New models of teaching, such as those that employ medical simulators, are needed to ensure that our schools continue to train the best possible physicians. The second crisis is disruption—competitors that are or will be disrupting our medical schools from four directions: foreign medical schools; alternative medical training such as osteopathy, whose focus is primary care; the training of nurse practitioners, physician assistants, and medical technicians; and in-house corporate medical universities. If our medical schools fail to implement the architectural improvements that we outline below (and we predict that most will fail to do these things), the progress of these disruptive competitors—especially the in-house corporate medical schools—will accelerate.

We predict that major integrated provider systems will begin training their own doctors because our medical schools couldn't do what had to be done. The training they provide will have a much stronger focus on how to design and preside over value-adding processes, and how to manage other professionals who are ensconced within those work flows. They will teach doctors how to function within professional networks and utilize patient-centric ones, so patients receive better care for chronic diseases. These "corporate medical schools" will be preparing students for practice in much less time than is required today, and the students will be more uniformly prepared for practice—meaning there will be much less graduate-to-graduate variability in what new doctors can do.

To support these assertions, in this chapter we'll first review the history of how our medical schools got to where they are today—and offer some measures of how well they're doing. Second, we'll introduce a very different theory of training—developed by none other than Toyota. This is not a theory of how to design and build cars, but a theory of training people. Third, we'll describe what a medical school organized around this theory might look like, and recommend to those administrators who would improve their schools along the sustaining trajectory how they must manage these changes. And fourth, we'll examine the entities that are disrupting medical education, and explain our prediction that in-house medical training is likely to supplant many of today's medical colleges.

A HISTORY OF MEDICAL TRAINING

Through the 1800s, most medical training in the United States was conducted in commercial medical colleges. That these were significant money-making opportunities for their founders is suggested in this comment by Henry J. Bigelow, professor of surgery at Harvard in 1871: "It is safe to say that no successful school has thought it proper to risk large existing classes and large receipts [of money] in attempting a more thorough education."[8] There was indeed a rapid proliferation of for-profit medical schools between 1810 and 1876—with 20 schools founded in Cincinnati alone—just to keep pace with the burgeoning need for heath care caused by America's growing population. "It is as easy to establish a medical school as a business college," complained an observer.[9]

A century ago, in 1910, medical training took a sharp turn toward self-policing responsibility for quality education when Abraham Flexner published his landmark report criticizing the "enormous variation in qualified graduates" being churned out by the medical schools of the day. Some of its conclusions:

We have indeed in America medical practitioners not inferior to the best elsewhere; but there is probably no other country in the world in which there is so great a distance and so fatal a difference between the best, the average, and the worst.... Our methods of carrying on medical education have resulted in enormous overproduction at a low level [of quality]. . . . Whatever the justification in the past, the present situation in town and country alike can be more effectively met by a reduced output of well-trained men than by further inflation with an inferior product. . . . If the sick are to reap the full benefit of recent progress in medicine, a more uniformly arduous and expensive medical education is demanded.[10]

Flexner's argument for widespread medical education reform was accepted by the Council on Medical Education of the American Medical Association. Among other things, this resulted in a standardized medical curriculum consisting of two years of basic science teaching followed by two years of clinical training, which are called "clerkships" or "clinical rotations" today.[11] This concept was essentially borrowed from the training hospitals and medical schools of Europe of the 1800s, during which time students enrolled directly out of high school. With the students coming from such disparate educational backgrounds, the only way for medical schools to ensure that they were adequately prepared to treat patients was to first provide education in the basic sciences, before tackling clinical skills. At the time the Flexner report recommendations were implemented, the only way to teach the basic sciences cost-effectively was lecturing to large batches of students in lecture halls. Johns Hopkins was one of the first schools to adopt this structure.

Two different faculty groups have emerged at most medical schools as a result of this temporal bifurcation in training. In about two-thirds of the schools, members of the science faculty teach the first two years of science courses, and typically conduct leading edge, NIH-funded research in the fields in which they teach. The clinical faculty members teach the bedside art of diagnosing and treating patients during the third and fourth years. Because the faculty are different, and because of student limitations as to how well they can retain what they learn, some of what is taught in the first two years, though deemed important by the faculty, is seldom if ever used in clinical practice. Some of the background students need to know in their clerkships is not learned in the first two years. And a lot of what they truly must know is often forgotten by the time they need to use that knowledge.[12] In other words, the first two years in these medical schools are *not* an efficient experience.

In the other one-third of schools, the science curriculum and clinical training are integrated in significant ways. This helps students deal with the "chicken-and-egg" problem of this phase of education: until students understand the clinical questions involved, they aren't prepared to grasp the potential significance of seemingly esoteric basic science. And unless they understand the physiology in normal and abnormal states, the clinical signs and symptoms may go over their heads.[13]

The clerkships or rotations, including those arrayed in Figure 10.1, typically consist of three weeks to three months spent caring for patients in various fields of medicine, under the bedside tutelage of the clinical faculty of the medical school. At the time this system was conceived, all medical students arrived in a "bolus"—a big mass at the same time, because they all completed their first two years of science courses together. And the reason students took their two years of science training in lockstep was that they needed to remain at home to help their fathers on the farm for the summer.[14] Meanwhile, at present, the typical hospital doesn't have the capacity for all the medical students to start their internship years in a particular department, such as internal medicine, or to move them uniformly as a group from one station to the next. So instead they parse out the incoming class of clerkship students across the departments, so that each major department gets approximately one-quarter of the student body.

The term "rotations" doesn't accurately describe what happens next, because the students don't "rotate" from one department to the next in a uniform sequence. Rather, they begin at any point, then can go from any clerkship to any clerkship, as depicted in Figure 10.1, based upon the students' interests and the availability of patients and teaching faculty.[15] There are, therefore, an almost infinite number of individual pathways a student can take through the last two years of medical school.

To the uninitiated, this system seems delightfully flexible. To those responsible for teaching and assuring that each student has mastered all that needs to be known, however, it is a nightmare. When students arrive at a given clerkship, each one has had a different combination of training experiences. Imagine being assigned to teach a graduate seminar in macroeconomics in which two students have not had calculus, three have had no exposure to matrix algebra, two have not yet taken statistics, one has no background in national income accounting, and only three have taken political science. And imagine that this variability in students' backgrounds changes from one month to the next. Not knowing what any of your students knows, you'd have to back up and reteach many things to many people, in order to get them all on the same page to be able to progress further.

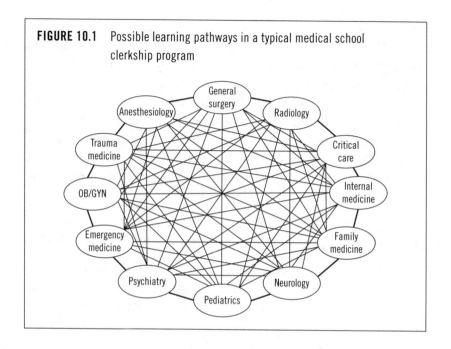

FIGURE 10.1   Possible learning pathways in a typical medical school clerkship program

This is what it's like to be a clinical faculty member at a medical school. Reteaching is as common as teaching. What's worse, it is almost impossible for the faculty to guarantee what students will know when they finish their particular clerkship. For instance, if a patient with trigeminal neuralgia didn't happen to present at the hospital or clinic during the weeks when the medical student was doing a neurology clerkship, she might not ever learn how to diagnose and treat that particular problem. If no patient needed a tracheotomy while a student was in his emergency medicine clerkship, he might graduate from medical school never having learned how to perform that procedure.[16]

Perhaps most important, however, the current system of medical education is designed to teach doctors how they as individual, independent actors, should care for patients—because at the time the architecture of medical education was defined a century ago, doctors largely worked independently of each other.

But today, doctors are ensconced within systems. There are processes through which multiple caregivers interact. There are myriad administrative processes, laboratory and imaging center processes, and triage processes, to name just a few. And these processes are embedded within value networks that define how other entities interact. It varies by hospital, medical school, and specialty department. But in general there is little in the medical training most doctors receive that teaches them how to create, administer, or improve the way people work together in the health-care system.[17]

SUSTAINING INNOVATIONS IN THE CURRENT EDUCATIONAL SYSTEM

An impressive body of research about the Toyota Production System (TPS) conducted by Harvard Business School Professor Steven Spear sheds remarkable light on how medical education might be redesigned so doctors can effectively deliver care in the health-care system of the future.[18] Spear has studied the Toyota system far more deeply than most other scholars—seeking not simply to learn how Toyota builds cars, but how its managers *think* when they design processes of *any* sort—processes for designing products, interacting with suppliers, maintaining equipment, training employees, and, of course, building cars.

To the uninitiated, it might seem that building doctors is far more complicated than the cut-and-dried world of building cars. But those who know both realms well conclude that, indeed, building a car is a very complicated endeavor. About 10,000 separate components must be made through millions of process steps by independent entities across the world, to degrees of precision that engineers of prior generations could not even measure. Each must be made and arrive at the assembly plant just in time to be assembled into the car. If one of the 10,000 components doesn't arrive in time or doesn't function properly, the entire factory must stop; the entire car won't work; or both. These pieces are made by people who speak different languages. Few of them are college graduates. Sometimes they show up to work drunk. Sometimes they don't show up at all. And the machines they operate actually have unique and stubborn personalities—proclivities to come out of adjustment in particular ways, tendencies to break at specific places, and so on. And yet every individual piece must be made perfectly, at exactly the right time. Designing and building cars is very complicated indeed.

Spear asserts that all processes consist of four elements: activities, connections, pathways, and improvements. *Activities* are the "islands" of individual work in which each of the discrete steps needed to achieve a complete result are performed. *Connections* define how these individual activities must interface or fit with each other in time, space, and properties. *Pathways* describe the flow and sequence of activities: who does what, who then performs the next step, and so on. *Improvements* are the methods that change the activities, connections, and pathways to come ever closer to the ultimate target of producing perfect products at zero cost.

Spear concluded that there are five "rules-in-use" at Toyota governing how its managers and employees design and conduct the activities, connections, pathways, and improvements in all of Toyota's processes.[19] Until Spear's work, these rules weren't written down anywhere. But it's as if these rules of process design are emblazoned everywhere at Toyota. Its managers behave as if these commandments were strapped like phylacteries to their foreheads. Spear and his associates have shown that following these rules has comparable impact on cost, quality, and safety in companies and industries as diverse as hospitals, semiconductor manufacturing, and aluminum processing.[20] They are, in other words, generally applicable principles, not methods for making cars:

- Rule 1 (Activities). Each value-adding step in a process must be completely specified, so that when a worker hands off what he's done to the next worker, the part is perfectly prepared for her to add the value that she has been assigned to add. When this rule is followed, it eliminates the need

to ever rework something that the prior worker did imperfectly. And it helps eliminate actions that do not add value to
the next step, because that is wasteful. There must be a clear
go/no-go verification at the conclusion of every activity, so
the worker performing the activity and the worker who will
perform the next activity in the process both know that they
have done exactly what needed to be done.

- Rule 2 (Connection). Never add value to a part that is
  defective. That means you should never work on a part until
  it is ready to be used in the *next* step. When you use the
  output of the prior step immediately, it tests whether the
  prior activity was perfectly done. This allows the worker to
  improve whatever element of the activity was responsible
  for the problem—so the activity isn't allowed to continue
  producing inadequate results.

- Rule 3 (Pathway). The sequence of steps that a part takes
  through the process must be completely specified as a series
  of one-to-one handoffs—the same worker always gives what
  he has done to the same worker to perform the next step.
  Any-worker-to-any-worker handoffs are not allowed. This
  creates unambiguous responsibility for doing it right, and
  makes it easier to correct the cause of problems.

- Rule 4 (Improvement). Perform each step in your process
  the same way every time—not to make the work mindless,
  but to scientifically test whether doing it this way, to these
  specifications, will result in perfection every time. It allows
  workers to conduct controlled experiments to improve
  toward the "true north" goal of making perfect products at
  zero cost.

- Rule 5 (Improvement). Never allow the cause of a problem
  to persist by working around it. We must change our
  methods whenever a faulty result occurs so that it cannot
  happen again.

At the Harvard Macy Institute program for academic health-
care leaders and medical school deans that Professors Elizabeth

Armstrong[21] and Clayton Christensen have conducted each summer for more than a decade at Harvard Medical School, many of the deans arrive believing the explosion in knowledge students need to absorb means that medical school will need to be lengthened to five years.[22] They are then given this assignment: "By the time you finish this program, we want you to have designed a medical curriculum capable of training better doctors, with much less variability from student to student, that requires three instead of four years." Most scoff that it cannot be done. They are then taught Toyota's rules-in-use. By the end of the course they realize, almost without exception, that by following those five rules, better doctors can indeed be trained in three years than those trained today in four.

In the text below we'll bring to light the conclusions that many of these deans reached while attending this program, after they understood how the rules of process governance Toyota has devised might be applied to medical education. These conclusions comprise our recommendations for the *sustaining* innovations that medical schools need to make. We'll then examine several disruptions that will affect medical education.

Integration of Science and Clinical Education

One of our most important recommendations relates to one of the fundamental interpretations of Flexner's report—that we must teach two years of science courses before clinical application of that science begins. This is a practice that Toyota would never tolerate, because it expects that students will efficiently hold that knowledge in "intellectual inventory," to be used years later. Rather, Rule 2 suggests that students will learn better when they learn something and then immediately use it; learn something more, and then immediately use it. In other words, the science curriculum and the clerkships should be conducted in parallel, knit carefully together, rather than taught in series. This would help faculty to teach the science students need to know when they need to know it. Students would be less prone to forget what they learned.

When medical education innovators created the existing pedagogical system a century ago, students had to arrive in a batch at the end of the summer after helping their parents on the farm. And the only pedagogical technology available a century ago was a live lecture—whose economics again favored teaching all students together in monolithic batches. Neither of these constraints is binding today. Students can easily arrive at medical schools in small groups rather than in a single large bolus, and can listen to the best lecturers in the world, anytime, anywhere, at the click of a mouse.[23] Learning the science can and should be knit together with learning clinical skills. Indeed, Harvard Medical School pioneered such an integrated program, dubbed "New Pathways," under the direction of then-dean Daniel C. Tostesen, nearly two decades ago. Perhaps a third of all medical schools have now begun similar efforts to integrate.[24]

True Rotations for Consistent Learning

Another recommendation that Toyota's rules prompt is to transform the last two years of today's medical training into true "rotations," during which students would "flow" into their clerkships in small groups, each starting in the same initial clerkship. Then, in terms of Figure 10.1, students would rotate from one clerkship to the next in an identical sequence—rather than crisscrossing back and forth as they presently do, and where the quality of students' educational experiences depends to a frustrating degree on "the luck of the draw."[25]

With greater predictability in the substance and sequence of each student's learning, each subsequent member of the clinical faculty would know that each student has the required background upon which to build. This is possible today, where it was not a century ago.[26]

The sheer number of scheduling combinations that today's students experience in medical school virtually *guarantees* that all students have a different combination of skills by the time they graduate. This extreme variability makes it difficult to teach students efficiently, even more difficult to adequately verify their skills before the students enter residency programs, and almost impossible to figure out which parts of the education process need to be fixed. Changing the clerkship years to resemble true rotations would enable our medical schools to follow Rules 1, 3, and 4. They could specify what scientific knowledge and clinical skills each student needs to bring *into* a clerkship, in order to learn what they need to master next, so they can progress to the next stage in the rotation.[27]

The fact that more and more patients are kept out of hospitals, except for the most severe episodes in their illnesses, exacerbates a challenge that has always vexed clinical faculty: students can rarely experience treating a patient across the full cycle of a disease; and they cannot learn to treat a problem if a patient with that problem does not appear at the hospital or clinic during their rotation. This means that if all students are to develop a set of skills the medical community deems necessary to function effectively in the health-care industry of the future, medical schools must be much more aggressive in their use of training simulators, which include online patient cases, simulated patient video encounters, and telemedicine encounters.

Widely used in pilot training and other professions, simulators offer a controllable teaching environment that helps students get the right lesson at the right time, rather than depending on the chance encounter with a particular patient.[28] A classic disruptive technology, simulators need to be deployed first in situations where patients with the disorder of interest are not coming to the clinic or hospital to be seen—where the alternative is that the medical student will not be able to learn to diagnose and treat the disorder. It will be a very long time, if ever, before simulators become as effective a learning experience as practicing on real patients. But little by little, like all disruptions, the technology will improve, giving *every* medical student the opportunity to experience a growing list of clinical encounters.[29]

Finally, we recommend most strongly that medical educators must begin teaching tomorrow's doctors to become much better at creating, improving, and managing processes and systems.

The idea that medical education is all about training individual artists who will practice their crafts independently of each other and in isolation from the work of nurses and technicians, pharmacists, administrators, and external service providers was appropriate a century ago, but is dangerously incorrect today. Even if our medical schools send forth perfectly skilled individual practitioners, care will be inefficient and costly if those doctors labor within dysfunctional processes in the hospitals and clinics in which they do their work.[30] Just as physicians are trained to arrive at a diagnosis through iterative experimentation, they should be taught to do the same with "ill" processes within the health-care system.[31] Work is effectively accomplished through processes comprised of activities, connections, pathways, and improvements. The curriculum of our medical schools today is largely focused on activities!

Variable Learning vs. Variable Time

Professor Spear shared an experience that has helped us understand the predicament in which nearly all our public schools, universities, and medical schools find themselves as they continue to utilize curricular architectures that were molded a century ago. At that time, the only cost-effective technology for learning was to process students in batches with monolithic instruction—teaching and testing all students at the same time in the same way.

As a doctoral student researching manufacturing systems, Spear took a job at a large American automotive plant, working at a station on an assembly line. Preparing him to install front passenger seats, his trainer demonstrated the proper sequence. "Every 58 seconds a car is coming down the line, and that's all you've got to get this seat in and be ready for the next one. Here's what you do. Start by picking it up like this. Turn it this way, adjust here, now do this, now that, and put it in just like so. Then quickly tighten this here, move this, turn that, and finally do this. Got it?"

Armed with a bachelor's and master's degree from MIT, Spear was no mechanical klutz, so he confidently picked up the approaching seat and followed the first few steps with ease. However, when he tried to install the seat in the car, it did not fit into the designated holes. Perplexed, he tried to redo and realign, using up the entire 58 seconds and causing his trainer to halt the assembly line to fix the problem. After demonstrating the sequence a second time, Spear tried again, but then something else didn't fit. In the course of an hour, he only managed to correctly install four seats. Assessing his experience, Spear came to understand why historically it was so important to test every product coming off the end of a production line such as this, where thousands of parts are used and one step builds upon another. A company with such a complex process simply could not be sure that each step had been done correctly, so the last step in the process had to be an end-of-the-line activity called "inspection."

In medical education, we call that last step "assessment" or "testing," rather than "inspection," but we do it for exactly the same reason. Thousands of students learn thousands of things from hundreds of people in thousands of situations. The only way we can assure ourselves that they have learned enough of what we want them to know is to inspect each student at the end of the line, through a standardized test. It is the only way—or so Spear thought.

Spear next went to Toyota, and though he got assigned to the same spot on the line—installing the front passenger-side seat—he had a completely different experience. At his training session he was told, "There are seven total steps required to install this seat correctly. We will start with step one. We will not teach you step two until you have proven mastery of step one. This may take you 10 minutes. This may take two hours. Even if this takes an entire day, we will not give you the privilege of learning step two until step one is mastered. It simply does not make sense for us to teach you the subsequent steps if you can't do the prior steps correctly and efficiently."

Rather than an end-of-the-line inspection, testing and assessment were an integral part of the instruction process. As such, when Spear finally took his place on the line, he was able to install each seat correctly the first time and every time. Toyota had built into its process a mechanism to verify immediately that each step had been done correctly, resulting in products that did not need to be tested at the end of the production line. Because it wastes no time or money adding value to defective products, the company's reputation for quality is well-earned.

What a contrast between the two methods for training Steve Spear! At the American plant, the time to learn was fixed, but the result of training was variable and unpredictable. At Toyota, the training time was variable, but the result was certain—every person who went through the training could predictably do what he had been taught to do. Toyota follows that principle in all its training, for every activity in the company. The philosophy is rooted in Rule 1 and Rule 2: never add value to anything that isn't perfectly ready to receive the next set of value. We should advance students to the next stage of learning only when they've verifiably understood the material that will be required to succeed at the next stage.

Because our medical schools continue to follow the fixed-time, variable-learning model that was the only economic option a century ago, we need to test students at the end of their work. Those tests essentially measure, of all the material we paid for and had hoped they would learn, the medical students actually did learn. In fact, the system purposefully seeks—and even *prizes*—variability in what the students learn. The process must identify the best students so they can then be tracked into the best residency programs. Students who master a smaller percentage of what we wanted them to learn get tracked to less desirable residency programs, in less desirable locations. This approach has actually perpetuated variability in the training of our physicians—which was the very problem that the Flexner report had sought to remedy.

While systems designed to cull the best from the rest might be desirable in situations like baseball's World Series, this ought not to be our design in the training of medical students. We want *each* medical school graduate to have mastered *all* the material considered important. At present, those doctors in need of remedial assistance are often not identified until some kind of ex-post screening process is undertaken, such as in-service examinations, specialty board certifications, or malpractice lawsuits.[32]

Changing the curricular architecture of our medical schools in ways that are consistent with the five rules in use at Toyota can result in better medical student education at significantly lower costs. Administratively this will be a challenge. To those who will be charged with these reforms, we strongly recommend an organizational tool developed by Professors Steven C. Wheelwright and Kim B. Clark called "heavyweight teams"—teams that have the authority to reach and implement decisions such as those noted above.[33] The typical academic response to challenges for curriculum reform is to convene a committee comprised of a strong-minded representative from each faculty group that might be affected by the change—and to expect them to agree on a new course of action. Wheelwright and Clark call such groups "lightweight" or "functional" teams. Their composition usually reflects the underlying departmental structure of the organization and the functions of each of those departments. Such committees typically are only able to recommend solutions that are the mirror image of the organizational structure the committee members represent. Any medical school administrator who attempts to implement our recommendations through a lightweight committee structure instead of a heavyweight team is condemning its members to a hellacious, frustrating, and fruitless endeavor.[34]

WHAT TYPES OF MEDICAL PROFESSIONALS WILL WE NEED?

What we've discussed in the pages above is an agenda of *sustaining innovations* that our present medical schools need to implement. The fact that our medical schools are also being disrupted compounds the urgency for change.

An important element of the future view of health care that we painted in earlier chapters is that the mix of health-care professionals we will need in the future is different than the mix we have at present. Specialist physicians need to be better trained to practice intuitive medicine in the multidisciplinary team environment of *coherent* solution shops. Primary care physicians will disrupt specialist physicians in a significant way. We'll need more primary care doctors and fewer specialists as more and more disorders move from the intuitive toward the precision end of the spectrum of medical practice, and as Internet-based decision tools bring the diagnostic capabilities of the world's best specialists into the offices of general physicians. Furthermore, much of the work that general physicians do today will be taken over by nurse practitioners, physician assistants, and medical technicians—suggesting that we need to train more of these professionals as well.

A century ago Flexner concluded, "The training of the doctor is therefore more complex and more directly momentous than that of the technician."[35] This observation certainly was true for the era of intuitive medicine emerging at that time. If we are correct about the future, however, the tide is likely to flow in the other direction. Those physicians who choose to practice in value-adding process clinics perhaps will need the technical training in how to use the equipment and devices of their chosen fields more than general knowledge of the sciences that must be mastered by the physicians who are still targeting careers in intuitive medicine.

What roles are today's leading medical schools playing in training the caregivers we'll need? In fact, they're training more and more of the doctors we won't need, and are leaving others to train the professionals we will need. The medical education system in the United States has no means of coordinated planning for training doctors to meet societal needs. Consequently, as recently as 2006 the Association of American Medical Colleges called for training 30 percent *more* physicians, even though other reports predict a severe excess of doctors—a problem that will become magnified if the disruption of specialists by general physicians and of general physicians by nurses comes to fruition.[36] The only resource allocation mechanism is that medical students, like the rest of us, choose to pursue careers that are intellectually and emotionally engaging, with the most attractive incomes and lifestyles. Similarly, students shun those fields like internal and family medicine, where reimbursement (for the present) constrains income.[37] This has led to a rapid expansion of subspecialists and a dearth of primary care physicians.[38]

Who is closing the shortage of primary care physicians our medical schools are creating, as their students march resolutely "up-market" toward higher-paying specialties? Three groups of disruptive competitors are filling that gap: foreign medical schools, schools of osteopathic medicine, and nursing schools. We mentioned at the beginning of this chapter that America's medical schools produce about 16,000 graduates each year, who then fill about two-thirds of the open residency positions every year. Much of the gap—positions primarily in internal and family medicine—is filled by graduates of foreign medical schools. Often, they are immigrants from countries where they received their medical training, but there have also long been medical schools in Central America and several Caribbean nations that readily admit students from the United States and elsewhere who were denied admission to U.S.-based schools. The science faculty of these schools were initially drawn from the ranks of faculty of leading North American medical schools who "moonlighted" by lecturing in their fields for a couple of months during the year and then enjoyed the real moonlight of the Caribbean in the evening. Increasingly, however, their science curricula have been augmented through online lectures recorded by the finest teachers in North American medical schools. The foreign schools have in fact been much more aggressive in using these disruptive means of instruction than mainstream U.S.-based medical schools.

These Latin and Caribbean schools then place their students in third- and fourth-year clerkship programs in North America—typically not in the best teaching hospitals, of course, but in positions that are good enough for these students who were so eager to become doctors that they would go abroad to get their training. Caribbean and Latin American degrees were initially derided. But graduates of these and other international schools comprised 27 percent of all residents in 2006.[39] And true to the pattern of disruption, they have a much higher "market share" of internal medicine and family practice residencies. Though these graduates were initially relegated to inner city and rural residencies abandoned by U.S. medical school graduates, their test scores and performance have continued to improve. In fact, international medical school graduates have begun to regularly outperform graduates of U.S. medical schools on important measures of knowledge and training.[40] Ross and St. George's are examples of schools that have developed good reputations and are moving up the chain. And this is occurring despite more stringent educational and regulatory requirements.[41]

Osteopathic medicine is the second disruptive competitor. In addition to incorporating osteopathic manipulative treatment, Doctors of Osteopathy typically emphasize "holistic" and homeo-pathic care, promoting wellness and preventive care as central elements of their practice. Osteopathy originated in the late 1800s, and over time its practitioners have adopted many of the research-based practices of conventional (often called "allopathic") medicine. Like Caribbean medical schools, osteopathic medical schools have traditionally been a route chosen by those who could not be admitted to mainstream American medical schools.

The profession faced an uphill battle while establishing its identity and legitimacy. But the gap created by the stampede of American medical school students into specialties has spelled opportunity for osteopathic doctors. Their medical education has long emphasized primary care as its core strength. By 2003, 46 percent of graduating osteopathic students planned to pursue allopathic residency training, and three-quarters of them were targeting primary care residencies.[42] As a partial reflection of the demand for doctors who can fill primary care positions, the number of graduates of schools of osteopathic medicine has nearly doubled, from about 1,750 in 1994 to about 3,300 in 2007.[43]

Nurse practitioners, physician assistants, and other so-called "physician extenders," comprise the third group of disruptors to our mainstream medical schools. Already, those with doctor of nursing degrees are allowed to sit for step two of the United States Medical Licensing Examination.[44] Long relegated to a sub-servient role in health-care delivery, nurses, nurse practitioners, and physician assistants are assuming increasing levels of respon-sibility in patient care as described in Chapters 1 and 4—so that they increasingly overlap with some activities of primary care phy-sicians. These professionals will in the future become the primary caregivers for patients with the growing number of diseases that are progressing into the realm of precision medicine.

However, America presently suffers from a severe shortage of nurses of every type. The American Hospital Association reported in July 2007 that U.S. hospitals faced a shortage of 116,000 nurses.[45] Within 15 years this will balloon to a shortage of between 500,000 and 1 million nurses.[46] It is a chronic problem that is driven by three factors. The first is the aging of today's nurse workforce: more than half plan to retire within 15 to 20 years.[47] The second is that there are many more attractive career options for women today than a generation ago, so fewer choose to pursue degrees in nursing. Historically, most nurses spent their entire careers working in a hospital unit. Medical adminis-trators felt little need to design attractive career paths for them. As other careers emerge with the promise of more attractive professional pathways, fewer young women and men choose to pursue nursing as a career—despite the centrality of this pro-fession in the health-care industry of the future. The third driver of the shortage is the limited (and declining) faculty capacity in nursing schools. In 2007 83% of nursing schools reported a need for additional faculty.[48] Yet few of our universities have viable programs for relieving this bottleneck.

As with the shortage of primary care physicians, America is turning to immigrants from foreign nursing schools, at least as a partial solution. In 2005, for example, the United States bowed to pressure from the hospital industry, found 50,000 unused immigrant visas somewhere, and dedicated them solely to nurses. Given their other career options, young men and women in nations like the Philippines—which supplies half of all immigrant nurses in the United States—choose nursing as a straightforward ticket to a more comfortable standard of living in more economically advanced nations.

IN-SOURCING MEDICAL TRAINING

Although there are clear needs for sustaining improvements to medical education as summarized in the first section of this chapter, and clear threats by the disruptive educators described in the second section, we are pessimistic that our leading medical schools will be able to act decisively on either front. More of the same is what we're most likely to see. The reason lies in the mechanisms of governance in these institutions—which are largely collegial and consensus-driven. The faculty cultures in most medical schools are very strong. There is broad consensus among faculty members about what they want from their participation in the enterprise, and broad agreement about what actions are required to get what they need. The tools to elicit cooperative behavior in this circumstance—like planning, negotiation, tradition, democracy, and folklore—are good at reinforcing the status quo, but only begrudgingly yield change.

When radical change is required, an executive with the power to convene heavyweight teams that can define and implement the new order of things is critical—and few such executives exist in our medical schools. In fact, the average tenure-in-position for medical school deans is about three years—suggesting that most of them can survive in their offices only until they try to take an action with which the faculty does not agree.[49] In other words, a well-informed oddsmaker would bet that most of our medical and nursing schools will not respond to the changes we'll need.

We suspect that in response to this inability to change, or change rapidly enough, the same fate that is befalling our graduate schools of business in the United States will soon hit the medical schools as well. Eventually, the corporations that historically hired our medical school graduates will conclude that they're better off training their own doctors, rather than continuing to wait and hope that their medical school "suppliers" will start giving them the doctors and nurses they need.

Disruption of Management Education

America's business schools are being disrupted by corporate universities, ranging from General Electric's extensive Crotonville campus in New York on the large end of the spectrum, to Salisbury, Maryland–based Perdue University on the smaller end.[51] The problem to which these corporate universities are responding is parallel to the one described earlier. Graduates of the leading business schools are flocking to the highest-paying subspecialties—hedge funds, private equity, leveraged buyout and venture capital funds, strategy consulting, and investment banking.

Mainstream operating companies that need to recruit tomorrow's general managers simply can't pay business school graduates the salaries they can earn in one of these specialties. The starting compensation packages in those specialty sectors, which in 2007 was approximately $150,000, simply don't fit within the salary structures of operating companies.[52] In response, operating companies have set up in-house management programs to train their own managers. While the number of course hours taken in MBA programs of every sort (including part-time and one-year degrees) is declining, the number of course hours taken in corporate universities is increasing at about 25 percent per year.[53] The number of corporate universities increased from 400 in 1990 to over 2,000 by the year 2000.[54]

Why, in an era of rampant outsourcing, are corporations increasingly in-sourcing the training of their managers? It's not just the prohibitive cost of luring specialty-bound MBAs into general management. When they train their own managers, corporations can equip the next generation not just with individual skills, but with the know-how to manage within the processes and culture of the company. These corporate universities began by tackling the simplest of skills that their mid-level managers needed to hone—and they continued to rely upon MBAs they hired from business schools to manage their complicated strategic and financial problems. But little by little these corporate universities have taken on more dimensions of management training, to the point that companies ranging from General Electric to Monitor (the Cambridge, Massachusetts–based consulting firm) voice an active preference for managers who were trained in-house, rather than those who received MBAs from traditional business schools.

Corporate Medical Schools

We anticipate that, given the need for more primary care doctors and nurses that our medical and nursing schools are not meeting, major integrated health-care providers will begin training their own caregivers. We predict that in 10 to 15 years the major, integrated health-care providers like Kaiser Permanente and Intermountain Healthcare will have begun training even their own doctors. The Mayo and Cleveland Clinics already have their own small medical schools affiliated with their world-class medical centers, of course. But in-house medical training will become commonplace.

As major providers come to grips with the likelihood that traditional medical schools will be unable to provide them with the professionals they need, it will be important for these provider systems *not* to launch a direct attack of sustaining innovation against medical schools—but instead, to *disrupt* them. Indeed, with the technological enablers of disruption fueling the handoff of work from expensive experts to less costly personnel, hospitals ought not to attempt training physicians at the outset. Instead, they should focus on training more nurses and arming them with technologies that allow them to do more sophisticated work— thereby providing them with the career paths that can make nursing an even more attractive profession. Likewise, if it proves too difficult to fill the nursing shortage, then hospitals will need to train more medical technicians and employ *them* in new disruptive models of care delivery. In other words, when faced with a skilled workforce shortage, the rule should be to *create disruption at the level of training immediately below the area of scarcity.* Then, the hospitals can notch up their in-house professional training in a series of small steps so that by the time they want to train their own doctors, it will be an incremental, logical extension of the training they have already been doing.

If hospitals were to suddenly jump into educating physicians, in contrast, the medical school and accrediting agencies would block them every step of the way. The Liaison Committee on Medical Education (LCME) of the American Medical Association and the Association of American Medical Colleges (AAMC) has been a barrier to accrediting new medical schools until very recently, and it is unclear whether the LCME would ever allow other delivery systems to get into the business of training doctors prior to residency. Until now, all M.D.-granting programs in the United States have had to be affiliated with a university. For example, Cleveland Clinic had to affiliate with Case Western University in order to launch its M.D. program (Lerner College of Medicine) in 2002. (The Mayo Clinic was an exception when it received permission to start issuing a limited number of M.D. degrees in 1972.) Furthermore, the systems of state medical licensing and specialty board certification are intricately tied together with the current system of medical education. These factors make it even more difficult for hospitals to immediately begin training physicians on their own. This must therefore come at the end of the disruptive path, not the beginning.

Most provider systems today would not list the training of their professionals as an activity that is core, or one in which they have competence. But the same arguments we advanced in Chapter 6 for why employers are integrating to provide the first level of health care for their employees apply here too. When provider systems cannot assure themselves of an adequate supply of appropriately trained professionals, they will make training a competence—because it will be core to their success. Most important, integration creates a more straightforward way to train caregivers about processes—how to design, troubleshoot, improve, and manage processes—in addition to mastering the individual skills in which physicians and nurses must be competent.[55]

In addition to addressing the shortages that stem from our medical schools not training enough of the right people, in-house training will bring two additional benefits. The setting of clinical practice has changed perhaps as much as the underlying science and technology of medical practice have changed since the Flexner report. Patients no longer remain in hospitals for extended periods, allowing for longitudinal observation. So much care has shifted to outpatient clinics and into the home that patients residing in hospitals today are much sicker than the average patient of yesterday. Further, doctors see only the "slice" of the disease that necessitated hospitalization—they typically don't see the beginning or the end, save for a half day per week or a few weeks per year carved out of their training calendar. Most care in the real world involves a much greater mix of chronic disease management and preventive care than can be seen in a hospital. Integrated medical systems will have greater ability and motivation than today's medical schools to train doctors and nurses to function in tomorrow's venues of care, across the entire life cycle of diseases.

Recall the four constructs that comprise every process: activities, connections, pathways, and methods of improvement. Medical schools are now set up primarily to help students learn and perform the individual activities of being a doctor. The science of connections, pathways, and improvements is not readily taught within the context, culture, and tradition of today's medical schools. This is the other driving reason why we predict that in-house schools are likely to emerge in the future. In-house programs will augment the disruptive waves from foreign medical schools, osteopathic medicine, and nurse practitioners and physician assistants, to diminish the role that many of today's medical schools will play in the health-care system of the future.

NOTES

1. Tu, H. T., and Ginsburg, P. B., "Losing Ground: Physician Income, 1995–2003," Center for Studying Health System Change. Community Tracking Study Physician Survey.
2. See Association of American Medical Colleges FACTS National Applicant Data Warehouse, "Total Graduates by Gender and Race/Ethnicity, 1992–2001;" and Association of American Medical Colleges FACTS National Applicant Data Warehouse, "Applicants, Accepted Applicants, and Matriculants by Sex, 1994–2005." These figures do not include osteopathic medical schools.
3. Association of American Medical Colleges Press Release, "U.S. Medical School Seniors Apply to Residency Programs in Record Numbers," March 17, 2005, available at http://www.aamc.org/newsroom/pressrel/2005/ 050317.htm, accessed July 29, 2006.
4. According to the Association of American Medical Colleges, the average educational debt of indebted graduates of the class of 2007 was $139,500.
5. Harvard Medical School Dean's Report, 2005–2006.
6. "New Paradigms for Physician Training: For Improving Access to Health Care," 18th Report, Rockville: Council on Graduate Medical Education, 2007. Accessed from ftp://ftp.hrsa.gov/cogme/18thCOGME.pdf on Aug. 23, 2008. Lim, J. K., and Golub, R. M., "Graduate Medical Education Research in the 21st Century and JAMA On Call," *Journal of the American Medical Association*, 2004, 292:2914. Chen, F. M.; Bauchner, H.; and Burstin, H., "A Call for Outcomes Research in Medical Education," *Acad Med.* 2004; 79:S68–69. Dickinson, T. A., "The Future of Financing Medical Education: Questions about Medicare's Role," *Am J Med.* 2004; 117:287–90.
7. Estimate made by Dr. Joseph Dorsey of Harvard Community Health Plan in a talk at the Harvard Macy Institute, June 1998. Dr. Dorsey also stated that it costs roughly $30,000 to retrain each medical school graduate. Though we know of no empirical studies on this issue, our more recent interviews with medical administrators support Dr. Dorsey's assertion that we're not training doctors with the skills needed to practice in today's environment. We refer readers interested in this topic to Wiest, F. C., et al., "Preparedness of Internal Medicine and Family Practice Residents for Treating Common Conditions," *Journal of the American Medical Association*, Nov. 27, 2002, 288 (20):2609–14.
8. Flexner, A., *Medical Education in the United States and Canada: A Report to the Carnegie Foundation for the Advancement of Teaching*. Boston, Massachusetts: Merrymount Press (1910), 9. Original source is Bigelow, H., *Medical Education in America*. Cambridge, Massachusetts: University Press (1871), 79.
9. Flexner, A., op .cit., 8.
10. Flexner, A., op. cit., 16, 18, 20.
11. Flexner's report actually did not separate the basic sciences and clinical sciences as starkly as it was interpreted by the medical schools at the turn of the century. As a teacher, Flexner argued for the importance of both content areas, but he also saw the need to have the two more closely linked in order to improve learning. Medical schools subsequently adopted the European model (largely German and French) in which there were very strong basic science departments performing world class research and also teaching their disciplines. This model appealed to Americans in that it was driving a strong research enterprise in Europe, and it could fulfill Flexner's calls that at least two of the four years of the U.S. medical school curriculum should be devoted to learning the basic sciences. It

was therefore the interpretation of Flexner's report by U.S. medical schools that created the chasm between the first and last two years of the medical school curriculum. It is also important to note that the strong departmental influence on the curriculum in many ways mirrors the health-care delivery system that remains so siloed today.

12. In fact, it has become a time-honored tradition to undertake a heroic study and review process to essentially *relearn* basic science principles in preparation for step one of the U.S. Medical Licensing Examination, which occurs after the second year of medical school. For many, this relearning continues during their third and fourth years and into their residency training.

13. Harvard Medical School's "New Pathways" architecture, developed and implemented under the leadership of Dean Daniel Tostesen in the early 1980s, was a pioneering program to achieve this integration, using the case method of teaching that was common at Harvard Business School. It has been remarkably successful, and many other schools have adopted the New Pathways system. We thank Dr. Lewis Hassell of the University of Oklahoma for his help in our understanding these issues.

14. Elsewhere in the world, including Europe, many schools have traditionally allowed two entry dates to medical school: one in the fall and one in the winter. However, students in each cohort still proceed through the curriculum in lockstep, with departments responsible for teaching their basic science subjects twice each year.

15. Students typically begin their clinical training with core clerkships, which include Internal Medicine, General Surgery, Pediatrics, Ob/Gyn, Psychiatry, and Neurology, and rotation through each of these is mandatory during the third year of medical school. Clerkships in the fourth year are much more diverse and elective, and only a sampling is included in Figure 10.1. The core clerkships will almost always precede the fourth year electives, but the order in which each clerkship is taken is otherwise random.

16. Many medical educators are aware of this problem, and as a result, the design of many post-medical-school continuing education programs is increasingly geared toward demonstrated competencies—because, we suspect, the professionals in those courses need to cultivate and demonstrate those competencies. The Accreditation Council for Graduate Medical Education Web site now defines specific competencies for each specialty. Hopefully this focus will trickle into the design of medical schools' curricula soon.

17. The Institute for Health Care Improvement Open School concept, launched Sept. 15, 2008, is attempting to address this problem in a disruptive manner, using free online modules about these topics that embrace all health-care professional students.

18. For those readers with an interest in Spear's work, we recommend first reading Steven Spear and H. Kent Bowen, "Decoding the DNA of the Toyota Production System," *Harvard Business Review*, Sept. 1999. In this narrative, simply for brevity, we attribute the insights from this work to Spear, who was the primary investigator. He was mentored throughout his work by Professor Bowen, who deserves substantial credit for the success of Spear's path-breaking work.

19. In this account we have taken a bit of liberty in rephrasing Spear's rules so they can be more readily applied to medical education.

20. Those who have become expert in the application of these rules in hospitals include John Kenagy and David Sundahl of Kenagy Associates. Steve King and Matt Verlinden of Innovo, Inc. have applied the rules in the semiconductor industry. Also see Spear, Steven

J., "Workplace Safety at Alcoa (B)," Harvard Business School Case #600068, Dec. 22, 1999.

21. We thank Professor Elizabeth G. Armstrong, Associate Professor of Pediatrics (Medical Education); former director of Educational Programs at Harvard Medical School, and presently with Harvard Medical International, for her tireless efforts to help us understand the problems of medical education around the world.

22. Interestingly, this isn't a new refrain. Even in 1905, the revered physician William Osler proclaimed, "To cover the vast field of medicine in four years is an impossible task." See Staropoli, J. F., "The Evolution and Evaluation of Modern Medical Education," *Journal of the American Medical Association*, 2004; 291:2138.

23. One of the deans of a leading medical school, in fact, recounted during the Harvard Macy program a stunning illustration of how obsolete the traditional lecture method for these science courses is, in competition against the other methods these bright students can devise to learn the scientific material. He said that the students in their school had persuaded the administration to record every lecture by every professor, and to make those recordings available to students online—so they could review the lectures again and again, if necessary, in order to master the material. Flattered that the students would see so much value in the lectures, the faculty of course agreed to do this. Once the lectures had been posted online, however, attendance at the lectures plummeted. One of the administrators later learned that the students had figured out a method to play the lectures at triple speed on their Apple iPods and were taking in the lectures in one-third the time that had been required when sitting through class. Many of them were multi-tasking (exercising, riding the bus, etc.) while listening to the lectures at triple speed! The administration noticed that these students' average scores on the national board examinations were just as high as in earlier years, when students were sitting at the feet of their professors in lecture halls.

24. The fact that a number of medical schools have attempted to integrate the science and clinical portions of their curricula in the ways we've suggested (often called problem-based instruction), has prompted studies of whether graduates of problem-based programs do better in their board examinations than graduates of programs that employ a conventional curricular architecture. The results do not show that integrating science with clinical instruction results in superior scores on these examinations. It is quite possible, however, that the examinations themselves are a reflection of the conventional segregated architecture, in which comprehension of science is taught and examined. The benefits of an integrated curriculum may not be well reflected in these tests.

25. A useful Harvard Medical School teaching case on this topic is Steven J. Spear and Marie Mackey, "Emily Wilson." Copies can be obtained from Professor Elizabeth Armstrong of Harvard Medical International.

26. Armstrong, E. G.; Mackey, M.; and Spear, S. J., "Medical Education as a Process Management Program," *Academic Medicine*, 2004; 79:721–28.

27. Clearly, the task of specifying what skills are necessary and desirable in our physicians is daunting. We will not attempt to define this list of skills, since they are (and should be) subject to constant debate. However, we believe this discourse will necessarily lead to experimentation that ultimately clarifies what these goals should be. Encouraging signs of outcomes-based education are already taking place, and this should lead to wider

acceptance and implementation. Should we continue to resist this change simply due to its complexity, we will do a disservice to future physicians, their employers, and, most important, their patients. Readers with further interest in this issue should study Johns, M. M. "The Time Has Come to Reform Graduate Medical Education," *Journal of the American Medical Association*, Sept. 5, 2001; 286: 1075–76; and Goroll, A. H., et al., "A New Model for Accreditation of Residency Programs in Internal Medicine," *Annals of Internal Medicine*, June 1, 2004; 140: 902–09.

28. See Ericsson, K., et al., "The Making of an Expert," *Harvard Business Review*, July–Aug. 2007, 114–21, for more about the importance of deliberate practice in developing proficiency in most essential professional skills. We also thank Dr. Peter Weinstock, a member of the faculty at Children's Hospital Boston, for sharing with us his expertise in simulation-based medical training.

29. See Christensen, Clayton M., Horn, Michael B., and Johnson, Curtis W., *Disrupting Class: How Disruptive Innovation Will Change the Way the World Learns* (New York: McGraw-Hill, 2008).

30. We refer readers with an interest in this problem to a video, "First Do No Harm," which was constructed from actual case studies under the sponsorship of the Institutes of Medicine. It is available from the Partnership for Patient Safety (http://www.p4ps.org/interactive_videos.asp).

31. Spear, S. J., "Fixing Health Care from the Inside: Teaching Residents to Heal Broken Delivery Processes as They Heal Sick Patients," Research in Medical Education, invited address, Association of American Medical Colleges, June 26, 2006.

32. Proposals have more recently been made to the ACGME to redesign the method of residency accreditation to include measures of clinical competence, essentially elevating the importance of outcome measures and continuous process improvement. In addition, some residency programs have begun to emphasize core competency assessments in place of time-based curricula. See Goroll, A. H., et al., "A New Model for Accreditation of Residency Programs in Internal Medicine," *Annals of Internal Medicine*, 2004; 140:902–909; and Johns, M. M., "The Time Has Come to Reform Graduate Medical Education," *Journal of the American Medical Association*, Sept. 5, 2001; 286:1075–76.

33. The original article on heavyweight teams was Clark, Kim B., and Wheelwright, Steven C., "Organizing and Leading Heavyweight Development Teams," *California Management Review*, 1992, no. 34, 9–28. The concept has been broadened by a number of scholars of innovation. See, for example, Christensen, Clayton M., and Raynor, Michael, "Is Your Organization Capable of Disruptive Growth," Chapter 7 in *The Innovator's Solution* (Boston, Massachusetts: Harvard Business School Press, 2003).

34. See "Forging a Consensus for Change" and "Giving Schools the Right Structure to Innovate," Chapters 8 and 9 of Christensen, Clayton C., et al., *Disrupting Class* (New York: McGraw-Hill, 2008).

35. Flexner, A., op. cit., 24.

36. Goodman, D. C., "Too Many Doctors in the House," *New York Times*, July 10, 2006, A21.

37. Remember that the levels of reimbursement that sum up to the incomes doctors in various specialties can earn are the result of fees for services that bear no relation to the supply, demand, or market value of their services. The rates are determined by formula and administrative fiat—a fairly flimsy, and even whimsical, basis for tomorrow's doctors to use in choosing careers.

38. We refer readers with additional interest in the underlying drivers of increased specialization to Martini, C.J.M., "Graduate Medical Education in the Changing Environment of Medicine," *JAMA*, 1992:268:1097-1105; and to Donini-Lenhoff, F. G., and Hedrick, H. L., "Growth of Specialization in Graduate Medical Education," *Journal of the American Medical Association*, 2000. 284:1286–87.

39. Brotherton, Sarah E., and Sylvia I. Etzel, "Graduate Medical Education, 2005–2006," *Journal of the American Medical Association*, 2006, 296(9):1154–69; and Kenneth, S., et al., "International Medical Graduates and the Primary Care Workforce for Rural Underserved Areas," *Health Affairs* 22, no. 2 (2003): 255–62.

40. Garibaldi, Richard A., et al., "The In-Training Examination in Internal Medicine: An Analysis of Resident Performance over Time," *Annals of Internal Medicine* 2002;137:505–10. Since 1995, international medical school graduates have consistently outperformed graduates of U.S. medical schools on the In-Training Examination in Internal Medicine (IM-ITE), which is administered annually to all U.S. medical residents since 1988. McDonald, Furman, S., et al., "Factors Associated with Medical Knowledge Acquisition During Internal Medicine Residency," *Journal of General Internal Medicine.* 2007 July; 22(7): 962–68. Factors significantly associated with IM-ITE performance included graduation from a U.S. medical school, which was associated with a score decrease of –3.4 percent (95%CI –6.5%, –0.36%; p = .03) compared to international medical school graduation.

41. *Accreditation Council for Graduate Medical Education, 2004-2005 Annual Report,* available at: http://www.acgme.org/acWebsite/annRep/an_2004-05AnnRep.pdf.

42. Singer, A. M., *2004 Annual Report on Osteopathic Medical Education, for American Association of Colleges of Osteopathic Medicine,* June 2005. Although most osteopathic physicians engage in primary care medicine, an increasing portion have begun competing successfully for *specialist* residency positions—a classic case of disruptive innovators moving up-market.

43. American Association of Colleges of Osteopathic Medicine, Annual Osteopathic Medical School Questionnaires, 1994–95 through 2003–04. The figure for 2007 is the sum of enrollments that each of the 20 schools of osteopathic medicine projected in 2004 as the size of their graduating classes in 2007.

44. O'Sullivan, A. L., et al., "Moving Forward Together: the Practice Doctorate in Nursing," *Online Journal of Issues in Nursing,* vol. 10 no.3, Sept. 30, 2005. Available at: http://nursingworld.org/ojin/topic28/tpc28_4.htm.

45. "The 2007 State of America's Hospials—Taking the Pulse," American Hospital Association, July 2007. Accessed at http://www.aha.org/aha/content/2007/PowerPoint/StateofHospitalsChartPack2007.ppt.

46. Biviano, Marilyn B., et al. "What Is Behind HRSA's Projected Supply, Demand, and Shortage of Registered Nurses?" Health Resources and Services Administration. Accessed at ftp://ftp.hrsa.gov/bhpr/workforce/behindshortage.pdf.

47. The 2006 Aging Nursing Workforce Survey, Bernard Hodes Group, July 2006.

48. Fang, Di and Stefanie Wisniewski, "Special Survey of AACN Membership on Vacant Faculty Positions for Academic Year 2007-2008," American Association of Colleges of Nursing, June 2007. Accessed at http://www.aacn.nche.edu/IDS/pdf/vacancy07.pdf.

49. See Christensen, Clayton; Howard Stevenson; and Matthew Marx, "The Tools of Cooperation," *Harvard Business Review*, Dec. 31, 1998. We will return to discuss this framework of organizational change in Chapter 11.

50. Clarkson, John G., "The Best Is Yet to Come." *Medicine*, Winter 2006.

51. Perdue University, operated by the chicken company Perdue Farms, should not be confused with Purdue University, which is located in West Lafayette, Indiana. The mascot of the latter university is the Boilermaker, whereas the mascot of the former would be the Broilermaker.

52. Data from Harvard Business School Class of 2007, accessed from http://www.hbs.edu/recruiting/mba/resources/career.html on Aug. 29, 2008. Median base salary for investment banking was $95,000, with a median signing bonus of $40,000; some received additional guaranteed compensation at a median of $60,000. Respective figures for hedge funds: $125,000, $25,000, $95,000; consulting (all fields): $120,000, $20,000, $20,000; private equity/leveraged buyout: $130,000, $35,000, $105,000; and venture capital: $127,500, $22,500, $45,000.

53. Olmstead, Helen, et al., *Opportunities in E-Learning*, (San Francisco: Ehrlrich Organization, May 9, 2000). Accessed at http://www.ehrlichorg.com/strt/s0509-28.doc on Aug. 23, 2008.

54. Morrison, James, "U.S. Higher Education in Transition," *On the Horizon* (2003), 11(1), 6–10.

55. We recommend Spear, S. J., "Fixing Health Care from the Inside: Teaching Residents to Heal Broken Delivery Processes as They Heal Sick Patients," *Acad. Med.*, 2006 Oct; 81 (10 Suppl): S144-49.

Chapter 11

Regulatory Reform and the Disruption of Health Care

The quintessential con artist of the nineteenth century was the snake oil peddler who sold sham elixirs to vulnerable patients—and it was the specter of his parasitical existence that ultimately spawned the Food and Drug Administration.[1] The FDA's essential oversight of certain elements of the health-care industry was just the beginning of regulatory influence, however. The tentacles of governmental control now stretch throughout America's health-care system in a deep, tangled, and pervasive way—to the point that health care isn't private enterprise in the sense that automobiles, semiconductors, and strategy consulting are private. Indeed, much of the current public discourse on health-care reform focuses on whether private industry can be expected to fix the current system—or whether the government will have to become even more deeply involved. In many other economically advanced countries, of course, the government *is* the health-care system.

In this chapter we will catalog the ways in which government policies influence health care for good and ill, and we'll recommend regulatory changes that are essential to successfully disrupting the system. To do this, we have reviewed the history of government intervention in a range of industries whose products or services have been considered "public goods"— where the public interest has been broader than what market mechanisms might be expected to serve autonomously. These include education, ground and air transportation, financial services, telecommunications, and health care. All policies can't be lumped together and treated alike, of course. But it seems that in general terms, the intent of schemes to influence and regulate these industries in the public interest evolves through three stages:

1. **Subsidizing** the foundation of the industry
2. **Stabilizing** and strengthening the companies involved, ensuring fair and equal access to their products and services, and assuring that their products are safe and effective
3. **Encouraging competition** to reduce prices[2]

We've organized most of this chapter around these three stages, because government's interaction with the health-care industry can also be grouped into these categories. Much of its energies to date have been expended in the second of these stages. In discussing those regulations, we'll show how the pattern that typified other industries is now at work in health care: regulations whose initial purpose was to protect the patient ultimately get used to protect the provider. After modeling these, we'll draw on our studies to suggest how private-sector innovators can cause policymakers to begin focusing on the third stage—and help them distinguish the types of regulatory reforms that can predictably lead to lower costs versus those that will predictably backfire.[3] Finally, we'll close the chapter by assessing whether adopting a government-led single-payer system will help or hinder the sorts of reforms we need in our system—and we'll apply those insights to the situation in other nations, where national health ministries already provide most health care.

SUBSIDIZING THE FOUNDATION OF INDUSTRIES

Governments sometimes conclude that a desirable industry cannot emerge on its own—so they subsidize or in other ways facilitate the investments required to cause that industry to coalesce. For example, under the Morrill Act of 1862, the federal government gave land to states that agreed to create "land grant" colleges; and under separate legislation that same year, it began giving land and cash to railroads that were willing to lay track to span the continent.[4] The 1925 Kelly Act initiated airmail service, which subsidized the establishment of the scheduled passenger airline industry. The Federal Home Loan Act of 1932, the creation of the Federal Housing Administration in 1934, and the Federal National Mortgage Association in 1936, were meant to help an affordable housing industry grow.[5] In 1957 the government did the same for the trucking industry, by building the Interstate Highway System.

Often, government subsidies of the cost of launching industries take the form of research and development spending. By illustration, funding of military cargo jet aircraft by the Department of Defense essentially paid for the design of the first commercial jet airliner, the Boeing 707. The research that enabled the commercial nuclear power industry was funded through military budgets—as was development of the Internet. Indirectly, through its regulation of pricing, the government "taxed" AT&T's customers to fund Bell Laboratories, whose inventions in microelectronics and telecommunications proved to be an extraordinary blessing to mankind.[6]

Funding the Science Underlying Health Care

The National Institutes of Health (NIH) have funded nearly all of the basic and much of the applied research that underpins modern medicine. Much of the knowledge that took many infectious diseases into precision medicine a generation earlier, and many of the insights in molecular medicine that are driving more diseases toward precision medicine today, have been developed in our leading research universities with NIH funding.

While everything can always be improved, we propose one enhancement to the methods used to allocate NIH grants. The NIH currently uses a single-blind referee system for evaluating grant proposals. When a researcher submits a proposal requesting that a project be funded by the NIH, the NIH sends the proposal to experts in the field in question. The reviewers evaluate the proposal's potential based upon their knowledge of the field, and will recommend that it be funded, that the project be reframed and resubmitted for further consideration, or that the grant simply not be made. The reviewers' names are typically not known to the researcher who submitted the proposal. The logic behind the single-blind method is that the reviewers need to know of researchers' track records in the field. But personal relationships and politics need to be kept from the decision-making process, ensuring that each decision is made purely on the merits of the science involved.

However, the inadvertent result of this system of sending proposals for review by the scientists with the deepest expertise in the specific topic is that it has "siloized" the structure of scientific work into ever narrower disciplines and subdisciplines—in our research universities and especially in our medical schools. The referees, as the experts in their particular subdiscipline, tend to view proposals positively if they extend knowledge in their known discipline even deeper. But if the proposal intends to push knowledge in a different direction—crossing the boundary into a different scientific domain—the proposal tends not to be viewed as positively. This is in part because most reviewers aren't comfortable vouching for the scientific potential of something beyond the boundaries of their own domain, and in part because it doesn't deepen knowledge in the direction in which their work and reputation are building.[7]

This shaping of the enterprise of science into ever more narrow fields generally facilitates the advancement of what the great historian of science, Thomas Kuhn, calls "normal science"—the incremental block-by-block construction of bodies of understanding upon the foundation of a paradigm.[8] But this specialization of knowledge and perspective flies in the face of over-whelming evidence that breakthrough insights nearly *always* come at new, unconventional *intersections* of scientific or technical disciplines. Breakthroughs rarely emerge from within individual disciplines. Rather, we get new perspectives when researchers from other fields examine old problems from their different, and novel, points of view.[9] Problems that have long vexed the experts are often resolved when someone in another field sees something that the first experts simply couldn't see or didn't think to look for.[10]

Typically, our instinct is to look to our own discipline as the credible source for solutions—and that is the *right* instinct when the issue is normal science. But it is the *wrong* instinct when breakthroughs are needed.[11] This is also why we proposed in Chapter 10 that the breakthrough structures we need in medical student education might not emerge from within our medical schools, but from corporate medical schools that might be more willing and capable of adopting principles that have already been discovered at Toyota.

There is no doubt that we need breakthroughs in health care. This means the NIH needs to create different tracks for funding, and different methods for evaluating research projects that stand astride multiple disciplines or propose tackling problems in one field through methods that have been developed in another. Projects like these can be accurately assessed and prioritized, but only by different and appropriate means.

REGULATING FOR STABILIZATION AND ASSURANCE

Once an industry has been launched, governments quite often then intervene in the name of the public good to stabilize it. The intent and effect of many of these "stabilizing" regulations is to *limit* competition in order to help companies become strong enough to endure. The purpose of other interventions is to ensure that everyone in the population that politicians believe ought to be served by that industry is in fact served. And many regulations, of course, are written to assure that the quality of products is adequate and won't harm consumers.

As an example, 44 years after the Bell Telephone Company was founded, the Willis-Graham Act of 1921 declared telephony to be a "natural monopoly." There wasn't anything "natural" about this monopoly at all: hundreds of local phone companies and equipment manufacturers populated the industry in the early 1900s.[12] But getting their mutually incompatible systems to work together had been a hellacious technological task. Willis-Graham allowed AT&T to acquire its competitors and suppliers to become completely vertically integrated—to make and manage every element of its system, from soup to nuts. Given the technological interdependencies across various pieces of equipment at the time, this integration was needed to give the company the scale and scope to make telephony reliable on a national scale.

The regulation of the securities and banking industries during the Great Depression had a similar intent. By setting prices, defining disclosure rules, regulating balance sheet leverage, requiring approval for new banks and securities firms, and mandating deposit insurance, the government limited the potential for fraud and risk-taking behavior that could damage consumers. The Interstate Commerce Commission and the Civil Aeronautics Board regulated pricing and route-by-route entry into the trucking and airline industries to avoid ruinous competition, and to assure that rural and urban consumers alike could access these services at fair prices. The Federal Aviation Administration assures passenger safety. The National Highway Traffic Safety Administration regulations that govern the crashworthiness of automobiles are likewise intended to assure our protection.

The intent of most regulation to date in the health-care industry has likewise been to stabilize and assure. The avenues of influence that the government has used to stabilize the industry and assure the availability and quality of health-care services are not dissimilar to what the financial, trucking, and airline regulators did to stabilize and assure quality and availability in their industries. The government regulates prices, licenses and certifies the people and equipment that provide the services, and determines who can and cannot enter the industry and who they must serve. In the following pages we'll describe these avenues of influence.

Setting Prices

We stated in Chapter 7 that the formulas and methods that the Centers for Medicare and Medicaid Services (CMS) use to set the prices of products and services constitute the most pervasive and potent regulatory controls in health care. The price at which CMS decides it will reimburse is an "anchor rate" of sorts, because most private insurers follow the lead of CMS in price-setting. This, then, determines the profitability of every product and service in health care—creating incentives for providers to sell more of what is most profitable and less of what isn't.

In a largely unintended way, the reimbursement policies of some large government payers even serve to prop price levels up by *discouraging* discounting in the rest of the health-care industry. For example, most states' Medicaid programs by statute pay drug companies a fixed percentage of the average wholesale price of each drug—a price that drug companies are free to set. Medicaid's reimbursement policies stipulate that at the end of each quarter, the prices paid for all of the products and services purchased must be rewritten to be as low or lower than the lowest prices offered to any other customers. This is accomplished through federally-controlled price ceilings and mandatory rebates from drug manufacturers.[13]

This seems like a smart deal for the government—it is the largest customer, and it ought to be guaranteed lowest prices. But consider, by illustration, its unintended, second-order effect. Suppose a chain pharmacy, which we'll call "MediQuik," negotiates a discount from a supplier of diabetes test strips, which we'll call "GluCorrect." Imagine that instead of paying GluCorrect 75 cents per strip (which would be marked up to a retail price of about a dollar per strip), MediQuik negotiates a 50-cent price, intending to pass those savings on to its customers in order to win more of the diabetes care business. But because government payers account for about 40 percent of the volume of this product,

GluCorrect, in agreeing to this new discounted price, would have to cut its price to 50 cents not just for the volume it sells through MediQuik, *but essentially and retrospectively cut the price to the same level on all of its government-paid business for that product—which amounts to at least 40 percent of its entire sales of those products that year.* At the end of the quarter, MediQuik would be required to send to the government a check to refund the excess price that it originally charged—25 cents per strip, multiplied by the total number of strips sold to it that year.[14]

While this policy on the surface seems to benefit the government—assuring it of the best prices in the market—the effect is to make any discounting by the providers of drugs, devices, and services extremely expensive. Executives in every industry wish that their counterparts in competing companies had the "discipline" to act independently to maintain prices at profitable levels. The policies of Medicaid and other payers actually instill this pricing discipline in the health-care industry.[15]

Regulation of Access

Another class of policies for stabilization and assurance defines who does and does not have access to particular types of care. In the United States, for example, medical expenses are the leading cause of personal bankruptcy.[16] Yet hospitals *cannot* deny lifesaving treatment to the uninsured or those who cannot pay for care. America, as a result, actually *already has* universal health insurance, in a sense—though the present system forces people to wait until they have no other recourse but to seek care in an extraordinarily expensive hospital emergency department. Not surprisingly, many of the bills for these services go unpaid; as a result, the regulation of guaranteed access to lifesaving services imposes a much heavier burden on hospitals in lower income areas, such as rural communities and inner cities, than on those in more affluent communities.[17]

The bad debt that accumulates from uncompensated care isn't relieved by the Internal Revenue System, however, but through a hidden tax collected through private insurance companies from their clients. Charges to those who are insured or who can pay must be high enough to cover the cost of uncompensated care. Ultimately, the impact of this regulation that funnels the neediest and sickest into our costliest solution shops is to significantly *increase* costs (and human suffering) through its inadvertent second-order effects. It's ironic. America's system, which popular opinion holds excludes the uninsured and the poor from health care, actually guarantees access—albeit access that is costly to the system. In contrast, government systems that are widely viewed as granting universal access often are good at providing access to primary care and other basic services but quite stringently ration more expensive care in an exclusionary way.

There is also substantial evidence that we've framed the problem of access incorrectly. It is the marked inconvenience of finding affordable basic care that makes it inaccessible to the uninsured poor, not simply its cost. Care is often free for those who can't afford it, but only accessible to those who have the patience and fortitude to endure the indignity and inconvenience of finding it. As an illustration, MassHealth, the Medicaid program in Massachusetts, provides comprehensive health coverage for those in need. In March 2002, under pressure to reduce spending, MassHealth reduced the amount it would reimburse dentists for a range of basic dental services—and the already small pool of dentists willing to accept MassHealth patients declined even further by 15 percent. Additional free care was still available in community health centers funded by the state through a different pool of funds, but these were much less convenient to access for many of the poor. Within three years of the reimbursement cuts, 100,000 fewer MassHealth patients received dental services that were reimbursed by MassHealth.[18]

One option that addresses this issue is to eliminate the unfunded obligation to provide free care. This is not to say that the sick and needy should be turned away—far from it. Rather, our system of charity care needs to ensure they have equal right to convenient, quality care that doesn't threaten them with bankruptcy or force them to wait until they're much sicker before they are allowed succor. One solution is to obligate the uninsured poor to purchase high-deductible insurance on a subsidized basis. They must also be equipped with health savings accounts that can be subsidized, when necessary. But this isn't enough. Regulators must promote—and pay for, when necessary—retail clinics staffed with nurse practitioners and dental technicians, in order to stabilize and assure that a system of convenient care is available and accessible to the uninsured poor, not just to the wealthy and insured. If we uphold our moral and societal obligations to cover the cost of health care for the uninsured poor but do not simultaneously make it affordable and accessible, we have in fact provided "coverage without care."[19]

Permitting and Certification

In addition to its power to set prices and control who has access to the goods and services of these industries, the government uses a third avenue to bring stability and assurance to health care—by approving, certifying, and licensing, and thereby determining which people and institutions can and cannot compete to provide different types of care.

The most visible form of permitting and certification is the authority of the Food and Drug Administration to approve the sale of drugs and devices. As we noted in Chapter 8, clinical trials for new drugs have traditionally been designed as a "final examination" of sorts, to see whether a drug adequately helped a sufficient portion of patients while harming them a minimal amount. If the result of a trial was that an inadequate minority of patients responded to the drug, then the drug often was not approved. The new perspective that molecular biology has given us is that when only a portion of patients respond to a therapy, it should be taken as a signal that those patients in the trial must have at least two different diseases and/or there is a genetic variation between subgroups that causes them to respond differently to the therapy. Clinical trials in the future therefore need to be managed not as one-off tests, but as research trials whose purpose is to assist the researchers in defining and diagnosing diseases more precisely.

In addition, clinical trials historically have been organized around diseases that were defined and diagnosed by observable physical symptoms in particular organs or locations in the body. As we explained in Chapter 2, it turns out that these categorizations sometimes run orthogonally to the true nature of the diseases being treated. The organization of clinical trials needs to adapt to changing and increasingly precise definitions of disease, so it is the efficacy of the drug in treating the underlying cause that is being tested, and not simply the extent to which the drug ameliorates a symptom that happens to be correlated.

In our opinion, the FDA has made significant progress already in designing new "fast track" processes for evaluating drugs, such as its Critical Path Initiative. These newer research programs and trials tend to incorporate biomarkers as end points, pursue drug-diagnostic codevelopment, enrich patient populations by first diagnosing them as precisely as possible, utilize bioinformatics, and retain specimens for future testing and analysis should the understanding of disease change.[20] There remains, of course, much to do.

Permits to People and Facilities

The FAA doesn't just certify new aircraft as being safe to fly after they've been designed and built. They certify pilots as having been thoroughly trained to operate them, and they certify facilities as being equipped to handle aircraft of various types. In the same way, governments don't just certify drugs and devices. They also certify people and places.

Because the nature of the technology available affects the skill required to use it, the fact that scientific progress pushes care from intuitive toward precision medicine demands different regulatory emphases over time, as illustrated in Figure 11.1. When a disease can only be treated through intuitive medicine, the *inputs* or *resources* used in the caregiving process are the critical points of assurance control. In this situation it is primarily the training and qualifications of the physicians that must be assured.

Over time, however, greater understanding and predictability arise from the cycles of qualified physicians repeatedly working

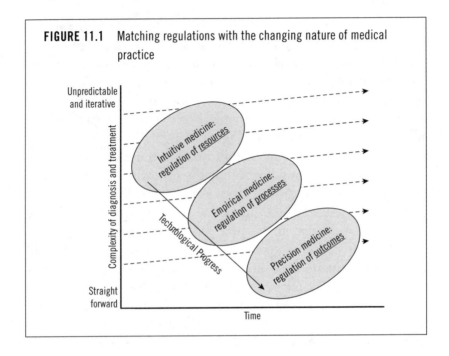

FIGURE 11.1 Matching regulations with the changing nature of medical practice

together to deliver outcomes in solution shops. Processes coalesce that embody the best of what has been learned about how to approach various diseases. A lot of know-how gets embodied in equipment and drugs. These mechanisms draw treatment into empirical medicine—where we can't guarantee the result, but can assert the probability of achieving a desired outcome *if a particular therapeutic process is followed, using particular drugs or devices.* When this happens, the emphasis of regulation needs to shift from a focus on the inputs and resources used, to a focus on the *process* used—to ensure that the best demonstrated practices are employed. This is what happens when an association of medical specialists or a hospital system proclaims new guidelines and standards of care for a certain condition, or an insurer declares that it will only reimburse if a specific procedure is followed. These are all regulations that govern process.

Often, the training of the professionals who provide care within these processes does not need to be as extensive as was formerly required in the regime of intuitive medicine. As regulators shift focus to process, therefore, they must simultaneously revisit their regulation of resources—because often caregivers with less training can do the job perfectly well.

When improved understanding has further shifted care into precision medicine, the focus of regulation needs to evolve again, toward a focus on *outcomes*, rather than on resources or processes. And because outcomes are predictable at this stage, regulators should focus on ensuring transparency and reporting relevant data from all providers. Regulating adherence to previously established standards for inputs and processes becomes less relevant, because competitive success typically compels adherence to these standards.

Many who have written about health-care reform urge in an undifferentiated way for *transparency*—for disclosure of outcomes data for individual hospitals and physicians. We have concluded that a key reason why such transparency hasn't emerged is that what these reformers have urged is not just overly simplistic: it is an impossible apples and oranges problem. For care of diseases in the realm of intuitive medicine that is provided in solution shops, the outcome is a diagnosis. But when care is provided in value-adding process clinics for diseases in precision medicine, the outcome is a cure. It is the latter in which outcomes data must be transparent and comparable. It comes as no surprise to us then that many physicians oppose the idea of pay-for-performance initiatives, often stating that their incentives are tied to processes and decisions beyond their control. This opposition arises not because they are opposed to quality care, but because a pay-for-performance system that attempts to encourage specific outcomes can *only* be effective for care that is fully in the realm of precision medicine.[21]

Regulatory insistence on compliance to inputs and process standards eventually can become a hindrance to further innovation if a pioneering company could potentially figure out a way to deliver superior outcomes by deviating from convention. A great example of an appropriate response to changing technology of this sort is in the FAA regulation that there must be an FAA-certified pilot and copilot in the cockpit for each commercial flight. The avionics on these aircraft and in control centers are now so sophisticated and comprehensive that much of the navigation, ground-air-ground communication, and piloting work is performed by computers, not pilots.[22] These advances are sophisticated and reliable enough that just a single pilot is needed at the controls. In the new microjets produced by Eclipse Aviation, Spectrum Aeronautical, and others for the emerging air taxi industry, the FAA no longer requires a copilot. There isn't even room for one.

Those who resist regulatory reforms such as these in health care have frequently told us, "Yeah, but it's *lives* that are at stake in health care." To which we reply, "You're right, and it is lives that are at stake on these planes too." Indeed, as the aviation regulations have shifted in emphasis to equipment, processes, and outcomes, the safety record of the technology is proving better than that of pilots.[23]

From Protection of the Patient to Protection of the Provider

We are not calling for wholesale deregulation of the health-care industry. Indeed, history has shown that when competitive markets can't create an industry that functions for the public good, regulation for stability and assurance has always been critical at a particular stage.

The dark side of this necessity for regulation, however, is that rules survive long after the public need for stability and assurance have been satisfied by technological progress. While the original intent of permitting and certification is a genuine concern for the patient, almost always the rules then come to be used to protect the economic interests of the providers—still invoked, of course, in the name of the patient, or of the passenger, or of the "public good." If regulators do not evolve the focus of their rules as science and technology progress, they will trap care in high-cost business models whose outcomes are less predictable, and are actually not as good as those that might otherwise be developed by innovators. Regulators must keep their vigil and adapt the focus and nature of the regulations to evolutions in medical practices, processes, and technology—but they rarely do.

For example, the Civil Aeronautics Board effectively "stabilized" the airline industry from the 1930s through 1977 by limiting the number and type of airlines that could fly on any given route, and by setting the fares they could charge. The Securities and Exchange Commission similarly "stabilized" the Wall Street brokerage firms as they emerged from the chaos of the Great Depression, by allowing the New York Stock Exchange to set at a profitable level the fees its member firms would charge to execute a trade. When Southwest Airlines and Charles Schwab sought approval in the 1970s to compete with the established firms in their respective industries through discount pricing, the lawyers for the established firms mounted eloquent arguments for why, in the name of the public good, the discounters should not be allowed to enter the market. Fortunately, they were allowed.

In a similar way, health-care providers regularly fall back on stability and assurance regulations to block competition. For example, in 2003, at the urging of the hospital industry, Congress imposed a nationwide moratorium on the construction of specialty hospitals such as heart and orthopedic hospitals. The argument was that in the event that a patient undergoing a cardiac bypass procedure suffered a stroke, for example, you needed to have within the hospital the ability to treat stroke, not just to repair hearts or replace hips. For the good of the patient, they claimed, all care needed to be delivered in general hospitals. It is interesting that the general hospitals have never militated to ban specialty psychiatric hospitals, even though, surely, patients in psychiatric hospitals on occasion have heart attacks, strokes, and hypoglycemia. Certainly, for the good of the patients, those with mental disorders also should be cared for in general hospitals. The reason for general hospitals' schizophrenic concern about heart and orthopedic hospitals but not psychiatric ones, of course, is that the procedures siphoned off by the former two are highly profitable, and psychiatric patients typically are far less profitable (and usually unprofitable). The actual reason for the 2003 ban was that these specialty hospitals could perform some of the general hospitals' most profitable procedures, but at much lower cost.[24]

As another example, out of concern for patient safety, many states still prohibit nurse practitioners from writing prescriptions without the direct supervision of a doctor, even for precisely diagnosable, rules-based disorders like strep throat. This effectively prevents retail clinics from competing against physicians' practices in those states—even though in the other states the patients are doing just fine, at less than half the cost. Worse still, patients who may not be able to afford the rates of physicians' practices or who do not have access to a primary care physician but might be able to afford a visit to MinuteClinic get shut out altogether—in the name of patient safety.[25]

Because assurance-oriented regulations initially limit rights of practice to those with the required expertise, a paternalistic culture often emerges in regulated industries that is built around the belief—validated at the outset—that people can't be expected to care for their own needs. This was the defense raised against discount and on-line brokerage firms. It is the fabric of the regulatory culture in legal services that to date has stymied disruption of that industry. And it pervades the defenses of the status quo in health care as well. In the realms of empirical and precision medicine people can actually competently assume responsibility for a growing portion of their care. This is a key reason for our call in Chapter 5 that patients with diseases in the "Chronic Quadrangle" be financially affected by their adherence to therapy. This is a critical change that regulators must allow. These diseases are decidedly in an empirical, rather than intuitive mode. We are no longer in the realm where paternalism is appropriate.

Ratification of Regulation Through Reimbursement

Many of the activities of certification, licensing, and permitting in health care are actually administered by trade or professional associations in the private sector, as well as by universities and various nonprofit organizations. The actions of these entities are given teeth when the ability to get paid for something—by Medicare or by private insurers—is tied to being credentialed. Among the best known and most influential agencies are the Joint Commission on Accreditation of Hospitals, which certifies hospitals for compliance with federal regulations and whose accreditation is required for Medicare reimbursement; the National Board of Medical Examiners, which tests the capabilities of medical school graduates and whose assessment is required for medical licensure; and the members of the American Board of Medical Specialties, which evaluates physicians in areas of specialty care and whose certification is necessary for physicians to be hired or credentialed by most hospital systems.

When Medicare or insurance companies follow a policy of paying only for services provided by licensed professionals, they can block disruptive innovations. There are many examples where technology has progressed to the point that procedures can be performed in clinics instead of hospitals, or by nurse practitioners instead of doctors, resulting in outcomes that are as good or better. Yet the rule of reimbursing only for services provided by certified caregivers makes it impossible or unprofitable to hand off care to lower-cost disruptive providers, because changes in certification typically lag many years behind changes in technology.

Toppling Regulations that Block Disruption: the Strategy of Starting Where They Aren't

When governments are democratic rather than autocratic, the entities that profit from the status quo typically have many more means of influencing elected and appointed officials to preserve the present system, compared to the more meager resources of disruptive entrants who petition to shift the focus of obsolete regulations away from resources like professionals and institutions and toward processes and outcomes instead. The $450 million the health-care industry spent in lobbying efforts with the government in 2007, in fact, exceeded spending to influence government policy by the finance, insurance and real estate, telecommunications and electronics, and energy and natural resources industries.[26]

The result of this massive imbalance of resources on the side of those resisting reform, based upon our studies, is that the reformers *almost always* lose head-on battles to deregulate what is regulated. Would-be disruptors who have directly petitioned the authorities to change regulation are left waiting on the sidelines for the regulation to one day change by fiat, or have simply abandoned their disruptive ideas. On the other hand, those disruptors that successfully dismantled the regulations that stood in their way succeeded by circumventing the regulation—by innovating in a disruptive market that was beyond the regulators' reach or was peripheral to their vision. Regulations ultimately change *in reaction* to the innovators' success in those markets— they rarely change to *enable* disruptive success.

For example, until 1980 Regulation Q profoundly shaped the structure and nature of competition in the consumer banking industry. It dictated that banks could not pay interest on checking accounts and capped the interest rates commercial banks and savings and loan associations could pay on savings deposits at 5.25 and 5.5 percent, respectively.[27] These regulations were broken when Merrill Lynch offered a cash management account that allowed customers to write checks against a "money market fund," and whose assets were short-term government securities that yielded more attractive interest rates. Fidelity quickly joined Merrill Lynch in offering interest-bearing checking accounts. Because they weren't banks and operated only on the periphery of bank regulators' vision, Merrill Lynch and Fidelity didn't attract the scrutiny that banks drew when they sought permission to pay interest on checking accounts. The disruptive Merrill Lynch and Fidelity products drew such enormous volumes of assets out of the conventional banks that ultimately the Federal Reserve had to change its regulations in response. Aggressive banks and consumer groups had lobbied for years to change these regulations from within the dominant value network, and they failed. It was the creation of a new disruptive value network, and the pulling of customers into it, that brought regulatory change.

As another example, until 1978 the Civil Aeronautics Board regulated the routes that airlines could fly and the prices they could charge. In 1971, Southwest Airlines began flying short routes within the state of Texas at very low prices, competing as a new-market disruptor to the major airlines by serving people who previously couldn't afford to travel by airplane. Because Southwest did not offer interstate travel, its routes and fares could not be regulated by the CAB. Furthermore, Southwest steered clear of the main DFW airport in Dallas, electing instead to fly in and out of the smaller, older, Love Field—where there were no established competitors. Southwest gradually started a few cross-border flights to adjacent states, but it minimized the opposition of established carriers by shuttling between smaller airports that weren't the bread and butter of the major airlines. By 1978 it became clear that the safety of discount airlines was just as good as—and the pricing for consumers significantly better than—what major airlines had been offering. So the CAB deregulated the airline industry. But once again, deregulation did not come from a direct appeal to the regulators.[28]

Note that in the earlier example of the virtual copilot in the minijets of Spectrum Aeronautical and Eclipse Aviation, even though similar avionics had long ago automated control on major aircraft, the mainstream pilots' union would have fought elimination of a required copilot to the death. But by going where they aren't—where the alternative is no pilots flying at all—the pilots and their passengers are delighted to see the regulation changed. Little by little, as Eclipse and Spectrum move up-market into bigger planes and grow from selling hundreds to thousands every year, the need for a copilot will be obviated.

And we see the same pattern in those few instances where the focus of health-care regulation has changed: you have to start where they aren't.

Drilling in Alaska

Consider this illustration. Despite the fact that it is preventable, tooth decay, the chronic disease that leads to most tooth loss, is present in over a quarter of all children between ages two and five, over half of all children between ages 12 and 15, and 90 percent of all adults over age 40.[29] Tooth decay plagues 5 billion people worldwide, disproportionately affecting low-income households. It accounts for 10 percent of all health costs in industrialized nations.[30] There *must* be an opportunity for disruptive innovation to address this global public health concern.

There is. But *for the good of the patients*, it's having a hard time getting to those who need it. Consider what's happening in Massachusetts as an illustration of how, when attacked directly, regulations get morphed to defend the professionals, not the patients.

Dental hygienists have been promoting legislation to allow specially trained hygienists to clean teeth and apply fluoride without direct supervision by a dentist.[31] The Massachusetts Dental Society has vociferously opposed this, citing concerns for public safety. But the MDS has proposed an alternative—the creation of a different class of specially trained dental assistants who could clean teeth and even place fillings *under direct supervision by a dentist*.[32] The Massachusetts Dental Hygienists' Association (MDHA) then voiced its opposition, concerned about how the introduction of dental assistants might "squeeze out more qualified registered dental hygienists."[33] All evidence points to a long battle in Massachusetts over these direct disruptive attacks. Organizations and professions will predictably fight to protect their livelihood.

Yet where fewer people are looking, dentistry is being disrupted. In 2000, to address the lack of dental services in rural areas,[34] the Alaska Native Tribal Health Consortium (ANTHC) persuaded the state to create a new type of dental provider called a dental health aide therapist (DHAT).[35] The model had been implemented in New Zealand over 90 years ago with demonstrable success, and similar programs existed in 42 other countries, including Canada and the United Kingdom.[36] In fact, the first Alaskan students to train in dental therapy went to the School of Dentistry at the University of Otago in New Zealand, since no such program was available in the United States. DHATs train for two years, instead of the minimum of four that dentists train, and at $60,000 per year, they make about one-third the salary of a typical dentist.

Since 2003, DHATs in rural Alaska have been providing services such as cleaning, drilling, filling, and extraction with only indirect supervision via periodic case reviews. Today, 10 DHATs serve 20 villages in Alaska—places that previously received dental care only one or two weeks each year from a visiting dentist. In 2005 a quality assessment by a professor of dentistry from the University of Washington School of Dentistry reported:

During my four-day site visit to the dental clinics at Bethel, Buckland, and Shungnak, I evaluated the clinical performance of the four dental therapists who have been providing primary care for Alaska Natives since the beginning of 2005. In every respect their performance met the standard of care I had established. Their basic training and subsequent preceptorships have produced competent providers. Each is equipped not only to provide essential preventive services but simple treatments involving irreversible dental procedures such as fillings and extractions. Their patient management skills surpass the standard of care. They know the limits of their scope of practice and at no time demonstrated any willingness to exceed them. On multiple occasions they demonstrated their ability to recognize and avoid clinical situations that might pose a threat to patient safety. My firsthand observations convince me that statements by dentists and dental societies suggesting that dental therapists cannot be trained to provide competent and safe primary care for Alaska Natives are overstated.[37]

The American Dental Association and Alaska Dental Society have predictably opposed allowing DHATs to provide unsupervised dental services, requesting an injunction from the Alaska Superior Court in 2006 to block their encroachment.[38] The judge ruled in favor of the ANTHC, stating that "a significant number of the enumerated health objectives . . . would continue to go unmet if the Alaska State Board of Examiners were placed in charge of dental health for Alaska Natives located in rural areas."[39] We expect that DHATs will soon be allowed in rural areas in the lower 48 states of America, where the population is not being well served by dentists. Eventually, the disruption will arrive in Massachusetts. But the shortest distance between two points is *not* a straight line.[40]

A View of Teleradiology

Over the past decade, there has been significant growth in the use of teleradiology, beginning with off-hours, or "nighthawk," radiology services, which allow hospitals to transmit digital images to anywhere in the world for interpretation. Even if the patient arrives in the dead of night, the radiographs can be interpreted within minutes by a radiologist at another center in the United States, or even in Australia, India, or France. This implementation of teleradiology has enabled hospitals to maintain reliable and efficient services around-the-clock and to meet the exploding demand for CT scans (growing at 14 percent annually) and other imaging studies, despite much slower growth in the number of radiologists.[41] The largest of these off-hours radiology providers, Idaho-based NightHawk Radiology Services, serves 26 percent of all U.S. hospitals.[42]

Teleradiology services began by targeting nonconsumption— radiologists gladly allowed the new services to manage their less desirable time slots on nights and weekends. However, once they began to offer daytime services, there was predictable opposition from radiologists. Leaders of the American College of Radiology raised concerns about ensuring the quality, accuracy, and accountability of personnel based in another state or country.[43] There were also concerns about communication problems when the radiologist and referring physician were so far apart. In 2002 an attempt by Massachusetts General Hospital to partner with a nonprofit company in India to shift some of its radiology work to Indian doctors resulted in hate mail and ultimate failure for the venture.[44] Legislators got involved, claiming that patient privacy was at risk, and placed restrictions on transferring patient data abroad.

In response to this reinforcement of the intuition-era regulatory focus on the doctor's qualifications, most teleradiology services, even if located abroad, have been compelled to employ only U.S.-trained and -licensed radiologists, who must also be credentialed at the hospitals for which they perform services.[45] Furthermore, their interpretations are often considered only preliminary until reviewed, or "overread" by a U.S.-based radiologist. The Joint Commission on Accreditation of Health Care Organizations also weighed in to require teleradiology services to meet licensing and accreditation standards that have long been in place for hospital-based solution shops of radiologists.[46] The result: a typical NightHawk radiologist has licenses in 38 states and is credentialed at over 400 hospitals. The company employs 35 to 40 people simply to manage all of this administrative overhead—and yet can still provide these services at lower cost than most of its customers can when they choose to perform them in-house.[47]

However, a funny thing is happening at the edge of this stalemate. A growing segment of work is no longer dependent on a radiologist's expert eye and clinical experience to interpret shadowy anatomical structures and link them to patients' clinical histories and physical symptoms.[48] "Functional" radiology, involving dynamic in-motion studies and molecular tracers rather than still pictures, and "quantitative" radiology—a related discipline based on measurements and scoring algorithms—have significantly enhanced the ability of nonradiologist physicians to elucidate physiologic abnormalities.[49] Starting with basic technologies like ultrasound and fluoroscopy, these machines automate image acquisition and analysis, embedding into algorithms some of the diagnostic skill that used to reside only in the intuition of radiologists. These machines also require less space, shielding, and power, so they can be integrated into the offices of cardiologists and orthopedic surgeons working in value-adding process clinics.[50]

The door was opened, in typical disruptive fashion, to nonradiologist physicians to begin performing and interpreting some of the simpler studies for themselves, and they are referring fewer and fewer patients to the radiology solution shops of the local hospital. So while radiologists were trying to figure out how to prevent the loss of work overseas, other physicians were beginning to perform some of that work for themselves within their very same offices and communities.

An important insight from this end run around regulation is that the cardiologists and orthopedic surgeons didn't *need* to seek regulatory approval. Radiologists make their money on a fee-for-service basis by interpreting images ordered by other physicians. Teleradiologists have been attempting a low-end disruption into this business—using a lower-cost business model to capture segments of the market—but still on a fee-for-service basis. The cardiologists and orthopedists working in capitation or fee-for-outcome models didn't need to worry about regulatory approval because they don't make their money interpreting images—they make it by repairing hearts and bones. Radiology simply helps them repair more hearts and joints better and faster.[51]

We suspect that after a few years of cardiologists, orthopedic surgeons, and others using these computer-assisted imaging technologies with results comparable to those of radiologists, regulations will eventually change to focus on processes and outcomes, rather than on the credentials of the physicians. Already, in fact, the initial fears about the safety of outsourcing radiology services to off-hours providers now seem unfounded.[52] The time will even come when point-of-care doctors won't need a radiologist as a copilot.[53]

Lao-Tzu framed the deregulation strategy of "Starting where they aren't" better than we have when he wrote, "Water is fluid, soft, and yielding. But water will wear away rock, which is rigid and cannot yield. As a rule, whatever is fluid, soft, and yielding will overcome whatever is rigid and hard. This is another paradox: What is soft is strong."[54]

REGULATING FOR COMPETITIVENESS AND EFFICIENCY

When stability and quality have become assured, governments often then shift their focus toward the third stage of government influence—to regulations that improve the affordability and convenience of the products and services in question. This can be achieved by deregulation, or the unwinding of restrictions on price-cutting and entry, that had been put in place when stabilization and assurance were paramount concerns. Antitrust action is another weapon used in the pursuit of competitiveness and efficiency.

Economists and economists-turned-deregulators have habitually employed a standard and simplistic formula for cost-reduction: $\uparrow$ competition = $\downarrow$ prices. Their simple creed is that in the absence of competition, companies will charge monopolists' prices. If you intensify competition it will drive prices down. It turns out that the hoped-for good news of this gospel often doesn't materialize. When deregulation or antitrust action pits new entrants against the established industry leaders from the regulated era in *sustaining* competition, it typically results in an enormous waste of resources and little impact on prices, because the entrants fail. It is *disruptive* competition that yields dramatic reduction in price and improved accessibility. The implication is that deregulators need to focus not simply on enabling competition—but on facilitating *disruptive* competition.[55] When regulators don't get this formula right, history has shown time and again that the results can be catastrophic. Let's look at three such cases, the scenarios of which are summarized at the end of the following section, in Figure 11.2.

Reducing the Cost of Computing

In the 1960s, IBM dominated the market for mainframe computers. It enjoyed a 70 percent market share, but captured about 95 percent of the industry's profit. This near-monopoly of course bothered the United States Department of Justice, and so in 1968 the DOJ sued to break up IBM into a set of smaller companies in the belief that more intense competition amongst mainframe computer makers would reduce the cost of computing. For 13 years the government spent hundreds of millions of dollars prosecuting this lawsuit, and IBM spent hundreds of millions defending itself.

While the lawyers were working on this problem, the disruptive minicomputer and personal computer value networks were emerging. As these ecosystems grew, they pulled more and more customers and applications from the mainframe value network in the back plane of the disruption diagram into the disruptive networks in the front. One day one of the lawyers noticed, "Hey! There aren't many customers back here using these mainframes! They're out there computing on those microprocessor-based machines!" So they closed their briefcases and went home. IBM's mainframe monopoly indeed had been broken—but not by the Justice Department. It was broken through disruption.

We invite our readers to pause at this point, boot up their notebook computers, and reflect on two historical possibilities. What impact would breaking up IBM's mainframe monopoly—in order to create more competition among mainframe providers—have had on the cost, availability, and quality of computing? How does that compare with the impact that disruption has had on these three variables? It's a great way to visualize how important it is for regulators and the economists who advise them to differentiate between sustaining and disruptive competition.

Breaking Up Microsoft

By the late 1990s an even more dominant near-monopolist named Microsoft had emerged in the personal computer operating system business. Its market share exceeded 90 percent, and the company was making extraordinary profits. This of course bothered the United States Department of Justice deeply, and so in May 1998 it sued to break up Microsoft in the belief that more intense competition among operating system and Internet browser vendors would reduce the cost of computing. The government spent hundreds of millions of dollars prosecuting this lawsuit, and Microsoft spent comparable sums defending itself. A decree in 2001 signaled that Microsoft had survived the first attack of the Justice Department.

While the DOJ's Antitrust Division is figuring out its next steps, a new disruptive value network is emerging in a new plane of competition. While it has many names, we'll call it Internet-centric computing. It is disrupting the enterprise-centric computer networks within which most of us have been computing during the last decade. Linux has become the operating system of choice in Web servers, and firms like Google, Yahoo, and Amazon have built their systems upon Linux. As these Internet-centric services are becoming faster, more convenient, secure, and reliable, more and more applications are being drawn out of the enterprise network in the back plane of the disruption diagram, into the Internet-centric value network in the front—customer by customer, application by application, from searching for documents on our hard drives to searching for them on the Internet.

One day soon some antitrust lawyer will notice that the government's latest legal briefs had been composed on GoogleDocs, not Microsoft Word, and will send out the message, "Hey! There aren't many customers left here using these enterprise networks! They're all out there computing on those Web servers!" They will then close their briefcases and go home. Microsoft's monopoly will indeed have been broken—but not by the Justice Department. It will have been broken through disruption.

Introduction of Sustaining Competition into the Telephony Industry

In the Telecommunications Deregulation Act of 1996, the United States government again attempted to enhance affordability and accessibility with the same naive theory—that competition per se will drive costs down. To promote competition, the act required that the independent local exchange carriers—also known as ILECs, comprising US West, Pacific Bell, Bell South, Ameritech, Southwestern Bell, and Bell Atlantic—share their networks with new entrants at discounted, regulated rates. These entrants, called competitive local exchange carriers (CLECs), were invited to create competition over the "last mile" to customers' homes and offices, and then "plug in" to the established ILECs' local networks that interfaced with long-distance networks. The hope was that a large barrier to entry—the creation of the physical "local loop" of communications lines and switches—could be circumvented by utilizing existing networks, thereby promoting competition in local telephone service that would hopefully result in lower rates for consumers.

Close to 300 CLECs garnered more than $300 billion in funding from venture capitalists and Wall Street, entering the markets of over 100 cities. By 2002 only 70 CLECs remained, and by 2007 nearly all of them were gone. High fliers like WinStar, Covad, NorthPoint, Rhythms, and Teligent all went bankrupt.[56] The sector became a poster child for the dot-com bubble burst. Indeed, rather than spurring more competition and lowering prices, a wave of industry consolidation occurred, and pricing for local telephone service remained high.

What happened? By enticing new entrants to use the prevailing business model, based on the existing local communications infrastructure, the regulators essentially pitted the start-up CLECs into head-on, sustaining-innovation competition against the ILECs on their home turf. Again, our research on innovation has shown overwhelmingly that when entrant companies attack incumbent leaders with a sustaining innovation, using a similar business model in the leaders' existing markets, the leaders invariably triumph. And they did.

While the regulators and their lawyers and economists have been using head-on sustaining competition as their tool for making telecommunications services more affordable and pervasively accessible, disruptive business models already are booming in a new disruptive plane of competition—without the subsidy of government. Using Voice over Internet Protocol (VoIP), Skype, to name just one example, is now one of the largest telephony providers in the world, with more than 350 million users. Its *premium* service offers unlimited local and long-distance calling starting at $35.40 per *year*—and its customers take their telephone numbers with them wherever they go in the world.[57] And we are only beginning to see the revolution in affordability and accessibility that will come with wireless VoIP and video over the Internet.[58] Meanwhile, in the rearmost plane of competition in the disruption diagram, the network companies and cable companies are engaged in multi-billion-dollar competitive battles of sustaining innovation, each striving to bring higher-definition television and more reliable wire-line telephony at higher prices to their most attractive customers in "Triple Play" bundled pricing.

The importance of applying the model of disruptive innovation to the challenge of improving the cost and accessibility of health-care services is presaged by Supreme Court Justice Stephen Breyer's opinion after the 1996 Telecommunications Act was challenged by a number of telephone carriers. Breyer offered an apt postmortem of the entire debacle: "It is in the unshared, not in the shared, portions of the enterprise that meaningful competition would likely emerge. Rules that force firms to share every resource or element of a business would create, not competition, but pervasive regulation, for the regulators, not the marketplace, would set the relevant terms."[59]

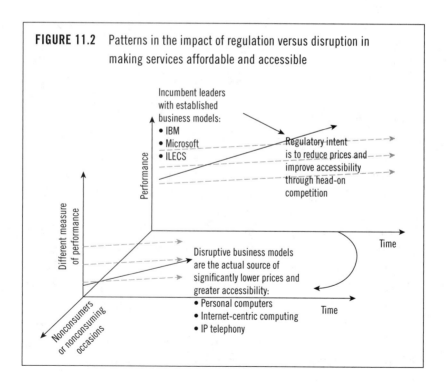

FIGURE 11.2   Patterns in the impact of regulation versus disruption in making services affordable and accessible

We could recount in detail for deregulators how air travel, trucking, stock brokerage, and many more regulated products and services have become significantly more affordable not by introducing head-on sustaining competition, but through disruption. The topic deserves a book in itself. Suffice it to say that there is a pattern here. Regulators and deregulators have not once—*not once*—brought significantly lower costs and better access by demanding enhanced competition among the established practitioners of existing business models. When regulations that were put in place to stabilize and assure subsequently need to be relaxed and refocused, significant improvements in cost and access have *only* come from disruptive business model innovation. When we read simplistic, undifferentiated calls for more competition, we all ought to invoke Yogi Berra's immortal phrase: "It's déjà vu all over again."[60]

The Path for Mitigating Medicare's Influence

In the decade over which we conducted the research that we tried to distill into this book, we've noted a growing sense of despair among doctors and executives about the counterproductive roles that Medicare policies play in the overall American health-care industry. Medicare has become so massive, the refrain goes, that it simply cannot be changed. We believe that Medicare can be transformed into a neutral force in the industry—still able to fulfill its mission of providing care to the elderly, yet not inhibiting innovation that can help everyone. This can be done by following the same rules: We need to initiate change in portions of the industry that are beyond Medicare's reach, rather than trying to change Medicare directly. And we need to control the ballooning costs of Medicare through regulatory change that enables or facilitates disruptive business models.

How does one create a value network beyond the reach of Medicare pricing mechanisms that create such powerful distortions in U.S. health care? One way is to internalize the market *within* the major integrated provider systems described in Chapter 6, where members pay a fixed annual fee for the health services they receive.

If organizations like Kaiser Permanente, Intermountain Healthcare, and Geisinger Health System create focused and disruptive business models appropriate for the different categories of disease, they can internally make decisions and direct patient care based upon efficacy and economics, not in response to distorting regulations on reimbursement.[61] As these delivery systems prove their efficacy and cost advantage, then one by one, patients can be drawn from the original plane of competition—where independent suppliers apply for Medicare reimbursement on a fee-for-service basis—into a new disruptive one. Ultimately, Medicare would assist its covered population in the payment of annual fees associated with care in the integrated fixed-fee provider system. Importantly, the fixed annual fee would be the only price that Medicare would be concerned with—and it would be a negotiated price between the payer and provider. Other prices would be set between vendors of drugs, devices, and services, and the integrated entities that buy from them, on a competitive basis.

In many respects the United States, with its hybrid public-private system, has a leg up in health-care reform over those democratic countries without a substantial private system. When the government is everywhere, innovators can't go where the regulators aren't, in order to initiate disruption. Reformers in those nations must tackle the system head-on—which, as the final section below will show, is a fight we wouldn't wish for our worst enemies.

NATIONALIZED HEALTH-CARE SYSTEMS

Our claim at the beginning of this chapter that "the tentacles of governmental influence and control stretch throughout America's health-care system in a deep, tangled, and pervasive way," actually might have been an understatement. CMS typically sets the anchor rates for medical reimbursement, which private insurers then follow. The NIH and FDA are essentially make-or-break supporters and gatekeepers for innovations in biomedical research and new technologies. Other institutions, including the Veterans Health Administration, Indian Health Service, and an extensive network of federally funded and state-funded public health centers, deliver care.

Given the pervasive influence of all these agencies, one might reason whether the government itself might be the only entity with the power and scope to solve the health-care crisis. In fact, nearly every decade brings a renewed push for the United States to emulate the system used by most industrialized nations—a government-sponsored, single-payer nationalized system.

The critical challenge we actually face is not *how* to pay for health care. Nobel laureate Milton Friedman long ago assured us that there is no such thing as a free lunch. Whether the check is written by individuals, employers, or government-run health-care systems, in the end it comes from the pockets of the people.

A second question of some import is *whether* to pay for health care. Overwhelmingly, American employers have chosen to pay for it. A key reason why health care accounts for a smaller share of Gross Domestic Product in other developed nations is that their governments have chosen *not* to pay for it: Almost every government with nationalized health care has been forced to ration access to advanced care in one way or another. The straits in which Canada's public, paid-for system finds itself, for example, prompted Chief Justice Beverly McLachlin of the Supreme Court of Canada to opine in 2005 that "access to a waiting list is not access to health care."[62] As a result, most countries with national health systems have had to develop alternative market-based channels for coverage as well—so people can choose for themselves whether to pay for certain services, rather than leaving that choice to bureaucrats.[63]

Government health systems in general do a better job not just of rationing, but also of controlling the salaries earned by doctors and nurses, because governments essentially are the *only* employers for most of those who pursue health-care careers—and monopsonistic purchasers have the power to dictate the prices they will pay.[64] Because of governments' tight control on caregivers' salaries, in many nations the best physicians establish themselves in private practice, where they can earn higher incomes by serving the wealthy. This is another paradox of national health systems: while the intent is to assure universal access, often it is the elite who see the elite, while the rest see the rest.[65]

Hence we come to the focus of this book: how to make health care *affordable*. We hope our readers are convinced by now that it is the business model within which the professionals work that is the major driver of cost, not just in health care, but in *every* industry. National health systems have *not* done a better job than America's system of making health-care costs affordable through disruptive business model innovation. Both, to date, have done poorly.

We believe that despite all the roadblocks we expect disruptive innovators to encounter in America, however, a decade from now disruptive reformers within America's system will prove to have been much more successful at making care more affordable and accessible than will those in most nationalized health systems. We therefore urge America's political leaders *not* to view further government control as a vehicle for solving our problems. Rather, it is time for America's government to foster disruption.

Most government health ministries are comprised of decentralized fiefdoms. Hospitals are administered independently of the physicians' organizations, which are administered independently of the drug pricing and distribution system, and so on. Though the administrators are civil servants and the doctors are employed by the ministry of health, these systems are not different in their basic administrative structure from the non-integrated system that characterizes most of the United States health-care industry. Those few public health ministries with a high degree of centralized, coordinative control, such as in Singapore and the United Kingdom, resemble in their structure the integrated providers like Kaiser Permanente, which we discussed earlier. In other words, the centralization of the power to orchestrate change is what is critical—and that power can be vested in either a government ministry or a private provider.[66] Most government health ministries are actually quite powerless to implement significant changes, because the political process of convincing the separate entities to fall in line in the new disruptive direction would stymie all semblance of reform.

Tools of Cooperation

To explain why the power to orchestrate is so critical, we'll draw on a final model from our research on innovation, which we call the "Tools of Cooperation." The essence of this model is that having the right vision for where your company (or a ministry of health) needs to go is just the start. Once you know the necessary future direction, you then need to convince all the other people and entities whose resources and energies are required to succeed in that journey to cooperatively work together to get there.

The effectiveness of the various tools that might be wielded to elicit this cooperation depends upon the extent of preexisting agreement along two dimensions. The first is the extent to which the people involved agree on *what they want*—the results they seek, what their priorities are, and which trade-offs they're willing to make to achieve those results. The second is the extent to which they agree with each other on *which actions will yield the desired result*.

For those who must manage change, there is no "best" position along these two dimensions of preexisting agreement. The key is recognizing the extent of agreement and then selecting the tools of cooperation that will work most effectively in that situation. We believe this simple model applies to units as small as families, to business units and corporations, to school districts, and even to nations.

Figure 11.3 maps these dimensions of agreement in a matrix, and describes the types of tools managers can wield in different situations, in order to elicit cooperation among the stakeholders to work in concert in achieving the needed change. The boundaries delineating the domains in which the various tools can work are not rigid, but the broad labels can give leaders a sense of which tools are likely to be more or less effective in various situations.

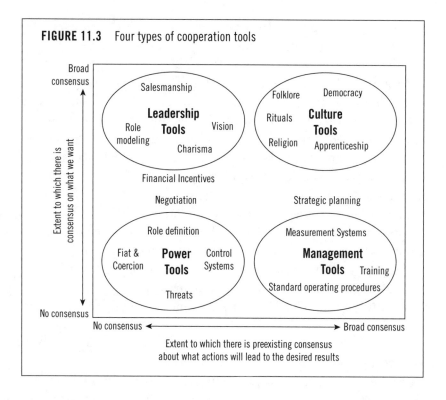

FIGURE 11.3   Four types of cooperation tools

Power Tools

When there are sharp disagreements among the concerned parties about what they want and how to get it, the only tools that will elicit cooperation in pursuit of a new course are "power tools" such as fiat, force, coercion, and threats. This is how Marshal Tito brought peace to the Balkan Peninsula, for example. After World War II, he herded the disparate and antagonistic ethnic groups in that region into a more or less artificial nation and said, in essence, "I don't care if you agree with me or with each other on what you want out of life or how to get it. I just want you to look down the barrel of this gun and cooperate with me and each other." It worked.

Tools such as negotiation, strategic planning, and financial incentives don't work well in situations of minimal agreement. As depicted in Figure 11.3, these will work only when there is a modicum of agreement on both dimensions of the matrix. In environments of antagonistic disagreement—whether in the Middle East or in the infamous clashes between the management of Eastern Airlines and its machinist union—negotiation does not work. A leader might use strategic planning to figure out where the organization ought to go next, but lacking some agreement on both dimensions, the strategic plan itself will not elicit the cooperative behavior required to get there. And financial incentives—essentially paying others to want what you want—typically backfire in a low-consensus environment. People will react indifferently, because they do not agree with the incentives' goals.

Only power tools are reliably effective in low-agreement situations. The key is having the authority to use them. In democracies, many of these mechanisms are outlawed. This hamstrings public-sector executives who face a mandate for change with little power to do what needs to be done. We will return to this point later.

Management Tools

The tools that elicit cooperation in the lower-right region of the agreement matrix of Figure 11.3 are coordinative and process-oriented in nature. We call these "Management Tools," and they include training, standard operating procedures, and measurement systems. For such tools to work, group members need not agree on what they want from their participation in the enterprise, but they must agree on cause and effect.

For instance, in many companies, unionized manufacturing workers come to work for different reasons from those of senior marketing managers. But if both groups agree that following new manufacturing procedures will result in better levels of quality and cost, they will cooperate. If there is no consensus among the people concerned that following the new methods or metrics leads to the desired outcomes any more effectively than the old ones, however, they are unlikely to behave differently after being trained in the use of the new routines. The effectiveness of training is more dependent on the level of agreement about how the world works than on the quality of the training itself.

Leadership Tools

In the upper-left region of Figure 11.3, results-oriented tools, as opposed to process-oriented ones, are more effective because there is a high existing consensus about what employees want from their participation in the organization. Charismatic leaders who command respect, for example, often do not address how to get things done; instead they motivate people to just do what needs to be done. The same actions that employees view as inspiring and visionary when they're in the upper-left corner of the agreement matrix are often regarded with indifference or disdain when the people are in the lower quadrants. For example, when people agree on what they want to achieve, vision statements can be energizing. But if people do not agree among themselves about what they want, vision statements typically induce a lot of eye rolling.

Culture Tools

People located in the matrix's upper-right region will cooperate almost automatically to continue in the same direction. This is the essence of a strong culture. Their common view of what they want and of how the world works means that little debate is necessary about where to go and how to get there.[67] But this very strength can make such organizations highly resistant to change. The tools of cooperation that are available in the realm of strong culture—including ritual, folklore, and democracy—facilitate cooperation only to preserve the status quo; they begrudgingly yield to change. When executives in this circumstance see big changes in the future and realize that the organization's momentum is propelling it in the wrong direction, the culture often fires the manager. Just ask former CEOs John Sculley (Apple), Durk Jager (Procter & Gamble), Carly Fiorina (Hewlett-Packard), and George Fisher (Kodak).

Where are health-care systems positioned in the agreement matrix? For the most part, they are in the lower-left corner of the diagram. Patients, doctors, regulators, IT professionals, hospital administrators, insurance companies, executives in pharmaceutical and medical device companies, small businesses, large businesses, and politicians all have divergent priorities and disagree strongly about how to achieve them.

The fact that health care is in the lower-left world of disagreement helps explain why certain remedies that reformers tried to introduce in the past have not worked. For example, reformers who advocate evidence-based medicine bewail the fact that many doctors continue to follow their own instincts rather than best demonstrated practices. But if those recalcitrant doctors don't agree that doing it a certain way brings the desired results, they won't follow the rules. Similarly, the reason why metrics of performance and value have been almost impossible to create is that the conflation of solution shops and value-adding process businesses within hospitals puts us in the lower-left portion of the matrix. Metrics of performance only work if there is strong agreement on cause and effect, and a modicum of agreement on what various parties want from their participation in the enterprise.

The scary thing about this situation is that democracy—the primary tool in most societies where health-care reform is at issue—is effective only in the upper-right circumstance, when there already is broad, preexisting consensus on what is wanted and how the world works.[68] And what's worse, like all the tools in the culture quadrant of the matrix, democracy is not an effective tool for radical change—it is a tool best used for maintaining the status quo.

So is it possible that changing our health-care systems is impossible? No, it can be done—if we use a fifth tool—that of separation.

Separation

There are instances in which disagreement among the parties that need to cooperate is so fundamental that it's simply impossible to reach consensus on a course of action—and yet no one has amassed the power to coerce cooperation. When all other tools have failed, there is a trump card to play, and it does not reside within the agreement matrix. We call it "separation"—dividing the conflicted parties into separate groups so they can each be in strong agreement with others inside their own group, yet don't need to agree with those in other groups. In the post-Tito Balkans, by illustration, no one could again successfully amass and wield the requisite power to maintain peace, as Tito had. So we tried the charisma of President Bill Clinton and sales skills of Prime Minister Tony Blair. We tried democracy and negotiation. We used economic sanctions and incentives. Nothing worked— except separation. Peace came to the Balkans when the need for cooperation across antagonistic ethnic divides was obviated by dividing the peninsula into nations and regions for each ethnic group.

In our studies of disruptive innovation, we have seen the same thing. The only instances in which an industry's leading company also became the leader in the following disruptive wave occurred when the corporate leaders wielded the separation tool. These companies survived disruption by establishing an independent business unit under the corporate umbrella and giving it unfettered freedom to pursue the disruptive opportunity with a unique business model, essentially placing it in competition with the parent company.

If employees responsible for sustaining the core business must work in the same business unit as those responsible for disruptive products, they are forever conflicted about whether new or existing customers are most important; whether moving up- or down-market offers more growth; and so on. Separation in these instances is the only viable course of action. In addition, it takes the power of the CEO suite to wield the tool of separation. As a result, only a few companies have ever successfully disrupted themselves.[69]

It is this model that provides the theoretical foundation for our recommendation of "Starting where they aren't" when pursuing deregulation. Situations requiring regulatory reform, by definition, are in the lower-left corner of the agreement matrix. Cramming deregulation down the throats of those who don't want it requires extraordinary power—and in a democracy, nobody possesses such power. In a health system such as America's, private entrepreneurs can find interstitial spaces in which to establish a disruptive foothold—out of the eyesight and earshot of regulators and influential competitors in the existing market. If America's government were to bring health care into a single-payer system, by definition it would make it impossible to incubate reforms in fringe areas "where they aren't." And it would strip from executives in the industry the ability to wield the tools of power that are critical to making things happen in situations where disruptive innovations will be unpopular to the established interests.

This is why we urge our readers, our lawmakers, and our fellow American citizens not to look to a government-controlled single-payer system as a solution to our health-care crisis. It is a route that is relatively easy to get onto, but it is in fact a one-way street heading in the wrong direction. And there is no exit.

SUMMARY: REGULATIONS THAT NEED TO BE CHANGED

The sections above highlight eight regulations or other mechanisms of influence that need to be changed in order to facilitate the transformation we call for in this book. We'll list these changes here, in summary.

1. The NIH needs to create a different methodology for evaluating research proposals that draw upon multiple disciplines. Otherwise, the peer review process will continue to push medical science into increasingly narrow silos of knowledge, and we will fail to capture the novel approaches and discoveries that only come from the intersection of *different* points of view.
2. The formulas by which CMS and private insurers determine the prices they will pay for services need to be replaced. Prices that reflect true value and actual cost must be allowed to emerge, as pure solution shops, value-adding process clinics, and facilitated networks contract for business directly with

employers and patients. Built into these prices are accountability of provider organizations and transparency of information for consumers—not equations of relative value administered by bureaucrats with false precision.

3. Reimbursement policies that unintentionally encourage disciplined price maintenance among competitors by rewriting prices based upon lowest-in-market rates each year must be discontinued. If health plans independently negotiate prices with suppliers and focused providers as we recommend employers do, overall pricing in the market will fall, not rise.

4. Because inconvenience *and* cost make health care inaccessible to the uninsured poor, the obligation of providers to provide uncompensated care should be eliminated. In its place, governments should mandate, with subsidies when necessary, the purchase of high-deductible health insurance and the use of health savings accounts by those who are now classed as poor and uninsured. At the same time, governments must foster not just a financial safety net, but expand the safety net of *providers* to include conveniently located retail clinics staffed by adequately trained nurse practitioners and dental technicians that are convenient, affordable, and accessible to *everyone*.

5. FDA clinical trials processes need to be redefined, when necessary, as research trials. At the same time, drugmakers should be encouraged to define the scope of clinical trials according to the molecular definition of the disease, and not necessarily by organ system or, in our parlance, symptom of disease.

6. The focus of regulations such as licensure and certification needs to keep pace with technological change and scientific progress. When care is in the realm of intuitive medicine, the focus should be on accrediting *people*. As care moves through empirical medicine toward precision medicine, the focus should shift to accrediting processes, and ultimately to guaranteeing outcomes.

7. The economists who advise deregulators need to abandon the simple, century-old, one-dimensional axis that pictures competition on one end and monopoly on the other. Rather, it is a particular type of competition—*disruptive innovation*—that will predictably bring significantly lower costs to health care. As soon as technological progress enables it, regulators must facilitate disruption. This is what will make health care affordable and accessible.

8. Employers need to be allowed to create financial incentives for healthy behavior. By illustration, they should be allowed to shift their contributions between high-deductible insurance and health savings accounts for individual employees as data on healthy or unhealthy behavior indicate that the long-term costs of insuring an employee are changing.

NOTES

1. The Food and Drug Administration's origins can be traced back to the Division of Chemistry in the U.S. Department of Agriculture, which began publishing its research on misrepresented food and drugs in the late nineteenth century. Regulatory powers were granted to the agency by President Roosevelt with the 1906 Food and Drugs Act, which authorized seizure of intentionally misbranded or adulterated food and drugs. The organization was renamed the Food and Drug Administration in 1930.

2. A significant group of Clayton Christensen's MBA students have written course papers and independent research project papers on this subject. In chronological order, these include Scott Anthony, Erik Roth, Dan Svoboda, Peter Šararík, Sara Dawes, and Privahini Bradoo. Each of these built upon the research of the prior students, culminating in many of the insights summarized in this chapter. We are deeply grateful for their hard work and very thoughtful contributions to our understanding of a portion of this extremely complicated field.

3. In his review of the manuscript of this chapter, Charlie Baker, CEO of the Boston-based Harvard-Pilgrim Health Plan, commented, "We need the government to do these things to permit disruptive innovation to flourish. Private enterprise alone, without decent, intelligent federal policy support, cannot find a way out."

4. The mechanism for doing this was the Pacific Railroad Act of 1862. It called for two railroad companies to complete the transcontinental line. The railroad would be a "land-grant railroad," meaning the government would give each company 6,400 acres of land and up to $48,000 for every mile of track it built.

5. The government's track record in creating new industries through subsidies and set-asides is mixed. There is strong reason to expect, for example, that the present subsidies of the ethanol, hydrogen, and solar and wind energy industries will ultimately be multi-

billion-dollar debacles and disasters. First, because consumption is so pervasive in economically developed countries, these nascent technologies cannot be commercialized in a disruptive way (targeted at nonconsumers). They can only compete head-on as sustaining innovations against well-established, mature, efficient, and reliable competing products and companies. For many reasons chronicled in our research on disruption, entrants almost always fail when pitted in head-on sustaining innovation against incumbents. In contrast, in the developing world where there are many areas of nonconsumption of electric power, we can expect solar and wind energy to thrive commercially. The second reason why we can expect these massive subsidies to fail is technological interdependence. Ethanol and hydrogen are not "plug compatible" with the existing infrastructure for distribution and use. These technologies will require building completely independent infrastructures—a proposition whose cost is extraordinary. However, a developing nation with no significant existing infrastructure will weigh its options differently and often choose the "leapfrog" technology—so called because it bypasses an entire generation of infrastructure requirements that had been necessary in the past.

6. The government's hits have been offset by a lot of misses, of course, and this topic deserves a Ph.D. dissertation, not just a footnote. But as a general rule, government funding of infrastructure upon which an industry can grow—highways, railroads, airports, etc.—results in successful economic growth. For similar reasons, government funding to develop scientific *techniques*—such as gene splicing techniques or synthetic biology techniques—typically creates more growth than funding to develop specific *technologies*. Anticipating which technologies will be commercially valuable is a much harder question to answer correctly, whereas subsidizing the creation of tools to enable companies to develop technologies seems to work better. When government funding of specific technologies seems imperative, those that are disruptive (such as the Internet and the transistor) also are often successful, because those technologies compete against nonconsumption—they find a much more ready market. However, when the government has funded technologies that can only be implemented in sustaining ways, in head-on competition with the conventional technology in common use, with just a few exceptions it results in a vast waste of financial and natural resources. This is because the steady, incremental advance of existing technologies in the value networks within which they function is persistent. and the new technologies are rarely plug-compatible in existing systems. Hence, the massive oil shale investments in the 1970s were a dramatic waste. We predict that today's investments in biofuels will similarly result in a waste of resources, a distortion of markets, and will have little beneficial impact on oil consumption or cost. It is a sustaining technology pitted into head-on competition against an established technology.

7. We thank Professor Emeritus H. Kent Bowen of Harvard Business School for his insights on these issues. He has pointed out that the funding of America's research universities by the National Science Foundation has had a similar "siloization" on institutions like the Massachusetts Institute of Technology.

8. Kuhn, Thomas, *The Structure of Scientific Revolutions* (Chicago: University of Chicago Press, 1962).

9. For readers with a deeper interest in this principle of intersections, we recommend Johansson, Frans, *The Medici Effect* (Boston, Massachusetts: Harvard Business School Press, 2004). This is a fascinating history of the technological intersections that led to many of the world's great scientific breakthroughs. And two case studies by Professor

H. Kent Bowen, "The Langer Lab: Commercializing Science" (Harvard Business School case # 9-605-017) and "The Whitesides Lab" (Harvard Business School case # 9-605-017), chronicle how two of the most productive biotechnology laboratories in the world (at MIT and Harvard, respectively) are structured to deliberately force a multidisciplinary perspective into each research project.

10. Consider, as an example of productivity at an unconventional intersection, the persistence of malaria in vast areas of the world, long the bane of infectious disease researchers and public health workers. Drawing upon the science of immunology to develop vaccines hasn't worked because the *Plasmodium* parasite that female anopheles mosquitoes inject into the human bloodstream, causing malaria, simply evolves too quickly; we can't keep up with it. One promising approach on the horizon for the prevention and treatment of malaria has been developed by a company in Havre de Grace, Maryland, General Resonance LLC. Its science comes from the study of nanotechnology and particle physics, not immunology or infectious diseases. Its founders have observed that a long-known property of materials called "resonance," whose effects are dampened or canceled in crystalline structures, actually become powerful among nanoscale particles of a material. They found that while human cells seem inert to the resonance generated by these materials, their resonance can be lethal to a very broad spectrum of these parasites. Whether this will prove to be the solution to eradicating this pernicious disease remains to be seen, of course. But it is an illustration of the principle that breakthrough insights almost always come at the intersections of disciplines, rather than from within one of them.

11. One of Thomas Kuhn's most prominent conclusions was that when a new paradigm is emerging from the work of scientists in other fields, the experts in the old paradigm remain convinced, even to their dying day, that the new paradigm cannot possibly be true. The reason is that the old paradigm has so powerfully shaped their beliefs about how the world works, and what is and is not possible, that their minds literally cannot see the phenomena that led to the articulation of the new paradigm. We would expect, as a result, that many leaders of our most prominent medical schools will discount the possibility of the reforms we have advocated, for reasons that are perfectly rational to them.

12. A useful summary of this early history, told through the language of disruptive innovation, can be found in Christensen, Clayton; Scott D. Anthony; and Erik A. Roth, *Seeing What's Next* (Boston, Massachusetts: Harvard Business School Press, 2004).

13. Under the Veterans Health Care Act of 1992, the Veterans Health Administration is also guaranteed discounts based on the non-federal average manufacturers price. However, in part because it is a closed system, the VA has also been able to establish other methods of discounting, including aggressive formulary management and national standardization contracts that encourage competitive bids. Medicare Part B previously had a similar "we get the lowest price" policy, but this was modified by the Medicare Modernization Act of 2003. Prices are now set at 106% of the average sales price, which is a statutorily defined price based on actual sales transactions, rather than a fixed discount of the average wholesale price. That same legislation also created Medicare Part D to expand prescription drug coverage, but included a "noninterference" provision that forbids the Department of Health and Human Services from negotiating drug pricing on behalf of Medicare beneficiaries. Instead, Part D encourages market competition by encouraging individual health plans to negotiate prices and discounts on behalf of their members, and offers no specific guidance on pricing. This "noninterference" clause is under threat

of repeal. See Jacobson, G., Panangala, S., and Hearne, J., "Pharmaceutical Costs: A Comparison of Department of Veterans Affairs (VA), Medicaid, and Medicare Policies," Congressional Research Service Report for Congress, Domestic Social Policy Division, April 13, 2007; and "Medicaid Drug Price Comparison: Average Sales Price to Average Wholesale Price," Department of Health and Human Services, Office of Inspector General, OEI-03-05-0020, June 2005.

14. We do not know the specific portion of blood glucose test strips purchased through government payers; but we've chosen to apply a simple assumption for ease of illustration.

15. The numbers in this example are very round and approximate ones, and not the result of a purposeful study on this topic. We have chosen this example for a purpose, however. Knowledgeable friends have informed us that while diabetes test strips indeed retail at prices near a dollar apiece, the cost to manufacture these strips is less than 10 cents. Of course there are *fixed* costs that must be covered from the gross margins on these strips, but situations like this are exactly where one typically sees price discounting as competitors vie for major contracts. And yet the competitors in this industry have maintained extraordinary discipline in raising and maintaining prices. We are not suggesting, nor has anyone else charged, that there has been collusion to set prices high in this industry. We're simply suggesting that a core reason why prices have risen and are maintained at such heights might be that Medicaid and similar systems of reimbursement have made discounting to *anyone* very expensive. Executives in industries like airlines, where rogue competitors routinely discount prices, can only dream of what it's like to compete against suppliers to the health-care industry, where pricing discipline is so pervasive.

16. Interestingly, according to a Health Affairs survey in 2005, medical bankruptcy affected roughly 2 million Americans (including dependents), and 75.7 percent of them had insurance when they first became ill. See Himmelstein, David, U., et al., "MarketWatch: Illness and Injury as Contributors to Bankruptcy," *Health Affairs*. Accessed at http://content.healthaffairs.org/cgi/content/full/hlthaff.w5.63/DC1. This is evidence that underinsurance is also a significant problem contributing to medical bankruptcy.

17. Public hospitals in the 100 largest metropolitan areas, considered key safety-net hospitals, comprise only 2% of all hospitals, but provide over 20% of all uncompensated care (Report of the Council on Medical Service, American Medical Association, December 2001). The burden of uncompensated care tends to fall on only a small number of hospitals, typically those that are: government-sponsored teaching institutions, rural non-profit hospitals, or serving areas with a disproportionately high number of uninsured patients ("Nonprofit, For-Profit, and Government Hospitals: Uncompensated Care and Other Community Benefits." U.S. Government Accountability Office, GAO-05-743T, May 26, 2005.

18. In the end, costs were merely shifted from one area to another, and any estimated savings to the state, at best $16.5 million out of a $3 billion MassHealth budget, came at the expense of increased suffering of patients due to untreated, and often preventable, dental disease. Dental coverage was reinstated in 2007, but reimbursement rates remain much lower than other dental insurance plans. See Pryor, C., and M. Monopoli, "Eliminating Adult Dental Coverage in Medicaid: An Analysis of the Massachusetts Experience," Kaiser Family Foundation, Kaiser Commission on Medicaid and the Uninsured, September 2005.

19. This is the phrase that Dr. Marcia Angell, former executive editor of the *New England Journal of Medicine*, used to describe the impact of the law in Massachusetts that mandates

health insurance for everyone, without taking any initiative to reduce the cost of providing that care. Source: Kuttner, Robert, "A Health Law with Holes," *Boston Globe*, Jan. 28, 2008 (editorial page).

20. For more about the FDA's Critical Path Initiative, we refer readers to http://www.fda.gov/oc/initiatives/criticalpath/initiative.html.

21. Astute readers will also recognize that once care reaches the stage of precision medicine, the intuition of physicians is no longer needed. At this point, rather than have insurers try to implement pay-for-performance for physicians, it would make more sense in many cases simply to have patients purchase their services directly from value-adding process clinics. If such a retail environment were to develop, market pricing could obviate the need for any pay-for-performance program imposed by a third party.

22. Unmanned Aerial Vehicles (UAVs) already in regular use by the military can fly and land automatically. They have become increasingly capable—even in combat situations that previously had required a pilot.

23. See Public Broadcasting System, "How Risky Is Flying? Commercial Aircraft Fatalities, 1982–2005," sourced at http://www.pbs.org/wgbh/nova/planecrash/risky.html. It shows how much safer flight has become in recent years. We know this book is about health care and not aviation, but check out this description of what the "virtual copilot" on these Eclipse jets does (taken from the company's Web site in August 2008): "Avio NG, Eclipse's exclusive Total Aircraft Integration system, incorporates technology never before available in general aviation. Avio NG centrally controls aircraft systems including avionics, engine operation, fuel system, flaps, landing gear, cabin pressure, and temperature. Beyond that, it acts as a virtual copilot, providing checklists and advanced navigation and avionics information, improving safety and dramatically reducing pilot workload—especially during single-pilot operation. Twin PW610F turbofan engines have an Automatic Power Reserve to boost power to one engine by 10 percent if the other should fail. Both engines are protected by Eclipse Aviation's exclusive PhostrEx next-generation fire suppression system. The Eclipse 500 features pneumatic de-ice boots, heated engine inlets, electrically heated windshields, and data ports that enable flight into known icing conditions. Reliability and redundancy are built into every system, from the four independent power sources to the electric trim motors and servos. So the pilot is never overwhelmed, and the passengers can relax and enjoy the ride."

24. Note that the general hospitals also have not militated against rehabilitation, cancer, senior care, women's, children's, and community hospitals either—even though an intellectually consistent approach ought to have raised some of the same concerns for patient safety against these institutions as well.

25. A 2008 RAND study revealed that only 38.7 percent of retail clinic patients reported having a primary care physician, compared to 80.7 percent of patients nationwide. See Mehrotra, A., et al., "Retail Clinics, Primary Care Physicians, and Emergency Departments: A Comparison of Patients' Visits," *Health Affairs*, vol. 27(5):1272–82.

26. Center for Responsive Politics, accessed from http://opensecrets.org.

27. The level of these rates could be changed, but they always were set by the Federal Reserve, and commercial banks always could pay one-quarter percent below what savings banks and savings and loan associations paid.

28. In fact, the famous Wright amendment, enacted in 1979 to protect the home base of American and Braniff at DFW Airport, essentially banned Southwest from DFW until 1996, when it finally was revoked.

29. "Oral Health: Preventing Cavities, Gum Disease, and Tooth Loss 2008," U.S. Department of Health and Human Services, Centers for Disease Control and Prevention," Coordinating Center for Health Promotion, February 2008, accessed from http://www.cdc.gov/nccdphp/publications/AAG/doh.htm on Aug. 5, 2008.

30. "Billions Suffer from Tooth Decay," *BBC News*, Feb. 25, 2004, accessed from http://news.bbc.co.uk/1/hi/ health/3485940.stm on Aug. 5, 2008.

31. S.2203 and H.2221: An Act Authorizing Dental Hygienists to Practice in Public Health Settings, filed by the Massachusetts Dental Hygienists' Association (MDHA). Our readers will of course note the similarities to the fight to allow nurse practitioners to examine patients and write prescriptions without physician supervision.

32. S.1216: An Act Relative to Dental Auxiliaries, filed by the Massachusetts Dental Society, would create new dental assistant classifications (registered dental assistants and expanded function dental assistants) and a new dental hygienist classification (expanded function dental hygienists), all of whom would be considered Dental Assistants with Advanced Training, accessed from http://www.mass.gov/legis/bills/senate/185/st01/st01216.htm on Aug. 5, 2008.

33. Massachusetts Dental Hygienists' Association Web site, accessed from http://www.massdha.org/news-events/legislative-updates.asp on Aug. 5, 2008.

34. According to the Agency for Healthcare Research and Quality, accessed from http://www.innovations.ahrq.gov/content.aspx?id=1840, on Aug. 6, 2008, Alaska Native children and adults suffer much higher rates of oral disease than other Americans. Alaskan children between ages two and four have a rate of dental decay five times the national average. In addition, 85,000 Alaska Natives are dispersed throughout small villages of less than 400 people that are relatively inaccessible. There are also fewer dentists available per capita, making access even more difficult.

35. Alaska Dental Health Aide Therapist Initiative, Alaska Native Tribal Health Consortium, 2000, accessed from http://www.anthc.org/cs/chs/dhs/index.cfm, on Aug. 6, 2008.

36. Nash, David A., and Ron J. Nagel, "Confronting Oral Health Disparities Among American Indian/Alaska Native Children: The Pediatric Oral Health Therapist," *American Journal of Public Health*, 2005; 95(8):1325–29.

37. Fiset, Louis, "A Report on Quality Assessment of Primary Care Provided by Dental Therapists to Alaska Natives," Alaska Native Tribal Health Consortium, Sept. 30, 2005. A second report in 2007 from a professor of dentistry from Texas A&M University found that care provided by DHATs were within the scope of their training and met the standard of care in dentistry. The study found no difference in the rate of complications resulting from care delivered by DHATs and dentists. See Bolin, Kenneth A., "Quality Assessment of Dental Treatment Provided by Dental Health Aide Therapists in Alaska," paper presented at the National Oral Health Conference, May 1, 2007.

38. Alaska Dental Society et al. v. *State of Alaska et al.* Complaint for Declaratory and Injunctive Relief. 3AN-06-04797 CI (Alaska Super. Ct., Jan. 31, 2006).

39. "Superior Court Judge Rules in ANTHC Favor June 27," *Mukluk Telegraph*, August/Sept. 2007, vol. 10, Issue 2, page 7; and "Judge Dismisses Case Against Dental Therapists," accessed from http://www.ktuu.com/global/story.asp?s=6720173, on Aug. 6, 2008. Although still opposed to the initiative, the ADA and ADS have since agreed to work with DHATs to promote dental care in Alaska's rural communities.

40. Our thanks to Dr. Keith Batchelder and Peter Miller of Genomic Healthcare Strategies for bringing our attention to this example.

41. Mullaney, T., "The Sensible Side of Telemedicine," *BusinessWeek OnlineExtra*, June 26, 2006, accessed from http://www.businessweek.com/magazine/content/06_26/b3990079.htm, on July 29, 2008.

42. NightHawk Radiology Services Web site and press release, accessed from http://www.nighthawkrad.net/ and http://biz.yahoo.com/prnews/080717/aqth080.html?.v=54, on July 29, 2008.

43. It's funny how the challenge of accurately interpreting images at night and on weekends was so simple that it could be done remotely without concern for patient safety, whereas the images that needed to be interpreted during weekdays were so complex that an on-site radiologist would be required.

44. Pollack, Andrew, "Who's Reading Your X-Ray?" *New York Times*, Nov. 16, 2003, accessed from http://www.nytimes.com/2003/11/16/business/yourmoney/16hosp.html, on July 29, 2008.

45. Mishra, Raja, "Radiology Work Shifts to Overnight, Overseas," *Boston Globe*, June 29, 2005.

46. Johnson, Douglas E., "NightHawk Teleradiology Services: A Template for Pathology?" *Archives of Pathology and Laboratory Medicine*, vol. 132, no. 5, 745–57.

47. Steinbrook, Robert, "The Age of Teleradiology," *New England Journal of Medicine*, vol. 357:5–7, July 5, 2007.

48. Our thanks to Dr. Keith Batchelder and Peter Miller of Genomic Healthcare Strategies for suggesting these technological enablers of disruption in radiology.

49. Prior to functional brain imaging, for example, even for a brain-dead patient images might often indicate a normal brain.

50. Our thanks to Joseph Camaratta of Siemens for his generous comments regarding this case study.

51. This is one of the inherent advantages of a value-adding process business model, which can be evaluated based on its outcomes rather than its component resources.

52. Wong, Wilson S., et al., "Outsourced Teleradiology Imaging Services: An Analysis of Discordant Interpretation in 124,870 Cases," *Journal of the American College of Radiology*, 2005; 2:478-84.

53. Radiologists, it should be noted, have not sat still, as forays into interventional radiology have enabled them to disrupt the low end of general surgery. Telemedicine services are similarly challenging the fields of pathology and intensive care, with others certain to follow.

54. Lau-Tzu, *Tao Te Ching*, circa 600 BC.

55. Our assertion here is that significant cost reductions typically do not occur within a business model. They occur when a new, disruptive business model is created to displace the old. A frequent reaction of those with whom we've discussed this assertion has been to cite significant price declines of products as they move from introduction to volume production. Intel, for example, frequently will drop the price of its microprocessors from an introductory height of $600 to a floor of $200 or so, as costs drop with increasing volumes. This is a different phenomenon than the one we are discussing in this chapter. As Intel moves from one generation of processors to the next, the introductory prices of the new-generation products tend to be as high as the prior ones; and the floors to which they drop tend to be similar to prior floors. The technology (and the corresponding business models in which it is embedded) that threatens Intel's hegemony in logic cir-

cuitry is the digital signal processor, or DSP chip, which is made by companies like Texas Instruments and is used in handheld devices like the RIM BlackBerry and wireless telephone handsets.

56. For more information on this history, see Doherty, Jacqueline, "Telecom Tightrope," *Barron's*, Jan. 8, 2001, 17-18; Darby, Larry F.; Jeffrey A. Eisenach; and Joseph S. Kraemer, "The CLEC Experiment: Anatomy of a Meltdown," *Progress on Point 9.23*, Progress & Freedom Foundation, Sept. 2002; and Christensen, Clayton, Scott Anthony, and Eric Roth, *Seeing What's Next*. (Boston, Massachusetts: Harvard Business School Press, 2004). Note that some companies predated the 1996 Act.

57. Skype's SkypeOut service started in 2006 at $29.95 per year for worldwide calls. Currently it costs $35.40 per year for unlimited calls within the United States and Canada. Skype's unlimited global plan is $119.40 per year as of August 2008.

58. If we went further back into the history of the industry, we could tell the same story. The cost of long-distance was made significantly lower by a disruptor, Microwave Communications Inc., or MCI.

59. *AT&T Corp. v. Iowa Utilities Bd.*, Supreme Court of the United States, Jan. 25, 1999. Accessed at http://www.law.cornell.edu/supct/html/97-826.ZX2.html.

60. We have sought a reliable source for this phrase that so frequently has been attributed to the venerable former catcher for the New York Yankees, but have not succeeded. Professors Michael Porter and Elizabeth Teisberg recently published a treatise, *Redefining Health Care* (Harvard Business School Press, 2006), in which they argue for enabling the better measurement of value and for enhancing competition among providers that will reward those that provide the best value. We hope that our research can bring more specificity to their findings, by contributing the notion that we should expect fundamentally different outcomes from sustaining and disruptive competition.

61. In his speech at a *Health Affairs* press briefing on Sept. 10, 2008, Glenn Steele, president and CEO of Geisinger Health System, described this perspective of integrated delivery systems in a comment about recent innovations at his organization: "It didn't matter who won financially. That's key. If the insurance company wins, or if the doctor group wins, which is rare, or if the hospital wins, it doesn't matter as long as the patient wins. Because we can do the internal transfer pricing. We can basically redistribute the financial benefits." See http://www.kaisernetwork.org/health_cast/hcast_index.cfm?display=detail&hc=2965.

62. "Unsocialized Medicine," *Wall Street Journal*, June 13 2005, A12.

63. Canada is the only country other than Cuba and North Korea where it is still illegal to purchase health care privately.

64. In the parlance of economists, monopolists are entities that are the sole suppliers of a product or service in a market. Monopsonists are the sole purchasers of a product or service in a market.

65. For example, see Anderson, Gerard F. and Peter Hussey, "Special Issues with Single-Payer Health Insurance Systems." Health, Nutrition and Population department of the World Bank Human Development Network. Discussion Paper. September 2004. In analyzing Sweden's health care system, the authors state, "Although most physicians are paid publicly, the share in private practice has increased, and public physicians can see private patients in their spare time. This may diminish access to care in the public system for poor patients if physicians spend more time with private-paying patients."

66. For example, see Zamiska, Nicholas, "China Thinks Small in Prescription for Health Care: Primary-Care Clinics to Become First Stop in Revitalizing System." *Wall Street Journal*, March 11, 2008, A10.

67. Schein, Edgar, *Organizational Culture and Leadership* (San Francisco: Jossey-Bass, 1987).

68. A moment's reflection supports this assertion. Whenever America has swooped into a country where there wasn't broad consensus on what everyone wanted or how to get it, and has tried to impose democracy—whether in Haiti or Nigeria, in Iraq or Afghanistan—the result has been a widespread breakdown in social order. The nations where fundamental regulatory changes have been implemented to enable rapid economic development in the last 50 years—including South Korea, Taiwan, Singapore, and Chile—were all governed by relatively honest dictators who could wield the tools of power to do what needed to be done. As those countries prospered, consensus on the two axes increased, and democracy gradually became feasible.

69. A good example is at General Motors. Its executives spun Saturn off in 1985 as an independent company under the GM corporate umbrella. Initially billed as, "A different kind of company, a different kind of car," little by little the organization's cultural power has pulled Saturn back into the General Motors cultural orbit. The corporate executives just haven't had or been able to wield enough power to keep it as separate as originally intended. Chapter 10 in Christensen, Clayton, and Michael Raynor, *The Innovator's Solution* (Harvard Business School Press, 2003), provides a listing of the few companies that have managed to disrupt themselves.

Epilogue

The need to transform expensive, complicated products and services into ones that are higher in quality, lower in cost, and more conveniently accessible is a challenge that is not unique to health care. Most modern industries started where health care is today, with products and services that were expensive and complex, but were transformed toward improved quality, cost, and convenience through disruptive innovation. Disruptive transformations were rarely initiated by the leading companies in these industries. The reasons? At the outset the disruptive innovations could not meet the needs of industry leaders or their customers. And the profits from disruption were unattractive when viewed from the perspective of the dominant business model. Instead, disruptions have always taken root by first addressing the simplest problems of the least demanding customers.

Disruptive technologies and business models have been the mechanisms that brought affordability, consistent quality, and convenient accessibility to most facets of our society. Disruption hasn't treated kindly the companies that have ignored it. But it has been good for mankind. In industry after industry disruption has made obsolete the trade-off that previously forced a choice between quality and affordability. It delivers both.

Every disruption is comprised of three components: a technology that transforms the fundamental technical problem in an industry from a complicated one into a simple one; a business model that can take that simplified solution to the market at low cost; and a supporting cast of suppliers and distributors whose business models are consistent with one another, which we call a value network. Disruptions combining these three factors actually have long been at work in health care, transforming the care of most infectious diseases into simple, affordable, convenient services of remarkable efficacy in much of the world.

More disruptive innovation is poised to be unshackled in other major sectors of health care. Precision diagnostics, often the prerequisites for development of predictably effective therapies, are emerging—transforming care from the realm of intuitive medicine into that of empirical medicine and ultimately into precision medicine—disease by disease, step by step. In the face of this technological progress, however, a host of factors have combined to trap the delivery of care in obsolete and costly business models. If health-care administrators and policy makers heed the call of this book for disruptive business model and value network innovations that complement this advance of technology, they can profoundly reshape the cost, quality, and convenience of health care. This industry is horrifically complicated. But in its essential elements, health care isn't substantially different from other industries that have already been transformed through disruption.

DISRUPTIVE BUSINESS MODELS

The general hospital is not a viable business model. In the absence of an array of cross-subsidies, restraints on competition, and philanthropic life support, most of them would collapse. The value proposition of general hospitals, which is to diagnose and treat any disorder that anyone might bring through their doors, has caused them to harbor each of the three generic types of business models under the same roof:

- Solution shops, which diagnose problems and recommend solutions, and must be compensated on a fee-for-service basis.
- Value-adding process businesses, performing procedures in which definitively diagnosed problems are repaired or treated through a relatively standard sequence of steps, and paid for on a fee-for-outcome basis.
- Facilitated networks, in which professionals and patients exchange with and help each other, and whose coordinators typically need to be compensated on a fee-for-membership basis.[1]

Cost Problems Are Due to Overhead, Quality Problems to Poor Integration

Trying to do anything for everybody has forced most general hospitals to organize their individual specialist physicians and their pieces of equipment to stand independently of each other and to *not* be tightly integrated. This enables patients to be routed from one department to the next in a maximally flexible, ad-hoc manner. It also means, however, that hospitals cannot be integrated in an optimal way to do well any of the jobs that individual patients need to have done. Hospitals therefore suffer from extraordinarily high, complexity-driven overheads as they attempt to manage the myriad patient pathways that snake through their facilities.

Hospitals need to disrupt themselves into the three types of business models, or they must be disrupted by others. The overwhelming burden of a hospital's cost is tied to its overhead. And inconsistent quality and safety stem from the patchwork integration of caregivers and equipment. Hospitals are ill-equipped to do each of their different jobs in an optimal manner. Creating coherent solution shops for the practice of intuitive medicine, value-adding process clinics for performing procedures after definitive diagnosis, and disease management networks for the care of many chronic illnesses, will both reduce overhead costs and enable appropriate integration. This is how the historically binding trade-off between quality and cost can be broken in health care, giving us significant improvement in both. *Affordability comes from reducing complexity-driven overhead, and quality stems from rational integration around the jobs of patients.*[2]

Primary care physicians' practices need to be dissected into these three business models as well—handing off rules-based care to value-adding process (VAP) retail clinics and the care of chronically ill patients to disease management networks. Primary care physicians can then focus on disrupting specialists in the practice of intuitive medicine.

Getting the Pricing Right

There are three perversions in the revenue models of today's system that combine to obfuscate value and misguide investment:

- Because hospitals conflate business models, they must price all services—not just solution shop activities—on a fee-for-service basis. And health assistance plans negotiate blanket contracts with providers, through which deep discounts for some services offset very high prices for others, in an opaque rather than transparent way.
- CMS and private insurers set prices based on formulas that do not account for supply, demand, systemic value created, or differences in cost associated with providing services via different types of business models.
- Nearly all Americans are cared for by business models that profit from patients' sickness, rather than wellness.

Who can pull off a rational reform of this system?

There are circumstances in which the perfect, atomistic competition of Adam Smith is an ideal mechanism for arriving at prices that accurately reflect supply, demand, and value. But today's health-care system, characterized by pervasive interdependencies, is not one of those circumstances. We need what Alfred Chandler calls "the visible hand of managerial capitalism"—the deliberate involvement of an integrated provider whose scope encompasses a complete system. Only with a systemic perspective can the real merit of specific activities such as precise diagnosis be assessed, and only then will prices that reflect real cost and real value be established.

Integrated fixed-fee providers can fulfill this role, profiting from patient wellness and the disruption of their own hospitals and specialist physicians by utilizing lower-cost caregivers and venues of care. We therefore urge the few providers that fit this profile to expand their geographic scope to a regional, if not national, scale and encourage providers that are not now integrated to become so.

In regions that are not served by integrated fixed-fee providers, employers will need to orchestrate the creation of disruptive value networks. Reimbursement needs to be replaced by true, high-deductible insurance and health savings accounts. In order to direct volume to the appropriate coherent solution shops, VAP clinics, and facilitated networks, employers need to negotiate directly with providers and begin playing a much more active role in directing employee care. This is how they can facilitate disruption.

MECHANISMS FOR ACHIEVING "CHRONIC WELLNESS"

Chronic diseases account for 70 percent of all health-care costs[3]— and as populations age this will only get worse. Employers who pay for the care of those with behavior-dependent chronic diseases with deferred consequences (patients in the "Chronic Quadrangle"), in particular need to find ways to tie those patients' adherence to prescribed therapy to their financial health. The reason is that, like it or not, financial well-being is a more pervasively held job-to-be-done for most people than maintaining physical health. Disease management networks, which are structured to profit from maintaining wellness, and patient networks need to be given much more prominent roles in the care of chronic diseases. The business model of the doctor's office simply was not designed to do this job.

The mechanism for coordinating care across this fragmented group of business-model-focused providers must be a personally controlled electronic health record—because the number and complexity of variables that must be orchestrated have simply surpassed the cognitive capacity of even the brightest physicians who have historically borne the responsibility of coordinating our care. To manage this Herculean task, integrated provider systems have already built proprietary record systems. But the open system that will make our health records portable across providers needs to be constructed from the point of view of the patient, and not the provider—just as Toyota organized its vaunted information system around the perspective of the car.

Drug companies and device manufacturers face extraordinary growth opportunities, in the form of technological enablers that transmit the ability to provide better care into the hands of lower-cost caregivers and decentralized venues of care. In concert with the NIH and the FDA, they are the institutions that can push diseases along the continuum from intuitive to empirical to precision medicine. We fear, however, that many of today's leading pharmaceutical companies are dis-integrating *away* from the stages in their value chain where these activities will originate—and where competitive advantage and attractive profits can be gained and earned in the future.

We also are not training the professionals that tomorrow's health-care system will need. Our chronic shortage of nurses will become even more acute because we simply lack training capacity, while our universities are investing elsewhere. America's medical schools are training more and more specialists, even while the dearth of primary care physicians is severe and getting worse. Though most politicians would never say it, we will: *thank goodness for international medical schools and for the well-trained immigrants from the Philippines, India, the Caribbean, and Latin America.* Without them we'd lose more than one-quarter of tomorrow's capacity to care for our health.

We need significant policy and regulatory changes from our federal and state governments to facilitate disruptive change. Despite Americans' faith to the contrary, democracy as a tool for eliciting cooperation around a course of action only works when little significant change is needed. The reason is that regardless of how badly broken things might be, there are always powerful entities that benefit from the status quo. Regulations always benefit someone, and democracy provides myriad levers that these entities with a lot at stake can pull in order to block change.

We hope, however, that the concepts in this book can give government officials a language and a deeper understanding of how the world works, so they can sort self-serving arguments from public-serving ones. In particular, we hope we've provided convincing theory and evidence that the solutions cannot come simply from demanding that existing providers operate more efficiently or compete against each other more intensely. Straightening the deck chairs on the *Titanic* might have been a good thing to do, but it wasn't the real problem. The health-care industry needs to be disrupted.

Because of the shackles that democracy imposes on those responsible for regulation, the employers that now pay for health care, and the companies that make health-care products and provide health-care services, need to initiate the regulatory changes that enable disruption. They must do this in the way that disruptive deregulation has always occurred—by innovating where the regulations can't reach, don't apply, or are off the radar screens that regulators most intensely monitor. Internalizing decisions and transactions that formerly occurred at arm's length between independent entities—which this book terms "integration"—is one way to do this. Competing against nonconsumption is another.

We are grateful, the three of us, for your patient willingness to read this book and consider what we've distilled to date from spending much of 10 years examining the health-care industry through the lenses of our research on innovation. This book is simply one milestone in a long and difficult process of learning. We're trying to understand the root causes of the industry's problems. We're struggling to articulate in a crisp and compelling way what needs to be done to address these problems. And we're anxious to watch and help those who follow our prescriptions, and to learn what they learn about what else needs to be done. We are confident that many of our recommendations are solidly grounded. We are also confident that we've not yet fully understood many other important issues. We have the greatest confidence, however, that you, our readers, have a lot more to teach the rest of us. We simply hope that this book can play a role in helping us all learn from each other about how to make health care higher in quality, lower in cost, and more conveniently accessible for all.

NOTES

1. This membership fee can be paid directly by the user; by an employer or insurer; or indirectly by users through advertisers.
2. We have touched on this theme in a number of places in this book. The key to Toyota's quality, for example, is in managing the activities, connections, and pathways of each process in an optimally integrated way. The mechanism by which AT&T came to offer the highest quality telephone service in the world, from 1925 to 1980, was through its optimal integration; and so on.
3. Health Care Costs. Fact Sheet. AHRQ Publication No. 02-P033, September 2002. Agency for Healthcare Research and Quality, Rockville, MD. http://www.ahrq.gov/news/costsfact.htm

Index